WE REMEMBER...

The Stories of Courage and Heroism,
Triumph and Tragedy,
from the Men and Women Who Served
their Country
during World War II
from the Antelope Valley, California

Compiled and written by

Dayle L. DeBry

With
Karla Archuleta

Edited by
Carol Fleming and Pat Holland

EAGLE EDITIONS
2004

EAGLE EDITIONS
AN IMPRINT OF HERITAGE BOOKS, INC.

Books, CDs, and more—Worldwide

For our listing of thousands of titles see our website
at
www.HeritageBooks.com

Published 2004 by
HERITAGE BOOKS, INC.
Publishing Division
65 East Main Street
Westminster, Maryland 21157-5026

International Standard Book Number: 0-7884-3182-X

This book is dedicated to the
men and women of courage who,
without hesitation,
and with no thought for their own personal safety,
have endured hardships and pain,
and who have given their lives for the freedom of America.
From the Revolutionary War to the Civil War,
World War I, World War II and
through Korea, Vietnam and Iraq,
they have unselfishly given of themselves and their families
in defense of their country and others,
to uphold the principles and values
we so cherish today.
May we never forget what you have done.
May you never be forgotten.
We *will* remember.

Table of Contents

Foreword

It has been about 60 years since the end of World War II. Little has been told about the young men and women who left the Valley during that period, to be stationed in all areas around the world. We World War II veterans are very grateful to Dayle DeBry for this publication in which she will tell more about what happened to these people during those years. She has spent hundreds of hours researching on her computer, spending time at libraries, writing letters and making phone calls. She has traveled around the Antelope Valley, interviewing many of these veterans.

Dayle and her husband, Michael DeBry, moved to the Antelope Valley in 1979. At that time, both of them worked for General Dynamics on the Air Launched Cruise Missile program at Edwards Air Force Base. Later, Dayle would secure a job with Lockheed, in Palmdale, as an illustrator and junior manufacturing engineer on the L-1011 aircraft program. Since then, they have been blessed with two sons, Dustin and Brett DeBry.

Upon her arrival in the Valley, Dayle soon became interested in the area history and began to learn more about the people of the Antelope Valley. She began researching her family history in the 1980's and later became a member of the Antelope Valley Genealogical Society, where she was inspired to record the stories of the World War II veterans.

As a native son of the Antelope Valley and having lived here for over 90 years, I have been saddened to hear about the loss of many of these veterans and their families. I have also been privileged to watch many of these veterans return to the Antelope Valley to take an active part in turning several towns into small cities with their own self-elected government officials.

We all can be thankful to the veterans, not only of World War II, but the veterans of other wars as well, for the freedoms we enjoy today. We are fortunate to live in a great country and enjoy the everyday way of life we live today.

Glen Allen Settle
Chief Specialist (A) (PA)
United States Navy, 1942 - 1945

Dayle DeBry has undertaken this project to put together a journal about veterans in the Antelope Valley. Apparently, this is a never-ending task, because in spite of our desire for peace, we seem, inevitably, to find ways to involve ourselves in military engagements somewhere in the world and the participants in these engagements become the veterans of the future.

All veterans are not necessarily heroes in the strict sense of the word. As a matter of fact, many of us served in non-combat positions and never even heard a gunshot. On the other hand, any individual who gives up a portion of his or her freedom to serve our country provides a vital service in the protection of our American privileges.

The Antelope Valley is very cognizant of military affairs. Our people are reminded daily about the American need to look to our National Defense by virtue of our involvement in the aerospace industry. So, veteran or not, we are ever conscious of our country's needs, and are ever conscious of our patriotism and our love for our country.

I am a product of World War II – America's last "popular" war, if there can be such a thing. I am a part of a vanishing breed. The people of the Antelope Valley should pay tribute to their veterans, and for that reason I am glad to urge Dayle DeBry to complete her work. But in my somber moments, I say a prayer that some day, wars will end; world strife will cease and then maybe we can strike the words "veteran" and "war" from our vocabulary.

Larry Chimbole
Staff Sergeant
U.S. Army Air Corps, 1943 - 1946

Acknowledgments

"Immortality lies not in the things you leave behind, but in the people your life has touched."

Author unknown

My sincere expression of gratitude and appreciation goes to all the veterans and their families who have touched my life by sharing their stories and friendship. It is my hope that your words and stories will inspire and touch others, as they have touched and inspired me. It has been a pleasure and an honor to get to know each and every one of you, by phone conversations, letters, through research, and in person.

A special thank you to veterans Harry Du Bois; Cece Ellison; Paul Wheeler; Walt Primmer and his wife, Mickey; and Marguerite Rowell, for their help in locating many of their friends and schoolmates found in this book.

A grateful thank you to the historians from the many World War II groups, the Navy historians, Army and Air Force, and others, who have helped me locate military records and photographs of these men and women, and the stories of the soldiers missing or killed during World War II.

Thank you to Karla Archuleta for her continued support and encouragement; to Nancy Mehaffie, Helen Mendler and Beverlee Gurel, thank you.

Many thanks to Jaime Goodreau, U.S. History teacher at Lancaster High School, and her students, for their support of this book, and the community support from H.W. Hunter Dodge dealership in Lancaster, co-owner, Tim Hunter.

To Carol Fleming and Pat Holland, your many hours of correcting my errors and editing are greatly appreciated.

To Army Air Corps veteran Bill Clutterham – Thank you for keeping me in your prayers.

If I have left anyone out of these acknowledgements, it is purely an error on my part. Thanks to all who have helped make this worthwhile and important project come to life.

"The willingness with which our young people are likely to serve in any war, no matter how justified, shall be directly proportional as to how they perceive the veterans of earlier wars were treated and appreciated by their Nation."

~ George Washington

Introduction

The Antelope Valley is located in the Southern California high desert, in the western portion of the Mojave Desert, approximately sixty miles northeast of Los Angeles. The Valley includes the cities of Lancaster, Palmdale, California City, and the unincorporated communities of Rosamond, Littlerock, Pearblossom, Lake Los Angeles, Mojave, Quartz Hill, Boron, Edwards Air Force Base, North Edwards, Acton, Leona Valley, Lake Hughes and Lake Elizabeth.

Military use in the northern Antelope Valley began in 1933 when Colonel Henry "Hap" Arnold, Commander of March Field at Riverside, transferred a small detachment of men to the area. Their job was to set up a bombing and gunnery range. A large "tent city" known as East Camp had been formed by 1935. The nearby town was called Muroc, so named after the Corum family moved to the area and homesteaded in 1910. The Post Office wouldn't accept their family name of Corum for a new town, so they reversed it, hence the name "Muroc."

The Army Air Corps conducted war game maneuvers near Muroc in 1937, and by 1940, with the possibility of entering the war on the horizon, government lands in the nearby area were turned over to the Army and the surrounding lands that were privately owned were purchased. The base was in full swing by the end of 1941 and known as Muroc Gunnery and Bombing Range.

Fred Corum, left, uncle of Army veteran, Alvin Coltzau.
Photo courtesy of Alvin Coltzau.

On December 7, 1941, the news rang out to the citizens of the Antelope Valley – the Japanese had attacked Pearl Harbor. The first of many casualties from the Valley was Seaman, 1st Class, Ivan Westerfield, lost on the *U.S.S. Arizona* at Pearl Harbor on that fateful Sunday in December.

From that time on, the citizens of the Antelope Valley developed into a large and industrious family. Rationing in the area was quickly established. The principal items covered in the rationing were gasoline, coffee, meat, sugar and tires. Delivery trucks reduced their stops, and long lines formed on the special, limited delivery days. In these times, many new friends were made while socializing during the long waiting periods in line. Butter, cream and milk were in short supply, but the people living on the hundreds of farms and ranches in the community were thankful for the cows they had to supply them with these scarce commodities. Gardens sprung up in the towns - urged by the government, the citizens grew their own vegetables to relieve the shortage of labor and dependence on out-of-town transportation diminishing since the start of the war.

In Palmdale, the California State Council of Defense set up the Ground Observation Corps, established to report all planes that passed over the Valley area. In 1942, the American Red Cross set up its first fund drive, led by Chairman Dr. Roy Knapp, Superintendent of Antelope Valley Joint Union High School and Antelope Valley Junior College. These are only a few of the many deeds the dedicated men, women and children of the Antelope Valley joined in together, unselfishly supporting all aspects of the war activity beginning on December 7, 1941.

Shortly after war was declared, Muroc Gunnery and Bombing Range was designated Muroc Army Air Field. One of the primary functions of the base during World War II was bombing and gunnery crew training. A 650' practice target was installed in the shape of a Japanese Navy heavy cruiser nicknamed the "Muroc Maru." During this time Muroc served as an advanced training base for P-38 fighter pilots and B-24 bomber crews, receiving final bombing practice on "Maru" and further training before being shipped overseas. Muroc AAF also functioned as the base for development and flight testing of America's first jet – the XP-59A – during World War II, with the first flight in October of 1942. Muroc Army Air Field was changed in the 1950's to Edwards Air Force Base in honor of Captain Glen W. Edwards, a test pilot who died while flight-testing the experimental YB-49 aircraft in 1948.

In the early 1930's, aviatrix and well-known socialite, Florence "Pancho" Barnes, purchased an alfalfa farm in the remote are of Rosamond, near Muroc. She established the Civilian Pilot Training (CPT) Program at the local airfield in Palmdale through Antelope Valley Junior College. In the 1940's, she built a roadhouse restaurant and bar catering to officers and pilots, including General James "Jimmy" Doolittle, Army Air Force Commander General Henry "Hap" Arnold, Captain Chuck Yeager, and many other top military fliers.

After opening in 1941, War Eagle Field, located in Lancaster, provided training for British and Canadian cadets. After the onset of World War II, it was used for training U.S. Army Air Forces cadets.

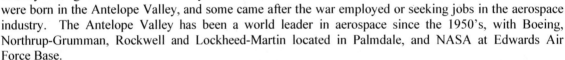

Young men who had never traveled outside their small communities, "farm boys," were now registered for the draft and entering into the service. Many of them willingly enlisted, heeding the call to duty and to serve with honor in this time of need in all branches of the service.

Women trained in the CPT Program, heading away from home – many for the first time. They trained as nurses, volunteered as Air Raid Wardens, worked as welders and riveters on numerous airplanes constructed during the war, and many supported their families while their husbands were away at war.

Within the pages of this book are the memories and stories of the men and women who bravely served their country during World War II. Many of these veterans were born in the Antelope Valley, and some came after the war employed or seeking jobs in the aerospace industry. The Antelope Valley has been a world leader in aerospace since the 1950's, with Boeing, Northrup-Grumman, Rockwell and Lockheed-Martin located in Palmdale, and NASA at Edwards Air Force Base.

In no cases are the veteran's stories intended to be full life stories of their achievements and services. Due to the great number of stories written, it was necessary to make them somewhat brief. Every one of the men and women in this book deserves mention as well as the deep appreciation of this community and country, no matter how large or small a part they played during their service in World War II.

Many of the stories include the thoughts and remembrances of the veterans or their families, spoken in the language that was acceptable during those times. Through research, the author has tried to, as accurately as possible, recall the lives of these men and women. If there are any errors in the following pages, sincere apologies are offered by the author. This book, by no means, includes all the men and women who served from the Antelope Valley. The author will continue interviewing and collecting the stories from the veterans and their families for a future publication.

"A soldier is not dead unless he is forgotten."
~Author unknown~

Antelope Valley Ledger-Gazette ad – August 23, 1945

Before the war...

...Antelope Valley Joint Union
High School
and
Antelope Valley Junior College
days

John Stege

George Campbell

Louis Massari

Back row, middle:
 George Bones
Back row, right:
 Bob Bright

Front row, left to right:
Stanley Washburn,
Paul Wheeler, Jack
Cozad

3

Cece Ellison

C. Wilber Lundy

Back row, left to right:
R.C. Franklin, Don McDonald

Front row, left to right:
Francis Batz, Don Bones

4

Jim Burns

Russell Godde

Clifford Burton

After the war…

THOSE WHO DIDN'T COME HOME...

"He stands in the unbroken line of patriots who have dared to die that freedom might live, and grow, and increase its blessings. Freedom lives, and through it, he lives – in a way that humbles the undertakings of most men."

~ Franklin D. Roosevelt ~

1st Lt.
Robert V. Batz
Army Air Corps

Ensign
Robert V. Bennett
U.S. Navy

S/Sgt.
Lorne C. Blasdell
U.S. Army

2nd Lt.
John W. Cozad
Army Air Forces

2nd Lt.
Edward G. Foote, Jr.
Army Air Forces

PFC
James Forsyth
Army Air Forces

2nd Lt.
Herbert G. Fritz
Army Air Corps

2nd Lt.
Russell H. Godde
Army Air Forces

MM/1st Class
Edward Henkel
U.S. Navy

2nd Lt.
Edward Patterson
Army Air Forces

Seaman 2nd Class
Earl M. Perkins
U.S. Navy

Ensign
Richard M. Rowell
U.S. Navy

Private
Walter E. Scates, Jr.
U.S. Army

AMM/1st Class
Laverne Shaffstall
U.S. Navy

S/Sgt.
Victor E. Thacker
Army Air Forces

2nd Lt.
Glen E. Thomas
Army Air Forces

QM/ 3rd Class
Donald S. Ulmanek
U.S. Navy

Seaman 1st Class
Ivan A. Westerfield
U.S. Navy

Killed or missing, no photos available:

2nd Lt. Thomas Bergin – U.S. Army
PFC Jack Marriott – U.S. Army
Horace L. Allen - Civilian

9

Circa 1947 photograph on Cedar Avenue, Lancaster – County building complex with
World War II Veterans Monument on the right.
Photo courtesy of Walt Primmer.

    The World War II monument pictured in the above photograph was a project of the Lancaster Chamber of Commerce. Today, after being vandalized, the monument is covered with stone, completely concealing the names of 709 men and women from the Antelope Valley who served their country during the war. On the following pages is a list, an "Honor Roll" of the names inscribed on the monument. The names were transcribed from the Antelope Valley Ledger-Gazette newspaper, published on May 10, 1945. It is *not* a complete list of all who served, only a list of names available at that time. The names are listed on the following pages as they were printed in the newspaper. Some of them are spelled incorrectly and are listed as found.

    On February 28, 1946, the Ledger-Gazette printed an article about the conception of this monument:

"Valley Service People Honored By Chamber"
~Beautiful White Silica Used In Making Monument Which Weighs Almost Eleven Tons As Completed~

    The World War II monument on the county property at the corner of 10th [now Lancaster Blvd.] *and Cedar Avenue has just recently been completed. A project of the Lancaster Chamber of Commerce, the monument was begun during the war and many difficulties were encountered in the construction.*

    Budd Aven, a member of the committee in charge of the project, was largely responsible for carrying through the building and completion. Many hours of his time were given to finding the proper materials and getting together the necessary workmen. But for the wholehearted cooperation of local citizens it would have been almost an impossibility to complete the project.

The Lancaster Chamber of Commerce is most appreciative of the generous help of Jack Orr in donating his labor to the forms; Charles Siebenthal for the donation of the native white silica of which the monument is made; Clifford and Cecil Burton for the use of equipment and labor in the crushing of the silica; W.I. Welsh for the donation of equipment and labor in pouring the concrete monument and walks; Clarence and Gene Welsh for their donation of labor on the concrete work; Fred Morton for donation of labor in polishing the monument, and last but not least, the donation of the beautiful hand wrought spiral atop the monument made by George Black.

The monument was conceived as a memorial to the men and women of the Antelope Valley who served in the armed forces in World War II. Their names are printed on the monument. In front of those who gave their lives is printed a gold star. The monument has been built to withstand the elements for many generations and weighs about eleven tons.

The monument committee states that the names of those who have entered service since the cessation of hostilities will not be added to the names on the monument. Only those who served during the war are eligible.

A

Wayne Abern
Leo E. Alexander
Ralph A. Alrich
Delbert O. Allen
Louelder Allen
Kenneth W. Allen
Richard Alley
Ruth G. Allington
John Almandoz
Charles W. Anderson
Chester G. Anderson
John M. Anderson
Lewis M. Anderson
Lonnie Anderson
Lovie Earl Anderson
Murton Anderson
Ray D. Anderson
Sherman Anderson
William H. Anderson
Gene E. Aronson
Jack E. Aronson
Joseph L. Asbury, Jr.
Oscar E. Austin, Jr.

B

William Babi
Glen M. Badgley
Ralph Earl Baehr
James M. Bagby
Frank E. Bailey
David L. Baker
Fred R. Baker
Marvin E. Barnes
William R. Barnes
Harley O. Barnett
Robert Barnett
George E. Bassler
Francis L. Bates
John E. Baty
Arthur Francis Batz
David J. Batz
Herschel E. Beard, Jr.
Gordon M. Beckwith
Kenneth Beckwith
Jack R. Beer
Howard W. Beery
Donald J. Beeson
Vincent E. Belvill
Charles J. Bennett
Claude Bennett
Francis W. Benson

G.H. Benson
Carl Bergman
Richard Bergin
William Bergin
Edward T. Beyer
John W. Beyer
Henry Billett
Kline R. Billet
R.S. Birch
Harry M. Blasdell
Robert L. Bliss
Dale Bocock
John Lee Bolin
Edwin G. Bond
Richard G. Bond
Donald R. Bones
Allan Lee Boyd
R.M. Boyd
Verdon Bragg
Max Breiholz
Don L. Brewer
Donald Bright
Robert H. Bright
Cecil M. Brown
David C. Brown
David L. Brown
Edward T. Brown
Franklin Brown
James M. Bugby
Jack Bull
Charlie H. Bunch
Buster Burges
Clifford G. Burton
James R. Bull
Vernon V. Bull
James H. Burns
Emil Burson
Kathryn Butler

C

Kendall Cahill
Courtney Calhoun
Calvin D. Camp
Clifford Campbell
George M. Campbell
John H. Campbell
John W. Campbell
Joseph W. Campbell
Lemuel Campbell
Paul C. Campbell
James A. Carlass
Alan S. Carp
Robert Carp
Howard C. Carter

Anthony K. Casamona
Brander Castle
Myles Castle
Rance Castle
Stephen Castle
James Cheney
Richard Cheney
Don Christiansen
Hans Christiansen
Robert S. Cissell
Vere D. Clair
James E. Clark
Melvin Clark
Thomas H. Clements
James R. Cleveland
O. Terry Cleveland
Nello C. Cluff
A.C. Cobb
George J. Cochems
Donald E. Cockrell
Guthrie Collins
Alvin M. Coltzau
Carence E. Cook
Robert L. Cook
Richard J. Coons
Henry C. Cooper
Jack Cooper
Lester L. Cox
Dean W. Craig
Everett Craton
Gilbert Craton
Leroy Craton
Harold Crawley
C.A. Cross
Raymond Cross
Wm. Joseph Cunningham
Duncan Currie
Raymond A. Curtis
Daniel O. Curtis

D

Hardin Paul Darling
Kenneth H. Day
Leaurence de Bejar
Robert de Bejar
Roderick J. de Bejar
Edward F. De Lemere
James H. Denney
M. Denney
Jack Diebler, Jr.
Anthony J. Dluzak
Carl E. Dodson
Royal Dorsett
Theodore B. Dorsett

Gillia V. Dowell
Harry S. Du Bois
Ralph Du Bois
Harry C. Dudley
Herbert C. Dudley
John Duhart
Louis J. Duhart
Robert Duhart
Frank E. Dunham
Price M. Dunn

E

Merle Edge
Paul J. Ednoff
Thurman Edwards
Ewald Eisele
Lawerence F. Ekker
Cris P. Eliopulos
John Eliopulos
Theodore Eliopulos
Charles B. Ellison
Robert B. Ellison
A.D. Evans
Conrad E. Evans
Harold L. Evans
Paul H. Evans
Preston L. Evans

F

George Faina
Otis Fairchild
Albert W. Farmer
Elbridge Faulkener, Jr.
Russell Ferguson
Orval Ferrell
Irwin H. Finck
Jack Fisher
Raymond L. Flory
Fred Foote
Ike Fox
Richard H. Francis
Leslie Frank
Harry L. Frazier
Maburn L. Frazier
Thomas R. Frazier
Roy S. Freeman
Malcolm Freeman
William H. Freeman
Verne M. Freeman, Jr.
Edwin H. Friend
Harold Frye

G

Wilfred Galloway
Herald C. Gagon
Roland H. Gantt
Jack T. Gardner
William E. Geile
Charles H. Gentry
Daniel L. Gibbons
Jesse G. Glouser
Charles Goldsberry
Fred T. Goldsberry
Maria Alva Gonzales
Ernest N. Gookins
Nathan A. Goodkins
Blas L. Gorrindo
Homer L. Graham, Jr.
Howard L. Graham
Lester M. Graham
George Gray
William J. Gregg
Burress Griffin
Morris N. Griffin
Joseph Grove
Edward J. Guill

H

Carl C. Hair
William R. Haley
Lloyd A. Hall
William J. Ham
John B. Hamblen
Jess C. Hamby
Ray S. Hamilton
Bobby W. Hanes
Sherman O. Hanks
Harold H. Hanson
George C. Harris
Lyle P. Hatley
Jack Hawke
Richard Haworth
Charles G. Henderson
David L. Herbert
Robert P. Herbert
Robert E. Hersey
David Hibbett
William High
Charles R. Hiller
Donald Hiller
Albert Hinojosa
Joaquin Hinojosa
Samuel Cox Hitte
Darrell L. Hobbs

Lloyd A. Hodge
Veryle E. Hodge
Victor R. Hofbauer
Gustavo Holquin
Raymond Holmes
William Walter Holmes
Vincent E. Hooper
James C. Horton
Willard V. Hosier
Jimmy Hronis
George C. Huffmire
Earl T. Hull
Charles K. Hulteen
John L. Humberd
R.E. Humphreys
Charles A. Hurd

I

Donald Lee Ikeler
Frank Ikeler

J

Carl C. Jackson
Joe H. Jackson
Donald L. Jaqua
L.S. Jaqua
Leroy Jackson
Ralph A. Jensen
Cecil Johnson
Robert A. Johnson
Ira Johnson
Jess Johnson
Oscar C. Johnson
Charles H. Jones
Edward Joseph

K

Anthony Kappas
Nick A. Kappas
Richard W. Keeney
Thomas B. Keeney, Jr.
Sam E. Keeton
William D. Keller
Jack R. Kellogg
Frank L. Kelly
P.H. Kenck
Kenneth Kennepohl
Ralph G. Kennepohl
Peter C. Kercher
Robert Kief

Bobby Carl King
Elbert L. King
Leeland S. King
Thomas C. King
Walter King
Bert Kirst
Floyd Klasson
Ronald J. Knapp
Carl Knoll
John A. Kostopulos
Sheldon Krave
Alvin Kreuger
Ray Kreuger
Louis E. Krubsack

L

Leslie H. Landin
Royal C. Lang
Stewart Lank
Walter J. Leake
Ernest B. Leidholt
Marion G. Lee
Donald Lewis
P.W. Lewis
Richard C. Lewis
Richard D. Lewis
Richard R. Lewis
Vernon E. Lewis
Lowell I. Lorbeer
J.C. Lindamood
John P. Lizarraga
Albert Llarena
Roy G. Logan
Clare P. Love
Robert L. Lowell
George Luby
R.L. Luby
John Lucero
C. Wilbur Lundy
Jack D. Lutes

M

Alexander Magowan
Euen Markam
Floyd Martin
George Martin
Jack Martin
O.W. Martindale
K.L. Marvin
Earl W. Masters
S. Matsubara
John A. Maynard

Verner E. Maynard, Jr.
Donald N. McAdam
W.J. McAdam, Jr.
Ashley McCaleb
C.T. McCaleb
Kenneth McCaleb
Robert McClaughry
Marvin R. McConnell
J.A. McDonald
Russel R. McIver
Glen R. McKenna
Dean A. McNeil
Richard L. McKinney
Vernon K. McKinney
Ralph G. McMurray
Byron C. Meline
Clarence Mendenhall
Elver V. Mendenhall
James R. Mettler
William G. Merritt
Alfred R. Michael
Carroll T. Migneault
Charles E. Miller, Jr.
Charles W. Miller
Edward L. Miller
A. Lee Mills
J.D. Mills
Martin V. Monia
Herbert Moise
John W. Moise
Jack R. Mojonnier
Chauncey A. Moore
George V. Moore
Harry E. Moore
James L. Moore
Thomas Moore
S.L. Moreno
Wilbur Moriarty
Albert Morris
Daniel J. Morris
George K. Morris
C.E. Morton
Curtis O. Moulton
James Wesley Mumaw
Carl E. Munz
Ward Myers

N

Louis Nastos, Jr.
Alvin E. Neilson
Charles Nepinsky
William H. Newell
Carl E. Newton
Dale Newton

James Nichols
Franklin W. Nicholas
Max D. Nicholson
Jim Nishimoto
W.J. Norris
F.F. Norton
W.R. Norton
Alex Nosik
Stanley Nosik
Donald Nourse

O

Franklin H. Oakes
Russell E. Ohneck
Wesley Victor Olds
Carmen Oliaz
Cliff Olson
Bernard Orlando
Michael T. Orlando
James E. Orr
John P. Orr
Homer F. Osborn
Robert O. Osborn
Jane Ottoson

P

George D. Padgett
Lester Pagluiso
Milton M. Pallock
George Palacius
James W. Pangborn
Boyd L. Parker, Jr.
Donald D. Parker
Claude A. Parker
Robert C. Parks
Gerald Parmer
Paul J. Patterson
Clyde Payne
Thomas B. Payne
Louis A. Pendley
Clarence Perkins
John D. Perkins
Charles Peterson
Ray Peterson
Ralph Peterson
Robert A. Peterson
James O. Phelps
Robert H. Phelps
David E. Pitts
Dale V. Pleake
Frank Plume
Herndon Polf

Leonce E. Pollard
Floyd B. Pond
Murray Pond
E. Allan Potter
Keith Potter
Nolan Price
Kenneth Prichard
Walter Primmer
Will J. Pritchard
Eldon J. Probert
George Pryor
Irving C. Purdy
Jack Puterbaugh
Edward Putman
Harold S. Putman
Willard Pyle

Q

S.M. Queen

R

William E. Rabe
Charles Rader
Norman Rader
John Glen Ralphs
Elias Ramirez
Jess Ramirez
Robert M. Randall
Donald Randleman
Jack Randleman
Raymond L. Rankin
Paul W. Rastawicki
William Rasterwicki
Burnis Reed
Galen W. Reed, Jr.
John E. Reuschel
Jack Reynolds
Virgil L. Rhodes, Jr.
Chester Rice
Ralph Ridgway
Norman Riess
Dean C. Ritchie
Charles Roberts, Jr.
Leonard A. Robinson
William A. Robinson
W.J. Robinson
Donald F. Roe
Charles E. Rogers
Charles S. Rogers
Randolph Rogers
Raymond D. Rogers
William A. Rogers

Jim W. Romine
Whiford Rose
Richard E. Rowe
Joe F. Rowles
John S. Rowles
Herman Rush
Allan Russell
L.M. Russell

S

Roy G. Sale
Ernest E. Samuelson
Clarence B. Scates, Jr.
Merrill Schaffert
Alexander C. Schneider
Leo L. Schwab
Edward H. Schwake
Eugene Schwake
Estelle Schwartz
Milton Schwartz
Merle T. Scofield
George B. Scott
Robert D. Scott
Joseph Seleya
Lawrence W. Sellers
Pete K. Semerenko
George Semerenko
Glen A. Settle
Jack Hurst Settle
Robert E. Settle
J.H. Shear
Robert E. Sherlock
Kenneth P. Sherrill
Elwood L. Shirk
Charles A. Shotts
Ernest P. Sievers
Roy J. Simi
John C. Sinn
Donald D. Skelton
Leland J. Skelton
John N. Skinner
Edward O. Smith
G. Kenneth Stanton
Floyd M. Smith
Harry D. Smith
Henry Harvey Smith
Ralph Smith
Roy C. Smith, Jr.
Russell L. Spangenberg
Paul Snyder
Charles Specht
R.A. Specht
Herbert E. Spencer
Russell Spitler

R.E. Stambook
O.M. Stark
Dean Leroy Stebbins
Gilbert D. Stebbins
John A. Stege
Jim A. Stemmons
Don R. Sterling
Arthur M. Stewart
Judson Stickney
William C. Stickney
Gene W. Stivers
Phil Stoore
Layard Philip Stoudt
Roy R. Stoudt
Clement W. Sullivan
Donald Swedlund

T

Emery L. Talley
Marion D. Talley
Mitchell G. Tanen
Gordon E. Taylor
Jean S. Taylor
Bob F. Tharp
Anthony J. Thomas
George C. Thomas
Orville Thomas
Lawrence Keith Tindall
Verne C. Torkelson
Russell G. Torrey
Clyde D. Townsend
Walter E. Tryon
Edwin A. Tucker
Mary Ellen Tullos

U

R.G. Uecke
George Ullman
Kurt F. Ullman
Minter Uzzell

V

James Van Sickle
Russell L. Van Sickle
Hugh Taylor Varty
Royal E. Varty
Kerns Vaughan
W.A. VerWeire

W

J.N. Wade
Robert W. Wade
R.W. Waldrip
Leslie H. Waldron
Jack L. Walker
T. Walker
Troy Wall
W.F. Walters
Francis G. Ward
Kenneth R. Ward
Leonard H. Ward
Robert R. Ward
Vernon Ward
Aaron Warkentine
George A. Washburn
Stanley Washburn
Clyde Watkins
Troy Watters
Arthur A. Weaver
Saul Weingarten
Clair S. Welch
Arthur Westcott
Lawrence A. Wheeler
Paul E. Wheeler
Edward Allen White, Jr.
Floyd Whitson
W.F. Whittlesey
Howard Earl Wilber
Clay O. Williams
George N. Williams
Harry F. Williams
Marion Williams
Perry N. Williams
Rodney F. Willingham
Asa C. Wilson
Esther Wilson
James H. Wilson
Kenneth Windbigler
Laurence A. Wiskerson
Ely M. Withers
Willard Withers
Jim Witte
Milton H. Wolf
C.C. Wohlquist
George E. Wolz
Gene A. Wolz
Charles Ware Wood
Joseph H. Wood
Robert G. Wood
Clayton W. Woodhull
Winifred Woodhull
Herbert Wright
Max C. Wurster

Y

Frank Young
Richard Young
James C. Youngblood
Edward J. Yrigollen

Z

Pete P. Zaro
Bernard J. Zarzana

~~~~~~~~~~~~~~~~~~~

Died in Performance of Duty

Lucius Fritz
James Forsyth
Edward Henkel

Killed in Performance of Duty

R.V. Bennett
Thomas Bergin
Lorne Blasdell
Russell H. Godde
John W. Cozad
E.G. Foote, Jr.
Richard Rowell
Walter E. Scates
Laverne Shaffstall
V.E. Thacker
Glen E. Thomas
Ivan Westerfield

Missing in Action

Horace L. Allen
Robert V. Batz
Edward Patterson

Prisoners of War

Orville E. Haworth

Jack Marriott
Donald J. McDonald
John M. Schaeffer
Donald Stout
Royal P. Smith

Honorably Discharged

John Almandoz
Rex Cecil Anderson
Robert Bland
Wayne Bocock
George T. Brinley
Margaret Walters Castle
C.M. Chaney
Virgil Cotton
J.K. Fuller
Henry Ivan Dorsett
Claude O. Frazier
Verne M. Freeman
Gary E. Gorsline
Lowell Guymon
William J. Harris
Donald M. Hosier
La Verne Hooper
William James
Herbert Kellogg
Harry Kirby
Vernon E. Maddox
Clarence D. Mapes
Paul Murtha
Joseph Nelson
James F. Nourse
E.E. Osborn
Jack H. Pangborn
Marcus D. Pendley
Justus C. Pickleheimer
William Prohaska
Thomas J. Puckett
Samuel Reeves
Frank B. Rutledge, Jr.
Hugh Slocum
Kenneth G. Spangenberg
Irma Story
Ralph Tanner
L.A. Thacker
N.W. Waldrip
George William Thomas
William Walz, Jr.
Logan B. White

On the steps of Antelope Valley Joint Union High School - Home from the war - 1946

Photo courtesy of Frank Stubbings

1. George Sheldon
2. Ray Hobbs
3. Bill Barnes
4. Dave Batz
5. Bill Geile
6. Ted Eliopulos
7. Vito (unknown)
8. Ernie Perria
9. Rod Willingham
10. Joe (unknown)
11. Merton Anderson
12. Jack Kugler
13. Al Krueger
14. John Duhart
15. Ray Krueger
16. Dean (unknown)
17. Anthony Batz
18. Eldon Probert
19. (unknown)
20. Glen Ralphs
21. Francis Batz
22. (unknown)
23. John Jackson

These posters were issued by the U.S. government during WWII to encourage enthusiasm and patriotism on the home front. Courtesy of the National Archives.

RICHARD FREDERICK "DICK" ALLEY

Richard Frederick Alley was born September 13, 1919 in Pomona, Los Angeles Co., California, the son of Fred Arthur and Olga Grace (Schisler) Alley. He had two siblings; Ruth and Marjorie Alley. By the time Dick was two years old, the family had moved to the Antelope Valley. Dick graduated from Antelope Valley Joint Union High School District (AVJUHS) in 1937.

On November 9, 1940 Dick married Maxine Moore in Nevada. They had two children; Gary Alley and Patricia (Alley) Newman.

Dick enlisted in the Army Air Corps and was assigned to the 11th Air Force. He traveled to the Aleutian Islands as part of the Aleutian Campaign in 1942-1943, and later attained the rank of Corporal.

Dick passed away April 2, 1983 at St. Vincent Medical Center in Los Angeles, California. He is interred at Joshua Memorial Park and Cemetery in Lancaster, Los Angeles Co., California.

JOHN "JOHNNY" ALMANDOZ

On January 18, 1910, John Almandoz was born in New Idria, San Benito Co., California, the son of Juan and Romualda (Aizpeurrutia) Almandoz. Juan and Romualda immigrated from Spain to the United States in 1908. John had two siblings; a brother, Joe, born in Spain, and a half-brother, Albert Llarena. Juan died in 1915 at age 35 in San Francisco Co., California. In 1926, the family moved from Inglewood, California, to the Antelope Valley, where they bought acreage on Avenue H in Del Sur. John's mother had remarried to Tomas Llarena, also from Spain. John and his brother, Joe, worked on their ranch as well as working for the Bell family.

John was drafted into the Army Air Corps in 1942. He was stationed at Merced Field, in the San Joaquin Valley, California, with the 90th Base Headquarters and Air Base Squadron.

On April 24, 1949, John married Mary Uarte in Las Vegas, Clark Co., Nevada. They had one child together, a daughter, Mary Jane. John passed away on December 1, 1987 in Lancaster, Los Angeles, Co., California and is buried at Joshua Memorial Park and Cemetery in Lancaster.

CARL COLUMBUS "BARNEY" BARNES

Carl Columbus Barnes was born on March 10, 1921, in Hugo, Choctaw Co., Oklahoma, the son of William Milton and Linnie May (Bowen) Barnes. Carl's siblings included two sisters; Velma Lorraine and Shirley Oneta Barnes; four half-sisters; Mary, Stella, Ellen, and Helen Barnes; and three half-brothers; Arthur, William and Leslie Barnes.

Shortly after Carl was born, the family decided to move west to Yuma, Arizona, where his father found work in the fruit orchards. After the fruit season ended, the family moved on to the Imperial Valley, near Banning, California. On the advice of Carl's Aunt Pearl, the Barnes family again picked up and moved – this time to Shafter, in Kern Co., California. It was there that they joined Carl's grandfather, Luther Steven Barnes, and great grandfather, William Cobb Barnes. With their help, the family began farming cotton and alfalfa.

Carl's interest in aviation began at a young age in Ojai, Ventura Co., California, where he would watch in awe each airplane that would fly over the valley. He began making homemade airplane "kites" with fishing line from his father's tackle box. As soon as he saved up his money, Carl would buy model airplane kits. It was with those kits that his study and understanding of flight began.

Carl's first aviation experience was at Kern County Airport where he refueled the airplanes coming through the airpark. He then moved on to work for a government pilot training school at the airport, working as a mechanic with the "Eagle Squadron" pilots, where he earned a Certified Aviation Mechanic ticket. On occasion, Carl was able to go along with an instructor who would let him handle the airplane controls, but not a landing.

In 1942, Carl attended Aviation Mechanics School, in Texas, where he earned credits to become a U.S. Army Air Corps aviation cadet. His basic training was in San Antonio, Texas, where he was assigned as a Flight Engineer and top turret gunner on a B-17 bomber. Carl's duties as Flight Engineer included assisting the pilot or co-pilot in landing the plane, if one was taken out of action. As a top turret gunner, Carl was encased in a plexiglas bubble on top of the fuselage of the aircraft. This was a vulnerable place for a gunner due to the cramped quarters and lack of vision that consisted of looking forward with a narrow field of fire. The peripheral vision was almost nonexistent.

Carl was assigned to the 8th Air Force, 351st Bombardment Group, 511th Bombardment Squadron, in Polebrook, Northamptonshire, England, where he flew 35 missions with his B-17 crew over Germany. Carl recalled one harrowing return from Mission #25, Leipzig, Germany, on November 30, 1944:

"The wake up call was unusually early for the day's mission. Seldom were we awakened at 01:00 and it deepened our concern for any chance of survival. As I staggered out for the breakfast of the usual French toast and coffee, I was having a very difficult time in rationalizing my personal outcome for the remaining ten missions.

It was a matter of physical, mental, and emotional stress that had really gotten to me. No human mind or body was supposed to go through such hell for as long as we had been fighting, flying over Germany, dodging the flak, and fighting off the many damned German fighters, and not be somewhat touched.

As the war dragged on, the German fighters, (ME-109 and Fock-Wulf) had become more determined to destroy our bomber efforts regardless of the target. At the morning briefing, the base commander gave us the word, 'Target for today is (our hearts dropped) LEIPZIG. There are several of the most important oil refineries on the outskirts of the city and we are going to blast them off the face of the German earth.' The Colonel could get pretty carried away when he was not going on a mission, and he put everything into the days briefing, telling us just how important it was that we do a great job.

Leipzig was deep in the heart of Germany, south of Berlin. The refineries were one of the most protected targets that we had to face, and the Germans let us know that we would pay one hell of a price in trying to bomb the area. There would be a lot of extra flak and every German fighter plane that was still serviceable would be in the air to meet us as we started our bomb run."

"Way before we were close to Berlin, the hard fighting began. ME-109's by the hundreds, Fock-Wulf fighters by the dozen, and a variety of twin engine planes came at us from every direction. We would have to fight our way into the target area and again fight our way back until we crossed into the English Channel. This would not be a good day. We began our bomb run right on course and on schedule. Just at the bomb release, we caught several damaging bursts of heavy flak which knocked out two engines and set them on fire. We had been bombing from 26,000 feet when we were hit, and it was a long way home.

The pilot put the plane into a steep dive in order to attempt to put the fire out. There is nothing that scares the devil out of you more than being in an airplane from that altitude, on fire in the No. 4 engine, with still lots of 100 octane fuel on board, diving almost straight down with the onrushing ground staring each of us in the face. We were sure that we had bought the farm [death] and it wasn't even our farm.

At 500 feet, the dive had blown the fire out and we struggled to level off just above the tree tops and hopefully avoid any remaining German fighters, as we groped our way across Germany, Belgium, Holland, and on to the English Channel. The Germans must have thought we had crashed, for none made their presence known.

The Channel allowed us to take our first deep breath and some measure of hope that we would soon be at our base and safety. We were still at about 500 feet over the Channel waters, and the White Cliffs of Dover were staring us straight in the face. Slowly we began to climb on the remaining engines, in order to have enough altitude to clear the Dover Cliffs at about 3,000 feet. At some ten miles from England, and still over the Channel, the remaining engines began to cut out and miss.

In a second, I called for emergency procedures to begin, and also called out for emergency landing instructions. With no other choice, I sent the remaining engine to the fire wall. We knew with full throttle on the one engine, our time was very limited and we just had the one choice. We had to glide to our base at Polebrook, and pray one heck of a lot - loud - so everyone and anyone could hear.

The runway at our base was almost straight in on the flight path that we were on, so we headed straight into the runway. Just as we were about to cross the approach end of the runway, the one remaining engine stopped dead. We were at stall speed before the engine stopped, and now with all engines out, we began to drop like a heavy rock. I had put the landing gear down and as we smashed into the runway, the landing gear folded up into the wing, and across the runway we slid, breaking into a ball of fire.

I knew all our numbers that we had counted on were about to end in one big bang. As the plane slowed down enough for us to gather our thoughts of survival, the first one to begin getting out was the bombardier. His home on the plane was in the nose, and he had to come by me in order to escape to the outside. As he crashed by me, he banged against my leg, waking me from the stupor I was in, and I came out of the haze. The bombardier was short and a little on the chubby side. I was afraid that he would get stuck in the bomb bay, so I jumped in front of him and kicked the aft side door open, hitting the ground at one heck of a run, out across the field, and as far away from the burning plane as I could get.

Somewhere, about in the center of the field, an ambulance raced along side me. A medic shouted, 'Get

in!' Several of the crew were running together shouting, 'Wait until we get farther away from the plane before she blows up!' Several times we had seen and been part of many such crashes and watched helplessly, as the plane exploded into hundreds of pieces. We did not want to be part of such a statistic.

The crew gathered many yards away from the plane and just collapsed in utter exhaustion, even to pray. No one said a word. Each crew member almost as one, got up and headed to the debriefing room and our double shot of 'medicine.' So ended our 25th mission. Now [with] only ten more to go, and if I survived - home. Tomorrow would be another day, and if the weather would cooperate, there would be another mission, somewhere into hell."

Carl cheated death several times before and after this mission, each time he stepped into the B-17. He later flew in C-46 cargo planes during supply missions in Korea.

Carl Barnes – proud of his Scottish heritage. Photo taken in Scotland.

During his service as a Technical Sergeant in WWII, Carl received the following awards; Air Medal – 7 times, in the European-African-Middle Eastern Campaign, with 5 Bronze Stars; European Victory Medal; Presidential Unit Citation for "extraordinary heroism, determination, and esprit de corps in action against the enemy"; World War II Victory Medal; and a letter of appreciation with a medal from France.

On June 14, 1947, Carl married Martha Rose Marple. In October 1954, the couple found a home in Palmdale, California. They had two daughters; Janet Kay and Robin Sue Barnes.

After serving 2 ½ years during the Korean War, Carl worked at North American Aviation, at Edwards Air Force Base, for seven years. National Aeronautics and Space Administration (NASA) hired Carl for the X-15 program as a field representative, after being impressed with his work while he was at North American. He stayed at NASA until his retirement in 1986, after 30 years of dedicated service with numerous achievement awards on the X-15, SR-71, and water tunnel programs.

Carl was a Veterans of Foreign Wars (VFW) post commander and also an active member of the First Baptist Church in Lancaster. He volunteered his time with the WWII Living History Project, speaking to thousands of young people about his experiences during the war.

Carl passed away on January 6, 2003. A memorial service was held at the First Baptist Church in Lancaster, California, where hundreds of friends and family members gathered to remember a true American hero.

ARTHUR FRANCIS BATZ, JR.

Arthur Francis Batz, Jr., was born July 20, 1918 in Riverside, Riverside Co., California, the third of eight children born to Arthur Francis Batz and Etta Louise (Kowalski) Batz. The family moved to the Antelope Valley from Riverside in 1932 to a ranch on the east side of Lancaster. Arthur Jr., graduated from AVJUHS in 1937. Arthur Francis Batz, born in Minnesota, and his wife, Etta, born in Texas, were successful in the farming community of Riverside.

Arthur enlisted in the U.S. Army in March 1941 in order to serve his country and to do some traveling. After basic training, he was sent to Camp Roberts, in California. Arthur was assigned to the 15th Army, 66th Infantry, nicknamed the Black Panther Division. Their uniform shoulder patch included a red bordered circle containing a black panther's head against an orange background.

When war broke out in December 1941, Arthur was at home on leave and was told to report back to Camp Roberts. While at Camp Roberts, the unit moved under darkness to a park in the San Fernando Valley and set up camp there. Arthur was in charge of guarding the water supply at the camp.

When stationed in England, Arthur was acquainted with a school teacher and was invited to Christmas dinner in December 1944. After the dinner, the 66th Infantry Division was shipped out, again under the cover of darkness, when "all hell broke loose." Arthur was on the second ship leaving England for France. The first troop transport, the *S.S. Leopoldville,* to cross the choppy waters of the English Channel, was attacked by a torpedo from a German U-boat. The torpedo ripped into the transport hull. Over 800 Black Panther officers and soldiers were lost in the channel that Christmas day, with many more to lose their lives in valiant attempts to save their buddies.

Arthur and the 66th proceeded on their assigned mission. When they landed in Cherbourg, France, it was wet and cold. The troops proceeded to the St. Jacque airport. From there, they re-organized and continued south to St. Nazaire and west to Lorient to contain the enemy. With the freezing weather, their fingers froze on triggers of the guns and their feet were numb from the cold, waiting for the Germans while in the foxholes.

The 66th carried out daily reconnaissance patrols, continually harassing and firing on enemy installations. In April 1945, the Germans attacked the Black Panthers but were defeated with several enemy positions taken by the 66th. Enemy troops surrendered to the Division upon the end of the fighting in Europe on May 8, 1945. Arthur was on guard duty in France when the news broke about the war ending.
The 66th moved to Germany on occupation duty, near Koblenz, on May 20, 1945. The troops sailed for home on October 27, 1945.

Arthur's time in the service was not all war duty. During his furlough in California, some of his most memorable times were spent at the U.S.O. clubs, where he met many beautiful starlets from Warner Brothers Studios. During furloughs in Hollywood, California and Atlanta, Georgia, the men were treated to excellent service with generous accommodations in local hotels.

Make-shift camp, San Fernando Valley, California

1944, Arthur Batz with Faye Emerson, left, and Andrea King, right, Warner Brothers Studio starlets. "It was nice to be home on furlough."

Arthur was discharged at the rank of Corporal on December 20, 1945, after over four years of military service. He was glad the war was over so he could finally go home and get back to work on the farm. He attended local schools supported by the G.I. Bill. During the service he met several close friends whom he has kept in contact with for over 60 years.

During his service to his country Arthur received the American Defense Service Medal; the American Campaign Medal; European-African-Middle Eastern Theater Medal; and the World War II Victory Medal.

Arthur married Jessie P. Coleman, December 27, 1967 in Marlin, Falls Co., Texas. He continued in the farming business after the war and currently lives with his wife, Jessie, in Belton, Bell Co., Texas.

Robert V. Batz was born September 26, 1922 in Riverside, California, the fifth of eight children born to Arthur Francis Batz and Etta Louise (Kowalski) Batz. In 1932, the family moved from Riverside, California, to a ranch on the east side of the Antelope Valley. Robert attended Redmond Grammar School and graduated from AVJUHS in 1939.

Robert enlisted in the Army Air Forces and graduated from the Advanced Flying School in Altus, Oklahoma in Class 43-E, on May 24, 1943 at the rank of Lieutenant. Robert was assigned to the 15th Air Force, 736th Bomber Squadron, 454th Bomber Group (Heavy) on a B-24 aircraft.

The 454th transferred in to San Giovanni, Italy from the United States, on Sunday, January 16, 1944 with their B-24 airplanes. Their first mission was carried out on February 8, 1944, bombing the airfields at Viterbo, Tarquinia, Orvieto, Piombino and Prato, Italy.

Nearly every day after the first mission, the 454th with their B-17 and B-24 bombers, hit several targets in Italy, France, and Austria. On Sunday, February 20, 1944, the B-24's blasted troop concentrations in the Anzio, Italy beachhead area. Again on March 2, 1944, the 15th Air Force, with nearly 300 B-17's and B-24's, supported the U.S. 5th Army's Anzio beachhead, bombing the Cisterna di Roma-La Villa area, Velletri, and military targets in the battle area at several key points.

In March 1944, the B-24's, escorted by over 100 fighters, bombed the air depot at Klagenfurt, Austria, with other B-17 and B-24's hitting the air depot at Graz, Austria, and marshalling yards at Knin and Metkovic, Yugoslavia. The Luftwaffe fighters provided fierce opposition along with anti-aircraft fire from below. The opposition shot down 17 bombers and one fighter, while the U.S. claimed 30 enemy fighters were destroyed in combat.

On Saturday morning, May 27, 1944, Robert and his crew, onboard their B-24, along with over 700 other bombers, hit France. The B-24's bombed airfields at Montpellier and Salon, and marshalling yards at Nimes, Marseille/St. Charles and Marseille/La Blancharde. This would be the last mission for Robert Batz.

Lt. Batz was flying in the No. 4 position in a "D" box formation, when his airplane was hit by several bursts of flak. The flak hit close to the nose wheel section. The shell burst and hit the front of the airplane. Immediately after being hit, the plane went into a shallow dive. According to witnesses from a nearby air crew, the plane spiraled down, eventually hitting the water at Cape Rouix, off the coast of southern France.

Pilot Lt. Batz, the co-pilot, navigator, and top turret gunner were believed to have been killed instantly according to eyewitness accounts recorded in Missing Air Crew Report No. 5413. The ball-turret gunner was killed after the aircraft exploded while awaiting his turn to bail out. The nose-turret gunner bailed out but his chute did not function. Four other crew members survived after they successfully bailed out. Upon landing, they were captured by German soldiers and taken to the prison camp Dulag Luft.

Robert was reported as Missing in Action after completing 21 successful missions. His body was never recovered. 1st Lieutenant Robert V. Batz is listed on the Tablets of the Missing at Rhone American Cemetery in Draguignan, France. He was awarded the Purple Heart Medal, posthumously.

In February, 1945, Robert's mother was an honored guest at Minter Field in Bakersfield, California, where Colonel Newton H. Crumley, Minter Field Commanding Officer, presented her with the Air Medal and two Oak Leaf Clusters, awarded by order of the President of the United States to her son. The presentation was made at a special review and retreat parade ceremony.

Charles Jackson Bennett, Jr., was born July 8, 1919 in Runnels Co., Texas, one of six sons born to Charles Jackson and Modesta Lea (Barnett) Bennett, both from Texas. Charles had nine siblings including brothers, Moody, Wayne, Mitchell, Robert Vance and James; and sisters Alice, Lyndal, Margaret and Mittie Bennett. The Bennett family moved to the Antelope Valley in 1932 where Charles attended AVJUHS.

In 1941, Charles was engaged to Martha Virginia "Babe" Burge. Martha was a 1942 graduate of AVJUHS. Charles was drafted into the U.S. Army Coast Artillery in November 1941. He was at Camp Wallace in Texas when he heard about the attack on Pearl Harbor. After boot camp, he was sent to Fort Dix, New Jersey, then to Norfolk, Virginia, attached to the 31st Artillery Battalion.

Charles spent 42 months in the South Pacific during the war, first serving as part of a gun crew for a large artillery, then later as convoy commander. He served at several duty stations including New Hebrides, New Guinea and the Philippines.

Charles was in Manila, Philippines when the war ended. He was honorably discharged in October 1945 at the rank of Staff Sergeant. Charles was awarded the American Defense Medal; Asiatic-Pacific Campaign Medal with 2 Bronze Stars; Philippine Campaign Medal with 1 Bronze Star; Service Award from the State of Missouri.

When he returned home, Charles married his fiancé, Martha Burge, on November 25, 1945 at St. David's Episcopal Church in North Hollywood, California. Charles was a farmer and cattle rancher in Lancaster and New Mexico after returning from the war. In 1960, Charles and Martha moved to Missouri where they continued farming. In 1972, they sold the farm and Charles worked as a real estate broker until 1974, when he secured a job in the trucking business as a long-haul truck driver, owning and driving his own rig. He retired from the trucking business in 1996.

Charles passed away on May 6, 1998 in Cassville, Missouri. He is buried at Oak Hill Cemetery, Cassville, Barry Co., Missouri. His wife, Martha, resides in Cassville.

Charles and Martha Bennett

GERALD L. "JERRY" BIGALK

Gerald L. Bigalk was born May 30, 1922 in Cresco, Howard Co., Iowa, the only child born to Newton Clinton and Susan Loretta (Rounds) Bigalk. His parents were married on July 4, 1917. The Bigalk family moved to Chino, San Bernardino Co., California in 1935.

Jerry attended school in Chino where he graduated from high school in 1941. While attending high school, he took a printing class and after graduation he got a job working for a newspaper as a printer. Jerry remarked, "I found my natural talent."

While riding in a car with his cousin in Long Beach, California, Jerry first heard about the attack on Pearl Harbor as it was announced on the radio. On October 16, 1942 Jerry was drafted into the U.S. Army, reporting at Fort MacArthur, California on October 30, 1942. He was sent to Camp Barkeley, near Abilene, Texas for training in the Medical Corps from October 1942 to January 1943. In basic training, one of his instructors was Lew Ayers, the well-known film star and conscientious objector of World War II.

Boot camp was a challenging experience for Jerry with cold showers under canopies, with wooden slats to stand on; tents for sleeping quarters for eight men and huts with twelve men. The weather from October to January was extremely cold, so cold that during a snow storm the ink in a bottle would actually freeze. On weekends the men would get a break from training with the USO (United Service Organization) entertaining the troops.

After basic training, Jerry went to Fort Meade, Maryland from January 1943 to July 1944. He served for three months with the 76th "Liberty" Division, 204th Infantry Battalion, Company K, and after that he was assigned to the 3rd Service Command in the motor pool. Jerry was transferred to the Station Hospital and worked in the message center. From there, he was transferred to Camp Ellis, Illinois where he stayed from July to October 1944, joining up with the newly formed 202nd General Hospital and was assigned to the motor pool. In October 1944, he was sent to Camp Miles Standish, Massachusetts for overseas embarkation.

On October 30, 1944 Jerry sailed out of Boston Harbor on the *U.S.S. West Point* (AP-23), and landed in Liverpool, England on the morning of November 7, 1944. Upon debarking at Liverpool, the unit was sent to Chester, England. On December 14, they moved to Southampton with the motor pool to board a Victory Ship bound for Le Havre, France. While in port, the ship broke a boom loading a Sherman tank. It took nine days to replace the boom on the ship, delaying their trip.

The unit left Southampton on December 24, and landed in Rouen, France on December 31, 1944. The Battle of the Bulge was in progress so they could not land at Le Havre. Consequently, they went up the Seine River to Rouen where they spent time at the Cigarette Camps "Pall Mall" in Etretat, and "Twenty Grand" in Rouen. Before reaching the camps, Jerry ate a steady diet of C-rations for three meals a day. While in Rouen, the troops had their first "real" food.

On January 5, 1945 the unit left for Paris, France. After arriving in Paris, Jerry was assigned to an ambulance pool. He took soldiers that were wounded and unable to return to combat from the trains to hospitals in Paris. If they needed any further medical treatment they were taken to hospital trains and then on to England. The U.S. Army had eleven hospitals in Paris. Patients were also taken to Le Bourget and Orly Field to be flown to England and the United States. The unit was quartered in school dormitories on the outskirts of Paris. Later, the motor pool drivers moved to the 48th General Hospital in Paris.

One day while sitting in his ambulance, Jerry recognized a man with a familiar walk. He jumped out of his ambulance and yelled, "Melvin!" Then he called out, "Burkhart" and the soldier turned around. Out of 84 graduates in his high school class, Jerry ran into one of his schoolmates who had been wounded in Frankfurt, Germany. During the war Jerry ran into another schoolmate who graduated with a later class.

Jerry remarked, "I drove the ambulance about 5,000 miles on a shift of 12 (hours) on and 12 off, then 24 off." In August 1945, Jerry was sent with his unit to Camp Philadelphia, near Reims, France. They were then sent to Marseille, France where a staging area was set up in preparation for the invasion of Japan.

When the war ended in Japan, Jerry only had 41 points, so he was assigned to Occupation duty in Germany, attached to the 3rd Army while under the command of General George Patton. It was during that time, General Patton was killed in an automobile accident. Jerry was part of a convoy sent to Wurzburg, Germany. "We crossed the Rhine River at Strasburg on a pontoon bridge. It took us five days to make the trip." Jerry joined the 124th Evacuation Hospital and spent five months driving a 6x6 truck. He made several trips to Munich and other parts of Germany to pick up supplies for the hospital. One trip was spent transporting troops from Southern Germany to Pilsen, Czechoslovakia. While in Wurzburg, Jerry was granted a seven day pass to go to Switzerland, which was "wonderful" he said, "It was a good experience, but made me very homesick."

Jerry left Wurzburg the first part of March, 1946 to return home to Chino. He was attached to the 102nd "Ozark" Division for his return to the States. He sailed from Le Havre onboard the troopship *U.S.S. General R.L. Howze (AP-134)* and arrived in New York around March 10. "Coming in to New York Harbor and seeing the Statue of Liberty is something I will never forget." After debarking, Jerry was sent to Fort Dix, New Jersey where he boarded a C-54 airplane to Fort Hamilton, California, and bussed to Camp Beale, also in California.

Jerry was discharged at Camp Beale on March 21, 1946 at the rank of Tech Corporal. When Jerry was discharged, he had to call information to get his family's phone number so he could have his mother pick him up. It had been a long time away from home and from making phone calls to his family. Almost immediately, Jerry secured a job working for the Claremont Courier as a typesetter and doing page make-up work.

On March 21, 1947 Jerry married Artis Mae Baudoin in Chino, California. They had two daughters, Barbara Joyce and Marcia Jean Bigalk. In May of 1953, Jerry and Artis moved to the Antelope Valley with their daughter, Barbara. Artis passed away February 1, 2003 at her home in Lancaster. For 36 years, Jerry and Artis operated their own business, the Printing Service Center. For 30 of those years, the business was located on Fern Avenue in Lancaster.

Jerry still keeps in contact with Pete Quiring, an Army buddy from World War II, in Denver, Colorado.

Jerry's patches and pins from World War II

Top left – 3rd Service Command – Three Point patch

Top middle – Tech Corporal patch

Top right – U.S. Army lapel pin

Middle left – 3rd Army patch - General Patton, Army of Occupation

Middle right – 18 months overseas patch

Lower left – Medical Caduceus branch lapel pin

Lower middle – European Theater Advance Base "Invasion" patch

Lower right – 102nd Infantry "Ozark" Division patch

DONALD L. "DON" BREWER

Donald L. Brewer was born May 3, 1918 in California. He was the son of John H. Brewer, from Missouri, and Catherine (Saultz) Brewer, from Illinois. Don had one sister, Jacqueline Brewer. John Brewer was a plumber, working in Lancaster, California, according to the 1930 Antelope Township census. Don attended the local grammar school and graduated from Antelope Valley Joint Union High School in 1937. He was a member of the high school football team.

Don was drafted into the Army in March of 1941. He was assigned to California's 40th Infantry Division, known as "The Sunshine Division." The Division assembled at Camp San Luis Obispo, in California, for basic training. After basic training, Don was sent to Texas for further training in the communications field.

Don spent the war running communication lines throughout the jungles and over the terrain of New Britain, New Guinea, and the Lingayen area of Luzon in the Philippine Islands. He spent over three years in the Army without coming home until after the war ended.

Around 1947, Don married Ann Gibas. Ann was a music teacher at the Lancaster Grammar School. They had three daughters; Lora Lee, Donna Lee, and Nancy Lee Brewer. Donald passed away on June 6, 1971, at the young age of 52.

DAVID CHAMBERLAIN "DAVE" BROWN

David Chamberlain Brown was born September 26, 1920 in Canon City, Fremont Co., Colorado, the only child born to Arthur Janney Brown and Anna Maude (Chamberlain) Brown. In 1923 the family moved to Tacoma, Washington. They stayed in Washington until 1927 when they moved to El Segundo, California. David's father worked for the Standard Oil Company in Los Angeles County, California.

In 1929, Dave's parents purchased 12 ½ acres of land south of Lancaster, in the Antelope Valley, where the family would spend the summer and weekends away from the city of El Segundo. In 1935, Dave and his mother moved to Lancaster permanently.

Dave graduated from Antelope Valley High School in 1937, followed by two years of junior college. He graduated from the Antelope Valley Junior College in 1939, with only eleven other graduates in the class. After college, Dave found employment with the Edison Company where he stayed for 2 ½ years as a meter reader.

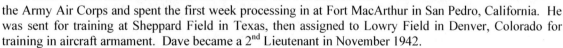

In June of 1942 Dave volunteered for the draft. He was drafted into the Army Air Corps and spent the first week processing in at Fort MacArthur in San Pedro, California. He was sent for training at Sheppard Field in Texas, then assigned to Lowry Field in Denver, Colorado for training in aircraft armament. Dave became a 2nd Lieutenant in November 1942.

After several months of training, Dave was sent to Miami, Florida, then on to Walterboro Army Airfield in South Carolina. As part of the 342nd Service Squadron, Dave was soon to leave on an adventure that would take him around the world. Dave sailed onboard the LST-326 (Landing Ship, Tank) on a trip across the stormy Atlantic Ocean. With high, churning seas, the ship almost turning on its side, the LST was disabled with a broken rudder. After repairing the damage, the ship sailed again, and in a long three weeks, landed in the Mediterranean at Arzew, the Port of Oran, in Algeria. While in Algeria, Dave wound up ill and was confined to the hospital there for three weeks.

In 1943, Lt. Brown was an armament officer stationed in Tunisia. He was scheduled to fly to Sicily for delivery of aircraft ordnance (machine guns, ammunition, bombs) to his group. Dave had information from his mother that his high school buddy, Lawrence Wheeler, who was with the Army, 3rd Division, was on R & R after the major campaign of Sicily was near an end.

The airfield where Dave landed was a few miles from the 3rd Division's camp. He borrowed an Air Corps Jeep and was able to find the bivouacked area where his buddy, Lawrence Wheeler's anti-tank outfit was located. To the surprise of Lawrence, there was Dave, standing in the tent! The former schoolmates had a great time talking for about an hour, reminiscing about the good old days in Lancaster. Dave was able to return to the airfield in time to catch his plane back to Africa.

In March of 1944, Dave was stationed in Southern Italy. From Italy, continually on the move by vehicle convoy, airplanes and ships, the Squadron traveled to Port Said, Egypt for two weeks of leave, before moving on again to Suez, Egypt, then to Bombay, India. Across India the 342nd Service Squadron traveled, this time by train. To Calcutta, then Assam, and on to Tinsukia. So far, they had traveled over 15,000 miles since the start of their trip. Traveling through dusty villages in the heat of summer, across the African desert, down towards the Sahara, moving and never unpacking, sleeping in tents and eating C-rations; through the winter with mud and cold, enduring flies and leeches, snakes and tigers. The group battled dysentery, black water fever, malaria, yellow jaundice, heat rash, and dozens of other diseases and infections while supplying the troops with their guns, ammunition, and bombs for their battles.

From the Indian Ocean, onto Ceylon, on a freighter loaded with jute, Dave sailed around the bottom of Australia for six weeks finally setting his eyes upon the Golden Gate Bridge in San Francisco, California. He was almost home after 2 ½ years away.

Dave went back to work with the Edison Company, after one month rest and recuperation from his travels during the war. On September 15, 1947, Dave married Alice Timm. Alice was employed at the CAA (Civil Aviation Authority) now the FAA (Federal Aviation Administration) at the Palmdale Airport. She was part of the communications group working the radios with the aircraft, reporting the weather. Dave and Alice had two children; Barrett C. Brown and Bonnie Jean (Brown) Duecker.

Dave was called up again to serve his country in May 1951, and again supplied the troops during the Korean Conflict. In August 1954 he was honorably discharged at the rank of Major. Dave currently resides in Yearington, Lyon Co., Nevada, retired from the Edison Company. He wrote a fascinating "travel story" several years ago titled, "Around the World in Twelve Hundred and Eighty Days," based on his experiences during World War II and Korea.

LST-326 – photo courtesy of the National Archives.

JAMES H. "JIMMY" BURNS

Jimmy H. Burns lived on a ranch in the Wilsona area of the Antelope Valley near 165th Street East. He graduated from AVJUHS in the class of 1938. Jimmy ran track and field and held the title of the first student to run the half mile in two minutes. He ran two miles every school day, from his house to Highway 38, where he caught the bus to take him to school. Jimmy was also Captain Elect of the high school football team in 1937, and in 1941 was the Captain of the Antelope Valley Junior College football team.

Jimmy enlisted in the Army and was sent to an Infantry unit in Europe. He was promoted twice with a Battlefield Commission. First, from Sergeant to Lieutenant; then from Lieutenant to Captain, all in only eleven months on the field.

After being captured by the Germans, Jimmy was held Prisoner of War (POW) in a camp near Leipzig in the southern part of Germany. He escaped late in the war and was picked up by the Americans further north in Germany. Jimmy was awarded the Silver Star Medal for bravery during World War II.

After the war, Jimmy used the GI Bill to further his education at the University of Southern California. He graduated with a degree in Electrical Engineering. He married a Hollywood gal, then moved to Missouri where he was employed by the Square D Electrical Company.

Silver Star Medal

Friend and classmate, Cece Ellison with Jim Burns, home on leave From service, April 6, 1943. Photo taken in front of Mrs. Ellison's home on Oldfield Avenue in Lancaster, California. (Photo courtesy of John Stege)

33

Alec Cecil Burton was born on March 2, 1926 in New Westminster, British Columbia, Canada, the son of Alec Geoffrey and Margaret May (Goodson) Burton, both born in England. Cecil had two siblings; a brother, Morris Sydney, and a sister, Judy Margaret Burton. In 1936, the family moved from Canada to Rosamond, Kern Co., California, where elder Alec would join up with his brothers, H. Clifford and Cecil F. Burton, co-owners of Burton's Tropico Gold Mine.

Cecil graduated from AVJUHS on May 26, 1944, and on May 27, at 5:30 a.m., he was on a train bound for Fort MacArthur, to be inducted into the U.S. Army. From there, he was sent to Camp Roberts for basic training in the Army Infantry. After basic training, Cecil was sent to Fort Benning, Georgia, where he was assigned to the 71st Infantry Division, 66th Infantry Regiment, 3rd Battalion, Company "M".

After further specialized training, the 66th moved to Camp Kilmer, New Jersey, a staging camp the soldiers were sent to before boarding the ships in New York. Cecil boarded the *U.S.S. James W. McAndrew,* one of over 60 ships in a convoy headed for Europe. The ship left New York Harbor, crowded and overloaded with soldiers. Cecil found a bunk, down below the water level. He knew it was below the water level as a leak had sprung right by the bunk! The bunks were stacked 7 high and the aisles were so narrow, the soldiers could barely walk around them.

Cecil recalled a part of the voyage, "Like all good sailors (which I wasn't) I got seasick. We headed up towards the sea into the North Atlantic, during the winter of January, 1945. I'm not sure what time it was, but it started to rain and the water was rough. It got to the point where I was seasick, I think about the first hour or two we were out there. It wasn't too long before everybody was seasick.

About the third day, I went out onto the deck, trying to get some fresh air with my buddy. We sat down by one of the bulkheads to get out of the wind. The water was just terrible. The ship was going up and down, up and down. I looked down the ship and they had life rafts, 25 man life rafts, stacked up on a pole. They had two or three poles on the ship itself, where they stacked these rafts. I was watching them and discovered that the only way to get a raft off the deck was for the ship to sink first, then the life raft would float off!

We were watching a few of the G.I.'s (Government Issue, slang for a U.S. soldier) along the rail, while sitting on the port side of the ship, when all of a sudden we were way up on top of the 'mountain' [the wave]. The next thing we knew, we were down in the "valley" and the water was coming in all around us. There was a huge wave, coming across the ship, and after it cleared, I looked over at the rail again and almost everybody was gone. I'm not sure if they were washed overboard or whether they were able to hang on to something. They never stopped the ship for anybody, we just headed on in the convoy.

Immediately after, there was a call for everybody to get below deck. I think we were below deck for about three days. Almost every time we hit rough seas, the propeller would come out of the water. Usually it would knock you off of your feet if you weren't hanging onto something. After about a week, it calmed down a bit.

They had chow onboard, but we were only fed two meals a day. It took about 2-3 hours for the line to go through. When we were seasick, we just didn't bother going through the line, but some people did. They figured after a few days we were pretty darn hungry. They didn't feed us anything but C-rations, hard boiled eggs and a cup of coffee – that was about it!"

After a 12 day voyage, the ship landed at Portsmouth Harbor, in Southern England, then went on to disembark at Le Havre, in Normandy, France. When they arrived at Le Havre, Cecil noticed that there were many ships sunk in the harbor, making the route to shore too difficult for their large ship. They had to use smaller boats to continue any further to shore. When they landed at Le Havre, it was raining. A camp had already been set up on a hard field, just off the coast. Each Squadron was assigned to a nine-man tent

34

set up with a small coal burner in the middle of the tent and folding cots for sleeping.

The conditions in the camp would change during the first week. It wasn't long before the hard field had turned into a sea of mud. Cecil recalled, "If you turned over in your folding cot, which had six legs on it, it wouldn't be too long before you were down on ground level. You'd just sink out of sight! The only place that stayed up on dry ground was where the stove was. They had a tank that went off the road and it started sinking. He got his tank belly to the top of the tractor until it was level with the ground. It just kept sinking and sinking."

Cecil's job assignment with the 66th was in the 81 Millimeter (mm) Mortar Platoon as a mortar man. While in Europe, he would travel over 800 actual combat miles, out of the over 2,000 miles he traveled with the 7th and 3rd Army. His first taste of combat would begin at Lemberg, France, in March 1945, when the 66th was strafed by several unidentified airplanes. This would be the first bloodshed in combat against the enemy, with two men killed and three others injured.

The 66th moved on, through several hilly areas, to valleys and into small towns. In the first few weeks, they passed through minefields and wooded areas and saw many dead Germans alongside the road. Cecil recalled an incident near Leisenwald, Germany. "We started to dig our holes and put our mortar in, and I started a foxhole just down by the gun. Just about the time Private Knapp and I got our holes dug down a bit, the Captain decided that we should have a guard set up near the road. Knapp and I got elected for that. I don't know what we were guarding because we had absolutely no cover at all – just a bare hill and the road went down through it. It was a paved road, but it went down through the town which was about ¼ mile away. We started to dig a foxhole and we hit hard rock at about six inches. There was nothing we could do but make a slit trench. Then, it started to rain hard. Knapp built his trench on one side of the road, and I built mine on the other side. I don't know if we could have stopped the German army or not, if they attacked!

Anyway, we got our slit trenches dug. I got my raincoat and put it over the hole, trying to keep the water out. It rained and it rained and it rained. The trenches were filling up with water. We were trying to lay in them so we wouldn't be seen. About every half hour or 45 minutes, somebody would shoot up a flare and light up the whole countryside. Then, some German started firing his machine gun. We watched for tracers going over us, but he never did spot our holes.

Thank God the Germans never tried to come across the road or tried coming up the road either. Everyone seemed to stay put. The next morning we went back down to the outfit. We'd found out that they'd shot a German soldier about five feet from the foxhole that I'd dug. I don't know if it was a good omen, or not, but we didn't have to confront anybody that was coming down the road."

The main event was on the horizon as the 66th moved on to the Maginot and Siegfried Lines near the borders of France, Germany and Austria. Cecil remembered an encounter with the Germans during this time. "We had walked all day under heavy artillery fire and finally reached the town of Grobestienhousen, near the Maginot and Siegfried Lines. We went through the town to the outskirts, and set up our 81mm mortars. By then, it was nightfall and M Co. Captain Ellison, detailed Pfc. Knapp and I to set up a Forward Observation Post (FOP). We were accompanied by a Sergeant and a 2nd Lieutenant. I do not remember their names, but I believe they were from an artillery unit in our support. Pfc. Knapp and I picked up a reel of telephone wire and a field telephone, and the four of us started out in the dark, toward the Maginot and Siegfried Lines, not knowing how far it was or where we were going. The reel of wire we had chosen had a squeak as the wire rolled out – not loud – but it had us concerned. We had cautiously gone quite a distance when we came upon a road. We stopped to listen and heard several people coming toward us. We quickly took cover in a ditch by the side of the road and blended ourselves in with the weeds and small brush. I would estimate there was at least a platoon of 'Krauts' walking by us. They were quietly talking to each other and never noticed us.

After they were some distance from us, we then proceeded across the road. Fortunately, we had heard them coming before crossing the road, otherwise, they would have tripped over our telephone line. There was a machine gun firing in the distance to our left front, but did not appear to be any threat to us.

We continued in the same direction, looking for a place to set up our FOP, still reeling out our line. The Lieutenant had a walkie-talkie, should we lose our communications. Soon, we came to a hole beside us, sloping down. We could see what appeared to be a bunker. This must be on the Maginot Line as it was facing the Siegfried Line. Leaving the reel of wire on the bank, under some small bushes, we went down the slope. We could see a stair-stepped impression in the face of the concrete bunker that sloped down to a small 3" x 10" steel window. To our left was a small tunnel running parallel with the face of the bunker. At a right angle to the tunnel was a steel door.

We decided this would be a good location to set up our FOP as this bunker should be close to the Siegfried Line. The Lieutenant tried the door, and to our surprise, we could see the light of a burning candle. He went in and determined that all was clear. There was a small, coal burning stove that was lit, and a can of Kraut ration heating on top. The Lieutenant shut the door and locked it from inside. We looked around, and judging from the gear on the bunk beds, there must be eight or nine Krauts occupying the bunker.

Two or three minutes had gone by since the Lieutenant locked the door, when we heard someone trying to open it. They made several tries for at least two minutes, before giving up, probably coming to the conclusion that somehow, they had locked themselves out. We were relieved when they left, but did not know what to expect. By this time, the stew that was warming on the stove was hot, and we decided that we shouldn't let it go to waste. It was a large can of ham and lima beans, so we shared it among the four of us. The Lieutenant decided we should stay there and told Knapp and I to get some sleep. We picked out a couple of cots, feeling secure with a Lieutenant and a Sergeant watching over us. We quickly went to sleep.

Around daylight, the Lieutenant woke us up. We opened the little window to look outside, but there wasn't much to see but the slope leading to the bunker. It appeared to be clear, so we ventured out of the bunker and crawled up the slope with our weapons ready. There was a small canyon in front of us, and the Siegfried Line on the opposite bank. Several Krauts were walking around. They were close enough that we could hear them talking. We hooked up our telephone line and made contact with the mortars. I don't remember if we fired any mortar rounds or whether the Lieutenant had the artillery do so.

We shelled them for a time, then we started to receive shelling from them. We retreated back to the bunker and when it quit, we went out again. The Krauts had disappeared by then. We had taken a couple of hits on the bunker, but no damage was done to us. Some time went by, and our troops moved up. We left the security of our 'happy home' in the bunker.

The area around the Siegfried Line where we occupied the bunker was relatively clear of heavy damage, but the area of the Siegfried Line that we actually made the crossing at, was really a 'no mans land.' It had received a tremendous amount of bombing in the past."

The 66th moved again with several skirmishes along the way. They came to the Rhine River, in Germany, where Pfc. Knapp and Cecil would begin to set up the mortars. They crossed the Rhine River next, one of six river crossings Cecil would make. He would encounter many attacks from machine gun fire and grenades, barely escaping death several times. Cecil would survive an ambush while on patrol with 24 other men, when "All hell broke loose. I saw the muzzle blast of a machine gun no more than 20 feet away. I am still puzzled to this day, how he missed me. I landed in the ditch on the south side of the road, grabbed one of my hand grenades and lobbed it over to where the machine gun fire was last seen. Others in our patrol were doing the same. I caught a glimpse of a Kraut 'potato masher' tumbling through the air. It landed short of the ditch, on the road. I quickly crawled under my helmet when it went off, about six or eight feet away. The explosion felt like it had broken my ear drum, but I believe the brute force went over us. (Several years later I found out that my ear drum had broken, and have lost all hearing in it since.)

There was continuous firing from both sides. I know that we passed the Krauts with a stream of bullets for several minutes, then about as quickly as it started, the firing stopped." The men in the patrol called out their positions where they had taken cover. The 2nd Lieutenant began looking for Major Spencer, who was no where to be found. Suddenly, someone yelled and said three Germans had just crossed the road, on Cecil's side, with one carrying a machine gun. The men had to get across the road, so Knapp and Cecil volunteered to see if they could intercept the Germans. The group covered them while they crossed, looking carefully around in all directions. They spotted the German soldiers and Cecil signaled to Knapp to take the one in the front, while he took out the second man. The third man nearly got away when both Cecil and Knapp shot him down. Cecil received the Bronze Star Medal "for meritorious achievement in the ground operation against the enemy" in this ambush.

Only eight of the 24 men on the foot patrol made it across the road when it was clear. They met up with Major Spencer a few hours later when he passed by with a truckload of G.I.'s after returning with help to rescue his patrol. When the men finally reached friendly troops they were given rations and got some much needed sleep. They moved out with them and after four days, they arrived back to Company "M." Upon their arrival, everyone was surprised to see them as they had been reported as being ambushed. The men had been gone so long that the rest of the Company had already divided up their belongings, thinking they weren't coming back!

The 66th battled from Bitche, France to the Maginot and Siegfried Lines; Lingenfield, Frankfurt, Coburg, Bayreuth, Amberg, Regensberg, Straubing, and on to Austria with battles at Reid, Lamback, Wels and Steyr. With eight river assaults, the 66th penetrated farther east than any other U.S. combat unit. They accepted the surrender of the German Army Group South on May 7, 1945. They liberated the concentration camps at Straubing, Gunskirchen, and several smaller camps in Austria.

Cecil was in Steyr, Austria, when they met up with the Russians on May 7, 1945. He was assigned to the Army of Occupation after the war ended, then to rest and rehabilitation camp. Cecil was honorably discharged at the rank of Private, 1st Class, on July 4, 1946, after over two years in the Army. He received the European-African-Middle Eastern Campaign Medal, with two Oak Leaf Clusters; the Bronze Star Medal - Rhineland Campaign; Campaign and WWII Victory Medal; Campaign and Service, Army of Occupation Medal; Efficiency, Honor and Fidelity Medal; Sharpshooter Rifle Medal; Marksman Machine Gun Medal; Combat Infantryman Badge; Good Conduct Medal; Letter of Commendation from General Eisenhower.

After the war, Cecil went to work at the Tropico Gold Mine in his hometown of Rosamond. He was a reserve Deputy Sheriff in Kern Co., and worked at Edwards Air Force Base employed with the Civil Service in jet engine test and development for the Air Force. Cecil earned a teaching credential from UCLA and taught mining technology and assaying classes at AVJC.

On September 8, 1988, Cecil was married to Letty in Rosamond, California. Cecil had three children from a previous marriage; Mike, Terry and Gary Burton. Letty brought to the marriage five children; Dave, Elaine, Don, Diane and Janene Mansker. Cecil and his wife, Letty, are currently living in Lancaster, California. Cecil belongs to the VFW Post 9657 in Rosamond.

A gunner in Cecil's Company M, PFC Leo A. Sims, tells the story of the men in the 71st:

Your combat days are over
The grim work now is done.
Your work in blood and glory
Will be told in years to come.

Mother Margaret, Cecil, and father, Alec Burton

Larry Chimbole was born May 22, 1919 in New Haven, New Haven Co., Connecticut, the first of four children born to Italian immigrant Anthony Michael and his wife, Adeline Ilvira (Johnson) Chimbole. Larry had two sisters, Lois Mae and Gloria Estelle Chimbole; and one brother, Robert Edward Chimbole. Larry attended school in Stamford, Connecticut, graduating from Stamford High School in 1937.

After entering the Army Air Corps in February 1943, Larry went through a daunting few weeks of boot camp. Larry, who had never been more than 50 miles away from home, was suddenly thrown in with a mass of other young men, and shipped half way across the country to Keesler Field, Mississippi.

His first few weeks were filled with shots and ill-fitting clothes, drilling and lectures, and learning to live among hundreds of other people without any privacy. This was a tremendous change for Larry, growing up in a small, close-knit community in Connecticut.

After basic training, Larry was trained as a radio operator and assigned the 58th Bomb Wing Group, (VH), known as the "Hellbirds", attached to the 20th Air Force. As a radio operator onboard a B-29 Superfortress, Larry was deployed to the Island of Tinian in the Mariana Islands chain, during the summer of 1945.

Upon arrival at Tinian, Larry's crew continued with training prior to beginning missions over Japan. They flew practice missions on small islands in the area that were still held by the Japanese. On the night prior to his first mission, Larry was assigned to stay with the fully loaded and armed B-29, scheduled to take off before dawn the next day. As was permitted, he laid down under the wing of the airplane, using his parachute as a pillow and fell asleep. Larry peacefully awoke to the sun peeking over the horizon, with his first thought being the war was over. The war wasn't over that morning, but the Enola Gay dropped the "bomb" and the war ended a few days later.

The crew flew over Hiroshima just days following the bombing by the Enola Gay, and Larry recalled the scene as "the bleakest, darkest devastation I have ever seen," something he would never forget. They landed on Iwo Jima and saw the scars of the terrible battles that had taken place, and could only imagine the fighting and suffering that cost thousands of American lives. As part of a relief operation in the days immediately following, the B-29 crews flew relief missions dropping food, medical, and other supplies to war prisoners who had been permitted to whitewash the initials "P.O.W." on their barracks. Suddenly, bomb bays which just days before had dropped lethal bombs, were dropping food, clothing, and medicine, all bringing comfort to the American servicemen.

B-29 Radio Operator's station

When General MacArthur led the signing of the peace accord on the Battleship Missouri, Larry was one of the thousands of young men manning his station on the B-29 as they flew over the scene in a massive show of strength. He was discharged at the rank of Staff Sergeant from the 6th Bomb Group in 1946 after three years of service.

Larry enjoyed his new found freedom in Southern California where he attended Glendale Community College. He moved to the Antelope Valley in 1957 to start a hardware and building supply business. After moving to the valley, Larry almost immediately became involved in community affairs as the president of the Palmdale Kiwanis Club, as well as president of the Palmdale Chamber of Commerce. He served as the first mayor of the city of Palmdale from 1962 to 1968, and then again from 1970 to 1973. Larry also served as a California state assemblyman from 1974 to 1978.

Larry had two children from his first marriage; a daughter, Patricia Lynn, and son, Harold Steven Chimbole. Larry and his second wife, Lelia "Vicky" (Roberson) Chimbole, currently live in Pearblossom, California, enjoying retirement, politics, and community service.

"The good Lord, with Harry Truman's help, has given me at least 56 years more than I might have had if I hadn't seen the sun come up on that fateful day [in 1945]. I am a grateful man!"

B-29 Crew 41, MacDill Field, Tampa, Florida, June 1945. Larry Chimbole, back row, second from right.

William F. Clutterham was born William Livern, August 1, 1924 in Denver, Colorado, the son of Speed Livern and Alice Loyd. Bill was placed in the Colorado State Orphanage where he was later adopted around the age of four, by Roy and Alma Clutterham. The Clutterham's adopted another child, Beverly, and moved to Billings, Montana. The next move would take Bill to Los Angeles, California, in 1934. It was there, as a teenager, he heard the dreadful news concerning the bombing of Pearl Harbor.

Bill had been interested in airplanes and flying as a youth and thought about becoming a pilot. When he turned eighteen, he went to the recruiting station in downtown Los Angeles to enlist in the Army Air Corps. Bill was told the enlistments for pilot training were closed indefinitely. After returning home, disappointed at not being able to fulfill his dream, Bill decided to return the next day and enlist as a crew member instead of a pilot. Upon his return, Bill was told they were opening up the enlistment for pilots for one day only. He quickly signed up and was on his way to pursue his dream of flying.

Bill was accepted as a cadet in the Army Air Corps. He was sent to Fresno, California to begin basic training. This was his first time away from home and Bill was somewhat fearful, facing an unknown road ahead. After two months of training he received orders to leave for Logan, Utah, to begin CTD (College Training Detachment). While in Logan, Bill received flight training in a Piper Cub airplane. From the college in Logan, he was transferred to Santa Ana Army Air Base in Orange County, California. After more training and testing, Bill was assigned to the Visalia-Dinuba School of Aeronautics at Sequoia Field near Visalia, California. After graduating from primary flight school, the next assignment was at Minter Field, near Bakersfield, California where he was trained in the large, single engine, basic flying trainer, the Vultee Vibrator BT-13.

Bill in his BT-13 Basic Flying Trainer

Bill's next stop would be Pecos Army Air Base in Pecos, Texas. In advance training Bill learned to fly the Cessna UC-78 nicknamed the "Bamboo Bomber", a twin engine, five passenger aircraft. After two months of difficult training, Bill received his silver wings and his officer's commission.

After several temporary assignments, Bill finally received orders to proceed to Hobbs Army Air Base near Hobbs, New Mexico to learn how to fly the B-17 Flying Fortress. He graduated from Hobbs, classified as a Pilot Aircraft Commander, and received new orders to report to Biloxi, Mississippi., where a new type of Air-Sea-Rescue unit was being developed. When Bill finished his month long training, he became part of the Sixth Emergency Rescue Squadron, the first of its kind, attached to the 5th Air Force.

The new unit was sent to Savannah, Georgia where they picked up eight B-17's newly fitted with twenty-seven foot boats mounted under the belly of the bombers. The final destination was Clark Army Air Base in the Philippines, just outside of Manila. While on this trip, Bill would just begin to experience the horrors of the war.

The long trip to the Philippines was broken up by landing and refueling on islands on the route. When the unit arrived at Biak, New Guinea, an overnight staging area for air crews moving up to the front, they were unprepared for what they were about to experience. Bill and several of the other crew members were sitting in a large tent used as a mess hall, eating and talking, when all of a sudden three loud explosions were heard and felt. A Japanese bomber had just dropped three "daisy cutter" type bombs – lethal bombs to any personnel caught in the blast zone.

The horror of war hit Bill hard. Several of the men in the mess hall were gone – limbs torn away – and many with crippling injuries. Bill realized he had escaped death by only inches. All through the night the Japanese soldiers hiding in the hills continued firing into the tent area. Thankfully, only the one Japanese plane made it through to drop the bombs, but that was enough to change Bill's life and the lives of everyone else around him. Only a year earlier Bill recalled his significant life experiences had been dating and driving a Model A Ford.

When morning finally came, the B-17 crews were ready to leave Biak and head for Clark field in the Philippines. Bill's Squadron would be based at Clark Field until the island of Okinawa was taken from the Japanese. While at Clark Field Bill and his rescue crew flew 35 missions – about one every seven to ten days. They dropped more boats and saved more downed crew members than any other rescue crew at Clark Field.

The next assignment would be at Ie Shima, an island off the northern end of Okinawa. While flying in the *Billie-Louise* Air-Sea-Rescue aircraft, the crews were usually alone except for four fighter aircraft, P-51's most of the time, to defend them in case of enemy attacks. On one mission, near the Japanese mainland, they were covered by P-38's instead of the P-51's. As a Rescue Squadron pilot, Bill would have to circle around while waiting to be called for a rescue or ordered to return to the base – on this mission the base was over 700 miles away from where they were circling and waiting. As the plane circled, the crew spotted a large Japanese ship, approximately eighty feet in length. It was armed and had plenty of radio aerials. Fearing this ship might have already reported their position, Bill took the plane down close to the surface of the water and proceeded to make passes at the ship with the B-17 crew firing their 50 caliber and top turret guns. The ball turret gunner joined in firing, along with the tail and waist gunner. They sprayed the ship with hundreds of bullets, hitting gas tanks on the ship.

After ten passes at the enemy, fire and smoke was billowing everywhere from the deck of the ship. The excitement of the situation mounted when top turret gunner yelled out "Zero, six o'clock high!" The Japanese Zero was making passes at the B-17, strafing it as he flew by. The bullets just missed hitting the plane. The P-38 pilots were called into action while Bill kept the rescue plane circling in a wide pattern, keeping the Zero in sight. The four P-38's had engaged the Zero in air combat. The Zero had made several hits on one of the P-38's – both engines were shot out and the plane headed in a nose dive, straight into the waters of the Pacific, sinking immediately.

The crew of the Billie-Louise, January 1945 – Command Pilot Bill Clutterham, front row, far right

Fortunately, the combat ended right then. The Zero climbed out of the area and headed west. That was the last they saw of him. The crew was ordered back to base on Ie Shima. The P-38's were low on fuel after engaging the Japanese plane in combat, so the B-17 was left on its own, without fighter escort, to get back to base safely. They had over 200 miles to fly over the Japanese mainland, unassisted, before they were out in the open sea. Bill took the plane down to just above the water, figuring that if a Zero took them on, this would be the best position to be in. The crew returned to base safely, but deeply saddened at losing one of their own fighter pilots.

Bill had come to realize that during the war he had two enemies as the pilot of a B-17: One enemy was the Japanese military, and the other was the severe weather conditions of the Pacific. Many of the flights had to be flown on instruments with 99% of the flying time over water. With those conditions, there was no room for error in flying or navigation. Every rescue mission Bill went on could be as dangerous as the missions were for the crews he was sent out to retrieve.

On the morning of August 6, 1945, the crew of the "Billie-Louise" would be an eyewitness to a historical event that would be imbedded in the minds of all who lived through World War II. It started out as an ordinary day – a routine flight, with the rescue crew providing a much needed safety net for the airmen bombing the Japanese targets. Bill was flying his B-17 along at 3,000 feet with the Japanese homeland below him. Somewhere nearby, unbeknownst to Bill or the crew, Colonel Paul Tibbets and the crew of the B-29, *Enola Gay,* had taken off from Tinian carrying the world's first atomic bomb, headed toward its target of Hiroshima.

"We didn't know they were dropping an atomic bomb on Hiroshima. We didn't even know what an atomic bomb was," recalled Bill of that fateful day in 1945. The crew was staring in amazement of what they saw before their eyes – a bomb with a nearly unimaginable destructive force producing radiation that would destroy everything in its path. "It was utter devastation."

The *Billie-Louise* was called back to base instead of circling around waiting to rescue any downed flyers. The B-17 touched down on Ie Shima five hours later, landing at the Army Air Corps 6th Emergency Rescue Squadron base. After landing, they were greeted by dozens of servicemen asking questions about the atomic bomb. Bill said, "What's that?" They weren't really sure what they had seen.

Bill was discharged from the Army Air Corps, on December 24, 1945. By the end of his tour, Bill had flown 65 missions. During one month he flew every day for 30 days. He received four Air Medals, numerous Campaign Ribbons, and twelve Battle Stars. His service included time spent in the Philippines, Tokyo, Japan and China. Bill enjoyed the camaraderie shared during war time, playing the card game of Hearts and listening to music on the radio provided by Tokyo Rose. He loved serving his fellow man and felt good in uniform being an officer. Bill would see another year of duty after World War II – this time in the Korean War.

On April 16, 1946 Bill married Mildred Louise Nordquist. They had five children, two daughters; Janice and Susan; and three sons; Bill, John and Robert Clutterham. In December 1948, Bill joined the Los Angeles County Fire Department, where he held the rank of Captain for eighteen years. He was the department Chaplain for the last five years of his career.

"World War II was of vast importance to me because I realized that God kept me from being killed 12-15 times. I wanted to know God and in the year 1967, at the age of 44, I received Christ as my Personal Savior." Bill continues to help others by sharing his life, faith and war experiences with school children and young adults at local junior high and high schools in the Antelope Valley. Bill, along with his wife and daughter, currently lives in Leona Valley, California.

Alvin Martin Coltzau was born January 25, 1921, in Los Angeles, California, the son of Edward J. and Carolyn D. (Knudsen) Coltzau, both from Iowa. He had one sister – Betty V. (Coltzau) Spotts. Al's father, Edward, was an alfalfa farmer and a veteran of World War I. After he was discharged from the service, around 1919, the family moved to the Antelope Valley where Edward worked on a ranch at 70th Street East and G-8. He eventually bought the ranch and started his own alfalfa farm.

Beginning in 1926, Al attended grammar school at the Roosevelt School on the east side of Lancaster. In 1938, Al graduated from AVJUHS. In September, 1939 through the spring of 1940, he joined the Civilian Conservation Corps (CCC) where he attained the rank of Corporal. During his school years, Al helped his father by working on their alfalfa farm.

Al was in Lancaster, driving his car and listening to the radio, when he heard the news about Pearl Harbor. In 1942, Al was drafted into the U.S. Army Air Corps. "A healthy farm boy – just what they wanted! My dad didn't want me to go into the service and go what he went through in World War I. He was in Germany, Belgium and France, and suffered through the man to man combat."

Al was inducted at Fort McArthur, California and sent to Fresno, California for basic training. He was already adjusted to the military life after serving in the C.C.C. which was run by Army officers. Al had a tough time with some of the drills as he had previously broken both feet when a horse fell on him. Al was sent to Glendale, California, for Airplane Mechanics School at Aero I.T.I. After graduating, he was stationed at Colina Army Base in Spokane, Washington. They didn't have any airplanes yet at the Army Base, so Al signed up for Bombsight School in Denver, Colorado. After returning to Spokane again, he saw a sign – "CFC (Central Fire Control) School, Denver – Students Wanted". Al knew what the class was about – the computer system for the Remote Control Turret guns – so off he went, back to Denver for training on the Remote Control Turret (RCT) system for the B-29.

Al quickly earned the rank of Corporal by attending school. His first job assignment was as Department Head for the RCT system. Al spent nearly four years in the Army Air Corps, with half the time spent training in the United States. He learned everything he could about airplanes before being deployed to the Pacific. As part of the 52nd Engineering Squadron, 330th Service Group, Al was sent to Saipan in the Northern Mariana Islands. The air bases in the Marianas were essential in order to accommodate the build-up of the new B-29 Superfortress in 1944.

When Al arrived on Saipan, the group saw the devastation left by the Japanese. They had to build their base from the ground up. Al recalled, "We had to cut the sugar cane down with our machetes. All of us in our group went out there and cut that stuff. The flies were really bad and the mosquitoes were terrible. After we got it [the sugar cane] cleared, we had to haul it away because of the flies. We were afraid to eat it because the Japs might have poisoned it. We didn't eat anything that wasn't part of our own supplies. We didn't drink the water there because the Japs poisoned all the wells. We got water from the Navy for a while. They made drinking water on the ships. We'd have to go down to the ocean, which wasn't very far away, to wash our clothes. You'd have to hang them up and beat the salt out of them. If you put them on before you beat the salt out, it would eat your hide out because of all the salt in the cloth!"

Al Coltzau, right.

Al's job was to keep the B-29's flying. His shop was inside a Quonset hut where he worked on the computer systems for the remote controlled gun turrets. A few times Al would fly in the airplanes to check the system out if the gunner complained about "not being able to hit anything!" He worked on the planes and fixed them up, no matter what shape they came back in. They had downed planes all over the base. If they needed a part or a whole section of an airplane, the men would scrounge around until they found the right part.

During his stay on Saipan the base was constantly being bombed by the Japanese. It only stopped when Iwo Jima was taken in 1945. Al recalled one night of bombing, "The Japs were bombing us every night. This guy, a red-haired, freckle faced boy, got so scared he'd sleep in his foxhole. You'd have to get the water out of the foxhole because it would rain so much, the water would just stay there. There he was, all folded up. He had his tin hat on and they would start bombing, strafing and everything and after about three nights of this, his hair turned whiter than mine [now]."

Al, back row, 2nd from left – Saipan CFC Repair Shop

"He got so scared, he had what they call the 'DT's'. They sent him back to the States. After that, everyone said they were going to get the 'DT's' so they could go back home. Compared to the front line guys, we had the 'gravy train.' We had it easy even being bombed every night. The bombing didn't last – it only lasted until they took Iwo Jima. After that, it was pretty peaceful on Saipan."

While on Saipan, Al received a letter from his mother telling him his friend from Lancaster, Harry Cecil, was in the Navy on a base in Saipan. Al met up with Harry and they shared the Navy chow – much better food than he had on the Army base! Harry visited Al one time at the Army base and suggested they eat the Navy food instead. The Navy had good food, served on stainless steel trays with compartments. All Al's group had were mess kits that required a balancing act to eat with. At the Army base they were served goat meat and mashed potatoes, maybe some corn or fruit, whatever came from a can, all served on top of one another, mixed together!

23 April 1945 – front half of a B-29 that broke in half after landing on Saipan. Hit by a Japanese suicide airplane, this B-29 crew flew all the way back from their mission and landed before it broke in two

At the end of the war, the Army base at Saipan became a station to load and drop supplies to the P.O.W.'s in Japanese camps. They used the planes to drop relief supplies instead of the bombs they had dropped just days before. The airplanes came from Tinian – another island in the Marianas – because the runway on Saipan was much larger and could accommodate more airplanes.

Al was discharged at the rank of Tech Sergeant. He received a Presidential Unit Citation; Bronze Star Medal; Asiatic-Pacific Medal; Victory Medal; and Good Conduct Medal. After his three month mustering pay ended, Al began working at H.W. Hunter Dodge & Chrysler in Lancaster. He worked as an auto mechanic, body and fender repairman, and eventually as the Painting Service Manager. In 1983, Al retired from H.W. Hunter after 37 years of service.

From his first marriage, Al had four children; Randy, Shelly, Laura and Jackie. He was married to his current wife, Lois Prouty, on April 29, 1964. Together, they have enjoyed many motorcycle and automobile trips across the United States. Al is still active in beautifully restoring antique and classic cars. He has respectfully earned the title of "The Oldest Teenager on the East Side."

Al Coltzau, late 1930's

OWEN CLIFFORD "CLIFF" COX

Owen Clifford Cox was born February 3, 1920, in Burksville, Cumberland Co., Kentucky, the son of Robert Hersel and Lizzie G. (Anderson) Cox. Cliff had one sister – Marjorie Helen Cox. He graduated from high school in 1937 and worked as a cook and waiter at a restaurant in Peoria, Illinois.

Cliff was drafted in 1941, at the age of 21. The plan was to be trained for a year, then after training, be released back into the civilian world and be in the reserves. All his plans changed after basic training when the war broke out. Cliff would remain in the service for the duration of the war.

Cliff was sent to Fort Francis E. Warren in Cheyenne, Wyoming [now known as Warren Air Force Base] for basic training. After basic training he was sent to Cooks and Baker School. Upon completion, he was assigned to Company C of the 2nd Regiment, as a Cook at the training center until 1943. Cliff was then assigned to the 56th Quartermaster Base Depot. He was sent to Camp Lee, Virginia before going overseas to England in the Spring of

1944. Cliff was assigned to three or four different camps before moving on to his next assignment.

The next stop would be Normandy, France. After arriving at Normandy, Cliff remembered the beach being cleared away of the bodies from the D-Day fighting, June 6, 1944, just days before his arrival. The Jeeps and trucks unloading the troops and supplies were greeted with deep, thick mud, causing many problems for them as they came off the transport boats.

The first thing to be done at the new camp was to set up the latrines. Next was to find water, then set up the cook's area for handing out rations. One of the most important jobs in the Army was to keep the troops healthy and supplied with nourishing meals to keep them going throughout the battles. Cliff usually ate well being either the Cook or Mess Sergeant.

While stationed in Cherbourg, France, December 24, 1944, Cliff remembered volunteering to cook 28 turkeys for the men as part of their Christmas meal. What was supposed to be a joyful day of celebration, turned into a horrific ordeal for the men of the 66th. Across the English Channel, men from the 66th Infantry Division boarded the ship *S.S. Leopoldville* to transport them over to France. While crossing the Channel, a German U-boat fired a torpedo, blasting a huge hole in the *Leopoldville*. 300 men were killed by the blast and more than 450 lost their lives when the ship sank two hours later. Over 750 men were lost from the 66th. Cliff remembers seeing hundreds of bodies brought up to the docks in bags to be taken to the cemetery.

The comradeship between the men was they way most of them got through the hard times during the war. The association with many of the local people in the small towns they camped near helped to make the time away from home more tolerable. A side job that Cliff enjoyed was the job of company barber.

Cliff recalled an interesting story involving a delivery of a case of whiskey to the captain at the Supreme Allied Headquarters in France. When he reached the room where the liquor was delivered to, a helmet with three stars was sitting on the table. "It was General Patton's room!" he recalled. "That was as close as I ever got to Patton."

On the rifle range having chow during basic training, October, 1941 – Cliff on the left

Cliff traveled through France, Belgium, Holland and Germany. After four years in the Army, Cliff was in Geissen, Germany, when he heard the news about the war ending. He was discharged in November 1945 with the rank of a Tech Sergeant, 4th Grade. During those four years, Cliff earned four Bronze Battle Stars for keeping the troops fed in Normandy, Northern France, Rhineland and Central Europe. He also earned the French Overlord Medal for the liberation of France; the WWII Victory Medal; the American Defense Ribbon; 1 service stripe; 3 overseas service bars and the Good Conduct Medal.

Cliff married Ada Jean Cirksena, April 30, 1952, in Cheyenne, Wyoming.. They had three children; Cheryl Lea; Ryan Alan; and Wendolyn Jean Cox. After the war, Cliff was employed at Joliet Arsenal, in Illinois, then moved to California in 1959. In 1966 he was employed by Atomic International and worked at Edwards Air Force Base. Cliff continued in the Civil Engineering-Maintenance field at Edwards until his retirement. He made many close friendships during the war and is a member of the VFW, Post 7283. Cliff and his wife, Ada, currently call Lancaster their home.

Drawing of Cliff Cox by Sgt. Lillie, April 2, 1943

JOHN W. "JACK" COZAD

John W. "Jack" Cozad was born in 1925 in Oregon, the son of John E., from Oklahoma, and Zora Cozad, from Nebraska. In 1930, the Cozad family was living in Los Angeles, California, with John E. employed as a salesman for a food company, and Zora as a clerk for an oil company. Shortly after 1930, the Cozad family moved to the Antelope Valley. Jack attended AVJUHS and graduated in 1941 while holding the position of class President.

By April 5, 1944, Jack was a 2nd Lieutenant in the Army Air Forces, stationed at Fowlmere, near Cambridge, England. He was attached to the 8th Air Force, 339th Fighter Group, 503rd Fighter Squadron. Jack flew in the Squadron with his P-51 Mustang. The first mission the Squadron flew was on April 30, 1944. This was a fighter sweep mission over South Central France. Many of the missions from April through July were escorting bombers, dive-bombing and strafing over France and Germany.

By July 8, 1944, the 339th Fighter Group had flown 78 missions. While taxiing down the runway on July 8, Jack was involved in an accident that would sideline his P-51 until repairs could be made. On July 25, 1944, Jack was on a training flight over England with his P-51. He was killed when the airplane crashed during the flight.

P-51 Mustangs, photograph by Bill Preddy, courtesy of the 339th Fighter Group Assoc. & Web-Birds.com

503rd Fighter Squadron insignia, courtesy of the 339th Fighter Group Assoc. & Web-Birds.com

RICHARD PIERCE "RICH" CULLETON

Richard Pierce Culleton was born August 12, 1922, in Los Angeles, California, the son of Pierce Henry and Mona Emiline (Green) Culleton. He had two brothers; Robert James and William Howard Culleton. Rich graduated from Los Angeles High School in 1941. While attending high school, Rich went through training with the ROTC as a cadet, learning General Orders, the Manual of Arms, and military drills.

On August 8, 1941, Rich enlisted in the Army. Due to the training he received in the ROTC, Rich by-passed the normal basic training. He was sent by train to San Francisco, arriving at Angel Island on August 9, 1941. On August 11, Rich was put on a steamer, the *S.S. President Taft,* and on his way to Hawaii. He arrived on August 17, without a uniform, dressed in his civilian clothes.

Rich's first assignment was with Battery A, 251st Coast Artillery Regiment, Anti-Aircraft Division at Camp Malakole, Oahu, Hawaii, where he drove a 2 ½ ton

searchlight truck. At age 19, Rich would be in the fight of his life on December 7, 1941, less than four months after joining the Army.

The 251st had been on alert for some weeks prior to December 1941, building up to a strength of 2,400 troops. They were assigned defensive positions around the west shore of Pearl Harbor and around the outside of Hickam Air Field, coordinating with the Navy and other Army units. However, on December 7th, the day of the Japanese attack, half of the Regiment were either sleeping or away from the Camp on a weekend pass.

On the morning of December 7, 1941, Rich was pulling guard duty near the beachfront at Camp Malakole. He went on guard with a truck-mounted machine gun and one single belt of ammunition, not expecting a surprise air attack by the Japanese. The machine guns were set up against a sabotage attack, not for an air attack. Since Rich had by-passed basic training, he'd never fired a weapon of any kind before - not even at a firing range. Rich recalled that Sunday morning as a day of "well organized confusion."

When the Japanese started their attack, the Regimental bugler went to blow "Call to Arms" and he realized he didn't know the call. The Fire Chief, Tom Showers, took the bugle and blew the "Call to Arms", but no one had ever heard it and didn't know what to do! What happened on that day was best described in the Legion of Merit Award Rich received in 1943: "For extraordinary fidelity to duty. During the attack at Camp Malakole, T.H., on December 7, 1941 [Private Culleton] was acting as gunner on the

camp 'sabotage guard' truck when the attack came. He [along with two other soldiers on the gun] opened fire as the second plane came over camp and was the first man in camp to fire on the enemy. When the truck's one belt [of ammunition] was exhausted, Private Culleton ran three blocks to the ammunition warehouse, obtained four boxes of machine gun ammunition and ran back to this gun and resumed fire."

What the award didn't state was that Rich first tried to obtain ammunition at a closer battery, but a by-the-book supply clerk wouldn't give Rich the ammunition because that particular ammo was assigned to another battery. He had to run to his Battery A warehouse to get the ammunition belts set aside for his group – three blocks away from his truck – while the Japanese planes were strafing and bombing the base.

Rich Culleton, right, with best friend, Bob Canfield – Waikiki Beach, Hawaii, 1942.

49

After Pearl Harbor, Rich was promoted to sergeant and was assigned to a supply unit. Not being a man who wanted to stay in a routine, government job, Rich requested a transfer to the Army Air Corps. He was granted his wish, joined up with the 7th Air Force where he graduated from flight school at Perrin Field, in Sherman, Texas. The first plane he flew was a Piper Cub. He later received training in a Steerman PT-17, the AT6 Texan, and in a B-25 Mitchell bomber and graduated from Cadet School at Enid Army Field, Oklahoma. Rich had just graduated from Pilot Training in class 45F at Enid, Oklahoma, when he heard the news that the war was over.

In October 1945, Rich received an honorable discharge from the U.S. Air Forces at the rank of 2nd Lieutenant. He received the Legion of Merit Medal, the Asiatic-Pacific Campaign Medal, American Campaign Medal, American Defense Medal, World War II Victory Medal and the Good Conduct Medal. He took a month long vacation to adjust to civilian life again after four years in the service. Rich loved taking his father flying in their Ryan PT-22 airplane, over Los Angeles, so he could see his home and business from the air. Rich recalled thinking, "He trusted his 23 year old son with his life – what an honor!" He went to work for his father for a while, then began attending college.

Rich landed a job with North American Aviation where he helped develop the XB-70 and the B1A and B-1B bombers. North American eventually became Rockwell International, which then became the Boeing Company as it is known today. During World War II, Rich's brother, Bob, provided home front help with North American Aviation on the hydraulic system design for the P-51 Mustang fighters and the B-25 bombers which helped the U.S. prevail in the Pacific and Europe.

On June 4, 1949, Rich married his sweetheart N. Teresa (Terry) Bibb, in Los Angeles, California. They had four children; William Patrick, Michael Pierce, Melinda Sue, and Dennis James Culleton. In 1962, the family moved to Lancaster with the XB-70 program for North American. Rich was employed in the Engineering-Design field while at North American, Rockwell and Boeing.

Rich currently lives in Lancaster and continues to enjoy traveling, airplanes and flying. He is a member of the Pearl Harbor Survivors, Chapter 29.

Richard in the AT6 Texan

Sergeant Richard Culleton on his 21st birthday, 1943, at Hickam Field, Hawaii. His mother contacted the Air Force about his birthday – the Air Force supplied the cake and the photograph. Official photograph, U.S. Army

Haldane C. Cummins was born March 25, 1918, in Sitka, Alaska, the son of Ralph Neil and Zilmah Vader (Gardner) Cummins. Haldane had one younger sibling, a sister, Mary Jean. Ralph was stationed in Alaska with the U.S. Army Signal Corps during the time Haldane was born. The family moved to California in 1920, settling in the Buena Park area of Orange County in 1930. Ralph was employed by the Standard Oil Company measuring the amount of oil held in the oil tanks. He later owned a filling station and a garage.

Haldane graduated from Fullerton High School in Los Angeles Co., California in 1936. After high school he attended Fullerton Jr. College where he graduated in 1938. After four years of hard work, Haldane graduated from the College of Dentistry, at the University of Southern California in 1942.

In 1942, Haldane joined the U.S. Army, with a commission as a 1st Lieutenant. His entire class at dental school joined the military determined to help serve their country in that time of need. Basic training began at Fort Sam Houston in San Antonio, Texas. The training consisted of field exercises, close order drill, discipline and 15-25 mile forced marches. Haldane remembered, "My feet still tingle when I recall a 25 mile forced march."

After basic training was completed, Haldane was assigned to duty as Battalion dental surgeon for the 16th Signal Operations Battalion. He was promoted to the rank of Captain. They shipped out to Australia for more training then proceeded to Papua, New Guinea in 1943. While on New Guinea, many of the men came down with malaria, dengue fever and dysentery. Haldane had all three at one time. The men were faced with torrential monsoon rains along with high humidity and sweltering temperatures. The swamps and muddy terrain were perfect breeding grounds for many tropical diseases. "Scrub typhus was a killer. 40% mortality rate if you were bitten by a tiny mite which infested the rats in the kunai grass. Falling trees took their toll during storms. Infected insect bites and fungus [jungle rot] were disabling. 300-400 inches of rain per annum kept us wet, caused accidents and flooded shelters."

Haldane was transferred to the 116th Combat Engineer Battalion with the 41st Infantry Division and sent to the island of Biak, north west of New Guinea. The 41st continued with intense fighting against the Japanese in the dense jungles of the islands. After Biak was secured, the 41st was shipped out in a convoy to the island of Mindoro in the Philippines. From there they landed at Zamboanga, on the island of Mindanao, southern Philippines. After bitter fighting, the 41st secured Jolo, Basilan and other nearby islands.

Haldane suffered a non-combat spinal injury and was shipped, via hospital ship, to Letterman General Hospital in San Francisco, California. He was transferred to Hammond General Hospital in Modesto, California, and in 1946 was given a medical retirement.

Being a dental officer, Haldane thought that he had it "easy," personally seeing no combat except for a "few bombing attacks." Although not directly in combat, the carnage, maiming and suffering of his fellow soldiers that he witnessed during the war continues to haunt him to this day.

Zamboanga, So. Philippines – Battalion Aid Station

For his time spent in the military in service to his country, Haldane received the following awards: the American Campaign Medal; Asiatic Pacific Campaign Medal; Philippine Liberation Medal; World War II Victory Medal; and an Honorable Service lapel button.

Waiting at home in California, was his wife, Betty Jo (Young) Cummins. They were married in 1941 before Haldane went into the Army. Together they had three children, Neil, Larimore and Anne "Annie" Robyn Cummins. Haldane went to work in Pomona, California, where he started a dental practice. In 1947, the family moved to the Antelope Valley after his wife became allergic to the smoke from the nearby citrus smudge pots. Since Betty Jo's parents lived in Pearblossom, Haldane explored the feasibility of opening a dental office in Palmdale. He discovered only one dentist in the Antelope Valley - Dr. Cowell, in Lancaster. Haldane built a dental office on Palmdale Blvd. in Palmdale which continued to prosper through to his retirement. He "officially" retired in 1998.

On October 15, 1974 Haldane married Jean (Naylor) Davis. In the summer of 1980, he and Jean sailed to Ketchikan, Alaska from Blaine, Washington in a 28' sloop rigged power boat, the *Annie Wiley*, built by Haldane. It was his dream to revisit Alaska, his state of birth, and with Jean's navigational adeptness they successfully completed the trip and fulfilled that life-long dream. Haldane and Jean, along with the *Annie Wiley*, currently reside in Palmdale, retired and enjoying the "fair winds" of the Antelope Valley.

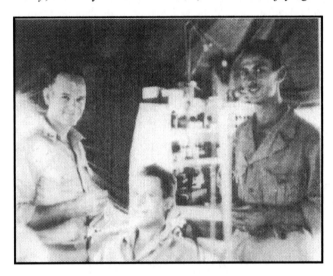

Ready for the dentist? "Doc" Cummins, far left
Zamboango, So. Philippines

WILLIAM FRANCIS DAVIS

William F. Davis was born February 20, 1917 in Bakersfield, Kern Co., California, the son of William O. and Nell Davis. By 1930, the family had moved to the town of Mojave, just on the outskirts of the Antelope Valley. William O. was working as a conductor for the railroad while Nell cared for their three children; Mary, William and Thomas. At age 13, William F. held the job of a news boy for the local newspaper in Mojave.

William attended AVJUHS, graduating with the class of 1934. He was an outstanding student and enjoyed participating in athletic events during his high school years.

William entered the Army Air Forces in 1942 where he completed training as a cadet at various military schools. In December 1942, William arrived at Greenville Army Air Base [later named Donaldson AFB] in South Carolina as a 2nd Lieutenant, where he served as a B-25 Bomber Instructor Pilot.

His next assignment would take him to the Southwest Pacific, where he flew B-25's in combat duty. There, he flew 43 combat missions and was commander of the 501st Bomb Squadron of the

5th Air Force. In October 1944, William received a serious eye injury while stationed in New Guinea. He was taxiing to take off on a bombing mission, with his head out of the pilot's window, when a sharp piece of runway coral was blown into his eye due to engine prop wash from the aircraft in front of his. His eye was seriously cut, ending his wartime service and nearly costing him his eye.

While in New Guinea, the Associated Press filed the following report on the 501st Bomb Squadron:

"A bold, ruthless band of medium bomber pilots, known as the "Air Apaches," were given the job of neutralizing enemy strongholds in the Halmahersas.

In little more than three weeks, these low-level strafers reported back to the Fifth Air Force bomber command their mission was completed. Japan's southern anchor in the Philippine defense line no longer is capable of defending itself from air attack and its shipping lanes have been badly disrupted.

In 533 sorties of this single bomber group, 13 cargo ships and small freighters were sunk and 17 luggers [small fishing boats] completely destroyed. Wrecked and damaged barges littered bays and inlets.

Eight B-25's and seven crews perished during the operations.

Lt. Charles A. Cates, Milan, Ga., former high school principal, destroyed a 700-ton cargo boat and probably another on one of the raids.

In another strike, Lt. William F. Davis, Travelers Rest, S.C., skipped a bomb clear through a lugger in Kaoe Bay and later blew a cargo ship in half."

William was awarded the Air Medal after this bombing mission, for "heroic action or meritorious service while participating in aerial flight."

After recuperating from his eye injury and having been voluntarily recalled from a short stint as a civilian, William was then stationed at Haneda Air Base in Tokyo, Japan, from 1946 – 1949. Returning to the U.S. in late 1949, he attended the Air Command and Staff College at Maxwell AFB in Alabama for a year. From 1951 – 1953, he was stationed at Andrews Air Force Base in Maryland. He was appointed Chief of the Budget and Fiscal Branch for Headquarters Military Air Transport Service.

In 1953, as a Lieutenant Colonel, William began a nine month Air Force advanced management course at the University of Pittsburgh in Pennsylvania. He attained a grade of "A" in all 14 subjects he studied. Major General Ralph P. Swofford Jr., Commandant of The Air University, described William's accomplishment as "an exceedingly rare academic performance."

William attained the rank of full colonel in early 1956, while working as Assistant Comptroller of the Western Air Defense Force at Hamilton Air Force Base, in California. His attainment of this high rank at the young age of 39 was a rare accomplishment for an officer during a non-wartime period. At the time of his promotion, he had completed only 12 years of active duty service.

In 1956, William was transferred to Pepperrell AFB, St. John's, Newfoundland, Canada, where he worked as the Comptroller of the Northeast Air Command, re-designated in 1957 as the 64th Air Division. In 1960, when Pepperrell AFB closed, he was reassigned with the 64th to Stewart AFB, Newburgh, New York. Two years later he was selected to attend the prestigious Industrial College of the Armed Forces in Washington, D.C. In 1963 he made his final active duty move to Ent AFB, Colorado Springs, Colorado, where he retired from the United States Air Force in August 1964.

During his military career he received the following awards: the Air Medal with one Bronze Oak Leaf Cluster;

Rose & William F. Davis

Army Commendation Medal; American Campaign Medal – WWII; World War II Victory Medal; Asiatic Pacific Campaign Medal; Air Force Commendation Medal with two Bronze Oak Leaf Clusters; WWII Army of Occupation Medal; and the National Defense Service Medal.

William met his wife, Rose Bishop, in 1943 at a party in Greenville, South Carolina. Rose was 19 at the time and attending Furman University, then located near downtown Greenville. They later had three children; one son, William Ernest, and two daughters, Linda and Bren. William and Rose were married for 46 years. Rose passed away in 1997 in Simpsonville, South Carolina, near Greenville.

After retiring from the Air Force in 1964, William moved to Greenville to reside. He was extremely active in business, church and civic affairs. He founded the Century 21 Golden Strip Realty and Insurance Company in Simpsonville, South Carolina. William was involved in many city affairs and served on Chamber of Commerce Boards in both Simpsonville and Greenville. He was elected to the position of Chairman of the Board of Trustees of the Greenville County Hospital System. He was also a member of Grace Presbyterian Church where he served as a deacon, treasurer and Sunday School teacher.

Colonel William F. Davis passed away at the age of 85 on October 30, 2002 in Simpsonville. William had requested that the following quote be read at his family memorial service, a quote that perfectly summarized his life and his devotion to his country:

"Colonel Davis was motivated by, inspired by, and lived by the words of the Military Academy – Duty - Honor-Country."

Colonel William F. Davis

54

CLETUS NORBERT "CLETE" DIDIER

Cletus N. Didier was born April 14, 1917 in Dayton, Montgomery Co., Ohio. His parents were Henry and Anna (Weber) Didier. Henry's parents were both born in France while Anna's father was from Germany. Clete had six siblings – four sisters; Rose, Alma, Agnes and Phyllis, and two brothers; Alfred and Raymon Didier. In 1920 the Didier family was living in the town of Dayton, Ohio with Henry employed as a machinist for the Delco Light Company. By 1930, the family had moved to Madison, Ohio where Henry was still employed as a machinist.

Clete entered the Maryknoll Society Catholic theological seminary in Cincinnati, Ohio as a student beginning in the 8th grade. For the next ten years Clete would devote his life to the church. He studied with the Maryknoll Society in Scranton, Pennsylvania and also in New York until having a change of heart in 1941, when he decided the life of a priest was not to be his vocation. While he stepped away from the church, Clete continued his devotion and faith to Christ and the church throughout the rest of his life.

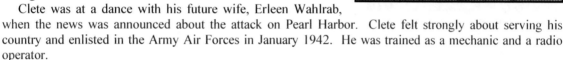

Clete was at a dance with his future wife, Erleen Wahlrab, when the news was announced about the attack on Pearl Harbor. Clete felt strongly about serving his country and enlisted in the Army Air Forces in January 1942. He was trained as a mechanic and a radio operator.

In February of 1943, Clete was attached to the 10th Air Force, 443rd Troop Carrier Group, 1st Troop Carrier Squadron. For the next year and a half, he would be serving his country in the China-Burma-India Theater of Operations (CBI), the largest single theater of operations in World War II. As part of the 1st Troop Carrier Squadron, Clete was onboard a C-47 as a radio operator, flying amongst the Himalayan Mountains. Many of the peaks and mountains in the area rose to greater heights than most of the aircraft of that era could reach, hence the danger in flying through what was nicknamed "The Hump". This area also had some of the worst flying weather in the world, causing many accidents and claiming many lives.

On February 3, 1943, the 1st Troop Carrier Squadron arrived at Chabua Airfield in India. On March 7th the 1st was transferred from Chabua to New Delhi, India. Severe weather conditions in April – June restricted 10th Air Force troop activities and attacks on enemy installations. In October of 1943, the 1st was again transferred – this time to Sookerating, India, with their C-47's. In 1944 and 1945, thousands of transport missions were flown in the CBI area carrying men and supplies to the front lines.

Clete was in Madison, Wisconsin when he heard the war was over. He was discharged from the Army Air Forces on August 31, 1945, at the rank of Staff Sergeant. During his service he was awarded the Distinguished Flying Cross with one Oak Leaf Cluster; the Air Medal with three Oak Leaf Clusters; and the Distinguished Unit Citation.

Clete was engaged to Erleen M. Wahlrab for three years while serving his country during the war. On February 10, 1945, the couple was married in Dayton, Montgomery Co., Ohio. During the war Erleen attended school to become a nurse's aide with the Volunteer Red Cross in Dayton, Ohio. Clete wrote hundreds of love letters to Erleen while he was away from her which she has kept close to her over the years. He sent her a crown embroidered with gold thread from India in 1943, for the lady he "hoped one day will be my queen."

From a letter written November 6, 1942:

Darling,

"Here's your flowers! It may be monotonous to you to receive roses every time I want to tell you how much I love you. But I never was much good at being original. Besides, I think God made roses especially so I could send them to you. You see, honey, the church uses the color red as a symbol of love and sacrifice and I have already told you what my definition of love is. That's why I use red roses as my messenger to you, my queen. Besides, honey, you're so much like a beautiful rose that it only seems natural that you and roses should go together.
So darling lady, take these flowers as a message of my love, on your birthday."

Clete

Throughout the rest of his life Clete would write Erleen beautiful love letters on every occasion.

Clete and Erleen had eight children together; Mary, Joseph, Kathleen, Patrick, Ruth, Anne, Cletus and Michelle. After the war, Clete was employed at Wright-Patterson Field in Dayton, Ohio as an instrumentation technician. In 1951 the Didier family moved to California where Clete was transferred to Edwards Air Force Base. He continued in the instrumentation field with the Civil Service until his retirement. In 1977, Clete was ordained a Deacon and served 15 years at Sacred Heart in Lancaster for the Archdiocese of Los Angeles. After retiring from Civil Service, he also taught classes in religion at Paraclete High School, in Lancaster, for eight years.
On June 30, 1992, Clete passed away in Lancaster, California. He is buried at the Good Shepherd Catholic Cemetery in Lancaster, Los Angeles Co., California.

Wedding day February 10, 1945 – Dayton, Ohio

56

DOYLE CHARLES "TEX" DRAPER

Doyle Charles Draper was born April 21, 1917 in Hot Springs, Arkansas, the son of Atis Alfred, from Kansas, and Estella Maye (Horndorff) Draper. He had six siblings; Gertrude, Alfred, Miller, Clifford, Estella and Sybil. In 1920 the Draper family lived in Lincoln, Garland Co., Arkansas. Atis owned a farm and earned his living as a farmer.

During the war, Doyle served in the European-African-Middle-Eastern Campaign with the U.S. Army. He was attached to the 101st Airborne Division. He received an honorable discharge on November 30, 1946 at the rank of Tech 5. While in the service he was awarded two Bronze Service Stars; the Purple Heart Medal; a Bronze Star for valor; the American Campaign Medal; and the World War II Victory Medal.

Doyle was married to Virginia and together they had four children; three sons, Doyle, Charles and Sammy; and one daughter, Mary Draper.

Throughout his life he was a professional boxer, truck driver, and electrician. Doyle also owned and operated several janitorial services. He enjoyed playing golf and shooting a game of pool. He belonged to the Disabled American Veterans (DAV) and the Moose Lodge. In his later years, Doyle enjoyed driving the Mayflower shuttle bus for the Mayflower Gardens Retirement Community in Quartz Hill, California.

Doyle passed away at home in Quartz Hill on April 20, 1997. He is buried at the Riverside National Cemetery, Riverside Co., California.

HARRY S. DU BOIS

Harry S. Du Bois was born May 1, 1918 in Seattle, King Co., Washington, the eldest child of Ralph Waldo and Catherine (St. Vrain) Du Bois. He had two younger siblings; one sister, Catherine Louise, and one brother, Ralph Waldo Du Bois, Jr. Shortly after Harry's birth, the family moved to California. The first exclusive family shoe store in the Antelope Valley was opened by Ralph and Catherine Du Bois in 1928. Later it was expanded to include men's wear.

The Du Bois family lived on Cedar Avenue in Lancaster where Harry attended Lancaster Grammar School. He was a member of the Honor Society in high school and graduated from AVJUHS in 1936. After high school, Harry was a student at the University of California at Berkeley. It was while setting tables for lunch in Bowles Hall at the men's dormitory, that he heard the news about Pearl Harbor.

Harry had always wanted to fly, so he took all of the tests for the Air Corps Aviation Cadet Program and qualified. He was listed as 1-A in the draft and the draft board granted him several deferments until he could be called in for training. He was sent to Santa Ana Army Air Base in Santa Ana, California, where he learned close order drill, military courtesy, military aircraft identification, navigation and other pertinent subjects, as Harry recalled, "with healthy doses of physical training thrown in."

From Santa Ana Harry was sent to Merced Army Air Base in Merced, California, where he was familiarized with the PT-22 (Ryan Primary Trainer). After ten days of ground school, the cadets were trucked to Eagles Field, the primary flight training facility at Dos Palos, California. Harry soloed after 8 hours and 23 minutes of flight instructor time. He had accomplished his first hurdle. The class was then bussed back to Merced Army Air Base to begin basic flight training. This would be a step up in flying due to the larger equipment, the BT-13 Basic Trainer and an introduction to instrument flying under difficult weather conditions. Harry soloed in that "bird" in only 5 hours.

On January 5, 1943, Harry's class arrived at Yuma Army Air Base, Yuma, Arizona for advance flight training in the AT-6. In spite of his request for twin-engine advance flight training, Harry was assigned to a single engine airplane. This was a disappointment because he never considered himself a "hot pilot." Harry's first impression of the AT-6 was one of awe! This was a lot more airplane than he had been used to flying. Soon he was learning aerial and ground gunnery techniques, aerobatics and perfecting instrument flying procedures. His solo time was 3 hours.

As the cadets approached the end of their training, an announcement suddenly showed up on the bulletin board advising that all cadets over 5 feet 10 inches tall, and weighing more than 160 pounds would not go to single engine fighter transition. This caused Harry great concern as he was above those specifications.

The second day prior to graduation a special meeting of the cadet class was called for volunteers for some "special" assignments. One called for 8 officers to report to the 6th Ferrying Group, Air Transport Command at Long Beach, California. Harry recalled "a round of laughter from the cadets. This assignment was close to home and I thought it might have some merit from the standpoint of broad flying experience. I bought the offer! Late that afternoon an assignment sheet revealed my selection to the 6th Ferrying Group. I had hit the jackpot but did not realize it until quite some time later."

On Wednesday, March 10, 1943, after 9 months and 218 hours of flying time, Harry received an aeronautical rating, his pilot's wings and his commission as 2nd Lieutenant, United States Army Air Corps, Officers' Reserve Corps. His first assignment was to move military aircraft from factories to modification centers, to staging area for combat areas and into theatres of combat operations. Harry recalled that the combat crew pilots referred to the Air Transport pilots as "Air Transport Command pilots - Allergic To Combat, jokingly, but it was doubtful that they realized the magnitude of the service [we] rendered."

6th Ferrying Command Crew, Long Beach Army Base, preparing to deliver a B-25 bomber to Brisbane, Australia. Left to right: 1st Lt. D.C. Ross, Pilot; 2nd Lt. Harry S. Du Bois, Co-Pilot; Lt. Keith, Navigator; Pvt. Larsen, Radio Operator - June 2, 1943.

A memorable flight for Harry occurred in December 1945. Harry remembered, "I was flying a C-54 (the largest passenger and transport plane in service at the time) with a load of passengers from Honolulu to Hamilton Field, north of San Francisco. We were arriving late at night after a smooth, virtually cloudless flight. Weather at Hamilton was minimum instrument and weather at Travis Field, Mather Field, McClellan Field and even Hammer Field in Fresno was not better! I debated as to whether to try to get into one of the other fields or not because of better instrument approaches than the one at Hamilton Field. Then I chucked the idea on the possibility that the field could close before I arrived leaving less fuel for another alternate.

Now Hamilton field is on the east side of the peninsula, north of San Francisco, and the approach is from the San Francisco Bay. There are hills on three sides of the field within very close proximity. The instrument approach was to fly over the beacon at 3,600 feet on a pre-determined northwesterly heading, then fly a rectangle letting down while doing so. At about 800 feet on final approach, we broke into the clear. My gosh, we were over a brightly lighted business district instead of the Bay! I was horror-stricken! We had to be over the east bay and there are mountains and a bay bridge also.

I spiraled back up to approach altitude while Hamilton Field Tower was calling for position reports. A check with the tower indicated 55-knot winds were affecting our let-down procedure! I call on the Lord for guidance. After correcting for winds, our second let-down put us on the runway. I thanked the Lord for getting that load of passengers on the ground safely. Somebody else besides me was guiding that plane."

Harry was overseas for several months at a time flying supplies and men to the combat areas. His tour included time transporting supplies and troops in Aden, Arabia (People's Democratic Republic of Yemen); Dakar, French West Africa (Senegal); and Bermuda. From Bermuda he flew to Florida, then Texas and on to Hamilton Field, California. He was thrilled at the opportunities to fly many of the twin and four engine aircraft used in the services for combat and transport services.

Harry and high school classmate, Don McDonald, wanted to stay active in the Air Force Reserve Program. Since there were no training units in the Antelope Valley, Harry and Don organized a unit for training Air Force Reservists as well as Army and Navy Reservists. Harry served 20 years as Flight Commander of this unit.

Harry retired from inactive Reserve at the rank of Lieutenant Colonel. He received the Asiatic Pacific Campaign Medal; the American Campaign Medal; Victory in Europe Commemorative Medal; World War II Victory Medal; and the Armed Forces Reserve Medal.

After the war, Harry went home to Lancaster and joined his father in the family business of retail men's wear. On April 20, 1946 Harry married his sweetheart, Barbara Marie Wright, in Pasadena, California. Together they had three daughters; Evelyn (Lynn) Marie, Janet Louise, and Patricia Ann Du Bois. Harry eventually took over managing the store after his father retired and continued on until his own retirement.

Harry and Barbara recently moved to San Diego, California so they could be closer to their daughters, after spending 74 years in the Antelope Valley.

October 7, 1943 ad, Antelope Valley Ledger-Gazette – R.. W. Du Bois men's store.

Charles W. Dungan was born July 8, 1921 in Brownwood, Brown Co., Texas. In 1930, at the age of eight, Charlie was living in Antelope Township on Sierra Madre Road with his uncle, Carl T. Olsen, and family. Charlie attended Lancaster Grammar school and graduated from AVJUHS in 1939.

Charlie entered the service in 1942 and began his pilot training. He was attached to the 20th Fighter Group, 77th Fighter Squadron. The group was established at March Air Field, California, in January 1943, where the group was equipped with the P-38 Lightning aircraft. The pilots served as part of the air defense, guarding the west coast before shipping out to England in August 1943, where they became a part of the 8th Air Force.

While stationed at King's Cliffe in Northamptonshire, England, the 77th was designated as a Fighter Squadron and entered combat operations in November 1943. Charlie joined the 77th as a replacement pilot in July 1944, flying a P-38J, Serial No. 42-68156. He was assigned to strafe and dive-bomb airfields, trains, vehicles, bridges, enemy barracks and many other targets mainly in France, Belgium and Germany. The 20th received a Distinguished Unit Citation for their performance on April 8, 1944 when the group struck several airfields in central Germany, while under attack by the enemy. After breaking up and shaking off the attackers, they re-grouped and began to hit railroad equipment, oil and power plants, factories and the German airdrome at Salzwedel. They became known as the "Loco Group" due to their numerous successful low-level attacks on enemy locomotives.

In June 1944, Charlie took part in the Air Offense Europe Battle at Normandy, in Northern France as part of the Normandy invasion. He flew patrols over the English Channel and supported the invasion force later in the month by escorting bombers on their way to strike targets in France, Belgium and Holland. On July 13, 1944, Charlie had to ditch his P-38 into the English Channel. After providing cover for heavy bombers returning from a mission over Munich, Germany, he was forced to bail out at 5,000 feet over the Thames Estuary when both of his engines quit. He was picked up by a small boat and brought to shore, safe and sound.

On October 7, 1944 Charlie would fly his last combat mission. He was on a mission escorting B-17 bombers to the synthetic oil plant at Politz, north east of Berlin, Germany in Red Flight of the 77th. While in his newly assigned P-51, "*Kathleen*," [named for his wife, Kathleen Stinson] he was hit by flak near Peenemunde, close to the secret German V-2 rocket plant and launching site. Before he was hit, he had made his only "kill" on the mission. He strafed the

runway at Peenemunde airfield and destroyed a German Ju 88 airplane on the ground. Charlie managed to bail out of the airplane at 8,000 feet, landing in the ocean near the coast of Denmark. Charlie was injured but able to swim to shore. As the story goes, he was aided by two padres and a young Danish boy who helped hide him in an attic, away from the enemy. Charlie was taken care of by the Danish underground, which arranged for his escape through Sweden.

Charlie was honorably discharged in 1950 at the rank of Captain with over 100 hours of combat time flown. He flew 27 missions with the 77th Fighter Squadron. His decorations included the Air Medal with two Oak Leaf Clusters; the Purple Heart; the American Campaign Medal; World War II Victory Medal; the European/African/Middle Eastern Campaign Medal; and the Japan Occupation Medal.

After his discharge from the service, Charlie, along with two friends, including veteran WASP, Irma "Babe" Story, formed the Antelope Valley Pest Control Company working as crop dusters. The company was located at the old Lancaster airport on Avenue I and 10th Street West in Lancaster. The firm was in business until 1953. Charlie became a salesman at Starksen Chevrolet, then later worked at H.W. Hunter Dodge where he retired after 25 years in the automobile business.

He was active in several community organizations including the Lancaster Elks No. 1625; Veterans of Foreign Wars; American Legion, Post No. 311; Air Force Escape and Evasion Societies; The Quiet Birdmen, and was a former president of the Antelope Valley Country Club. He was given membership in the Caterpiller, Goldfish and the Boot, an organization with the member requirements of having to bail out during combat action, parachute into the sea and walk out of enemy-occupied territory.

Charlie passed away in 1994 at the age of 70, in Lancaster, California and is buried at Joshua Memorial Park in Lancaster, California.

NEIL GLENN "STUBBIE" EARL

Neil Glenn Earl was born July 3, 1922 in Wilmot, Roberts Co., South Dakota, the son of Harold Allen and Mae Gwendolyn (Walker) Earl. Neil had three siblings; two brothers, Allen Eugene and James Dale; and one sister, Audrey Gwynethe Earl. Neil was living in Hollywood, California when he heard about the attack on Pearl Harbor. On July 4, 1942 Neil married Ardith Jo Beavers in Hollywood, California.

Neil was drafted into the U.S. Army Air Corps and inducted at Ft. MacArthur in San Pedro, California on December 21, 1942. He entered into active service on December 31, and was sent to St. Petersburg, Florida for basic training. After basic training, he was transferred back to Los Angeles, California for six weeks of clerical training at the Roslyn Hotel.

Neil enjoyed the great camaraderie while in the Air Corps and also the benefits of a cadet in training. He was stationed at Santa Ana, California while training as a cadet. Neil recalled, "As a cadet stationed at Santa Ana, California, one night while serving at the dinner table, I noticed a head pop out. Since the cadets had to sit at attention, with no talking, I was afraid I was going to have to report him. It turned out he was a good friend from my home town of Wilmot, South Dakota. Also while stationed in Santa Ana, I was fortunate to be able to play in the marching band. I would go home on Friday night. On Sunday, my wife and I would take the bus back to Santa Ana where she watched me march with the band, then I would put her on the bus to return home."

He received specialized training as an Aerial Gunner at the Army Air Force Gunnery School in Kingman, Arizona and was attached to the 3505th Army Air Force Unit, Squadron A-9. In 1944, Neil graduated from Primary Flight Training at Ryan Field in Tucson, Arizona. He was stationed in Deming, New Mexico and Scott Field in Belleville, Illinois during his time in the service. Neil was serving at Scott Field when the war ended. He remained there and helped with the separation of the military personnel from the service.

Neil was honorably discharged at Jefferson Barracks Separation Center in Missouri, on February 18, 1946, at the rank of Corporal. He was awarded the American Campaign Medal; World War II Victory Medal; Good Conduct Medal.

After his discharge, Neil returned home to Hollywood, California to his wife and son, Larry. He went to work at Lockheed Aircraft and also attended Television and Radio School in Hollywood. Neil later entered into the building trade where he became a plastering contractor. He and Ardith had four children, including sons Larry Allan and Lonny James, and daughters Robin Jo and Susan Irene Earl. Neil and Ardith are enjoying retirement in Mojave, California.

Neil's thoughts on the war included, "I don't like war, but our generation did not hesitate to fight for freedom. I learned discipline and a work ethic which benefited me the rest of my life."

Neil Earl, in center kneeling – 1944 - graduation from Primary Flight Training at Ryan Field Tucson, Arizona

World War II Victory Medal

Cris P. Eliopulos was born March 16, 1924 in Lancaster, Los Angeles Co., California, the son of Greek immigrants Panos George and Stavrula (Karatzas) Eliopulos. In April 1930, the family had grown to include six children; sons Andy, George, Cris and Ted; and two daughters Angele and Helen – all born in California. A fifth son, Charley was born in September 1930. Panos worked the land in the Antelope Valley and made his living as an alfalfa farmer on 70th Street West and Avenue H in Lancaster.

Cris attended grammar school in Lancaster and graduated from AVJUHS in 1943. After graduation from high school in 1943, Cris was drafted into the U.S. Army. He was inducted at Fort MacArthur in San Pedro, California and sent to Fort Lawton, Seattle, Washington for basic training.

When he received his orders to go into the Army, Cris recalled that "my emotions were excitement because I was doing something for my country. I was worried because I wondered if I would be coming home – wondering what it would be like to leave the farm and all my family relatives and friends. I was eighteen years old and really had never been out of California."

Cris left Lancaster by train for Fort MacArthur in December 1943. It was a whole new experience for him. He arrived in Los Angeles then went on to Fort MacArthur. When he received a few days off, he went home to say goodbye to his family. Upon returning to Fort MacArthur, Cris was told he would be going to Seattle, Washington. He trained there from January 1944 to March 1944. After basic training he received a furlough and went home for two weeks. After his return to Seattle, Cris was told that he would be leaving for Europe. He had no idea where he was going.

The Army put his group on a train and they headed East. Cris had never been back East before and when he went through Montana he saw his first real, live antelope! Even though he lived in the Antelope Valley, Cris had never seen an antelope there. He enjoyed traveling through the beautiful countryside on the way to his first destination – Chicago, Illinois. They arrived in Chicago near the stock yards and were not allowed to venture out into the city. Instead, they were made to exercise and did plenty of marching around the stock yards.

Later that evening, the train pulled out, again heading East. They ended up at Camp Kilmer in New Jersey. While Cris was there, he and three other GI's went off to New York to see the "Big Apple." While waiting for the train to New York, they stopped at a small café and had dinner. "After some time I mentioned to my friends that this restaurant must be owned by a Greek family. My friends asked how I knew , and I told them that a Greek can always tell another Greek. When I asked if the owner was Greek, they said 'yes' and came over to talk to us. We ended up with extra dessert and a free meal."

In April 1944, Cris finally was onboard a ship bound for Europe, landing in Southampton, England. "Our assignment was to make a last stop for our Army in England. We were getting everything needed for an invasion of France. The first time we did this was early May and it was a practice run. On June 6, 1944, we did it again, but this time we found out that it was the real thing. From our temporary camp we were called back so we could get ready to go over to France. We landed in France at the end of July 1944. We went in on Omaha Beach and had to walk all the way to Saint Lo [nearly 40 miles]. The next day we were sent to Chartre from Saint Lo, and from there we were split up into small numbers of about 15 men."

1944 – France

From Chartre the troops went on to the town of Pontorson/Dinard. While in the town, Cris saw a truck with an Air Force ID. He asked one of the guys in the truck if they knew a Sgt. Nick A. Kappas, a cousin of his. The name sounded familiar to them, so Cris gave them a note to pass along to Sgt. Kappas, telling him to come and visit with him. A few days later, Nick showed up and the two of them had a long visit together over lunch.

A month or so later the group was split in half and sent to the small town of Dol, near Mont St. Michel. The area was a scenic place with a beautiful castle out at sea – a castle where you could only enter or leave when the tide was out. In December 1944, as part of the transportation group, Cris was called on to drive Lt. Cook to Paris. This would be the first time he had been to Paris. It had been snowing and Cris recalled what a beautiful place the city was. On December 15, Cris was at the Paris Opera House waiting for the band leader, Glen Miller to arrive for a show. An announcement was made that Glen Miller's plane had gone down in the English Channel.

While stationed in Pontorson, Cris was called away for basic training in the Infantry to support the Battle of the Bulge. Before he completed his training the fight was over and Cris was sent to Paris to work. A visit by his cousin, John P. Eliopulos, came as quite a surprise to Chris. They spent an afternoon taking in the sights of the city.

In 1945, a high school friend, Dale Scott, from Lancaster, was walking down a side street near the Arc-de-Triomphe, in Paris, and happened to look into a room where Cris was working. "When he walked in and I saw him, I looked up and called him by his nickname of Scotty. The officer in charge came over to bawl me out because Scotty was a Lieutenant. The Lieutenant told the officer who he was and I apologized. I should have said, hello Lt. Dale Scott! Everything went well after that and I was given the afternoon off. We had a good time sitting and having drinks on the Champs-Elysées."

By January 1946, Cris was on a ship bound for home. He was discharged at Fort MacArthur in February 1946. His family met him in downtown Los Angeles and they made the journey back together to Lancaster. Cris went to work on the family farm picking melons. In September 1946 he was hired by the Southern California Edison Company (SCE). Cris attended night school supported by the G.I. Bill and continued working for SCE for over 37 years at various jobs. He joined the American Legion, Post #311 in Lancaster, California.

Cris married Anne Pappas on June 11, 1950, in Los Angeles, California. From this union, three children were born; Cristine, Pete and Stephanie Eliopulos. Cris is retired and currently lives in Torrance with his wife, Anne.

Cris and buddy – France

IRWIN HOWARD FINCK

William L.P. Finck immigrated from Germany to the United States in 1902 with his parents, Henry and Wilhelmina Finck. In 1910 the family was living in Los Angeles, California, where Henry was employed at a plumbing shop. By 1920 the family had moved to the Antelope Valley. William was living next door to his parents, with his wife, Jessie, and daughter, Pearl. In 1930, William and his three children were living on a ranch in the Esperanza District of the Antelope Valley. William was a rancher/farmer and made his living farming the land with alfalfa. Irwin Howard Finck was born February 28, 1921 in Lancaster, Los Angeles Co., California, the son of William Ludwig Peter and Jessie Elma (Dunham) Finck. Irwin had two sisters, Pearl and Florence Finck.

Irwin attended the Esperanza Grammar School in Lancaster and graduated from AVJUHS in 1939. When the news was announced about the bombing of Pearl Harbor, Irwin was at his home in Lancaster. Irwin was drafted into the U.S. Army in November 1944. He was inducted into the Army at Fort MacArthur, California. For 15 weeks he went through basic training at Camp Roberts, near Paso Robles, California, training to be a soldier in the Infantry.

After basic training, Irwin was sent to Fort Ord Debarkation Center in California. The troops left on a ship bound for the Philippine Islands. After a month at sea, they arrived at Manila Bay. Irwin was assigned to Clark Field where he joined up with the 126th Infantry Regiment, 32nd Red Arrow Division.

Irwin spent most of the war in the South Pacific, in the Philippines and New Guinea as part of the Morotai "mop-up." When the war ended Irwin recalled, "Another Sergeant and I were chosen to carry the white flag to the Japanese forces letting them know the war had ended. I had a very uneasy feeling not knowing what kind of reception we would get." Close to the end of 1945, Irwin was transferred to the Army Air Forces with the 5th Air Force, 36th Fighter Squadron. He spent one year in Japan in the Army of Occupation. He was a Staff Sergeant in charge of airplane armament in a P-51 Squadron.

In November 1946, Irwin was honorably discharged from the Army Air Forces at the rank of Staff Sergeant. He received the following awards for his time in service to his country: Army of Occupation Medal; Asiatic-Pacific Campaign Medal with 1 Bronze Star; Liberation Ribbon with 1 Bronze Star; World War II Victory Medal; and the Good Conduct Medal.

After the war Irwin went back to his home in the Antelope Valley where he was self-employed in the farming business. He married Nan Christine Smillie on November 15, 1947, in Los Angeles, California. They had four daughters together; Leigh Ann, Gail Eileen, Debra Jane and Cinda Joyce. In 1965, after 44 years in the Antelope Valley, Irwin and his family moved to Pasco, Washington. Irwin and his wife, Nan, currently call Pasco their home.

32nd Red Arrow Division patch

ADOLF MICHAEL "ADIE" FIX, JR.

Adolf Michael Fix, Jr., son of Adolf Michael and Magdelena (Walters) Fix, Sr. was born August 26, 1922 in Brooklyn, Kings Co., New York. Adolf Sr., an ornamental ironworker, landed in New Jersey from Ludwigshafen, Germany in October 1905. Magdalena came to the United States from Hungary in 1915 at age 17. Adolf Jr. was the eldest of six children including 5 sons; Michael, Jackob, William and Robert; and one daughter, Eleanor Fix.

After graduating from East Islip High School in New York, Adolf was employed by the Republic Aviation Corporation in Farmingdale, New York, as an airplane mechanic. He entered the Army Air Corps on December 7, 1942 at Yaphank, Long Island, New York. Basic training at Atlantic City, New Jersey, consisted of numerous drills and field marching along with plenty of calisthenics.

Adolf's first assignment upon completion of basic training was at Seymour Johnson Field in Goldsboro, North Carolina. There, he went through Aircraft and Engine school, then on to the Henry Ford Plant, Detroit, Michigan for Engine [aircraft] school. The next stop was Aerial gunnery school at Las Vegas, Nevada where in November 1943, he received his gunner's wings. Prior to volunteering for overseas duty, Adolf attended aerial gunnery instructors school at Fort Meyers, Florida, aerial gunnery flight training and crew flight training at Avon Park, Florida.

After completion of flight training, Adolf's first assignment was aerial gunner for a B-17 Flying Fortress crew. The crew arrived at Hunter Field, Savannah, Georgia, assigned to a brand-new B-17G. They left Hunter Field for an over night stop at Bangor, Maine. The next stop was Iceland, then on to England. They arrived in England and were assigned to the 8th Air Force, 447th Bomber Group (a unit of the 3rd Bombardment Division), 708th Squadron, at Rattlesden Air Base in Suffolk Co., northwest of London. Adolf was promoted to Staff Sergeant after his arrival in England.

During his time with the 8th Air Force, Adolf and his crew completed 30 missions over Germany, with the last 15 of the missions as lead crew. The lead crew was responsible for leading the 447th Bomber Group over their targets. Adolf dealt with many combat hours as the waist-gunner while on these missions. Two of the missions he recalled stuck out in his mind the most, "First, we got shot down by a German jet – a brand new ME-262. They hit us with about five shots. The jets went by us so fast that we could hardly see them.. We spiraled down and finally made it back to Belgium with a safe landing. Our plane was heavily damaged and had one engine shot out. The second time we got hit with flak over the target area and once again, made it back to Belgium and safely landed with our damaged aircraft. Belgium had just been liberated and the field runways were being hastily repaired and were very bumpy." On the first

mission he described, Adolf was injured by the flak bursts with chemical burns to both eyes. He was sent to a hospital in England for three days with his eyes closed shut from the powder burns. He also had flak in the back of both legs. Adolf was laid up the on "flak leave" for a week in a large English home with other GI's until he was well enough to fly again.

B-17 waist-gunner, Adolf Fix

Co-pilot Colby checking engine damage from interception with German ME-262's – photo by Adolf Fix.

Tail damage from German ME-262's – photo by Adolf Fix.

Adolf was on a ship in New York Harbor, waiting to dock, when he heard the war was over. On V-J day he was at Chanute Field, Illinois, in training for a B-29 flight crew assignment to the Pacific area. Adolf was honorably discharged on October 10, 1945 at Chanute Field. He received the Purple Heart Medal; the Air Medal with three Oak Leaf Clusters; the European Theater Ribbon with a Bronze Service Star. The 3rd Bombardment Division was cited by the President for the historic England-Africa shuttle mission, bombing Messerschmitt factories in Europe.

During the war, all five children of Adolf Fix, Sr. were in the service. Michael was in the 8th Air Force working as a Crew Chief for a P-51 Fighter Group; Jackob was a paratrooper in the U.S. Army with the 101st Airborne; William was in the Navy in the Pacific Area; Robert joined the U.S. Army and was in the U.S. Army of Occupation in France following the war.

After the war, Adolf drove home to Islip, New York from Chanute. He enjoyed home life once again and applied for school through the GI Bill. He attended radio school in Mineola, New York. On October 18, 1947, Adolf married the girl he had known since the third grade – Evelyn Dolores Hitt. They were married in Islip, Suffolk Co., New York. Together they had two sons; Richard Lauren and Allan Michael Fix.

In April 1956, Adolf and his family moved to Lancaster, California where he worked as an Instrumentation Technician at Edwards Air Force Base for over 30 years. He also worked for General Electric and General Dynamics, then at age 65 was hired by Northrop for the B-2 program. Adolf is a life time member of the American Legion, Post 411, in Islip, New York; an 8th Air Force life member, and a 447th Bomb Group life member. In December 2001, the Consul General of France awarded him with a "Thank you America" certificate in appreciation for the Liberation of France in WWII.

Speaking on his military experiences during the war, Adolf stated, "Everyone should put time in the military and remain patriotic to our country, enjoy our mixed cultures and learn English, but not forget their ethnic beginnings. The war made me appreciate what we have in our country and I wish people would understand what it means to be free and stand behind all it represents – without the negative attitudes."

Adolf and his wife, Evelyn, currently live in Lancaster where they both enjoy attending church, Elk's Lodge functions, and reunions with the remaining five B-17 crew members.

Four of the five Fix brothers in WWII uniform. Left to right – William, Jackob, Adolf and Michael.

Edward G. Foote, Jr., was born about 1922 in Illinois, the son of Edward G. and Margaret Foote, Sr., from New York and Illinois, respectively. By 1930 the family was living in the South Gate area of Los Angeles Co., California where Edward, Sr. was employed as a salesman for an oil refining company. The family included Edward's wife, Margaret, and sons Edward, Jr. and Fred Foote.

While attending AVJUHS, Edward was involved in many activities including three years of Varsity football, and two years of basketball. In his junior year he was elected the Jr. Class yell leader and was also a member of the Letterman's Club. Edward graduated from AVJUHS with the class of 1941.

On March 20, 1942, Edward enlisted in the U.S. Army and served with the U.S. Army Air Forces before attending Officer Candidate School. In 1943, Edward was commissioned a 2nd Lieutenant in the U.S. Army after the successful completion of the Officer Candidate course at the Infantry School in Fort Benning, Georgia. He held the rank of corporal before being commissioned.

As part of the 5307th Composite Unit (Provisional), Edward was sent to Myitkyina, Burma. The group later became known as "Merrill's Marauders" named after its leader, Brigadier General Frank Merrill. The jungles of Burma were thick with vegetation – no room for the jeeps and trucks needed to carry supplies. The men had to carry all their equipment and supplies over 800 miles, marching over jungle and mountain roads. All the equipment was carried by the soldiers, on their back, or on the backs of pack mules. They were re-supplied by air drops after clearing the thick jungles areas below. Landing strips were hacked out to allow small planes in to evacuate the sick and wounded. At the end of the Burma Campaign, all remaining soldiers were evacuated to hospitals suffering from tropical diseases, exhaustion and malnutrition.

On July 2, 1944, Edward was killed in action. He was awarded the Purple Heart Medal and the Bronze Star. For their accomplishments in Burma, the Marauders were awarded the Distinguished Unit Citation in July 1944. The Marauders also have the rare distinction of having every member of the unit receive a Bronze Star, duly awarded for their "heroism and outstanding achievement in a combat theater."

2nd Lieutenant Edward G. Foote, Jr. was buried at the Honolulu Memorial, in Honolulu, Hawaii, where his name is joined with thousands of other soldiers who died in World War II.

Merrill's Marauders patch

Battle of Myitkyina – Author unknown

At Myitkyina today they lie at rest
There were soldiers all and gave their best
They fought and died in days of rain
And prayed for sun that never came.

Through mud they crawled to find their foe
They cursed and swore but on they go
As days went by and night fell
They all slept on the walls of hell.

Artillery shells with their melody of death
Whizzed by with each and every breath
As dawn came to light the earth
Amid sniper fire through dirt
In falling rain they fought on
                    Hope to live by
those had gone.

Myitkyina has fallen at last
They would be glad to know of the finished task
But the trails are filled with Yankee blood
Of gallant men who fought, died in Burma mud
Courageous men these, they fought and fell; Bless them all, God; treat them well.

Bronze Star

★

WE'VE BEEN HITTING 'EM
WHERE THEY LIVE, FOLKS,
and the future looks a great
deal brighter. Here's wish-
ing all our friends Health,
Happiness and Prosperity
in 1944.

E. G. FOOTE

DISTRIBUTOR SIGNAL OIL PRODUCTS

December 30, 1943 ad from the Antelope Valley Ledger-Gazette
E.G. Foote, Distributor of Signal Oil Products

RUFUS CLARENCE "R.C." FRANKLIN, JR.

R.C. Franklin, Jr., was born in 1921 in Oklahoma, the son of Rufus Clarence, a native of Arkansas, and Willie (Ross) Franklin. In 1920, elder Rufus was living in Muskokee City, Muskogee Co., Oklahoma with his wife, Willie, and three children; Clarence, Vivian and Roberta. By 1930, the family had moved to Martin Township in Muskogee Co. and the family had grown to include R.C., age eight. Elder Rufus was employed as a general manager for a coal mine during that time.

R.C. attended Antelope Valley Junior College in 1938 while living in Mojave, California. He played on the baseball team along with future veterans Donald McDonald, Francis Batz and Donald Bones.

R.C. originally joined the Army Air Forces 8th Air Force, 55th Pursuit Squadron, 20th Pursuit Group, in late 1942 or early 1943. He was serving as an instructor and had requested to be entered into combat action.

On August 11, 1943, R.C. joined up with 20th Pursuit or Fighter Group at March Field in Riverside, California. Soon after, R.C. departed by train to Camp Miles Standish, Taunton, Massachusetts, a European staging area, en route to England onboard the *HMS Queen Elizabeth (QE)*. The luxury ship *QE* had been refitted to accommodate over 19,000 men. Captain Don Reihmer, also on the *QE* the same time as R.C., recalled, "We slept in five-high bunks in a two-person room and ate twice a day, in shifts. The enlisted men slept either on the enclosed boat deck or in bunks on alternate nights. We young 2nd and 1st Lieutenants spent a lot of our daytimes on the open decks. Some used their time at the poker table. Franklin stood out as a leader and a really good man from the onset."

After five days onboard the ship, the *QE* dropped anchor on August 25, 1943. The men were transported to the docks at Greenock, Scotland, then went on by train to RAF Wittering, then to King's Cliffe in Northamptonshire, England to join up with the 79th Fighter Squadron. King's Cliffe had one of the poorest airfields in England. The buildings were old and inadequate for the job they had to do.

Captain Arthur W. Heiden recalled R.C. as "a great combat leader whose mind kicked into high gear when the pressure was on. He had outstanding flying abilities and was a superb teacher. Instead of coming down hard on someone for not doing something right, R.C. would make a joke out of it, get everyone laughing, then make the guy feel like he was the best in the world at what he was doing."

On January 26, 1944, R.C. was promoted to the rank of Major. He was assigned to the 79th as the Squadron Commanding Officer for a short time – from February through May 14, 1944. He was then transferred to the 8th Air Force Fighter Command Headquarters. R.C. left a huge impression on his men at the 79th. Captain Heiden remembered him "leading the 79th Fighter Squadron and often the whole of the 20th Fighter Group. His effort wasn't at an easy time or circumstances. The 20th FG had been beat up badly, stood down from combat for a week for reorganization, and now short of pilots and aircraft. R.C.'s enthusiasm, leadership, ability, encouragement, especially for us new replacement pilots and ground crews, was a great gift. Being confronted with four or five to one of our escort force could, and occasionally was, heartbreaking – pull your socks up and do it again, tomorrow."

"Noticeable also," recalled Heiden, "R.C. was always gentle and instructive to young pilots. He certainly never let his older flight commanders get away with stupid things and would come down on them very hard. Of course, we enjoyed that! Later when he finished his tour, he assigned his P-38 airplane, *'Strictly Stella's Baby'* [named after R.C.'s wife, Stella Actis] and ground crew to me. It was renamed *'Lucky Lady.'* Crew Chief Max Pyles went on to win the Bronze Star with that airplane by going 300 combat hours without an abort and on original engines. Also, it was honored by being placed on a United States Post Office stamp and card."

The 20th Fighter Group stayed in the United Kingdom well after the war with R.C. as it's Wing Commander. In the 1950's, Captain Heiden remembered seeing a photo of R.C. as the Captain of the 20th's gunnery team at Nellis Air Force Base.

71

During his time in the service, R.C. received numerous awards including a Distinguished Flying Cross with one Cluster, and the Air Medal with six Oak Leaf Clusters. As a Major, his claims were three German aircraft destroyed while in the air and, along with Capt. Heiden, seven German aircraft on the ground. The 20th received the Presidential Unit Citation on April 8, 1944.

R.C. married Stella Actis, a 1942 graduate of AVJUHS. Together they had four children; three daughters; Cathy, Victoria and Valerie; and one son, Russell Franklin. R.C. passed away in 1969, leaving behind many friends with memories of their service together with him during World War II.

R.C. Franklin (center) with the crew of "Strictly Stella's Baby"
Left to right – Jim Cavalier, Isadore Jaffe, Major R.C. Franklin, Max Pyles (Crew Chief) and Charles Fink.
Photo use courtesy of Capt. Arthur W. Heiden

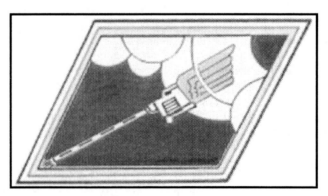

79th Fighter Squadron patch

Robert Maurice Fritsinger was born December 8, 1925, in Kirksville, Adair Co., Missouri, the son of Fred J. and Buena Clarice (Murphy) Fritsinger. In 1943, he graduated from Kirksville High School in Kirksville, Missouri.

Shortly after Robert turned 18, he enlisted in the Army Air Corps for pilot training and was sent to Jefferson Barracks in St. Louis, Missouri for basic training. As soon as his group completed training, they were told no more pilots were needed, so they would have to make another choice. Robert stayed in the Air Corps and shipped out to Godman Field at Fort Knox, Kentucky. He was assigned to the U.S. Army Airways Communication Systems in the Asiatic-Pacific Theater. He was sent to McClellan Field in Sacramento, California, then on to a quarantine area in Pittsburg, California where he subsequently joined units floating down to Mare Island, in the San Francisco Bay, on a barge.

At Mare Island they boarded the *U.S.S. Republic*, a German passenger ship captured during World War I and converted into a transport ship. At that time, convoys traveled at 10 knots, but since their ship could only make 6 knots, they had to travel alone and via a different route – down the coast passed Mexico, across the equator, and west to New Caledonia. One night while cruising near a small island, they wandered close enough to a naval battle to hear the big guns and see flashes of light, but they slowly slipped away from the area without being detected.

Robert arrived at New Hebrides where he was in charge of a motor pool and power plants. The food there left a lot to be desired, but after he found a 16' boat and repaired it, he got permission to take it out to catch fish as long as they caught enough for all of them. It was a treat to be invited aboard the visiting ships as they had "real" food. After a year, Robert (now a Private, 1st Class) was transferred to Guadalcanal where he remained until the end of the war. While there, he attained the rank of Sergeant. When the troops were being reassigned to return to the United States, his unit was given orders to escort 13 American prisoners back to Hawaii for trial. They were provided a new ship, the *U.S.S. Oglethorpe*, which was equipped with a brig.

Once again, they couldn't take a direct route. They went to New Hebrides and back to New Caledonia, but due to a rapidly moving storm, they left there hurriedly (leaving some of the unit behind) to ride out the typhoon at sea. For five miserable days, everyone was sick, including the captain. Robert remembered coming out of the storm near the Fiji Islands, and eventually headed home on a flight in a C-54 transport plane out of Hawaii, landing at Hamilton Field, near San Francisco. From there, he traveled by train to Fort Leavenworth, Kansas where Robert was discharged on March 12, 1946. A bus ride back to Kirksville, Missouri completed his wartime journey. It was a shock to find his parents had moved, but they left directions to the new place!

On January 19, 1947, Robert and Lorene Sue Carpenter were married in Kansas City, Missouri, and soon afterward moved to Pasadena, California. They had four sons; Robert, Jr. of Lakewood, California, and Stephen, David and Keith Fritsinger, all of Lancaster, California. In 1948, Robert graduated from the Los Angeles Police Academy and went to work for the Pasadena Police Department, progressing from patrolman to detective. From 1950 to 1953 he studied police science at the University of Southern California, and in 1954, Robert became a California Highway Patrol officer, Badge #1570. His first assignment was in Bakersfield, followed by Barstow and then Salinas, California.

Robert and Sue moved their family to Lancaster in 1962 when he was assigned to the CHP office. In 1982, after 26 years with the CHP, Robert took a disability retirement due to an accumulation of job-related injuries. Following a brief battle with cancer, he passed away on April 21, 1999. Robert's wife, Sue, died in 2000, but their sons, Stephen, David and Keith, remain in Lancaster, and a number of their ten grandchildren and six great-grandchildren reside in the Antelope Valley.

HERBERT GARDNER "BUD/LUCIUS" FRITZ

Herbert Gardner Fritz was born April 24, 1917 in Poulsbo, Bainbridge Island, Washington, the son of Lucius L., from Iowa, and Mayme M. (Tucker) Fritz, a native of New Mexico. In 1920 the Fritz family was living in the city of Mount Vernon, Skagit Co., Washington. The family numbered five – Lucius and his wife, Mary, along with four children; two sons, Orville L. and Herbert; and one daughter, Melba M. A second daughter, Doris Fritz was born later. Lucius was employed as a house painter.

Bud was a 2nd Lieutenant in the Army Air Corps assigned to the 9th Air Force, 565th Bomber Squadron, 389th Bombardment Group (Heavy), nicknamed "Sky Scorpions." In December 1943, the group was activated at Davis-Monthan Army Air Base in Arizona. From February to June, 1943, the 389th trained and prepared for overseas duty. They flew their B-24 bombers to Hethel, Norfolk, England via Iceland in June 1943, where they were assigned to the 8th Air Force. The group was detached to North Africa, to Benghazi, Libya in June/July 1943, flying missions over Crete, Sicily, Italy, Austria and Rumania.

The group received a Distinguished Unit Citation for their participation in the low-level attack, "Operation Tidal Wave," on the oil refineries at Ploesti, Rumania, August 1, 1943. All the crews received the Distinguished Flying Cross. They also flew supporting missions for the invasion of Sicily.

From General Order No. 78, November 15, 1943:

"The 389th Bombardment Group (H) is cited for outstanding performance of duty in action against the enemy. Arriving in the Middle East theater with less experience than any of the more veteran organizations and without many of its needed ground personnel, this organization by intensive training and preparation studiously mastered a novel and experimental form of aerial attack and simultaneously familiarized all personnel with the details of a hazardous objective planned for 1 August 1943. After having departed on the 2,400 mile flight for Ploesti, Rumania, this unit became separated from the advanced elements of the massed formation while avoiding cumulous cloud conditions over mountainous country, but with the determination of its airmen unimpaired, the flight proceeded to its target. Arriving in the area as the last element, they found the entire area surrounding Ploesti swarming with enemy fighter aircraft, much of the area covered with dense oil smoke, and all defenses completely alerted and actively opposing them. Though having lost the element of surprise upon which their safety depended, they bombed and strafed their target with an efficiency, thoroughness, and intrepidity that left this oil refiner, plants, and installations a mass of blazing wreckage. The courage, skill, efficiency, and heroic scorn for personal safety with which the personnel of this organization struck this devastating blow against our enemies exemplified the noblest qualities and finest traditions of our armed forces."

By Order of the Secretary of War:
G.C. Marshall,
Chief of Staff

On August 25, 1943, the 389th flew back to their base at Hethel, England, arriving on August 27th. On September 13, 1943, B-24D, *"Yours Truly"* No. 42-40716R, crash landed at Hethel, England. Five crew members were killed including co-pilot 2nd Lieutenant Lucius H. Fritz. He is listed incorrectly as Lucius H. Fritz. The Fritz family bible names him as Herbert Gardner Fritz. He is buried at Cambridge American Cemetery, in Cambridge, England.

Douglas Gilmore was born in Albuquerque, New Mexico on May 20, 1926. His parents were George and Edna (Sudderberg) Gilmore. When Doug was six years old, his father died. He lived with his grandparents until June, 1942, when he moved to the Antelope Valley to live with his cousins, Fred and Margaret Witte. Their son, Jim, was in the Army Air Corps and since he was away from home, they needed a helping hand on their ranch.

Doug attended AVJUHS, where he lettered in track, and graduated with the class of 1944. Upon graduation, he went into the Pre-Cadet Program with the Army Air Corps. To enter this program, the government signed a contract with the Pre-Cadets giving them cadet training to become pilots. Doug went through basic training at Keesler Field, Mississippi, and was then transferred to Sheppard Field, Texas.

The Pre-cadets were awaiting assignment to Cadet training, but due to V-E and V-J Day, their orders were "put on hold." Doug was transferred to Hill Base in Salt Lake City, Utah in September, 1945. He was sent to the Base Hospital for a few days with a viral infection. When he was returned to his unit, he found that they had shipped out to Japan. Doug stayed at Hill until December, 1945, when he was discharged at Ft. Douglas, Utah. He and many other Pre-Cadets were honorably discharged because the government could not fulfill the original contract with them.

Doug married Norma Jean Blair on December 28, 1945, in Mancelona, Michigan. They were the parents of four children: George, Glenn, James, and Anne. While in Michigan, Doug attended Michigan State University majoring in Forestry. He also enrolled in the ROTC [Reserve Officers Training Corps] and received a commission as 2nd Lieutenant in May, 1948. He graduated from Michigan State University with a Bachelor of Science degree in June, 1950. During the next few years he was employed by the Tom Schweigert Company, in Michigan; the U.S. Forest Service in Hat Creek, California; Burney Lumber Company, Burney, California; and Southwest Lumber Company based at Flagstaff, Arizona. While at Flagstaff, he also attended Arizona State College (Northern Arizona University), and received a Master of Arts degree in Education. Doug taught Science and Math at the Middle School in Flagstaff and later in Traverse City, Michigan.

While in Traverse City, Doug enrolled in the Graduate program at Michigan State University and received his Doctor of Education degree in 1963. Due to daughter Anne's handicapped condition, the family lived in Wichita, Kansas for three years where Doug was the Director of Special Education at the Institute of Logopedics. He also taught at Michigan State and Central Michigan Universities.

Doug and Norma were divorced in October, 1969. In 1974 Doug married Bea Brenton and they resided in Kalamazoo, Michigan. He later became a school Psychologist for the Intermediate School District at Centreville, Michigan. Doug retired from the school system in 1988, and he and Bea moved to North Carolina, the state they now call home.

Russell H. Godde was born in Lancaster, Los Angeles Co., California on March 8, 1918, the son of Anthony Frank and Marie Theresa (Wolff) Godde. The family included three brothers; Forrest, Lawrence, and Jerry, and two sisters; Margie and Barbara. Russell was the grandson of Max and Elizabeth (Sommers) Godde, early Antelope Valley pioneers who immigrated to the United States from Germany in the 1880's.

The Godde family lived in the Del Sur area on the west side of the Antelope Valley. Russell attended AVJUHS, graduating with the class of 1936. Following graduation he improved an 80 acre ranch on the Westside. As a young boy, Russell showed an enthusiasm for flying. He already had his pilot's license at the time he enlisted in the U.S. Army Air Forces in 1941.

Russell was sent overseas in June, 1943. As a 2nd Lieutenant, he was attached to the 9th Air Force, 415th Bomber Squadron, 98th Bomber Group, Heavy. The group was also known as "The Pyramiders". In 1943, the group was stationed in North Africa under the leadership of John R. "Killer" Kane.

After one week at the base, Russell was flying as a replacement bombardier on a B-24 Liberator, the "*Yen Tse*" sent to destroy the oil refineries at Ploetsi, Romania.

During the war, the Germans received almost half of their oil from the refineries in Romania and had heavily fortified the oil fields. President Roosevelt had called for a joint 8th and 9th Air Force attack on these oil fields to be secretly carried out from a North African base. Three experienced heavy bomber groups from England's 8th Air Force flew to North Africa to join the local bomber groups in low level practice missions over the desert on simulated oil fields built by the Americans. This would prepare them for their mission to the oil fields in Romania.

On August 1, 1943, 178 B-24 Liberators took off from North Africa – Target: Ploetsti, Romania – Code Name: TIDALWAVE. The 8th and 9th Air Force set out to bomb the oil fields at dangerous altitudes of less than 100 feet. This attack was an unprecedented, low level attack, unexpected by the Germans.

Thirty-nine of the forty-six 98th Bomb Group aircraft that had set out from North Africa, led by Colonel Kane, headed for Target "WHITE 4", Astra Romana, the largest refinery in Europe. The outlook was grim. Colonel Kane's group had to attack a refinery already damaged by an earlier group.

Lawrence, Barbara, Margie, Russell, and Forrest Godde

They attacked at 120 – 250 feet, but with exploding bombs, heavy flak, and black clouds of burning oil restricting their view, the Germans had the advantage. The *Yen Tse,* one of six aircraft in the fifth wave of attacks, would not return. The B-24 was hit over the bombing run and burst into flames. Russell's plane was shot down with only three crewmembers from the back of the plane surviving - the only men with any chance to bail out, then captured, becoming Prisoners of War.

One of Russell's crew mates who survived, Sergeant Waltman, said Russell "died a very brave man after dropping his bombs directly on the target, completely demolishing it. We were told by the Rumanians

76

that our men were buried in their heroes cemetery where they buried their own heroes who had died in the war."

Russell was awarded the Distinguished Flying Cross and the Purple Heart Medal. He was listed as Missing in Action on August 1, 1943. His name is inscribed on the Tablets of the Missing at Florence American Cemetery, Florence, Italy. A memorial plaque honoring 2nd Lieutenant Russell Godde was obtained through the American Battle Monuments and the Department of Veterans Affairs to be placed on a memorial at the Lancaster Cemetery District, in Lancaster, California.

Ploesti bombing raid photo, photo from www.b17sam.com, used with permission.

Distinguished Flying Cross

Purple Heart Medal

ROBERT JOHN "BOB" HADDEN

Robert John Hadden was born March 6, 1921 in Springfield, Hampden Co., Massachusetts, the son of James Jennings and Ethel (Munsell) Hadden. James immigrated from Ireland to the United States in 1888, while Ethel was born and raised in Massachusetts. Bob was one of nine children in the family which included sisters Helen, Elizabeth, Mary Jane, Barbara and Marion; brothers Raymond, Kenneth, and Howard Hadden.

Bob was at home in Springfield when the news of the attack on Pearl Harbor was announced. He enlisted in the Army Air Forces and was sent to basic training in Atlantic City, New Jersey. From basic training Bob went on to Radio School in Madison, Wisconsin. His first assignment was as a Flight Radio Operator.

Bob was attached to the 561st Army Air Forces Base Unit. During 1943 through 1945, the Unit was flying C-47's, loaded with supplies, back and forth from India to China as part of the China-India-Burma Theater of operations. He kept in touch with his family through letter writing and was fortunate to see three U.S.O. shows featuring entertainers Jackie Coogan, Pat O'Brien, and Jinx Falkenberg. Bob considered the food very good, considering the conditions they were living in and the area they were stationed. One enjoyable memory Bob had of India was his visit to the Taj Mahal.

Bob was discharged on April 3, 1945, at the rank of Corporal. For his honorable service he received the Presidential Unit Citation; the Asiatic-Pacific Theater Campaign Ribbon, with two Battle Stars; and the Good Conduct Medal. After the war, Bob enjoyed being home with his family and friends. He went to work for a short time at Buxton, Inc., a leather goods manufacturer, in Springfield, Massachusetts.

On July 1, 1950, Bob married Shirley A. Gordon. They had one son together – Mark Robert Hadden. Bob went into the landscaping business after the war, then took an electronics course, which led to a career at Lockheed. In 1961 the family moved to California where Bob worked for Lockheed until his retirement.

In retrospect, Bob recalled his feelings on his time in the service – "You see so many dreadful things at such a young age. It's an experience and a learning process. Wars should be avoided at all costs."

Bob passed away February 3, 2004 in Lancaster. He is buried at the Riverside National Cemetery, Riverside Co., California.

HOWARD W. HANAWALT

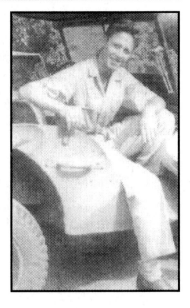

On June 27, 1925, Howard W. Hanawalt was born in Burbank, Los Angeles Co., California, to Charles H. and Laura Bell (Webster) Hanawalt. Charles was born in Pennsylvania, and Laura was born in Illinois. In 1920, Charles was living in Burbank, employed as a building contractor. By 1930, he was still living in Burbank, married, with five children; Genevieve, Charlotte, Howard W., Ray and Charles. Another daughter would be born later, named Stella. Charles was working in the contracting business as a mason.

The Hanawalt family moved to Agua Dulce near the end of 1930, where Howard attended Agua Dulce grade school. He graduated from AVJUHS with the class of 1943. Howard was drafted into the U.S. Army in March, 1944 and inducted at Fort MacArthur in San Pedro, California, where he was almost drafted into the Navy after physical processing. He showed the Admiral his Army Specialized Training Program [ASTP] letter and was referred to the Army Colonel for his assignment. The ASTP was established by the U.S. Army to "identify, train and educate academically-talented men as a specialized corps of Army officers during World War II." Through this program, they provided a four-year college education along with specialized Army technical training. The Army cancelled this program early in 1944, and Howard was sent to Camp Barkeley, near Abilene, Texas, for medical training boot camp.

Howard's first job assignment was that of a medical instructional cadre/platoon leader and acting Field Sergeant at Camp Barkeley. Howard was assigned to several different duty stations in the United States before being transferred overseas to India.

While in India, Howard was involved in a terrifying incident. "I was caught in the riots of Calcutta in 1946. We were riding our bikes and took a shortcut through the corner of Black Hole in Calcutta. We were suddenly trapped at an intersection by mobs, then stoned, and like a miracle we were saved by a British lorry [truck] coming through the crowd with rioters bouncing off the hood. We fought our way into the back of the vehicle and they cut on through to freedom. The next day they found two GI's drowned in a pond at that corner."

Howard would enjoy an elephant ride in the Assam jungle and would befriend the Naga Indians, headhunters from Nagaland in Northeast India. One day, he convinced two Naga Indians to let him take their photograph. The Nagas believed that taking a photograph of them would capture their soul. Howard convinced them that he would give them the photograph. They were very pleased that he did, but of course, he had the negative. He won first prize in a photography contest with the photo titled, "Naga Indians of Assam."

Also while in Margherita, Assam, India, Howard would kill a Krait, one of the most venomous snakes in the world. One bite can kill a human. Howard's "kill" was done with stones, near the coal mines, and in the eyes of the locals he was considered a local hero.

Howard was onboard a ship in the Indian Ocean when he heard the news that the war had ended. He was honorably discharged at the rank of Staff Sergeant, in June of 1946, after 29 months of service. He received the Asiatic-Pacific Campaign Medal and the Good Conduct Medal. Howard went back to his home in Agua Dulce, then traveled to Santa Barbara College to attend school. He graduated from the University of California, Los Angeles, with a degree in Meteorology. Howard worked as a designer and engineer before he was called up by the U.S. Air Force for service during the Korean War in 1953.

Howard was assigned to several different duty stations with the Air Weather Service as a Weather Officer and Climatologist. He worked for the 15th Air Force Headquarters as a Jet Stream Specialist at March AFB in Riverside, California, then was sent to Harmon AFB in Newfoundland and Goose Bay in Quebec, Canada in support of the Strategic Air Command. Howard would serve 50 months in the U.S. Air Force, honorably discharged in 1958 at the rank of First Lieutenant.

Howard married Jacqueline Marie Curotto, on January 27, 1951, in Westwood, Los Angeles Co., California. They had two children together; a son, Howard W. Hanawalt, the II, and a daughter, Deborah Marie Hanawalt. Howard worked for IBM in Haymarket, Virginia, retiring after 24 years. He moved to Colorado in 1973 where he and Jacqueline are both retired and live in Colorado Springs.

Jack Elwin Hawke was born May 27, 1920 in Montford, Wisconsin. He was the son of Bert and Tillie (Buttries) Hawke. Jack's siblings included one brother, Sidney, and two sisters, Bessie and Myrtle Hawke. The Hawke family moved to the Antelope Valley in 1935. Jack attended AVJUHS where he played on the tennis team. He graduated with the class of 1939. Jack also attended Antelope Valley Junior College where he earned his pilot's license through the CPT (Civilian Pilot Training) program. Pancho Barnes, the female aviatrix, gave Jack his first lesson followed by CP trainers.

After graduation, Jack enlisted in the Army Air Corps. With extensive training in various aircraft, he was awarded his "wings" and commissioned Lieutenant at Luke Field, Arizona, in August, 1942. Jack was sent to Philadelphia for further training as a fighter pilot, issued a P-40, and was assigned to the 33rd Fighter Wing of the 15th Air Force.

The P-40 airplanes were loaded on a British ship converted into a make-shift air carrier. With nearly experimental catapult action, they were launched off the carrier, flew to Africa, and landed at Casa Blanca for the North African Campaign. After defeating the German Army led by General Rommel, the 33rd Fighter Wing was sent to Sicily, then on to Italy. During this time Jack's P-40 was hit. He was not wounded, but Jack, along with the entire Squadron, was awarded the Purple Heart Medal by General Doolittle.

When victory was declared in Europe, Jack was sent to the China-Burma-India Theater. After two years, he returned to the U.S. where he served two more years at several different Air Bases. Jack was discharged in September 1946 and joined the Reserves. He retired from the service at the rank of Captain. Jack received the Air Medal; the Presidential Unit Citation; the American Combat Medal; Purple Heart Medal; Asiatic-Pacific Campaign Medal; European-Africa-Middle Eastern Campaign Medal; and the World War II Victory Medal.

Jack married Betty Randleman on August 27, 1942 in Phoenix, Arizona, while he was stationed at Luke Field. They have two children; a daughter, Jacklynn, and a son, Randle. Jack passed away on November 30, 1990, in Concord, California. He was cremated, with his ashes spread over Lake Tahoe in California. His wife Betty currently lives in Bay Point, California.

Jack Hawke – CPT Program

The following is a letter written to the Antelope Valley Ledger-Gazette newspaper, printed in the October 14, 1943 edition:

September 11, '43

Dear Sirs:

The last few days have made me feel quite at home here due to the heat, wind and dryness of the country. Around here is more like the foot hill country around the A.V. All grain and no irrigation with the exception of about 15 A. (acres) This 15 A. is an irrigated field planted to potatoes and melons. The potato crop is good and certainly stands out compared to the brown grain fields. There seems to be very little alfalfa over here.

I was very glad to hear of Captain Stege's promotion, nice going John.

There were three of us that went through flying school together and flew in combat together, but one was lucky and is now in the States thus splitting up our threesome.

The things we of California miss most over here is the fresh fruit. There are large grape vineyards here along with olive groves and a little later on there will be oranges, but the peaches and apricots are small and seem to have very little taste. I passed through one valley here that had very good cherries and it reminded me of A.V. when I used to go up towards Littlerock and pick them.

I have just been informed there is a plane to be test hopped so I had better close and get back to work.

Thanks so much for sending me the paper, I sure enjoy it.

Sincerely,
Lt. A.C. Jack E. Hawke

Lt. Jack Hawke, center, in Egypt

Forrest Edgar Hull was born September 8, 1911 in Los Angeles Co., California, the only child born to Frank Edgar, and May M. (McLaughlin) Hull, M.D. Forrest attended the University of Southern California School of Medicine and interned at the San Diego General Hospital in San Diego, California, following in the footsteps of his father Dr. Frank Hull, a physician with his own practice. Forrest's mother, May, worked as a teacher in a public school.

On May 12, 1938, Forrest was commissioned as a First Lieutenant in the Army Medical Corps. After intensive training in military medicine and Army procedures, he was assigned to the First and Fifth Infantry Divisions located in Georgia, Louisiana and Texas. In 1941, he served as Battalion surgeon in the 10th Infantry Regiment in Iceland. On April 15, 1943, Forrest was part of a group assigned to organize the medical service of the newly activated 75th Infantry Division at Fort Leonard Wood, Missouri. He then attended the Command and General Staff School, Fort Leavenworth, Kansas for three months of intensive training in military strategy. After graduating, Forrest returned to the 75th Infantry Division to assume command of the 375th Medical Battalion. The 375th was sent to Wales for staging until they crossed the English Channel shortly after D-Day.

In December 1944, the 75th Infantry Division landed in Le Havre, France and moved north to the Ardennes Forest in southeast Belgium. The troops arrived on Christmas Eve during heavy winter conditions, with snow and sub-freezing temperatures, and engaged in combat in one of the worst battles in terms of men lost during the war - the Battle of the Bulge. During the long, rigorous battle, Forrest's mobile hospital was overrun with numerous battle casualties.

During the siege of Colmar, the 75th was attached to the French First Army where Forrest's work earned him the French Medal, Croix de Guerre avec Etoil de Vermeil. The Division was then sent to liberate southern Holland and Belgium. During those battles, his medical mobile hospital treated many captured enemy soldiers. After Germany surrendered, Forrest received the Bronze Star for "outstanding leadership, devotion to duty, and ingenuity in executing every assignment."

While being transported on the *H.W. McAndrew* from Marseille, France, the troops onboard learned from sealed orders that they were being sent to the Philippines. Their duties included organizing a strike force and securing the beachhead so Paratroopers and Marines would have a safe landing spot on the heavily defended island of Honshu. To Forrest, this appeared to be a suicide mission. This was all changed by the atom bomb which Forrest believed saved his life and the lives of the other soldiers in his group.

Forrest's next assignment led him to the Surgeon General's office at the Pentagon. He completed his residency at Walter Reed General Hospital in Washington, D.C., then a year of post graduate work at the University of Pennsylvania in Philadelphia. This was followed by an assignment in Tokyo, during the Occupation of Japan, where he served as the Chief of Ophthalmology, Far East Command, under General Douglas MacArthur. He then became involved in the Korean War where he was responsible for treating combat soldiers suffering from eye injuries. His last assignment was as Chief of Ophthalmology at Letterman General Hospital in San Francisco, California.

In 1953, Forrest left the regular Army and joined the California National Guard until he completed his military service in 1971, retiring at the rank of Colonel.

In 1997, Forrest married Martje Van Wachem in Lancaster, Los Angeles Co., California. Forrest had two sons by his first wife, Kathryn (Ballas) Hull, who died in October 1992 - Stephen Nelson and Frank E. Hull. Stephen became an ophthalmologist, like his father, and shared a practice with him at the Hull Eye Center in Lancaster until his death in 1990. Younger son, Frank, named after his grandfather, is a dentist and currently has a practice in Santa Barbara, California. The elder Frank E. Hull, father of Forrest, conducted First Aid classes in Lancaster for the American Red Cross during World War II.

Forrest was one of the members of the first Lancaster City Council when it was formed in 1977. After the war, he joined the American Legion organization. He made several close friendships during the war and continued to keep in contact with them for many years.

In February of 2004, the Forrest E. Hull Park was formally dedicated with a ceremony attended by Forrest and his son, Frank, along with friends and several former and current dignitaries from the City of Lancaster. The 10-acre park is located at 30th Street West and Avenue L-12 near Paraclete High School in Lancaster.

Speaking about his time in the service, Forrest said his experiences made him realize that "war is Hell and never solved anything". Forrest and his wife, Martje, are currently enjoying retirement in Lancaster.

CONRAD CLYDE "CONNIE" JOHNSON

Born July 17, 1920 in Portland, Oregon, Conrad C. Johnson was the son of Hiram Clyde and Elsie Ann (Deyoe) Johnson. Hiram was born in South Dakota while Elsie was from North Dakota. In 1930, the Johnson family was living in Lomita, Los Angeles Co., California with Hiram employed as a transfer driver. Conrad had three siblings; a step-brother, Richard Little; a step-sister, Louise Little; and a sister, Elsie Johnson.

The Johnson family settled in the Littlerock area of the Antelope Valley in 1936. Conrad graduated from AVJUHS in 1938. He attended AVJC, enrolling in the CPT program and in 1941 received his pilot's license. It was Conrad's acknowledgment that "Pancho Barnes taught me how to fly."

Conrad was working in Boron, a town east of Mojave, in 1942, when he enlisted in the Army Air Corps. His cadet training began at Cal-Aero Flight Academy at Ontario, California. From there he went to Luke Field in Arizona, and received his commission in September 1942.

On June 1, 1943, Conrad married Roberta (Bobbie) Blickenstaff, in Lancaster, California. Bobbie graduated from AVJUHS with the class of 1940.

Shortly after the marriage, on July 1, 1943, Conrad was whisked off to Attu, Alaska with the 11th Air Force, 343rd Fighter Group, 54th Fighter Squadron. In Alaska he would fly his P-38, "Bobbie," named after his wife, as part of the air defense in the area for the Aleutian Campaign. When he returned home after a year in Alaska, he spent a brief time at Redmond, Oregon as an instructor. Conrad was transferred to McChord Field in Tacoma, Washington where he flew with a Ferrying Group transporting surplus airplanes to various places in the West. He was in Tacoma when he heard the news that the war was over.

In September, 1946, Conrad's next orders would take him to the Philippines. He was stationed at Florida Blanca Army Air Base in Luzon. After one year in the Philippines, he was again transferred to Johnson Air Force Base in Tokyo, Japan. While in Japan Conrad played football for the 5th Air Force. Conrad had joined a photo reconnaissance group flying the P-61 Black Widow taking aerial photos over Korea. His wife, Bobbie, joined him there in September 1947.

In 1949, Conrad returned to the United States and spent most of his time as an instructor. From 1951 to 1953 he spent much of his time at Los Alamos, New Mexico, and Indian Springs, Nevada, involved with an atomic energy group. He was stationed at Kirtland Air Force Base in Albuquerque, New Mexico.

Conrad's time in the U.S. would end again with an assignment in France to aid in restoring the Air Base near Rouen. After six months, the base was abandoned and Conrad was off to Ramstein, Germany. His wife and sons were able to join him two months later. A wonderful time was spent traveling and sightseeing. Conrad was an avid skeet shooter and spent time at skeet competitions. One night, at the Officers Club, he was happy to see his high school friend, R.C. Franklin, and his wife, Stella.

In 1957 Conrad was assigned to Reese Air Force Base in Lubbock, Texas. In 1961, while at Reese, Major Conrad Johnson was presented with an Air Force Commendation Medal. He was "honored for his meritorious service as operations staff officer of the 3500th Pilot Training Group from Sept. 11, 1957, to Feb. 6, 1961, and from July 18, 1961, to Feb. 15, 1962, and as executive officer of the Maintenance and Supply Group from Feb. 7, 1961 to July 17, 1961." Conrad was presented the Commendation Medal and citation by Lt. General James E. Briggs, ATC commander. The citation stated, "Through his ingenuity, professional knowledge of the training program, understanding of accident cause and prevention, and cooperation with flying safety agencies, Major Johnson contributed immeasurably to the excellent flying safety record of the 3500th Pilot Training Wing."

Conrad remained at Reese AFB until his retirement on March 31, 1962. After 20 years of service he retired as a Lieutenant Colonel. He was a dedicated pilot and Air Force officer. After retirement, they moved to Urbana, Missouri, where Conrad built the family a beautiful home in the woods. Conrad and Bobbie had three children – all boys – James, Jerry and Frank Johnson. He returned to college in 1964 at Southwest Missouri State University in Springfield, Missouri. Conrad graduated in 1966 with a degree in Industrial Arts and taught for 13 years at Conway, Missouri. He was forced to retire due to the need of a hip replacement. He did not return to teaching, but he and Bobbie enjoyed a considerable amount of time traveling.

Conrad passed away on June 1, 1998, at the VA Home in Mt. Vernon, Missouri. He is buried at the Cory Cemetery in Dadeville, Missouri. His wife, Bobbie, currently lives in Urbana, Missouri.

"Connie" Johnson next to his P-38, "Bobbie" – Attu, Alaska

Peter Craig Kercher was born to Peter and Alma Jennie (Dunham) Kercher on December 18, 1918 in Fresno, California. Pete had five siblings; two brothers, Frederick and Paul; and three sisters, Elma, Myrtle Jean and Bernice Kercher, all born in California. In 1920, the family was living in Hardwick, Kings Co., California, where elder Peter was working on a farm. By 1930, the Kercher's were living in Armona, Kings Co., where Peter owned his own dairy farm. Pete's grandmother, Mary Jane Dunham, was also living with the family.

On May 7, 1940, Pete married Bessie Katherine Price in Reno, Nevada. Pete was living in Lancaster when he registered for the draft. He originally wanted to enlist with the Marine Corps, but the quotas were full. Pete was working as a truck driver at the time he was called to serve. On December 9, 1942, he was inducted into the U.S. Army at Los Angeles, California.

Shortly after basic training, in March 1943, Pete qualified as a Sharpshooter with the M-1 rifle. In November 1943, Pete was stationed at Camp Howze, Texas, with the 103rd Infantry Division, 328th Engineer Combat Battalion, 2nd Platoon, Co. C – Third Squad. They were known as the "Cactus Division."

The last week of September, 1944, Pete left Camp Howze and arrived at Camp Shanks, New York, to prepare for boarding on the troop transport ship, *U.S.S. Henry T. Gibbons*. They sailed on the morning of October 6, 1944, bound for Marseilles, France. While on board, the troops were kept busy with drills, calisthenics and orientation. The sea was rough for several days and many of the men began to get seasick.

On the morning of October 20, the Port of Marseilles finally came into view. The troops were forced to land on LST's that night, decked out in full field equipment. After spending 14 days at sea, the men had to march for 12 miles over the rocks and hills to get into the Division area. Pete was a truck driver (light) during this time. The weather was extremely dismal at the camp, cold and wet with half the tents flooded.

The first week of November saw the Division move towards the combat area. They traveled north to Avignon, then up the Rhine Valley. By the second week in November they had come within 8 miles of the front. They witnessed destroyed German transports and equipment along the way. The Battalion's job was to cut a clearing through the pine trees, in the snow and rain, for 155 guns to fire.

On November 17, the 103rd Division began its first battle by launching an offensive attack. Pete and his buddies were driving close behind, "driving off into the valley of death," in support of the 2nd Battalion, 411th Infantry. As they watched the infantry advance from a nearby hill, they witnessed many of the young men fall. The Squad's job was to remove the roadblocks ahead and remove any mines along the road. By November 19, with their job complete, the Squad sat down to enjoy some chow. The cooks had set up in an open field and just as they were starting to eat, they were fired upon by enemy artillery. They all scattered and, luckily, no one was hurt. They moved back into the hills for the night.

Pete and his buddy, Corporal Robert Kerley, spent many days and nights together, routing by-passes around dangerous areas thought to be booby-trapped and investigating forward areas to make sure the road was clear for the troops. Unbeknownst to them, they were under enemy observation most of the time, with the Germans playing a "waiting game," according to Kerley.

The men would witness numerous attacks on their way through France while chasing after the Germans. Bridges were to be built and crossings to be made, so they pressed on from Mietesheim to Uttenhoffen, still under watch by the Germans, passing burning buildings and listening to the cries of the wounded soldiers nearby.

By mid-December they were passing through the main forts of the Maginot Line, with the whole platoon crossing into Germany on December 18. On Christmas eve the weather was cold and damp. The men celebrated with two cans of beer. The next day a turkey dinner was served and all was quiet for the moment. A few of them played a game of poker with matches since they hadn't been paid since November 1st.

103rd Infantry patch – Cactus Division

On January 10, 1945, the 3rd Squad went into town, following the 411th with TNT for foxholes. As Cpl. Kerley remembered, "When we returned home, Pete had a radiogram announcing the birth of a baby girl, Mary Anne, born the 6th of January, red-headed, blue eyed."

In mid-January, the troops were on the move once again. As troops were withdrawing, the 3rd was preparing to blow road blocks and several bridges. The weather was miserable and with about 15" of snow on the ground, traffic was jammed up for miles. As they set up another defensive position, the 3rd was helping the 411th once again, hauling planks and ties for foxhole covers.

"The 1st Squad lost three men, killed, and about 10 injured when their one truck load of English mines exploded. Pittman, Wisdorf and Beckley were killed. Lt. Neal, Swai and Doc Hunter were seriously injured. The pins had been pulled on the mines and about 60 went off and the truck disappeared. On the 25th, Swaggert and Ennis were hit by artillery fire while putting up barbed wire; Swaggart lost a leg. It seems our luck is running short," remembered Corporal Kerley.

At the end of the month, on January 28, the 3rd was sent out to support the 2nd Battalion. On their way back they were told of a terrific explosion in town. When they returned to town, their Company was in shambles with 34 casualties and many injured, both civilian and military. A truck had backed up into a mine dump and ran over it causing 150 mines to explode.

In February, most of the time was spent on the roads doing routine jobs. March brought a move to Ingwiller, then on to Mulhausen. The town was a wreck, littered with G.I. equipment and desecrated buildings. The 3rd's job this time was to clear the mines beyond the nearby bridges. They found hundreds of mines planted along the side of the roads while listening to small arms fire and shelling nearby. Near the end of March, long convoys of troops began the race to the Rhine. Payday was on the 30th and each man was also given a quart of champagne. The reports were that "combat was finished."

The first week of April brought a move across the Rhine to a larger occupation area. They crossed the Rhine and set foot in the town of Modau. They crossed the river at Ludwighaven and Mannheim, witnessing the bombing destruction first hand. The streets had to be cleared of the rubble before any trucks could pass. Most of the trucks were hauling the infantry men.

On April 24th, "Kercher pulled out an abatis, (an obstacle made by laying felled trees on top of each other, with sharp branches, facing the enemy) and after he had finished someone shot a Kraut who had been hidden right beside the obstacle," Corporal Kerley recanted. Heading south toward Mittenwald and Innsbruck, they passed hundreds of prisoners on the road making truck progress slow.

June 30th brought surprising news to the 3rd – they were to be sent to the 120th Engineer Corp Battalion (Combat), with the 45th Infantry Division. On the 1st of July, the men turned in their equipment, rifles and extra clothing in preparation for their departure. July 3rd, they arose early to make ready for the train trip from Innsbruck to Munich, where they were met by trucks from the 120th Engineers.

Pete was discharged from the Army at Camp Beale, California, on November 7, 1945, at the rank of Private, 1st Class. For his service during the war he received the European-African-Middle Eastern Campaign Medal; the American Campaign Medal, World War II Victory Medal; and the Good Conduct Medal.

Pete and Bessie had two more children along with Mary Anne – a son, Peter and

Pete Kercher, far right, Bertchesgarten, Germany - 1945

daughter, Petra Elaine Kercher. Following the war, Pete continued farming in Hardwick, Kings Co., California. He kept in close contact with many of his buddies from the 103rd. Pete passed away on February 15, 2001, in Riverdale, Fresno Co., California. He is buried at Oak Grove Cemetery in Laton, Fresno Co., California.

HELEN KATHARINE KRIEG

Helen Katharine Krieg was born to Lasalle and Esther (Magnuson) Krieg on January 2, 1914 in Minneapolis, Hennepin Co., Minnesota. Lasalle was born in Iowa, the son of German immigrants. Esther, the daughter of Swedish immigrants, was born in Minnesota. In 1920, the Krieg family resided in Minneapolis, renting a home, with Lasalle employed as a foreman in a garage. The family included son, Arthur, and two daughters, Helen and Dorothy Krieg.

On December 7, 1941, Helen was attending nursing school at St. Barnabas Hospital in Minneapolis, Minnesota, when the bombing of Pearl Harbor had commenced. In 1944 she enlisted in the Army Nurse Corps where she was assigned to the 251st Station Hospital. Station hospitals received battle casualties from evacuation hospitals and performed surgery and specialized treatments.

As an Army nurse in charge of a ward, Helen served in Cape Gloucester, New Britain; Australia, and other islands in the South Pacific. Helen was one of the first white women to set foot on Cape Gloucester, New Britain after Pearl Harbor. She performed her duties in a tent where the wounded were flown in to be attended to. Helen recalled to her family, "The dust was terrible. We had to cover the patients with sheets and then shake [the dust] off all the blankets." The men she cared for were evacuated from the jungle campaign moving towards the Japanese garrison at Rabaul, New Britain, one of the greatest Japanese strongholds in the Southwest Pacific.

According to Army military historians, "The Army nurse in the Pacific theater was known to perform her tasks efficiently, compassionately, and courageously whether she was caring for casualties in the field or patients evacuated from the front lines. These nurses prevailed over dangers and difficulties not experienced by nurses in other theaters. They became ill with malaria and dengue fever; experienced the rigors of a tropical climate; tolerated water shortages; risked kamikaze attacks; adapted to curfews, fenced compounds, and armed escorts. They dealt with medical corpsmen's hostility. Nurses in the Pacific demonstrated their ability to overcome adversity and reached the front lines of a uniquely dangerous theater before the end of the war."

Helen was discharged from the Army Nurse Corps at the rank of 1st Lieutenant in 1947. She returned to private duty as a nurse at St. Barnabas Hospital in Minnesota. In 1978 she retired from nursing and moved to California close to Lancaster where her sister, Dorothy (Krieg) Philbrick, had lived for 22 years. Along with Helen's two siblings, she also had a half-brother and sister, Robert and Lorraine Hartke, from her mother's second marriage. Her half-sister, Lorriane, was also living near, in Bellflower, California.

Helen never married, but passed on many stories about her service during WWII. She told her niece, Barbara Parkhurst, how proud she was to have served her country, and that she made many life long friends whom she continued to keep in contact through the years.

Helen passed away on February 17, 2001, in Seal Beach, California. She is buried at the Westminster Memorial Park, Westminster, California.

Robert Neale Lee was born August 31, 1925 in Mountain Park, Otero Co., New Mexico, the son of John Owens and Ella Catherine (Crowell) Lee, Jr. They were married April 16, 1898 and together they had 12 children with Buddy being the 10th child born. Buddy's siblings included Ethel J., Daisie, Walter C., James O., Beulah, Mildred, Raymond, Mary, Johnnie, Ada and Ida Lee. The Lee family was living in the High Rolls Village in Otero Co., New Mexico in 1930, with John supporting his wife and children as a farmer.

John moved his family to the Antelope Valley in 1935. On December 7, 1941, at age 16, Robert was driving in his car from Burton's Camp to Rosamond, listening to the radio, when they announced the attack on Pearl Harbor. In 1943 he was a junior at AVJUHS. He was drafted into the U.S. Army in February 1944.

Robert was inducted at the Palmdale induction office and then sent to Fort MacArthur, San Pedro, California. This was the first time he had ever been away from home. After 17 weeks of training at Camp Roberts, San Luis Obispo, California, he had learned a lot about the regimented military way of life.

Robert's first assignment was as a rifleman and radio repairman. He joined up with the 343rd Infantry Regiment, 86th Blackhawk Division in Louisiana on September 18, 1944. In October 1944, the Division was sent to Camp San Luis Obispo for amphibious training at Morro Bay. In November 1944, a note was sent from AVJUHS Principal, Roy A. Knapp, to Private Lee requesting a letter be sent back to be included in an Alumni Bulletin. Robert sent the following note to be included in that bulletin. "I have been in the Infantry ten months. I am now taking amphibious training and will be overseas soon."

In January 1945, the 86th prepared for movement to the east coast, to Camp Myles Standish near Boston, Massachusetts. In February they sailed from Boston to Europe and landed safely in Le Havre, France March 1, 1945. From there the men of the 86th were trucked to Camp Old Gold, near Doudeville, France. At the end of March, the 86th Division was ordered to join up with the newly formed 15th Army and prepared for combat. On its way to the combat area, the 86th Division rode through Belgium, Holland and Germany. In Cologne, Germany, they relieved the 8th Infantry Division and assumed its mission of defending the 23 mile front on the west bank of the Rhine River.

Robert recalled, "On occasion, while advancing or taking a small village or countryside, coming around a corner or turn in the road, you would find a German 88mm anti-aircraft gun pointing directly at you. On

another occasion while advancing through a small backyard, I saw what I initially thought were two life size dolls, a boy and a girl, both dressed in German costumes. However, on closer inspection, it was two small children, pale, appearing slightly swollen, no gross injury. Just a few feet away was a small bomb crater and the children were evidently killed by concussion."

In April 1945, the troops crossed the Rhine River at Bonn, Germany. They fought in the Ruhr Pocket, attacking the German forces on April 6. The 86th captured the major cities of Attendorn, Luderscheid and Hagen. From there the troops moved into Bavaria assisting Patton's 3rd Army, and in 16 days covered 110 miles, crossed over six major rivers and captured the cities of Ansback, Ingolstadt, Freising and Oberdorf. They entered Austria and arrived at Randensburg on May 8th 1945.

The 86th passed through Munich, Augsburg and Weidelburg on the return trip to Mannheim, Germany. They returned to Camp Old Gold and then to Le Havre for transport back to the United States. The troops landed at New York on June 17, 1945. They were then sent to Camp Kilmer, New Jersey where they were granted a 30 day leave.

After the 30 day recuperation leave, the 86th Division was reformed at Camp Gruber, Oklahoma. In August 1945 they were shipped to Camp Stoneman, in Northern California. The troops sailed from San Francisco, California August 29, 1945, headed for the Philippine Islands in preparation for the invasion of Japan. Even though the Japanese had surrendered on September 2, 1945, the 86th continued on to the Philippines for occupation duty. The first stop was Eniwetok, Marshall Islands on September 10. Next, Tacloban, Leyte, and on to Batangas, Luzon, Philippine Islands. The Division moved on to Marikina where they relieved the 38th Division and occupied the Island of Luzon in October 1945.

The 86th continued its duties on Luzon until December 30, 1945, at which time it was inactivated. The troops were then sent home. Robert recalled the food as being "generally good." He dined in mess halls and field kitchens and ate C and K rations. He enjoyed Red Skelton's performance at a U.S.O. show and went to numerous U.S.O. canteens for donuts and coffee.

Robert was honorably discharged from the Army May 9, 1946. He was extremely happy the war was over and that he was out of the military. After the service, Robert made arrangements to continue with his education at Antelope Valley Junior College. While attending school he worked as a school bus driver and as a correctional officer at a state prison. He graduated from AVJC and continued to further his education at La Sierra College where he earned his BA degree. Robert met Helen Dean while attending college. They were married and had one child together, Kenneth Lee. Robert received the Doctor of Osteopathy degree from the College of Osteopathic Physicians and Surgeons, and in 1963 was granted the MD degree.

On December 31, 1962, Robert married Juanita Frances Cortez in Redlands, San Bernardino Co., California. They had eight children; Cynthia, Martha, Patricia, Vanessa, Robin, Roberta and Frances. Robert continued in the general medical practice field for 36 years. Always fond of flying, Robert pursued his passion and attained his single engine land/sea helicopter ratings. He is now retired and currently lives with his wife, Juanita, in Hemet, California.

Robert recalled an interesting side light to his military service, "You are probably familiar with Bill Mauldin's books and cartoons about World War II soldiers. Bill and myself were born in the same small mountain community of Mountain Park, New Mexico. Bill was about 3 ½ years older than I. My brother Johnnie and I would visit him and his brother, Sid, often. My wife and I went to visit Bill in Newport Beach a few months ago at the convalescent hospital where he was living. I'm sorry to say he died recently." Bill Mauldin died at age 81 on January 22, 2003.

"Just give me the aspirin. I already got a Purple Heart."
Drawn by Bill Mauldin - From the newspaper, Stars and Stripes, 1944.

Orion Martin "Skip" Lippert was born June 29, 1922 in Napa, Napa County, California, the son of Rudolph and Dorothy Viola (Dickman) Lippert. Rudolph was born in Chicago, Illinois, of Swiss ancestry. Dorothy was born in Defiance, Ohio, with both of her parents also born in Ohio. In 1920 the Lippert family was living in Los Angeles, California, where Rudolph was a minister. By 1922 they had moved to Napa, California, where Skip was born.

On May 29, 1939, at age 16 and underage to enter into military service, Skip joined the California National Guard. His sister, Virginia, had a boyfriend, the Recruiting Sergeant, who "stretched the truth" about Skip's age. After boot camp at Seaside Park, Ventura, California, Skip was assigned to the Regimental Band as a drummer (in peace time). On September 16, 1940, the 251st Coast Guard Artillery (Anti-Aircraft) was inducted into Federal Service. In November 1940, after staging in Ventura, California, the 251st left the Port of Los Angeles for duty on the island of Oahu, Hawaii. Upon arrival on Oahu, the 251st trained for two months at Fort Shafer.

The Regiment constructed their permanent location at Camp Malakole. The days began with training on the firing line for half a day, then with clearing the land to make way for camp construction in the latter part of the day. They built their own quarters in spite of inadequate water supplies and dense growth of the Hawaiian kiawe tree. The motto of the 251st Regiment was "We Aim to Hit" – a motto that would hold true in the months to come.

With the potential of an upcoming conflict looming on the horizon, the Regiment was ordered on full alert in the field whenever sight of the Japanese fleet was lost. On November 26, 1941, the Regiment received a warning. They were assigned to defensive positions around the west shore of Pearl Harbor. Their job was to provide anti-aircraft defense alongside the Navy and other Army units. This warning turned out to be a false alarm.

On December 7, 1941, Skip recalled a beautiful, sunny day – a typical Hawaiian morning. He was eating the typical Sunday morning breakfast of green, dehydrated eggs and coffee when he heard what sounded like bombing in the distance. He saw planes diving down, but thought it was just a practice drill. When the Regiment's medic was hit, they realized they were under attack. Most of the men were sleeping or away from the Camp on a weekend pass. Skip jumped into a truck along with his buddies and headed down to the harbor. When they arrived at the harbor, they couldn't get through the main gate so they drove to Hickam Field where they knocked down the fence to get in. They were about 50 yards away from the *U.S.S. Shaw* in the harbor when it exploded. The explosion blew them out of the truck. They proceeded to get back in the truck and set up a position to cover the harbor mouth.

Skip was aware of tremendous fires, hearing people screaming for help, badly burned from the attack. The noise was indescribable with bombs exploding and every type of gun imaginable going off. He admittedly was not scared – just extremely mad. He was too busy to be scared, he recalled, trying to

Skip Lippert – 2nd from right, Malakole, 1941.

set up positions, which was what he was trained to do. He saw the *U.S.S. Arizona* on fire with secondary explosions going off. It was when they had used up all their ammunition that they were afraid the Japanese were coming back soon.

At Hickam Field, Skip recalled seeing the huge, garrison flag riddled with shrapnel holes, torn and tattered, but still proudly flying. At age 18, Skip had become a man and at that moment, after seeing the flag, he thought of all the previous wars, from the Battle of Lexington and Concord to World War I. He thought of what that flag meant to him – freedom.

In May of 1942, the 251st was sent to the Pacific Theater with duty on the Fiji Islands, and Guadalcanal in the Solomon Islands. On Viti Levu in the Fiji Islands, they established the anti-aircraft defense for the islands only airfield, Nandi Air Base. All the weapons and housing of the troops was hidden under thatched native huts. While stationed on Fiji and Guadalcanal, Skip was transferred to the U.S. Air Corps, 20th Communication Squadron, Nandi Air Base, Fiji Islands. The food on Fiji consisted of mainly Spam and tea. "Even the starving dogs wouldn't touch the Spam!"

Skip remembered his homecoming – finally seeing the shore of California and home at long last! But Skip would miss his service buddies. He had served with "a great bunch of guys who could see humor in everything – what great, wonderful pals they were." Skip was in Tucson, Arizona when he heard the news that the war was over.

Skip was honorably discharged at the rank of Sergeant. He received numerous awards and medals for his service to his country: The American Campaign Medal; American Defense Medal; Asiatic-Pacific Campaign Medal; U.S. Army Commemorative Medal; World War II Victory Medal; Combat Service Medal; National Guard Reserve Service Medal; Victory in the Pacific Medal; and the Pearl Harbor Congressional Medal. Skip felt the military "taught me discipline and it made me understand and appreciate being an American - to love this great, wonderful country, the freedom to be ourselves. Even at [age] 81 I'd serve again in a heartbeat."

Skip Lippert – Hawaii, 1942

After the service, Skip went to work for the Federal Aviation Agency (FAA) as an Airport Traffic Controller [tower operator] in Tucson, Arizona. On June 10, 1949 he married Lois Irene Gillies in Yuma, Arizona. They had two children – Lorion Marty and Craig Martin Lippert. Skip also had a son from a previous marriage, James Scott Lippert.

In 1952, Skip and Lois settled in the Antelope Valley where he was employed as a Control Tower Operator at what is now U.S. Air Force Plant 42 in Palmdale. In 1974 he went to work as Director of Campus Security at Antelope Valley High School in Lancaster, California for 14 years. Skip and Lois worked as ushers for Magic Mountain Theme Park for 11 years where they also were Mr. and Mrs. Santa Claus during the Christmas season. Now retired, he volunteers at local schools telling his stories of World War II to students as part of the Living History Program.

Skip married Audrey Studts-Fuller on March 14, 2003. They currently live in Palmdale, California.

Claude Wilber Lundy was born August 10, 1917 in Malad, Oneida Co., Idaho, the son of Claude Wilson and Clara Edith (McDougall) Lundy. In 1920, Will was living in Lancaster at the home of his grandmother, Mary McDougall, born in Canada, of Scottish ancestry. Will's mother, Clara, also born in Canada, was employed as a telephone operator. By 1921, Clara had remarried to Samuel A. Ming, a foreman for the Southern California Edison Company. Will's siblings included sister, Lorene Lundy and a half-sister, Ina Mary Ming.

Will graduated from AVJUHS in 1935. While attending high school he played and lettered in football, basketball, baseball and was on the track team. After high school, Will attended Antelope Valley Junior College for two years, with one semester as class president. He then went on to the University of California, Los Angeles (UCLA) and graduated in 1940. Will had signed up for the draft and was inducted on Armistice Day, November 11, 1941. He immediately enlisted in order to get into his choice of service - the Army Air Corps. Will was in basic training at Keesler Field, Biloxi, Mississippi, when he heard the news about the attack on Pearl Harbor.

After basic training, Will was assigned to Aircraft Mechanics school for five months at Keesler Field. After graduating from AM School, he was transferred to the 44th Bombardment Group at Barksdale Field in Shreveport, Louisiana, as an Aircraft Mechanic. He was assigned to a crew servicing B-24 Liberators. Two months later, the 44th Bombardment Group was sent to Will Rogers Field in Oklahoma City, Oklahoma for five weeks. In October of 1942, the 44th Bombardment Group was transferred to England for service with the 8th Air Force. Will served on a crew with seven other men at Shipdham in Norfolk, as part of the 44th Bombardment Group (Heavy), 67th Bomb Squadron, 2nd Air Division.

Will saw plenty of combat as part of the B-24 ground crew during the 31 months spent with the 44,th although he did not fly on any combat missions. The Group was awarded the Distinguished Unit Citation for an extremely hazardous bombing mission against the U-boat naval base installations at Kiel, Germany, on May 14, 1943. In June of 1943, the Group moved to North Africa to help with the invasion of Sicily, by bombing airfields and marshalling yards in Sicily. In August 1943, they participated in the dangerous, low-level raid on the Ploesti oil fields in Romania for which they received another Distinguished Unit Citation.

Proud of his Scottish heritage

On May 8, 1945, when the war in Europe was declared over, Will was in Bristol, England visiting a wounded friend, Herman Rush, also from Lancaster. Will was helping Herman onto the hospital ship for his return to the United States. Herman died before Will returned home from the service. When the war with Japan was over, Will was in Albuquerque, New Mexico, waiting for orders to return home. In September, 1945, Will was honorably discharged from the service at the rank of Staff Sergeant. He was at Fort MacArthur in California, 80 miles from home, scheduled to be discharged at noon. With all the military red tape, he was delayed until after dark – not exactly what Will had expected. He was discharged on a Friday and went to work at Southern California Edison Company on Monday, thankful to be home.

On January 26, 1947, Will married his English sweetheart, G. Irene Haines, in Lancaster, California. Will met Irene in November, 1942 while in Norwich, England. They had three children together; Kerry Lee, Lynn Dee, and Kevin Alan Lundy.

Will received many awards and decorations while serving in the Army Air Corps including the Presidential Unit Citation with one Oak Leaf Cluster; six Battle Ribbons for both Africa and European activities – France, Belgium, Germany and Norway. After the war, he joined the 44th Bomb Group Veterans Association and the 2nd Air Division Association to keep in contact with the many friends he made while in the service. Many of his friends are now deceased, but over the years they kept in touch with visits and reunions, with several of the reunions attended in Norwich, England.

Will spent thirty-three years with the Southern California Edison Company, first as part of their construction crew, then as a senior clerk in the office. He moved several times in order to be promoted with the company. The last eight years at SCE he worked in the general office as a senior accountant specializing in state rate cases with the Public Utility Commission for the state of California. For the past twenty-five years Will has worked as the 44th Bomb Group Historian. He has collected most of the details of the 850 airmen who were killed in action and 1,500 others who were prisoners of war, wounded or evaded. Will is in the process of revising his "*Roll of Honor*" book which will include the detailed information, photographs, and stories he has collected thus far, about what happened to the airplanes and airmen lost during the war. Will also compiled another book titled, "*History of the 67th Squadron.*"

"When I returned to Lancaster, I never wanted to leave there again. I could see so many possibilities for growth in the Valley, a great place to live, that I wanted it to be home forever. But a few years later, I was 'forced' to move in order to obtain promotions. By the time such opportunities opened up in Lancaster, things had changed and there was better work elsewhere.

When the war was finally over, I was amazed at the great 'luck' that so many of my friends and associates had survived the war. Nearly all of my close friends had survived! Many had become pilots, and they, too, returned. We were blessed.

Never again should the U.S. permit our defenses and might to become so inadequate. For over a year I watched our brave men fly against nearly hopeless odds and severe weather knowing their chances of survival was ZERO! Most of those 'pioneers' were killed or POWs. It was heartbreaking to watch them."

Will currently calls Cool, El Dorado Co., California, in Gold Rush country, his home. He and his wife, Irene, spent each summer in Bridgeport, California, enjoying the cool, mountain area. Irene recently passed away in March 2004.

GLYNDON LLOYD LYNDE

Glyndon Lloyd Lynde descended directly from a long line of U.S. military members including Lieutenant Benjamin Lynde who served in the American Revolutionary forces. His ancestor, Thomas Lynde, emigrated to Charlestown, Massachusetts in 1634. Glyndon's grandfather, Stephen C. Lynde, first came to Nebraska in 1879. He operated a livery stable for 20 years. He was also involved in the grain and coal business. Stephen married Elizabeth Griffith, a native of Wales, on February 23, 1887. The couple had four children, including Lloyd who married Lillian in 1913 in Wynot, Cedar Co., Nebraska. Lloyd Lynde was a cashier for the Wynot bank. Lloyd and Lillian later had a daughter, Margaret, who was born in Ponca, Nebraska.

Glyndon was raised in Dixon and Cedar Counties in Nebraska. He graduated from the Hartington High School in 1932. His father, Lloyd, was president of the school board. Glyndon participated in a declamatory contest where the topic for debate was 'war or peace'. As an extemporaneous contestant, he took the position that war may be a necessary evil and would continue to be so. He continues to believe that war is a generally ineffective means to settle international disputes but has some redeeming features such as "stimulating the collective intellect resulting in a marked acceleration of new technology."

Glyndon served with the Nebraska National Guard over a period of four years, starting in 1932. He attended the University of Nebraska, graduating in 1936. He was a member of the Reserve Officers Training Corps while attending Nebraska University. He married Charlotte Fisher on July 3, 1940 in Omaha, Douglas Co., Nebraska. Charlotte was a member of the Mayflower Society. Glyndon worked for the Federal Land Bank in Omaha for three years. He moved to California in 1941, taking a position with Lockheed Aircraft Corporation. He volunteered for the Army Air Corps in May 1942 after the Pearl Harbor attack, and joined the service at Grand Central Airport in Glendale in May 1942.

Glyndon was sent to Nashville, Tennessee for basic training where he was assigned to a psychological research unit which screened aptitudes of potential aircrew members. Next, he was assigned to the U.S. Air Force meteorological school at Grand Rapids, Michigan, after serving as a cadet at the Boca Raton Club in Florida. The school was later moved to Chanute Air Force Base. As a new Second Lieutenant he took command of a weather station at Lemoore Army Air Field in California. After six months he was assigned to Headquarters, Air Weather Service at Asheville, North Carolina as an operations officer.

Air Weather Service was tasked early during wartime operations to provide accurate forecasts to support military operations. Headquarters, Air Weather Service (Hq. AWS) was located at the city building, Asheville, North Carolina. About 30 key personnel were assigned to this headquarters. One of the most critical responsibilities of the AWS was to assure that the Allies would be provided with the most recent advances in meteorology and the best operational expertise available. Lt. General [then Colonel] William O. Senter commanded AWS and was responsible for providing the best weather team available to support General Eisenhower. Glyndon was honored to accept assignment to Hq. AWS about May 1944. Glyndon remained at Asheville until the war was over. Later, Glyndon was assigned to the Continental Weather Wing at Tinker Air Force Base, Oklahoma.

Glyndon stated his own thoughts on World War II and the purpose of the Air Force Weather Service, "Perhaps the most significant event that occurred during World War II was the D-Day invasion on June 6, 1944. This event signaled the turn of the war for the United States and its allies." He continues to believe that President Woodrow Wilson had the proper perspective. Wilson's slogan was to "Speak softly and carry a big stick."

"Weather was the key to a successful movement of troops and materiel across the English Channel during the Normandy invasion. Inclement weather prompted Hitler to visit his mountain retreat, Berchesgarten, in the Alps. Goering, commander of the German air forces, and many of the German high command felt secure, thinking that no military operations would be planned or executed during unusually severe weather. Had the Germans been alerted to the Allied plans, large German forces would undoubtedly have been defending Normandy, including Omaha Beach and other invasion sites. A defeat of the allies would have been a disaster and may have turned the tide of the war. Domination of Europe by the Germans would have left the United States in a vulnerable position that in turn may have resulted in a major change in the course of world events.

General Eisenhower relied on weather forecasts to assure a successful launching of the Allied forces to cross the English Channel and to mount a landing during a thinly manned German contingent at various invasion sites. The strategy of the invasion of Europe was planned early during the war and was well concealed from the enemy forces by various means of deception. Keeping the enemy speculating over where a possible invasion could be mounted enabled the Allies to focus on the Omaha Beach area to assure minimum resistance by the enemy. The deception strategy included studies of past weather conditions in the English Channel area. Weather studies were conducted by the best meteorologists that were available in the U.S. and the U.K. Cal Tech and MIT were among the universities to provide the best technology to support the invasion. Rossby, Fletcher, Kaplan, Austin and Krick were among the brilliant meteorologists selected to identify and predict suitable deceptive weather conditions for the invasion."

After the war, Glyndon moved his family back to Glendale, California. Daughter Catherine was born in 1946. Glyndon worked for U.S. Treasury Intelligence until June 1948. He was then commissioned as a First

Lieutenant in the regular Air Force about June 1948. He was immediately assigned to Hq. AWS Weather Wing in Tokyo. Son Tom was born in August 1948. Glyndon served in Guam as a Detachment Commander for 15 months. He was then reassigned to the Weather Wing in Tokyo. Daughter Patricia was born in Tokyo in September 1949. Again, General Senter was his commander while serving in Tokyo.

Glyndon and his family returned to Hq. AWS at Andrews Air Force Base about March 1950. He served there as AWS Communications Officer. He then attended MIT to pursue a course in micrometeorology where he received a Master's Degree. He was assigned to Dugway Proving Ground, Utah in 1952 as a micrometeorologist for the U.S. Army. He was then reassigned to Eglin Air Force Base in Florida about 1953 to command a Weather Center which supported the Air Force Proving Ground Command and the Air Force Armament Service. He further served as Staff Weather Advisor for three years while at Eglin Air Force Base.

Glyndon was next assigned to Wheelus Air Base in Libya were he was assigned as Operations Officer for the Middle East area. At Ankara, Turkey he represented the United States at a NATO conference. He hosted several Arab League members at Wheelus Air Base. Later, he was sent to Ramstein Air Force Base in Germany as AWS Squadron Operations Officer and later as Commander of 12th Air Force weather support team located at Kinsbach, Germany. Returning to the U.S. in 1958, he became commander of the Air Force Weather Center at McGuire Air Force Base, New Jersey for three years. While still at McGuire he became Staff Weather Advisor to Eastern Transport Air Force for three years. In this capacity he helped to develop a computer flight plan system, which was widely adopted within the USAF about 1961. While assigned to McGuire he was fortunate to fly in Air Force II from Andrews Air Force Base. This back-up aircraft followed President Kennedy's Air Force I to Palm Springs, California.

A conference was held at Fort Ord, California commemorating the 50th anniversary of the June 6, 1944 D-Day invasion. Glyndon assisted in arrangements including invitations to former enemy and friendly weather forecasters who were involved in the D-Day forecasts. Some of the festivities were broadcast on national television.

Glyndon retired in 1964 with a rank of Lieutenant Colonel. General Senter later visited Del Mesa Carmel, where Glyndon also lived, during which time reminiscences of service life were exchanged. In a humorous note, General Senter thanked Glyndon for helping to win World War II. Glyndon joined both the Air Force Association and Veterans of Foreign Wars.

Glyndon continued to be associated with the Defense Department after his retirement from the USAF. He developed a night light prediction system in support of night vision devices while with Litton Scientific Support Laboratory. He was associated with simulated F-14 and F-15 aircraft combat exercises at Nellis Air Force Base, Nevada. He finally moved to Carmel, California, then to Lancaster in 1999.

Louis Massari, the son of Donato and Maria D. (Moneta) Massari, was born on July 28, 1921 in the small town of Pietragalla, Potenza, Italy. In 1933, Louis immigrated to the United States, coming directly to Palmdale, California. Louis had two younger siblings, a brother, Rocco and a sister, Anna.

In 1941, Louis graduated from AVJUHS. During high school, Louis was a well-rounded student who participated in student government, Lettermen's Club and other groups. He played both baseball and football.

Louis enlisted in the Army Air Force in 1942. After boot camp, Louis was assigned to the 385th Bombardment Group (Heavy). The 385th was activated on November 25, 1942 and formed in February, 1943 at Geiger Field in Spokane, Washington. The Group trained for two months at Geiger Field.

On May 27, 1943, Louis was assigned to Captain William Tesla's crew at Great Falls Army Air Base, located in Montana. The crew's B-17 was named "*Slo Jo.*" The 385th

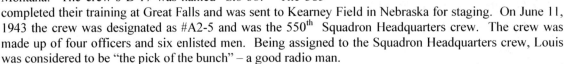

completed their training at Great Falls and was sent to Kearney Field in Nebraska for staging. On June 11, 1943 the crew was designated as #A2-5 and was the 550th Squadron Headquarters crew. The crew was made up of four officers and six enlisted men. Being assigned to the Squadron Headquarters crew, Louis was considered to be "the pick of the bunch" – a good radio man.

They left for Great Ashfield, Suffolk, England, where they were attached to the 8th Air Force, 3rd Bombardment Division, 93rd Combat Wing. Louis was assigned to the 550th Bombardment Squadron of the 385th Bombardment Group (H) as a radio operator.

The first mission flown by the 385th was on July 17, 1943 with the target of Amsterdam. While in England, from 1943 – 1945, the Group flew 296 missions, dropped 18,494 tons of bombs and 184 tons of food all across Europe. On August 28, 1945, the 385th was deactivated after three years of service. The 385th was awarded the Distinguished Unit Citation twice - on August 17, 1943 for their bombing efforts at Regensburg, Germany, and again on May 12, 1944, for Zwickau, Germany.

Louis was one of the founding members of the 385th and was in the last group to leave Great Ashfield. Louis, then a Master Sergeant, returned home to Palmdale.

After the war, Louis attended the University of Redlands. While at Redlands, Lou was again active in student government. He also participated in baseball and football. He was a member of the 1949 football team that played in the Pineapple Bowl on New Year's Day in Hawaii. As a member of the 1949 team, Lou was inducted into the Redland's Athletic Hall of Fame.

After college, Louis returned to the Antelope Valley and began a life-long career as an insurance broker and community leader. At the age of 33, Louis married Maria M. Pappas of Lancaster on January 11, 1953. Louis and Mary had four children; Dan, Marina, John and Barbara.

Louis was President of Insurance Associates, located in Lancaster, for over thirty years. While maintaining his business, Louis stayed involved in the community in many ways. He coached youth baseball for many years. He was the President of the Board of Trustees of Antelope Valley College during the early 1960s. He was a founding member of the Antelope Valley Country Club. He served as a Board of Director for the Antelope Valley Savings and Loan. He was also the Director for the Lancaster Parks and Recreation during the formative years of the City of Lancaster.

Throughout the years since the war, Louis stayed active in the 385th Bombardment Group Association. He participated in many reunions. Several of the reunion trips were visits back to Great Ashfield in England. He was fortunate to be in England for the 50th celebration of VE-Day.

On June 1, 2001, Louis Massari died at the age of 79 in Lancaster, California. He is survived by his wife, Mary Massari. He is also survived by his children; Dan and LuAnn Massari, Marina Massari, John and Laura Massari, and Barbara and Tom Horton. Louis and Mary have eight grandchildren; Alex, Michael, Nicholas, Joseph, Thomas, Gabrielle, Natalie and Alexa.

Louis Massari, center, with the B-17 "Slo Jo"
The "Slo Jo" was shot down on December 11, 1943.
Photo courtesy of Ray Bowden, USAAF Nose Art Research Project

ROLAND JOSEPH "RON/MATT" MATTISON

On May 2, 1922, in Chicago, Cook Co., Illinois, Roland "Ron" Joseph Mattison was born to Allen and Margaret Mattison. Ron had three younger siblings; one brother, George and two sisters, Dolores and Theresa Mattison. In 1930, the Mattison family was living in the city of Chicago, Illinois. Ron's father, Allen, was a native of Arkansas while his mother, Margaret, was from Southern Ireland, immigrating to the United States in 1914.

Ron was at home in Chicago, listening to a football game, when he heard the news about Pearl Harbor. He was drafted into the U.S. Army Coast Artillery (Anti-Aircraft) on May 12, 1943. Ron was inducted at Camp Grant, in Illinois. He remembered the induction center as being like a military school. He enjoyed basic training – he felt as if he was being trained for a football team!

After basic training, Ron was sent to Camp Irwin [now Fort Irwin] near Barstow, San Bernardino Co., California, for desert warfare training and maneuvers. The Battalion was being trained to join General George Patton's forces in North Africa. He was first assigned to Battery "A" of the 797th Anti-Aircraft Artillery, AW Battalion as a member of a 40 Millimeter Anti-Aircraft Gun crew.

General Patton's troops secured North Africa quickly and the Battalion was re-trained for non-desert warfare. Ron was sent to several locations for training, including Camp Haan and Camp Cooke, both in

97

California. He was reassigned to Battery "D" of the 485 Anti-Aircraft Artillery AW Battalion and sent to the South Pacific. Ron engaged in combat during the Battle of Leyte Gulf in the Philippines in October of 1944. His anti-aircraft gun crew shot down one enemy plane and shared credit with another gun crew in the destruction of a second enemy plane. He also saw combat duty at Okinawa, for the liberation of the Ryukyu Islands, an island chain southwest of the main islands of Japan. He entered into occupation duty in South Korea at the end of the war.

Ron, kneeling at far right – Leyte, October 1944

Ron kept in contact with his family through regular mail and V-mail. Among the best entertainers at the U.S.O. shows were comedian Danny Thomas at Camp Grant, Illinois, and at Camp Haan, California he saw Lucille Ball and Desi Arnaz. He recalled the food he ate as being good while he was in camp, but while on maneuvers, it was average and during combat it was poor.

On the lighter side Ron said, "Almost all outfits had one or more clowns. For instance, one soldier with a deep, authoritative voice, would startle unsuspecting recruits by shouting, 'Look alive there soldier!' Another amusing guy would imitate the voice of a Philippino newscaster. He would do 'spoofs' on nonsensical bits of local news of the Leyte Island."

Ron was near the beach on the island of Okinawa where his anti-aircraft gun was 'dug in', when he heard the news that the war was over. However, the officers warned them not to become complacent until the news was verified. On January 26, 1946, Ron was honorably discharged from the Army due to the demobilization after the war, at the rank of Private, 1st Class. He received the Asiatic-Pacific Theater Ribbon with two Bronze Battle Stars; three Overseas Service Bars; the American Campaign Medal; the Philippine Liberation Ribbon with two Bronze Stars; Good Conduct Medal and the World War II Victory Medal.

In the days following his discharge, Ron went home to Chicago, Illinois where he enjoyed his mother's home cooking. After several weeks at home, he enrolled at the Columbia College of Radio where he was trained in the radio broadcasting field. With the onset of the television, Ron's radio broadcasting career was unsettled. Most of his work after the war came as a security officer. His military training and experience helped him quality for employment for security duty at a motion picture studio.

Ron settled in California in 1952 and on June 2, 2002, he married Darlene Parrett. They had both been previously married, and she had three children from her first marriage; Daniel J., Steven M., and William Edward Parrett. Ron and Darlene currently live at Mayflower Gardens Retirement Community in Quartz Hill, California.

Ron and his brother, George – February 1946

WILLIAM JOHN "MAC" McADAM, JR.

William John McAdam, Jr. was born December 4, 1915 in Pasadena, Los Angeles Co., California to William John and Ethel (Neer) McAdam. William was born in North Dakota, of Scottish descent, and Ethel was born in California. Bill's parents were married around 1913, in California, and had the following children, along with Bill: Dorothy, Donald, Christine and Mary McAdam.

In 1908, Robert McAdam, a fruit farmer and the father of the elder William McAdam, became interested in the Pearland area, near Littlerock, California. Robert, along with his two older sons, Frank and William, began to acquire parcels of land, some purchased and some acquired by homesteading. The property became known as the San Andreas Ranch, consisting of over 1,000 acres of land.

By 1920, the family had settled in the Antelope Valley where elder William was a fruit farmer, growing mainly pears. William served a term as president of the Antelope Valley Fruit Growers Association in the mid 1920's. During the 1930's, the pear market grew depressed, so William began a real estate business which would develop into a successful venture for the next 15 years.

The McAdam children attended primary school in the Antelope Valley. Bill graduated from AVJUHS, and after graduation he attended Willamette University in Salem, Oregon. He enlisted in the Army Air Corps as part of the Cadet program in 1939 in Pasadena, California. Basic training began in Ontario, California, at the Ontario Army Air Field. After training, Bill was sent to Randolph Field in San Antonio, Texas for flight training, then on to Kelly Field, also in San Antonio, for continued training.

On July 13, 1941, Bill married Donna Stewart in Santa Monica, Los Angeles Co., California. They had four children; two daughters, Christine and Nancy, and a son, William John McAdam, III. After the marriage, Bill was sent to Chico Army Air Field in Chico, Butte Co., California. This base was mainly set up for bomber crew and fighter pilot training. His next assignment would take him to the West Coast Training Command Center in Bakersfield, Kern Co., California. He was then sent to Ontario Army Air Field for fighter training. Bill was stationed at Moffett Field in California when he heard the news that the war had come to an end.

Bill was honorably discharged at the rank of Major in 1945. He kept in contact with many people he had made friendships with during the war. After his discharge, Bill went to work in Chico, California where he owned a drive-in restaurant. He was part owner of a car agency, then he worked in the real estate business. William returned to the Antelope Valley in 1949, living there until his death on June 24, 1990. He is buried at the Joshua Memorial Park and Cemetery in Lancaster, California.

Donald J. McDonald was born March 12, 1920 in Mojave, Kern Co., California, the son of Dan and Eliza Lillian (Taylor) McDonald. Dan was born in Boston, Massachusetts, and Eliza was born in Wroxton, England. They had six children, including Don; daughter Lily, twins Mary and Mable, Joseph and Ethelbert McDonald.

Don attended Mojave Grammar School and graduated from AVJUHS in 1937, where he played football and baseball and was captain of the Varsity basketball team in his senior year. He was the President of the "Knights" organization and for one semester, President of the Lettermans Club. Don attended AVJC in 1939, then transferred to Santa Barbara State College (now the University of California, Santa Barbara) where he participated in college football and basketball programs.

Don was drafted in October 1941 and was inducted into the U.S. Army at Fort MacArthur, San Pedro, California. He was given the opportunity to transfer into the Army Air Corps and immediately "jumped" at it. Don was sent to Wichita Falls, Texas for recruit training. From there he went to Mather Field, Sacramento, California to serve as a mechanic on the flight line. At Mather Field, he took and passed the tests for the Aviation Cadet Program. Don was then sent to Ellington Field, Texas to the Cadet facility for indoctrination.

Next, came flight training, all of which was in Texas. First, to Ballinger Field for Primary Flight Training, on to Randolph Field for Basic, then back to Ellington Field for Advanced Flight Training and graduation in April of 1943. After graduation, with his new gold bars and "gleaming pilot wings", Don departed for B-17 training at Malmstrom Air Base, Walla Walla, Washington, then on to Geiger Field in Spokane, Washington for further training.

In October of 1943, Don was assigned overseas duty and sent to Ridgewell, England, attached to the 8th Air Force, 381st Bombardment Group, 534th Bomb Squadron (Heavy). He participated in eight combat bombing missions beginning on December 11, 1943 at Emden, Germany to January 5, 1944 at Tours, France.

On January 7, 1944, Don was the co-pilot on the B-17 "Winsome Winn" on his eighth mission with the 534th. This was Mission 58 for the 381st Bombardment Group , with the target at Ludwigshaven, Germany. Don recalled, "We had dropped our bombs and were leaving the target area, when the No. 2 engine was hit by anti-aircraft fire (flak) and was put out of commission. Apparently, the No. 1 engine had also received some damage too, as it soon caught on fire and we were not able to control this. The result of losing all this power was that we soon dropped behind the main bomber stream. The awaiting fighters – ME-109s – took advantage of this and finished the job. Adding this to the worsening condition of our aircraft, order was given to 'bail out'.

As this order was given, I set the autopilot to help hold the aircraft as a steady platform as the crew members left their positions. Being the size I was – 6'2" and 220 pounds – I chose to go out through the open bomb bay doors. On the way aft I stopped to help our engineer/top turret gunner, Sergeant Embach, free himself from his oxygen equipment so he could leave the aircraft.

As I fell towards the ground, I remembered our escape and evasion training which taught: 'Do not open your chute until in the clouds below you, as this will help in evading those on the ground who will be looking for you.' Following this advice I did as instructed and in the cloud received my second big scare of the day as a ME-109 passed by so close that I could see the pilot.

Coming out of the cloud, I found myself over a town where it seemed that all the inhabitants were in the streets looking up and gesturing towards me. Thinking that we might have made it to France and that they were friendly, I started waving back. It didn't take long for me to see just how wrong I was!

Hitting the ground on a small slope on the edge of a town, I lost my footing and began to tumble. As I was arising, I was immediately surrounded by hostile civilians who didn't appear to be the nice, friendly

Frenchmen whom I was hoping for. As one gentleman started tugging me around by my parachute harness, another came up and started striking me with his fist. A third person came up to join in and luckily, I was able to grab his arm and keep him between me and the striker. At this time, a man with a swastika arm band and a mighty big looking hand gun arrived and I figured that this would be my end. Instead, he ordered the others away from me – by this, he instantly became my friend.

Before marching me up to the jail, I was made to empty out my pockets. During this act I was really provoked when one person slapped my Hershey bar out of my hand and stomped it into the ground. I bet later he was sorry that he hadn't kept it for himself.

Later that day, all surviving crew members were picked up and put in the rear of a truck for transport to a fort in Metz. Also in the truck and covered, was the body of one person. Others told me that it was Sergeant Kucher, although it could have been Sergeant Greco.

Before being transported from the fort to our next destination, we were lined up to be lectured to by a German Army Colonel. While he was berating us and telling us that, 'we were not real soldiers but merely murderers, and should be taken out and hanged as such', Sgt. Embach smiled. This infuriated the officer who then struck the Sergeant across the face with his gloves. The Colonel then wanted to carry out his desire for execution, but he was stopped by over-coated civilians who were present and seemed to carry some authority.

While traveling on to Dulag Luft for interrogation we were joined by a U.S. Air Corps Captain who spoke very good German. This made us very suspicious of him. He said that he had been a member of the P-38 flight which was coming to answer our call for help. On the way at max throttle, one of his engines failed and caught fire. He too, had to bail out.

During our conversation, I learned that his flight leader was a past schoolmate of mine [R.C. Franklin] from California. He knew enough about this other officer and his family that we decided to accept him at face value. This pilot was Captain Joseph Marsiglia, from New York. In Stalag Luft 1, he was the interpreter and trader for his compound.

After Dulag Luft, all the officers of the crew with the exception of Lieutenant Joseph Connolly, were transported to Stalag Luft 1. The train ride took nine days in old coaches with guards in each one. Connolly was retained in a hospital until his broken leg healed and then, he too, was sent to Luft 1.

On arrival at Luft 1, I was interviewed by the camp intelligence officer, Major von Miller. Noting my home address of Mojave, California on my ID tags, he proceeded to tell me that he knew the area well. Supposedly, he'd had an interior decorating shop on Sunset Boulevard in Hollywood.

My initial residence in Barth was a room with ten other POWs. I was soon moved to another room with only seven others, but as the war went on we increased the total to twelve. The room was 16' by 16'.

An interesting moment was when the Camp Commander, Hauptmann von Beck, brought his fencing foils into the compound for a friendly match with one of the 'Kriegies' (prisoners) who had fenced at the University of Southern California. This was enjoyed by all who were fortunate to see it. H. von Beck was admired and respected by all officers in the camp.

Another incident, not so happy, was my week in solitary for participating in the construction of one of the many escape tunnels. Needless to say, it was not a success."

On May 1, 1945 the men from Luft 1 were liberated by the Russian Army. They were transported in B-17's to France for a two week stay at Camp Lucky Strike. They sailed from Le Havre to Newport News, Virginia via Liberty Ship. Next, they boarded trains that took them across the country, to Camp Beale, near Sacramento, California. Don boarded a bus that took him to Bakersfield where he caught a train to Mojave – home at last!

All Prisoners of War were given a ninety-day rest and relaxation leave. After the leave, Donald reported back for a medical and physical evaluation to assess his placement for further duty. He passed the tests, but the war with Japan had now ended and he was released to the inactive reserves.

Don completed his education under the G.I. Bill at UCSB, graduating in 1948. He became a member of the physical education staff with AVJUHS, where he coached baseball, and at AVJC where he coached football and basketball. In the summer of 1951, he was hired as the Assistant Athletic Director at Edwards

Air Force Base where he was assigned to assemble and coach the football and basketball teams representing the Base.

In March of 1952, Don married Darlene "Pidge" Hoskins. Darlene was a fellow teacher at AVJUHS, and during World War II she had served as a pilot with the Women's Air Service Pilots (WASP). His recent marriage and job assignment at Edwards Air Force Base was cut short when he received orders to report for active duty once again. Don remembered, "When I was recalled to active duty, Pidge out-ranked me in reserve grade and also had more flying hours than I did!"

In April of 1952, Don was called up to serve as a B-29 pilot during the Korean War. He reported to Randolph Field, Texas for training and was transferred to the 20th Air Force, 19th Bombardment Group, 30th Bombardment Squadron at Kadena Air Force Base in Okinawa. While stationed there, he flew thirty bombing missions over Korea, mainly at night. A highlight for Don in Korea was when he stumbled upon AVJC schoolmate, Major Dave Brown, while at an air base.

After Korea, he remained on active duty flying KC-135 tankers on fighter support missions in Vietnam. Don was assigned to the 93rd Bomb Wing at Castle Air Force Base, Atwater, California. He flew many ninety-day temporary tours (TDY) including duty at Elmandorf AFB, Eileson AFB, Goose Bay, Harmon AFB, Greenland, Guam, and several other stations.

In 1962, Don's wife, Darlene, passed away. They had one child together, Michael McDonald, born in 1954 at Castle AFB, Atwater, California.

Don was promoted to Lieutenant Colonel in 1966 and moved to Operations Officer for the 321st Air Refueling Squadron, then went on to serve as Commander of the Alert Force and Deputy Commander of Operations Training. He completed his military career as a Staff Officer in charge of scheduling flight and ground duties of the flight personnel in the 301st Air Refueling Wing at Rickenbacker Air Force Base in Ohio.

Don retired from active duty with the Air Force in October 1972, holding the rank of Lieutenant Colonel. He received the following awards for his service during World War II, Korea and Vietnam: Air Medal with 2 Bronze Clusters; Purple Heart Medal; Presidential Unit Citation; Prisoner of War Medal; Air Force Longevity Service Award with 3 Bronze Clusters; Air Force Outstanding Unit Award with 2 Bronze Clusters; American Defense Service Medal; American Campaign Medal; European-African-Middle Eastern Campaign Medal with 1 Battle Star; World War II Victory Medal; National Defense Service Medal with 1 Bronze Service Bar; Korean Service Medal with 1 Bronze Star; American Forces Reserve Medal.

In July of 1975, Don married Mary Elliot of Columbus, Ohio and in 1976 they moved to Florida to be closer to Mary's father who was in ill health. Tragedy struck in 1988 with the death of Don and Darlene's only child, Michael, killed in a train/auto accident.

The "Winsome Winn" B-17F, No. 42-3078 before she was lost on January 7, 1945. AKA "Winsome Winn Hilda" – the Hilda was added by Lt. Arden Wilson for his wife. Photo courtesy of the 381st Bomb Group (H) Memorial Association, Inc.

Erinnerungsfoto Die Crew der „Winsome Winn" im Jahr 1943.   FOTOS: ARCHIV WILHELM

„ . . . und ich winkte den Leuten zu"

Der Copilot der abgeschossenen B 17, Donald J. McDonald, erinnert sich

The above photograph and text is from the German newspaper, "Neunkircher Rundschau" dated January 7, 1997. The article printed was titled "…and I Waved at the People" a story written about the memories of Dr. Horst Wilhelm who, at age 14, was an eye-witness to the crash of the "*Winsome Winn*" B-17 on January 7, 1945.

The crew of the "*Winsome Winn*" included: Back row, beginning at the far left: Sgt. John Embach, S/Sgt. Dick Espit, Sgt. Walter Sussek, S/Sgt. George Hawkins, Sgt. Robert Garaghty, Sgt. Anthony Greco. The officers in front of the crewmembers are: left to right, Lt. Joseph Connolly, Lt. Arden Wilson, Lt. Donald McDonald and Lt. Harry H. Ullom. Radio-Operator S/Sgt. Peter Kucher was killed in the airplane, along with tail-gunner Sgt. Anthony Greco.

Don and his wife, Mary, are retired and now reside in Holly Hill on the eastern coast of Florida with children, grandchildren, and great-grandchildren living nearby.

P.O.W. Medal

103

On November 03, 1923, Donald Leland McLaurin was born to James. H. and Grace (Brown) McLaurin. James was born in Canada and immigrated to the U.S. in 1906. Grace was born in Missouri, with her father born in Kentucky and mother born in Tennessee. By 1920, the McLaurin family was living in Los Angeles, California. James and Grace had three children at that time; two sons, Elden and Peter, and a daughter, Nadene. James was working the land as a farmer, living next to Grace's parents, Thomas and Elizabeth Brown.

In 1930, the McLaurin's owned land in Owensmouth, (now Canoga Park) California, where James made his living as a grape rancher. Don had one other sister, Geraldine, born in 1935. Don also lived in the Antelope Valley for a short time with his parents in the 1930's where he attended Lancaster Grammar School.

Don graduated from Owens Valley High School in 1941 while assisting his father in the operation of a 500 acre poultry farm in Independence, Inyo County, California. He fed and cared for over 2,000 turkeys, planted, cultivated and harvested grain, crops, and operated a tractor and other farming equipment. When Pearl Harbor was attacked, Don was living in El Monte, California, with his parents.

Don was drafted into the U.S. Army in April of 1944. He was sent to Camp Roberts in San Luis Obispo, California for four months of basic infantry training and training as a rifleman and guard patrolman. After seventeen weeks of more training at Camp Roberts, from May 8, 1944 to September 2, 1944, he would qualify as a cannoneer. He was then promoted to Corporal. Don was sent to the east coast where he boarded a ship that would take him to the Mediterranean Theater of Operations - to Italy with the 34th Infantry Division "Red Bull", 135th Infantry Regiment.

Don entered into combat almost immediately in Italy in October 1944. In April, 1945, he was a part of the Po Valley offensive battle in northern Italy. The 34th took control over this important area in May of 1945, just before the end of the war in Europe. Don was reassigned to the 88th Infantry Division and promoted to Tech Sergeant. He served as Platoon Sergeant and "supervised 16 enlisted men in the operation of two 105 MM Howitzer Artillery weapons. He was responsible for the control, coordination, and tactical deployment of these weapons."

After the war ended, Don served one year in the Army of Occupation. He also played baseball with other military teams during the occupation time. He was honorably discharged at Camp Beale Separation Center in California, on July 5, 1946. He earned the rank of Tech Sergeant with the following awards: European-Africa-Middle Eastern Campaign Medal; a Bronze Star Medal; World War II Victory Medal; Army of Occupation Medal; Good Conduct Medal.

On November 15, 1946, Don married Betty L. Dawson in Glendale, Los Angeles Co., California. After moving to the Antelope Valley in 1947, they had two children together, daughter, Nancy, and son, Craig Bradley McLaurin. When they moved to the Valley, Don worked in Lancaster for four years with Southern California Edison Company until he found a job at Edwards Air Force Base as an Instrumentation Technician.

Don passed away in Lancaster, California on June 16, 1998. His wife, Betty, currently lives in Lancaster.

In 1935, Charles and Ida (Dunn) Mills uprooted their family and moved from Texas to Lancaster, California to pursue the life of the alfalfa farmer. There were five children in the family; three sons and two daughters. Son Josh "J.D.", was born July 30, 1916, in Nocona, Montague County, Texas, before the move west.

Jobs were scarce in the Antelope Valley, so J.D. looked for employment further north in Searles Valley. In November of 1936, he found a job in Searles Valley at an industrial chemical plant owned by the Westend Chemical Company. J.D. was working there when he was drafted into the U.S. Army in March of 1941.

In basic training at Fort Lewis, Washington, he received training as a combat rifleman and qualified to carry a Browning automatic rifle, a highly effective 30mm weapon. J.D. was assigned to the 161st Infantry and was scheduled to go to Manila in the Philippine Islands in December 1941.

The December 7th attack on Pearl Harbor changed those plans, and the 161st was held on the docks at San Francisco, California, for ten days, waiting for orders. The regiment was then assigned to the 25th Infantry Division and shipped out to Kaneohe, Oahu, in the Hawaiian Islands.

Soon after their arrival on Oahu, they were shipped out again to an unknown destination. After more than a week at sea, they were advised that their mission was to relieve the Marines at Guadalcanal. At this time a shoulder patch was issued to the troops. The design was a taro leaf, familiar to the Hawaiian Islands, with a bolt of lightning striking through it. The Division became known as the "Tropical Lightning Division."

During the many battles on Guadalcanal, the 161st established itself as an effective, rapid, fighting machine. One of the battles at the Mantanikau Pocket found the entire company stranded, 100 feet above the Mantanikau River, with no where to go except down the cliff. All the men removed their rifle slings and joined them together to form a "rope." They had no choice other than to go hand over hand, down the side of the cliff using the rifle slings to repel. J.D. was one of the men who made it down the cliff and returned to continue fighting.

While the 25th was on the Philippine Islands, J.D. was part of a firefight. During this battle, a comrade of J.D.'s was wounded and pinned down by enemy gunfire. J.D. ran to his position and carried the wounded soldier to safety. J.D. received the Bronze Star for heroic action under fire that day.

More combat action followed at New Georgia, Solomon Islands and at Luzon. The Luzon campaign lasted 165 days. Balete Pass, on the island of Luzon, was where some of the fiercest fighting of the Pacific took place. It was at Balete Pass on February 18, 1945, that J.D. was wounded while in combat by a Japanese grenade. Despite his injuries, J.D. was able to shoot the enemy soldier who tossed the grenade – a fact that he was always proud of.

J.D. was sent to Hawaii for hospitalization and recuperation. After almost six months of recuperating J.D. rejoined the 25th Infantry and found himself back in combat. Due to the severity of his previous wounds, his tour of duty only lasted a few days. He was discharged and sent home on his 29th birthday, July 30, 1945, at the rank of Staff Sergeant.

J.D.'s military decorations and citations included the Bronze Star for heroic action under fire, and the Purple Heart, received after being wounded at Balete Pass. He also received the

American Defense Service Medal; the Asiatic Pacific Campaign Medal with three Stars; and the Philippine Liberation Ribbon with one Bronze Star.

J.D. married Peggy "Pearlie" Ford on June 11, 1949, in Las Vegas, Nevada. From this union two sons were born – John David and Michael Ray Mills. After his discharge, J.D. returned to his previous job at the Westend Chemical Company. He remained there until his retirement in 1982. J.D. had worked his way up to the position of Shipping Superintendent when he retired after 46 years of loyal service.

J.D. passed away on June 18, 2002, in Lancaster, California, where he was interred at Joshua Memorial Park, in the Avenue of the Flags. The Avenue of the Flags was designed to honor the four branches of the United States military. J.D. was buried with military honors in the Army section of the memorial.

Drawing from "165 Days – A Story of the 25th Division on Luzon," by William de Jarnette Rutherfoord who dedicated his book to the combat infantrymen. He followed the doughboys to the battlefield of the Luzon campaign and recorded real life as it was in combat. "Many of my sketches were actually done under fire, while some had to be done from memory, because of such things as rain, darkness, and the violence of sudden, unexpected actions" – September, 1945. Submitted by Michael Mills.

ELMER M. MORSE

Elmer Morse was born May 20, 1920, in Brunswick, Cumberland County, Maine, the son of Charles Moody Morse and Anna Grundy. He had four siblings – Gladys, Robert, Charles, and George Morse. Elmer has lived in California for over forty years, settling here in 1963.

Elmer arrived at Park's Air College, East St. Louis, Illinois, on a Friday evening, February 14, 1941, entering the Army Air Corps in the Flying Cadet program. He started flying lessons in an open cockpit Stearman bi-plane. A few days later, he continued his training in the PT-19 Trainer. Elmer soloed after only eight hours of instruction. Upon completion of his training at Park's, he was transferred to basic training at Randolph Field, Texas, and then onto advanced training at Kelly Field, also in Texas. He graduated September 25, 1941, and was commissioned a 2nd Lieutenant in the United States Army Air Corps.

Elmer's first assignment was with the 13th Bomb Group, 41st Bomb Squadron, at Orlando Air Base, Florida. After the Pearl Harbor attack he was temporarily assigned to patrol duty at West Palm Beach, Florida, until January 20, 1942. Upon completion of the temporary

106

duty he was assigned to the 34th Bombardment Group (Heavy), 4th Bomb Squadron, at Pendleton Field, Oregon.

The 34th Bomb Group had B-24 (LB-30) and B-17E aircraft. Elmer was checked out as an instructor on the B-24 with only seven hours of flight instruction, then checked out on the B-17E in only three hours and twenty minutes. All new incoming pilots had no B-17E flight time. They were checked out very fast to build up the 34th Bomb Group, which later formed several other new groups.

On April 16, 1942, Elmer received secret orders to proceed with a B-17E and crew to join the 10th Air Force in India. The crew departed Pendleton Field on April 17th and arrived in Karachi, India, May 7, 1942. The B-17E and crew were assigned to the 7th Bomb Group (Heavy), 436th Bomb Squadron.

Shortly after arriving in Karachi, India, most of the 7th Bomb Group personnel and aircraft were dispatched to the Middle East. Elmer's crew was scheduled to go with them, but the aircraft they were assigned to was not flyable. Several days later when the aircraft became flight worthy, their orders were cancelled and they remained in India.

The living conditions in Karachi (Tent City) were primitive, warm, and dusty during the dry, hot period, and sultry during the rainy season.

During June and July of 1942, there wasn't much flying done since the Allied Forces had withdrawn from Burma leaving no threat of Japan invading India. The men had time to visit the city of Karachi which helped relieve the boredom of inactivity.

B-24 crew of the 436th Bomb Squadron (H), 7th Bomb Group, 10th Air Force China-Burma-Indian Theater, late 1942 - Standing in back row, far left, 1st Lieutenant Elmer M. Morse

In late July, 1942, the 7th Bomb Group (H) was moved to Allahabad and were housed in the British Bengal Lancer's vacated barracks. With the few B-17E aircraft available, they flew several missions to Rangoon and the Andaman Island. These missions were basically for crew training.

In September, 1942, the 7th Bomb Group (H) received B-24 aircraft which were picked up in Karachi. The crew then started training and planning for the secret Lin-Hsi (Linsi) Coal Mines Mission, one of the most remarkable missions of the war. The coal mines supplied more than two-thirds of the coal used in the production of high grade steel in Japan. If the electric power station was taken out, it would have a devastating effect on Japan.

1st Lt. Elmer Morse, piloting a B-24, was among the first of seven crews to arrive at Dinjan, India, leaving Karachi under sealed orders. The B-24 crews, led by Major Max Fennell, flew over the Himalayan mountains (the Hump), into Kunming, China, where they waited for the weather to clear. The next stop was Chengtu (Hsinching Airfield), where the aircraft were fueled and loaded with modified Russian bombs. After another wait for the weather to clear, the crews proceeded to fly over 1,000 miles northwest to bomb the electric power station at the Lin-Hsi Coal Mines, just on the border of Manchukuo, in Japanese occupied China.

On October 21, 1942, the bombs were dropped from the aircraft at 14,000 feet, hitting the target and inflicting considerable damage to the power station. With the destruction of this power station, the coal mines were put out of operation for a long time. The B-24 crews on the Lin-Hsi mission flew a twelve hour mission with nearly eight hours over enemy territory. They were 800 miles deep into Japanese occupied China, and bombed the coal mines which were within 500 miles of the Japanese mainland. This was the first use of heavy bombers in China.

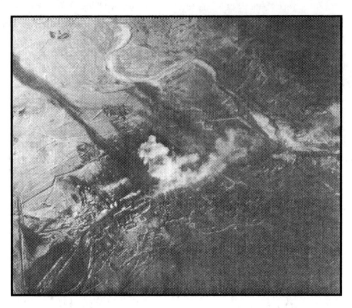

Elmer received the Distinguished Flying Cross and an Air Medal during his service in the war. He retired from the U.S. Air Force in August, 1963, as a Lieutenant Colonel.

Elmer married Marian Rae Arbuckle on September 19, 1943, in Indianapolis, Indiana. They had three children; Ray, Gary, and Susan Morse.

After his retirement from the Air Force, Elmer owned and operated his own business manufacturing metal fasteners for several companies in the aviation industry.

In 1981 Elmer and his wife, Marian, moved to Tehachapi, Kern County, California, north of the Antelope Valley.

Lin-Hsi power plant after the bombing on October 21, 1942

Chinese soldiers with Russian bombs, modified to fit on the B-24 Liberators, Chengtu, China, October 1942

Flight crew members with Chinese guards and the B-24D Liberator, Lin-Hsi Mines Mission, Kunming Air Base, China, October 1942. At left of the group playing cards is Lt. Kenneth Trout, Lt. Elmer Morse, Lt. Taylor, Lt. Milatzo, Capt. Werner (in pith helmet), and Lt. Lewellyn Daigle (navigator for Max Fennell, mission leader). Poker games were used by many crews to pass the time during missions.

108

Marshall Edward Mullens was born May 2, 1923, to Arnold Richard and Ada Lily (Brook) Mullens in Cheyenne, Laramie County, Wyoming. He had six siblings, Marshall being the second to the youngest child. Marshall's brothers and sisters were; Victor Irving, Lucile Ethel, Gladys Emma, Richard Arnold, Glenn Brook, and Frank Ager Mullens. His father was a store department official for the Union Pacific Railroad and Marshall spent his childhood between Wyoming, Idaho, and Nebraska.

When the United States entered World War II, Marshall knew that he wanted to fly for the Army but was too young to join. He attended the University of Wyoming for one year and the University of Nebraska for six months until entry qualifications for the Army were relaxed. He enlisted in February of 1943 in Omaha, Nebraska.

From basic training in Jefferson Barracks, Missouri, he went on to Superior, Wisconsin and then on to Santa Ana, California where he was chosen for pilot training. From there he went to Twenty-Nine Palms, California, then to War Eagle Field in Lancaster, California. He wanted to fly P-38's because they were considered to be "hot" aircraft. One way to do this was to volunteer for reconnaissance work.

Marshall went to Williams Air Force Base in Phoenix, Arizona to train as a pilot in the P-38, then to Will Rogers Field in Oklahoma. He then went on to Hunter Field, Georgia for more training, finally ending up at Hamilton Field in San Francisco, California. At Hamilton Field he learned photo reconnaissance and ended up in Oahu, Hawaiian Islands, where he learned to photograph beaches and islands to prepare for deployment in the Central Pacific in December 1944.

On January 3, 1945, Marshall arrived at East Field on Saipan. He was a replacement in the 28th Photo Reconnaissance Squadron, part of the 7th Army Air Force, 318th Fighter Group. This squadron was concentrating on collecting information on several islands in the Mariana chain that were still held by the Japanese. The goal was to gain control of those large islands where huge air bases could be constructed to hose the B-29 bomber flights targeting Japan. It was clear that Iwo Jima, 800 miles north of Saipan, would have to be taken due to its strategic position halfway between the Mariana Islands and Japan. The recon pilots began taking photos of Iwo Jima prior to the invasion in February 1945.

Marshall standing next to his P-38, the "Lucky Lu"

Okinawa was the next island targeted to support the invasion of Kyushu. The 28th Recon Squadron not only photographed the island before the invasion in April 1945, but also served as intelligence support to the Marines fighting northward across the island. Toward the end of the war, the 28th Squadron flew intelligence missions to Japan and the Sea of Japan.

It was 11:02 a.m., August 9, 1945. Marshall Mullens was flying a P-38 photo reconnaissance over the southeast corner of Kyushu, photographing port installations, shipping activity, and anything else of military interest, when he saw the atomic cloud rising over Nagasaki, 130 miles away. He was to make 3 or 4 passes over the bay, but cloud cover under his plane was making his mission difficult. He didn't know what the cloud cover was, but was told in preflight briefing to stay away from the west side of Kyushu because there was going to be some activity over there.

Seeing the mushroom cloud, he knew it was an opportunity not be passed up. His plane was equipped with two vertically oriented high-resolution cameras, one with a 12 inch lens and one with a 24 inch focal length lens mounted in the belly of the plane. He banked his plane sharply to the left, bringing it around 180 degrees and standing it up on its left wing, hoping to catch an oblique photo of the cloud. The cloud would ultimately rise to 42,000 feet where it would top out at 3 miles above his aircraft.

Marshall had been flying for over three hours from his base at Yonton Field, Okinowa, and was now about at the end of his normal range. His maneuver to take the photo of the mushroom cloud had allowed the Japanese anti-aircraft gunners below him to draw beads [taking aim] on his plane. He headed back on his three hour return flight to Okinawa, unaware that two B-29's were also on their way back to Okinawa from Nagasaki.

In Marshall's own words, he describes the action – "I was flying north over the southeastern coast of Kyushu at 25,000 feet when I was startled by a bright flash off to my left. I figured something big had happened over that way, so I kept my eyes on the clouds in the direction of the flash. Suddenly, a huge, hemispherical ball came up through the clouds, an orange ball, dark orange and white. It was coming fast! A mushroom tower formed as it boiled up. It was awesome!"

11:45 – 12:15 "News in Review" – KBON, Tuesday, March 20, 1945.

A 7ᵗʰ AAF FIGHTER BASE IN THE MARIANAS – Playing an important role in Iwo Jima invasion preparations, 2ⁿᵈ Lt. Marshall E. Mullens, Omaha, Nebraska, a 7ᵗʰ AAF P-38 Lighting reconnaissance plane pilot, flew daring, low level photographic sweeps over the island, providing close up pictures of Jap defenses and prospective beachheads.

Lt. Mullens, during the final mission of the campaign raced across the center of the island flying so low and arriving so unexpectedly that he nearly collided with a Jap bomber taking off. He was forced to veer from his course to avoid a head-on collision.

Skimming the island at 300 miles per hour only 50 feet above the muzzles of Jap weapons, Lt. Mullens' plane, equipped with a high speed camera in lieu of guns, clicked off pictures at the rate of three per second. During the three months campaign the squadron shot 1,170 negatives from which 17,170 pictures were printed. Marine, Naval, and Air Force units cooperating in the invasion then formulated plans for the attack after exhaustive study of the pictures...

Lt. Mullens actually had to dip under the nose of the approaching Japanese bomber in the incident mentioned in the Inland Broadcasting Company news brief. The Japanese nose gunner was quick and executed a few shots, but couldn't get his guns trained on Mullens before he was gone.

Lt. Mullens, and the other thirty pilots in the 28th Photo Reconnaissance Squadron, mission was to take intelligence photos for pre-invasion assessment or flying close in reconnaissance of the front lines. The photos allowed strategic planners to assess troop and supply movements and appraise changing enemy defense capabilities.

During the incident described in the radio report (to the right of the preceding photograph), the 28th was based at East Field on Saipan. The strategy was for the pilots to approach the target individually. About an hour out, around 200 miles distance away, the pilot would drop to just over the wave to avoid radar detection. The pilots would race across the island, cameras clicking, at 300 mph, and be gone before the enemy could get a decent shot at them.

Flying the front lines was much worse. If enemy defenses were particularly strong, fighter aircraft would precede the photographers at treetop level, strafing the landscape ahead to disorganize the defenders and suppress their fire. Fighter support was rare. Most of the time the photo pilots flew alone at tree top level parallel to the front, about 500 yards back of the line. In some cases the ground troops marked their forward positions with banners so the pilots knew just how close to come in. The photo runs continued throughout the battle, with the pictures developed and distributed to the officers in charge as soon as possible.

Mullens realized while on Okinawa, how lucky he was to be flying rather than part of the ground troops. At the end of the day he slept the night in a dry tent, well behind the lines, while the ground troops he flew over during the day spent day after day in monsoon rains, mired in deep mud and laying in fox holes half filled with water.

Marshall Mullens mustered out of the Army Air Forces on February 26, 1946, after flying 64 missions, 157 combat hours, and 560 flying hours. He achieved the rank of 1st Lieutenant and was awarded the Air Medal with 5 Oak Leaf Clusters. He spent another six months at the University of Nebraska and then transferred to Ohio State University. Ohio State University was one of the few schools that offered Aeronautical Engineering, a relatively new field. He graduated in June 1948. While at the university, Marshall met and eventually married Doris Helen Williams. They were wed on December 18, 1948.

In 1951, after working a few years at Wright-Patterson Air Force Base in Ohio, they moved to Muroc (now Edwards Air Force Base) in the Antelope Valley, California. There he worked as an engineer in flight research, including time on the B-52 project. He was employed at Edwards Air Force base for 28 years.

Marshall and his wife, Doris, had four children, all born in Lancaster, California. They had one daughter, Christine Louise, and three sons; Douglas Edward, Paul Arnold, and Craig Marshall Mullens. Marshall Mullens died March 15, 1998, in Lancaster, California. His ashes are interred at Joshua Memorial Park in Lancaster.

Plaque at the USAF Museum, Wright-Patterson AFB, Dayton, Ohio, honoring the 28th Photo Recon Squadron

James Wesley Mumaw was born May 26, 1916 in Lancaster, California, in a tank house behind the Mumaw Funeral Home. He was the son of Roy S. and Florence M. (Rector) Mumaw. In 1930, Roy Mumaw was working as a salesman for the Standard Oil Company in Lancaster to make ends meet during the depression, while also working with his father, Wesley S. Mumaw, in the undertaking business.

The Mumaw family came to California from Pennsylvania in the late 1890's. Wes's grandfather, Wesley S. Mumaw, was asked to be the town undertaker when they found he had helped his cousin as an undertaker back in Pennsylvania. He opened the doors of their home in 1913 to become the first "real" full-time undertaker in the Antelope Valley.

Wes graduated from AVJUHS in 1934. In 1936 he earned his embalmer's license. With generations of undertaking experience behind him, Wes knew that he could make a difference in the Armed Forces.

He enlisted in the U.S. Army in 1941, prior to the attack on Pearl Harbor. He went through training at Fort Ord in central California, and was on a transport ship bound for Hawaii when Pearl Harbor was attacked. The ship returned for an armed escort, then continued on to Hawaii.

Wes was the Morgue Master at Honolulu, Hawaii, for the Hawaii Army Mortuary. He helped lay out the process for retrieval, identification, and processing of the war dead. With his experience he was able to revamp the graves registration procedures for the Army. Wes was also stationed at Canton Island, in the Pacific, as part of the Quarter Master Unit. Canton Island was a major link in the U.S. military air supply ferry running from Hawaii to the South Pacific and Australia.

On the way to Canton, Wes was stationed for a short while at Christmas Island, also in the Pacific. He recalled to his son that the island was loaded with "armies" of red land crabs, some large, and some small. The crabs would march across the islands and would actually keep everyone awake at night as there were so many of them clanking together!

Wes was honorably discharged from the Army in 1945, at the rank of Tech Sergeant. After returning home, he went back into the family business. In 1957 he married Marian Hintz with the ceremony conducted in the chapel at the Mumaw Funeral Home in Lancaster. Also in 1957, Wes and Marian purchased the family undertaking business from Wes's father. The business continues on today owned and operated by their only child, James W. Mumaw. He is the father of Katrina M. Mumaw, currently at the U.S. Air Force Academy, and Nicolas W. Mumaw.

Wes never left Lancaster except for his time away during the war. He passed away October 25, 1986 at Antelope Valley Hospital, in Lancaster. He is buried in the History Garden section of Lancaster Cemetery next to his wife, Marian.

Walt Primmer & Wes Mumaw – Oahu 1943

MERVEN LELAND "FRITZ" NEIS

Merven Leland Neis was born January 27, 1921 in Hope, Dickinson County, Kansas, son of Clarence Herman and Emma (Luedeman) Neis. Merv had two sisters, Elaine and Marilyn, and one brother, Dean Neis.

In the late 1930's and early 1940's, the chances of war were imminent. Merv's father advised him to join the service and get trained before a war *did* break out. He enlisted in Denver, Colorado, in November 1940, with the Army Air Corps and started training as a radio operator. The pay was only $21.00 per month and with many men enlisting at the time, the training facilities were overcrowded, the food was substandard, and they were fitted with only fatigues, not standard uniforms.

After radio school, Merv was assigned to the 38th Bomb Group (Medium) in Jackson, Mississippi. When the war broke out, the 38th Bomb Group was made up of the 69th, 70th, and 71st Bombardment Squadrons. The group started out as, and were on paper, a "combat ready" group, but without any airplanes they were not ready to go to war.

In January 1942, the group was sent out to San Francisco, by troop trains where the combat crews were decided. The officers stayed in hotels, while the enlisted men were sent to Angel Island, in the San Francisco Bay. The ground personnel of the 38th were sent to Australia. At this time, Merv was part of the 71st Bombardment Squadron.

In April 1942, the crews were sent to Patterson Field, in Dayton, Ohio, so the pilots could learn to fly the B-26 aircraft. Merv was sent to gunnery school in Harlington, Texas. He was trained for about four weeks as a top turret gunner, then sent back to Ohio in May. After about two weeks, Merv was assigned to a flight crew and received orders to ship out to the South Pacific.

The crew flew to Hawaii, via Nebraska, Wyoming, Utah, Sacramento, and San Francisco. It took them four days to reach the west coast and Merv was worried with all the stops they had to make before crossing the ocean to Hawaii, that the B-26 would never make it to the South Pacific! The day they landed on the island of Oahu, the Battle of Midway broke out.

Merv's crew was ordered to stay on Oahu while two other planes were sent, by the Navy, to Ford Island where they were quickly refitted as torpedo bombers. The two planes were sent directly to Midway Island where they took part in the Battle of Midway. One was lost at the battle location while the other was shot-up so badly they had to crash land at Midway Island.

The 38th then moved on to the South Pacific, via Christmas Island, Canton and Fiji Island, landing at New Caledonia, just east of Australia. While stationed at New Caledonia, the 38th became part of the 13th Air Force, 69th Bombardment Squadron after arriving to find the 38th ground personnel stationed there. While en route to New Caledonia, the crew often times did not have any sleeping quarters when they landed. Portable cots were used for sleeping under the airplane at night to keep dry from the rain.

On New Year's Eve, 1942, Merv was sent on his first combat mission to New Georgia, Solomon Islands. He was scared, but had no problem with Japanese enemy fighters as the 38th had Naval escorts, along with several U.S. fighters to defend them. With B-25 aircraft now assigned to the group, the crews were strafing the jungles and airfields at dangerously low altitudes, and "skip-bombing" Japanese ships [dropping a bomb such that it literally skipped off the water like a stone, hitting its target from the side].

Merv spent time on Efate, an island in the New Hebrides chain, Guadalcanal, and Fiji. Around August 1943, the crew was assigned to the 311th Bomb Group in Fiji. He was sent back to the United States in September 1943 and spent the balance of the war in Greenville, South Carolina, as a Radio Operator Instructor. He received an Air Medal, Good Conduct Medal, and several Theater Medals during his service in World War II.

Merv married his sweetheart, Ruth Mae Emig on September 13, 1943, in Wichita, Sedgnick Co., Kansas. He was discharged from the Army in 1945, with his first child born the day after his service ended. After a few months, the family moved to the Los Angeles, California area where Merv found employment as a security guard with North American in Long Beach. In 1947 he was hired with the Los Angeles County Sheriff's Department where he continued working for 26 years until his retirement at the rank of Sergeant in 1973. Merv and his family moved to the Antelope Valley in 1961 when he was transferred with the Sheriff's Department. Merv and Ruth had three children together; Merven L., Jr., Robert D., and David C. Neis.

Serviceman Clark, Jim Orr, and Merv Neis "The Leather Jacket Brigade"
Sitting on a dugout in Guadalcanal 1943

Although Merv thought his life in the service was uneventful, he often wondered why he survived when many of his friends did not. He played an important part in winning the war and was proud of his service, just as his father before him, and his son since. Merv and his wife, Ruth, currently live in Quartz Hill, California.

FRANCIS F. (FRANK) NORTON

On December 2, 1921, in Flatrock, Crawford Co., Illinois, Francis F. Norton was born to Robert A. and Bessie R. (Fuller) Norton. The family moved to Lancaster, California in 1926. Frank attended Terra Bonita grammar school and graduated from AVJUHS in 1939.

Frank entered the service with the U.S. Army Coast Artillery on November 7, 1942 at Fort MacArthur, California. He was stationed at Camp Callan (a Coast Artillery training camp) and after thirteen weeks was sent to Camp Haan at Riverside, California, adjacent to March Army Air Field. Frank was sent for advanced training to Camp Irwin in the Mojave Desert, California. There, he was assigned to the 195th Anti-Aircraft Automatic Weapons Battalion (AAA AW) attached to the 2nd Armored Division, nicknamed "Hell on Wheels." This was the first Battalion to be trained with these weapons – 250/450 caliber machine guns and 40 millimeter machine guns attached on a ½ track turret, used to provide air cover for the 2nd Armored Division.

On December 2, 1943, Frank left Camp Irwin on a troop train, with their equipment, bound for the Port of Embarkation at Camp Kilmer, New Jersey. On Christmas Eve, 1943, the 195th boarded the *Isle de France* troop ship and departed in a convoy. The ship experienced engine trouble which in turn, started a fire and had to be towed back to port. One week later, the troops boarded the *Queen Elizabeth,* traveling alone, headed for Green Oak, Scotland. They arrived seven days later, and from there boarded another troop train bound for Tidworth Barracks in Hampshire, England. The 195th trained there until June 6, 1944 when they were sent to Omaha Beach on D-Day + 6. They settled in on the beach head for twenty-five days.

114

Frank next saw action during the breakthrough at St. Lo, France. Then, it was on to Belgium, Holland and into Germany. They were there until the Ardennes Campaign in December of 1944. Frank and the troops of the 195th drove 100 miles at night, in a blizzard, to meet the point of the German counter attack. They pushed the Germans back ten miles and were there until the end of the Ardennes Campaign in January, 1945.

From the Ardennes, they advanced to the Elbe River where they met the Russians. It had been agreed upon that the Russians would be allowed to take Berlin because the Allies felt they had suffered the most from the German armies. The 195th remained at the Elbe River until Berlin fell.

The next event was the Potsdam Conference where the 2nd Armored Division stood Honor Guard for President Harry Truman, British Prime Minister Winston Churchill and Soviet Premier Joseph Stalin. They met at an undamaged suburb of Berlin, July 17 through August 2, 1945, to discuss the details regarding the division of Germany and, among other things, to issue a proclamation demanding the unconditional surrender of Japan, or face "prompt and utter destruction." The conference plans also divided Berlin into four sections for occupation duty. The 2nd Armored Division occupied the American section until October, 1945, when they were relieved.

An interesting note to Frank's military service was in the final stages of the war, when his Company Commander was Captain Ralph J. Hallman. Ralph Hallman was Frank's American History teacher at AVJUHS class of 1939. Ralph went on to be a Professor of History at John Muir College in Pasadena, California.

Frank traveled back to Frankfurt, Germany where the troops turned in their equipment, boarded a troop train, and headed for Marseilles, France. There, they waited for thirty days, then boarded a liberty ship back to the United States. They landed at Camp Shanks, New York, where they caught planes and trains to get back to California.

On December 1, 1945, Frank was honorably discharged at Fort MacArthur, San Pedro, California. He received a Bronze Star Medal for his part in the April 12, 1945 capture of fifteen enemy officers, including one full Colonel and 265 German soldiers, in the town of Renie, Germany. Frank also received a Unit Citation (the Belgian Fourragere) from the Prince of Belgium, for participating in the liberation of Belgium and the liberation of the German counter-offensive in the Ardennes. This citation was the first award ever presented to a foreign Division.

On April 16, 1948, Frank married June Verlain Crall in Las Vegas, Nevada. They had two children together; a daughter, Lynn, and son, Steven Norton. They have three grandchildren; Crystal Ingledue, Brandon Wray, and Jarod Norton; five step-grandchildren, Ryan Vise, Brenda, Rachel, Joey and Terry Smith; and one great grandson, Dylan Ingledue.

For several years after the war, Frank worked for the Antelope Valley Hay Growers where he managed the alfalfa seed mill. In 1956, he went to work for Meadow Gold Dairies in Lancaster. Frank moved to Medford, Oregon in 1964, where he retired from Williams Bakery in 1983, and where he and June currently live.

Frank with damaged German fighter – shot down, but landed intact with a broken oil line.

Wilbur Ray Norton was born March 20, 1917 in Flatrock, Crawford Co., Illinois, the son of Robert A. and Bessie R. (Fuller) Norton. After the family moved to Lancaster in 1926, Ray attended Terra Bonita Grammar School and graduated from Antelope Valley Joint Union High School.

Ray enlisted in the U.S. Army in order to serve his country. He was inducted at Fort McArthur, California on March 28, 1941 at the age of 24. After basic training, he was sent to Fort Lewis, Washington to complete one year of rigorous combat training even though war had not yet been declared. Ray was assigned to the I Company, 163rd Regiment, 41st Infantry Division.

In March 1942, orders arrived for the 163rd to depart for overseas duty. At that time Ray was serving as a Second Cook. The 41st was sent to Australia first, then to Papua, Sanananda, and on to Buna and Gona, all in New Guinea in the South Pacific. The troops began arriving on the Sanananda-Buna front on December 30, 1942. By the end of 1943, the 163rd Regiment, 41st Infantry Division, had lost 102 men, 238 wounded, and 584 sick in action during the Sanananda-Buna Campaign.

Many of the men were ill with malaria due to the appalling living conditions on the tropical islands. The weather was hot and humid with bush and swamplands perfect breeding grounds for many tropical diseases. Food was scarce and the men ate whatever was available to them with most of the provisions coming from Australia. Ray was among the many servicemen who contracted malaria. He spent nine months in a malaria camp in Australia.

Papua, Sanananda area – "Home was never like this." An American in the early morning surveys what had been a dry area when he selected it for his camp the previous night. Inches of rain fell in the meantime.

This was only part of the hostile environment the servicemen had to endure during World War II in the South Pacific.

Photo no. 14254, D of I; courtesy of Ray Norton.

Some of the most vivid memories of the war for Ray come from the landing at the Zamboanga Peninsula of Mindinao Island, Philippines. He was aboard an LST (Landing Ship Transport) that conveyed supplies to the island troops. The crew was watching the pre-landing bombardment at Zamboanga. Along with the LST, there were destroyers, cruisers, and one battleship involved in the pre-invasion bombing. Aircraft were shelling the beach and further inland to where the Japanese troops were entrenched. The LST landed as part of a second wave of troops. They unloaded the supplies and returned to Mindinao Island where they reloaded the ship over a period of a few weeks. The ship returned to Zamboanga with the supplies for the troops.

After the ship was loaded, Ray was sent to Takloben on Luzon Island, Philippines, where he was among the men eligible for rotation back to the States. He was assigned to a Navy transport ship and returned to the U.S.

Ray also spent time in Byak, Netherlands, and in the East Indies during his tour of duty. When he came home he was on "temporary" duty in the U.S. While at home, the point system was initiated and he was discharged after spending 37 months overseas. On June 18, 1945, Ray was released from the Army having attained the rank of Staff Sergeant.

The 163rd Regiment, 41st Infantry Division, received the Presidential Unit Citation for the campaign at Sanananda, which was the first defeat the Japanese suffered in the war.

Ray went to work for Bandhauer's Market, in Tehachapi, California, (north of Lancaster) transporting groceries to Los Angeles. It was at Bandhaver's that Ray met his future bride, Edith "Dorothy" Painton. Dorothy was working in the meat department at the market.

Ray and Dorothy were married in December 1945, in Las Vegas, Clark Co., Nevada. After the wedding, Ray was employed by his brother in Buttonwillow, California, then went to work in road construction in Fresno and Merced, California, finally settling in Lancaster at the Union Oil bulk plant.

In 1950, they moved to Oregon where Ray returned to grocery work. He went into partnership with two other men and together they owned five grocery stores. He eventually owned his own store, but then sold it, and in 1975 returned to work, this time selling commercial real estate, mainly grocery stores. He retired in 1980 and moved to Boise, Idaho. Ray and Dorothy have two children; a son, Robert, and a daughter, Jane. Now retired, Ray and Dorothy are currently living in Boise, Idaho.

CARMEN D. OLAIZ

On January 2, 1921, Carmen Olaiz was born in Inglewood, Los Angeles Co., California, the daughter of Timoteo and Gregoria (Aizpeurrutia) Olaiz. She had one brother, Santos Olaiz. The Olaiz family came to the Antelope Valley in 1932 where Carmen graduated from AVJUHS in 1939, then from Antelope Valley Junior College in 1941.

Carmen was training to be a nurse at St. Vincent's Hospital in Los Angeles, California, when she heard the news about the attack on Pearl Harbor, December 7, 1941. Her training covered three years of living, working and studying in the hospital – including every phase, from kitchen (nutrition) to the morgue. From her graduating class of 23 students, only eleven finished with a Registered Nurse (RN) degree. Out of the eleven RN's, six of them volunteered for military duty in the Army Nurse Corps.

Carmen enlisted in the Army Nurse Corps in February of 1944, in order to serve her country by aiding the sick and wounded soldiers. Basic training started at Fort Lewis, Washington where Carmen was sent on bivouac (an outdoor camp with tents). The training began with following a Sergeant, marching in the woods. They dug fox holes and set up for a field hospital; were fitted with gas masks and went through a gas chamber with them on, then had to take the masks off for two minutes - carrying a tent, canteen, shovel and helmet while going through the chamber.

During her first days as nurse with the Ninth Service Command, Carmen was issued her uniform and sent to a hospital ward with 40 patients. After receiving orders from the Medical Doctor, she went to work. After boot camp, Carmen boarded a troop train and was sent to Madigan General Hospital in Tacoma, Washington where her first job assignment was caring for soldiers with all types of combat injuries. She spent much of her time traveling all across the U.S. on troop trains that had been converted to moving hospitals with 14 men to a car. The soldiers were flown to a port then transferred to a train with their destination being a hospital nearest to their home.

The nights were extremely difficult for Carmen. She dealt with men who had horrible nightmares and injuries. She had bandages to change and medications to dispense along with consoling the men. The patients who had just arrived back from Prisoner of War camps were grateful for any word from her or just a touch, to help them through until they arrived home. Each nurse had one Sergeant Medic to help and even soldiers, who were able, helped them through the long days and nights.

Carmen feels the war taught her to be more compassionate for anyone in her care and also to be more organized. She was honorably discharged at the rank of 2nd Lieutenant in July of 1946, after two years of service.

On July 6, 1946, Carmen married Edwin E. Wasil in Tacoma, Washington. Edwin was in the Army Air Corps and had served as a fighter pilot on a P-38, "*Mama's Boy*," and a P-51, "*Mama's Boy II*" while overseas with the 20th Fighter Group in Kingscliffe, England. Carmen and Edwin had two children together; a daughter, Rita, and son, Gregory E. Wasil.

Carmen, far left, February 1945, in field gear

After the war, Carmen traveled and went to work as a Registered Nurse in an ex-military hospital. She worked at Harbor General Hospital near Los Angeles, California; she worked as a school nurse; and administered first aid while she was employed in the motion picture industry. She made many friends while in the service and still keeps in touch with them today. Carmen joined the American Legion, "Women in Military" organization to also keep in touch with nurses who served during the war.

Carmen and her husband, Edwin, currently live in Rancho Palos Verdes, California. She continues to stay in contact with the many friends she made while living in the Antelope Valley.

Lt. Olaiz, 1945, Fort Lewis Surgery Ward

St. Louis, Missouri – troop train stop

On October 28, 1922, Edward Lee Patterson was born in Long Beach, Los Angeles Co., California, the twin son of Leslie J. and Etta May (Wilson) Patterson. Edward's twin brother was Paul Jean Patterson. In 1920, Leslie and Etta May were living in Long Beach where Leslie was employed as a machinist in a factory. The Patterson family moved to the Antelope Valley in 1932 and settled in the Littlerock area.

Edward graduated from AVJUHS in 1941. While attending high school he played basketball, football, ran track, and was a member of Stamp Club and the Boys' League. He was a Letterman in his junior year.

After graduating from high school, Edward entered the Army Air Forces. In July 1944, he was stationed at Westover Field, Massachusetts. Edward was a co-pilot, with the rank of Flight Officer, assigned to the 8th Air Force, 852nd Bombardment Squadron, 491st Bombardment Group (H), nicknamed "The Ringmasters." After training in Savannah, Georgia and at the Army Air Base in Charleston, South Carolina, he left for England in October 1944, and arrived at North Pickenham Airfield in Norfolk, England, in early November.

Edward became good friends with 1st Lieutenant Andy T. Wilson, pilot and crew leader of their B-24 Liberator, *The Green Hornet.* During his time in the service, Andy Wilson wrote home to his wife, Betty, nearly every day, expressing his love for her and keeping her informed of the daily events in his life away from home. Upon meeting his crew in July of 1944, Andy told her, "I have a pretty good bunch of boys. My co-pilot (Edward) seems a little bashful." This "bashfulness" would change as throughout their time in the U.S. and England, Andy and Edward enjoyed watching several movies together, visited the local pubs, listened to "good American swing records in the clubs", and were entertained by playing the occasional friendly poker game in-between flying on their dangerous bombing missions.

Andy described their living quarters when they first arrived on November 8, 1944 at North Pickenham Airfield, "We live in tin huts with ten officers in each hut. The stove, which is in the center of the room (or rather, hut) is about the size of a large (pregnant) stove pipe and is 2 feet high. Last p.m. was really cold but it is surely colder here. In fact, we use 4-5 blankets on our beds. The amount of heat is small, but I feel lucky in having what we have."

After they arrived in England, Edward and the crew went through more training with practice in target identification, communications and other ground school subjects. In mid-November, they began with formation checks and flying practice missions. They flew their first combat mission in December 1944.

In March of 1945, the 491st Bomb Group flew twenty-six missions – more than any month since June 1944. They were responsible for bombing marshalling yards, airfields, oil refineries, an armament factory in Berlin, a tank plant, and the railroad viaduct at Bielfield. They were also responsible for the attacks on Naval installations at Wilhelmshavaen and Kiel, Neuburg's jet aircraft assembly plant, and the headquarters of the German General Staff at Zossen. Not every plane in the Group flew every mission, therefore, crew mission counts did not necessarily match the Group mission counts over any given period.

On the morning of March 24, 1945, Edward and the crew of the *"Green Hornet"* took off from North Pickenham on a low-level re-supply drop to the U.S. and British forces near Wesel, Germany. This was their 23rd mission. The British troops had parachuted and landed gliders earlier in the day to secure a crossing of the Rhine River. Since this was a low-level mission, the supply drop was made from an altitude of 200-400 feet. The German Army was waiting for them and began firing at the B-24. First Lieutenant Andy Wilson reported his aircraft was severely damaged by ground fire and he was going to crash-land approximately ten miles west of the Rhine River.

No contact was made with the crew after that radio call. All nine crew members onboard the *"Green Hornet"* were reported as Missing in Action. The following is an excerpt from a letter written by U.S. Army Brigadier General Leon W. Johnson to Mrs. Sutcliffe, wife of crew member Technical Sergeant Charles B. Sutcliffe, dated June 11, 1946, over a year after the report of the crash:

"...the B-24 (Liberator) bomber departed from North Pickenham, England on a mission to re-supply the 17th Airborne Division which landed near Wesel, Germany by parachute and glider a few hours earlier. The flight was made at an altitude of 200 feet above the terrain on a heading of approximately 180°. This unusually low altitude was necessary to prevent the supply bundles from falling into the hands of the enemy on a bitterly contested battlefield. The success of this mission was demonstrated by the fact that over ninety percent of the supplies fell in the American zone, thus lending support to our troops in the speedy capture of the Ruhr industrial area and greatly reducing the number of American casualties.

As the B-24s dropped their bundles, they encountered very intense ground fire from machine guns and rifles as well as some small caliber anti-aircraft fire. The plane sustained damage, fell to the earth, and was completely destroyed. All the occupants of the plane were killed. In view of the circumstances, it is reasonable to presume that death came instantly for all members of the crew.

Identification of all the occupants of the plane was not possible immediately following the crash which explains why several members of the crew were buried as unknowns and were not reported as killed in action until Graves Registration Units had completed a thorough investigation. Many casualties occurred in the area in which your husband's plane crashed which made it difficult to identify each crew member unless his identification tag was found on his body...

...May I assure you that the personnel of the Army Air Forces share the sorrow caused by the untimely passing of Sergeant Sutcliffe."

Mrs. Patterson had hoped that her son would be found alive and return home. She worried about her son, Paul, away in the service with the Army, stationed in the Pacific. Her husband, Leslie, had also recently passed away in February 1945. She kept in contact with the families of the crew, and developed a close relationship with Andy Wilson's wife, Betty, and infant son Andy, born while his father was overseas. In the closing from a letter written by Mrs. Patterson to Betty, dated October 26, 1945, she states:

"They say time heals, but I think time has lost her power in this case. I think I will stop now and write to Paul who is still in Japan. Sunday, the 28th is my boys 23rd birthday."

Before Edward was killed, he had applied for his commission as Second Lieutenant and had passed the required physical. He was awarded the commission, posthumously. His remains were buried in the Netherlands American Cemetery, Margraten, Netherlands, Plot L, Row 17, Grave 10. Edward was awarded the Air Medal with two Oak Leaf Clusters, the Purple Heart Medal and numerous other awards.

Edward Patterson, back row, far left with unidentified crew. The photo was probably taken by Andy Wilson in England. Two rolls of film went undeveloped until 2003, when son Andy found them in his father's footlocker and had them developed.

Crew of the "Green Hornet", undated. Edward Patterson, kneeling on the left, behind Andy Wilson in front row with cigarette. Other crew members are not identified. The crew included Navigator James Conway (not on the mission of March 24, 1945), Bombardier Charles Goodacre, Engineer Charles Sutcliffe, Radioman Martin Cuff, Gunners Delbert Carr, Charles McKinney, Kenneth Mann and Harold Gardner. Photo courtesy of Allan Blue and the 491st Bomb Group Association.

Air Medal

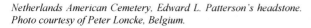

Netherlands American Cemetery, Edward L. Patterson's headstone. Photo courtesy of Peter Loncke, Belgium.

PAUL JEAN PATTERSON

Paul Jean Patterson was born October 28, 1922 in Long Beach, Los Angeles Co., California, the twin son of Leslie J. and Etta May (Wilson) Patterson. Paul's twin brother was Edward Lee Patterson. The Patterson family came to the Antelope Valley in 1932, where they settled in the Littlerock area.

Paul graduated from AVJUHS in 1941. While attending high school, Paul played basketball and football; was on the track team, and a member of the Lettermen, Stamp Club and the Boys' League.

He was working at a shipyard in San Pedro, California, when he heard about the attack on Pearl Harbor. Paul felt it was his duty to join the service and enlisted in the United States Army on August 31, 1944.

Basic training was hectic and after completion of training as a rifleman, and with his experience as a carpenter, he was shipped off to the Philippines attached to the 836th Engineer Battalion (Aviation), "Americal" Division. His training earned him a medal as a Sharpshooter with an M-1 Garand rifle.

Paul saw duty on the Philippine Islands and Japan. He was honorably discharged on June 16, 1946, after "1 year, 9 months and 5 days." For his time spent in service to his country, Paul received the following awards: the Asiatic-Pacific Campaign Medal; American Campaign Medal; World War II Victory Medal; and the Good Conduct Medal.

In the days following his discharge, Paul returned home to the Antelope Valley where he attended Antelope Valley Junior College under the G.I. Bill. He was a self-employed fruit grower (peaches) and continued in that profession until his retirement. Paul joined the American Legion organization after the war.

On June 4, 1949, Paul married Norma Joyce Bullock, in Littlerock, Los Angeles Co., California. They had three children; two sons, Dan Edward and Mark Paul; and a daughter, Jill Maria Patterson. Paul and Norma are retired and live in Fair Oaks, California, a suburb of Sacramento.

FOSTER DEVON PHEBUS

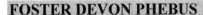

On May 4, 1924, Foster Devon Phebus was born in Tippecanoe, Marshall Co., Illinois, the son of Howard and Orpa (Harley) Phebus, both from Indiana. Foster had three siblings: two brothers, John and Max, and one sister, Kate. In 1930, the Phebus family was living in Tippecanoe with Howard self-employed as a farmer. Foster attended Tippecanoe High School in Indiana, and graduated in 1942.

Foster was drafted into the United States Army March 8, 1943. Basic training was spent in Texas where it was extremely hot and dusty, nothing like his home in Indiana. After basic training, Foster was sent for duty in Africa with a mortar squadron attached to the 34th Infantry Division "Red Bull", 168th Regiment, Company I. This Division would receive more Medal of Honor decorations and would see more days in combat than any other U. S. division during the war.

As a Light Mortar Crewman, Foster's job was to "set-up, aim, and fire a 60-mm mortar to place toxic or explosive shells upon enemy positions." He would "emplace mortar and sight in on the aiming stake, adjust the mortar for elevation and deflection, and fire the weapon by dropping a shell into the mortar to strike the firing pin."

Foster would experience and endure more than any man should have to during the war. He relived some memories from that time:

"Combat was hell. I lost many friends who were killed or wounded. One thing I won't forget was when I was in combat, one of our Lieutenants got hit in the leg and the Sergeant asked me to get two people and take him back to the aid station. They gave me a white flag and told me to hold the flag high and pray. We got back to the aid station o.k.. One of the letter carriers had received some mail from home and was sitting on a dirt bank when the Germans threw in a shell. I looked up and saw him get up and then fall. He was hit in the spinal cord and probably never knew what hit him.

I went into combat in September of 1943 in Italy. I was in combat for 14 months until I got wounded – it was near the Po Valley (below the northern Apennines, in Germany). I was wounded severely – lost my right leg and my left leg was badly broken, plus I had many, many other wounds. I came back to the States on Christmas day."

On February 20, 1946, Foster was honorably discharged from the U.S. Army at the rank of Private, 1st Class. He was at Lawson General Hospital in Atlanta, Georgia, recovering from his wounds. Foster was awarded the Purple Heart; a Bronze Star; Combat Infantry Badge; European Theater Ribbon with 3 Battle Stars; World War II Victory Medal; Good Conduct Ribbon; and numerous other ribbons and decorations. Foster was extremely happy the day of his discharge because, at times he thought he never would return home.

In the days and weeks following his return home, Foster spent time recuperating and healing from his combat wounds. On December 6, 1947, he married Portia Radke in South Bend, St. Joseph Co., Indiana. They had two children, David and Diane Phebus. Foster attended business school, supported by the G.I. Bill, in South Bend, Indiana which helped him secure a job with a finance company as an accountant. He made many lasting friendships during the war and continued to keep in contact with several of his buddies. He joined the Disabled American Veterans and the American Legion after moving to the Antelope Valley in 1950.

The military changed his life, Foster recalled, "When I went into the service I was a farmer. When I came out I went into business school and I became an accountant." He felt that "We should avoid war if at all possible." Foster passed away on February 17, 2004 in Lancaster, at the age of 79.

WILLIAM RICHARD "BILL" PROTEAU

William Richard Proteau was born January 23, 1920, in Thompsonville, Windham Co., Connecticut. He was the son of William Henry and Jane Cecelia (Landry) Proteau, both of French-Canadian descent. Bill had two siblings, Jane and Gilbert Proteau, both born in West Virginia. In 1930, elder William was working as an electrician, with the family living in Connecticut. Bill's father would later go on to do engineering work at the Electric Boat Company in Groton, Connecticut. He helped build the Submarine Base in Enniskillen, Ireland for World War II.

In 1936, Bill quit high school and enlisted as a Private in the Connecticut National Guard (CNG). Shortly before reporting for duty, Bill had appendicitis which delayed his reporting to the Guard. On May 2, 1939, Bill's group, the 118th Quartermaster Regiment, Co. F, was called up and the Regiment was mobilized to start preparing for war. On February 24, 1941, Bill was ordered into Federal Service as a member of the Connecticut National Guard. Bill was sent to Camp Blanding, Florida, where the Unit restored the Camp and built facilities for the troops who would begin training there.

The Regiment then moved to Camp Shelby, Mississippi. There, Bill went into the Aviation Cadet program where he was trained in the North American T-6 Texan and the Martin B-13 airplane.

Bill took part in the Air Offensive in Europe beginning in July of 1942. At the close of 1942, he was sent to Harlingen Army Gunnery School in Harlingen, Texas, where he completed Aerial Gunnery School with the Army Air Corps. In 1943, Bill completed Aircraft Armament school, and in January, 1944, he was sent to the European Theater of Operations with the 458th Bombardment Group (Heavy) at Horsham St. Faith Airfield, Norwich, England. The 458th helped prepare for the Invasion of Normandy by striking gun batteries and airfields in France. They also attacked enemy airfields in Germany to assist the Allied assault across the Rhine.

Bill was assigned duty as an aerial gunner on a B-24, attached to the 8th Air Force, flying on bombing missions over France and Germany. He participated in one of many memorable missions during the war - the bombing of the Peenemunde Rocket Research Laboratory near the Baltic Sea in northern Germany. Peenemunde was the location where the German V-1 Buzz Bomb and the V-2 Rockets and their launching rails were developed. Werner von Braun was one of the infamous rocket researchers using this facility.

This bombing mission had an almost immediate reaction from the Germans. After Bill's eight hour mission, he and the crew were completely surprised by the attack of two German twin-engine planes that followed their B-24 bomber back to England. The German planes strafed the B-24, just as it was landing. The right engine exploded into flames, and the bomber crash landed on the runway. Bill jumped out of the plane as it was rolling, smashing both his ankles. In spite of his injuries, Bill ran off the landing field to the nearest building, which turned out to be a pub. The Military Police found him there, being tended by the local citizens.

After he had flown 10 missions, Bill was on a ship bound for Germany when he heard the news about the war ending. He was on his way to Germany to help "clean up the mess." Bill was stationed at a P.O.W. Camp after the war and on October 21, 1945 was honorably discharged at the rank of Sergeant from the Army Air Corps and from the Connecticut National Guard. The discharge order was officially signed on November 2, 1945.

B-17 Crew – Bill Proteau, 2nd from left

Not satisfied with mundane civilian life, Bill rejoined the National Guard. He was called back to action in 1951 and was sent to Armament School. He served as a BB Stacker [weapons loader on an aircraft] and was sent to Korea on July 1, 1952, only to be evacuated back to the United States, to a hospital, with a parasite infection.

From May, 1952 through April, 1953, Bill was on combat duty in the Korea Summer-Fall and the Third Korean Winter effort with the Far East Air Forces. He was sent to Lackland Air Force Base, in Texas, where he was in the Security Squadron serving two additional years after Korea. In 1954, Bill completed a Management Indoctrination Course at Lackland AFB.

Bill served two enlistments after Korea, re-enlisted again, then was transferred to Kelly Air Force Base in San Antonio, Texas. A tour of Vietnam, beginning in 1964, was his next assignment where he was sent to Bien Hoa, just northwest of Saigon. Bill was a Weapons Supervisor and Weapons Technician at Bien Hoa and Nha Trang Air Bases, flying in Secret missions on AC-47 Gunships, in charge of the SUU-11A mini-guns. The mini-gun could fire 3,000 or 6,000 rounds per minute.

The final assignment for Bill was at Lowry Air Force Base, Colorado, where he retired after over 30 years of service and 148 missions. He was honorably discharged from active duty at the rank of Tech Sergeant on October 31, 1969 and retired on November 1, 1969. For his service in World War II, Korea and Vietnam, Bill received the following awards: Air Medal with two Oak Leaf Clusters; European-African-Middle Eastern Campaign Medal; American Campaign Medal; World War II Victory Medal; Good Conduct Medal, Army and Air Force, with five Loops; American Defense Service Medal; National Defense Service Medal; Korean Service Medal; Republic of Korea Presidential Unit Citation; United Nations Service Medal; Vietnam Service Medal; Air Force Commendation Medal; Vietnam Gallantry Cross with Palm; Air Force Longevity Service Award Ribbon; Small Arms Expert Marksmanship Ribbon.

The next stop for Bill was in Arizona where he was employed as a facility inspector for the Arizona Veterans Service. After three years there, he worked at a local sporting goods store as a gunsmith. As a hobby, Bill created beautiful silver jewelry set with turquoise, obsidian, ironwood and opal, commanding high prices for his work. Bill married Letha June Cadwalleder, and together they had three children; two daughters, Jeanne and Mazelle; and one son, Guy Proteau. They later divorced in 1963. Bill moved to the Antelope Valley in 1999, then to Barstow, and is now residing in San Diego, California.

CHARLES PEARCE "CHARLIE" RADER

On November 2, 1920, Charles Pearce Rader was born in Lancaster, Los Angeles Co., California, the son of Jason I. and Leona (Pearce) Rader, both from Missouri. The Rader family moved to the Antelope Valley around 1910. Jason was an alfalfa farmer, and he and Leona were the parents of three children; two sons, Charles and Richard; and one daughter, Nola Rader.

Charlie graduated from AVJUHS in 1939, and on November 30, 1941, married Mildred Mills, daughter of Charles and Ida (Dunn) Mills. They were married in Las Vegas, Clark Co., Nevada. The next week, Charlie was at his wedding reception when he heard the news about Pearl Harbor.

On August 26, 1942, Charlie was drafted into the U.S. Army Air Corps. He was inducted at Fort MacArthur in San Pedro, California and shipped off to basic training in Texas. Training camp was "early up – late to bed, total confusion and shots, lots of marching, running and drilling." After basic training, Charlie was sent to Sheppard Field, near Wichita, Texas, to Aviation Mechanics School. From there he went to Willow Run, Michigan to B-24 School. Ford Motors built the B-24 Liberators at Willow Run. After B-24 School, it was on to Harlingen Army Gunnery School in Harlingen, Texas.

The next stop would be at San Antonio Aviation Cadet Center for classification. He was then sent to Tampa, Florida, where he was assigned to a crew with the 88th Bombardment Group, and sent for B-17 overseas training at Avon Park Army Airfield, Avon, Florida. Charlie landed in Wales, then arrived at Duncan Hall, near London, England, on September 5, 1944. His next assignment was with the 15th Air

Force, 483rd Bombardment Group (Heavy), 840th Bombardment Squadron, "Rum Hounds" in Foggia, Italy.

His first job assignment was as an Engineer and Top Turret Gunner on a B-17. The sleeping quarters were tents for almost a year in Foggia. From October 12, 1944 to December 17, 1944, Charlie would fly on 10 missions, from Bologna, Italy; Skoda, Czechoslovakia on October 6; to the Mooshierbaum oil refinery in Austria on November 6; and the oil refinery at Blechhammer, Germany on December 17, 1944.

December 18, 1944, started out as another mission day, the 11th mission, with the crew bound for Odertal, Germany to bomb oil refineries and storage installations. While over the target area, Charlie's B-17 was under attack by German aircraft. They were hit hard, and on the way down were attacked again with anti-aircraft fire from below. What transpired during this time is best told in the Silver Star Citation Award narrative:

"As part of the strategic campaign of the Fifteenth Air Force to destroy sources of enemy oil supply, a formation of B-17 type aircraft was dispatched on 18 December 1944 by the 483rd Bombardment Group (Heavy) to attack and destroy vitally important enemy oil refinery and storage installations at Odertal, Germany. Technical Sergeant Charles P. Rader participated in this mission as aerial engineer-top turret gunner on a B-17 type aircraft.

In the target area, Sergeant Rader's aircraft was aggressively attacked by enemy fighter type aircraft. On the first pass made by the enemy aircraft, shellfire struck Sgt. Rader's top turret, shattering the plexiglass and severely wounding him about his head, shoulders, and arms. Shards of plexiglass and shell splinters and fragments became imbedded in his face and neck, causing him to bleed freely. In addition, the terrific concentration of enemy machine gun and cannon firepower severely damaged the number one, two, and four engines, destroyed the oxygen system from the waist forward, severed the aileron controls, destroyed the pilot's controls, shot out the nose turret, seriously wounded the navigator, shattered the plexiglass in the cockpit enclosure and almost completely destroyed the instrument panel.

Despite the severe pain from his wounds, Sergeant Rader steadfastly remained in his battered turret, refusing proffered first aid and manning his guns until the enemy was driven off. Although his face was covered with congealed blood and a shell splinter directly beneath one eye seriously impaired his vision, Sergeant Rader made a complete check of his badly crippled aircraft for battle damage, secured an emergency oxygen supply for the crew and then took a position on the flight deck behind the pilot, who was now flying from the copilot position, as only those controls were operating.

The three damaged engines were consuming fuel at an exorbitant rate and throughout the flight, Sergeant Rader kept a constant check on the rapidly dwindling fuel supply and on the damaged engines. Twice he transferred fuel in order to keep his almost unworthy aircraft in flight. As the aircraft was alone

and unescorted over enemy territory, he kept an alert lookout and instructed his gunners to do likewise, for another attempted attack by enemy fighter aircraft.

Careful inspection of the aircraft convinced Sergeant Rader that it could be flown for some time if necessary precautions were observed and he reassured his pilot that they could reach friendly territory and secure aid for the seriously wounded navigator. Despite the pain from his wounds and the additional hazard and discomfort from snow which came through the shattered plexiglass into the flight deck and coated the cockpit installations, Sergeant Rader gallantly fulfilled his duties as engineer. When the fuel supply became almost completely exhausted and it became evident that the aircraft could not reach home base, Sergeant Rader thoroughly briefed the crew on crash landing procedure and by his competent instructions, assisted the pilot in effecting a crash landing in a boulder-strewn field

without further injury to the crew. By his gallant heroism in the face of overwhelming enemy opposition, outstanding professional efficiency, superlative devotion to duty and determination to bring his crippled aircraft and crew safely back to base, Sergeant Rader, who has flown more than one hundred thirty (130) combat hours on sixteen (16) combat sorties, has reflected great credit upon himself and the Armed Forces of the United States."

The B-17 was flying at a high altitude when hit by the enemy fighters. The oxygen system was knocked out, so they only had a limited amount of oxygen and time to descend and try to land. Charlie had a "bail-out bottle" of oxygen he always carried with him. He gave his bottle to the pilot which provided him with oxygen to help maintain his breathing through the descent to around 12,000 feet. The navigator's papers were sucked out of the nose of the B-17 when the fighters attacked the plane. "They hit the nose area and it just looked like it was cut off," Charlie recalled. He saw the papers fly by him and knew that the navigator would have to rely on his knowledge and skills. At that time, they were in the clouds when the navigator started to try and plot their way back to base. They hit a clear spot in the sky and just at that time they were "peppered by anti-aircraft fire from below."

The B-17 crash landed in Yugoslavia, where Charlie was the first man out of the plane. "There were Tito's Partisans with guns - men and women - waiting for us. Luckily, they were on our side and took four of us to a small hospital. The nose gunner was in very bad shape." He was taken to the same hospital as Charlie and another crewman who spoke French. The rest of the crew was taken to a hide-out for safekeeping from the enemy.

They were taken to Zara, Yugoslavia where they were picked up by the British radar ship, *H.M.S. Columbo*. The French met them further on, and took them to another hospital. After three days, Charlie was released from the hospital. Charlie stayed in a "tent city," a place where people who were down and out stayed, to keep hidden. There, they had a bed and food to eat, but they were on the coast and needed to get back to their base at Foggia, Italy, in the middle section of the country. Charlie had met up with another gunner from a different Squadron, who had stayed at the same hospital.

They hitched a ride to an American base where they spoke to a Major who told them about a nearby base with "red-tailed" planes, forced down due to weather. Charlie and the gunner hitched a ride with this group, back home to their base in Foggia.

While in Italy, Charlie flew on 23 missions and was shot down twice. The second time was on his last mission, high over the Alps. They were sent to bomb a bridge in Maribor, Yugoslavia, and unbeknownst to the Squadron, the enemy had moved in "a bunch of guns along the railroad." More guns than they had expected. Luckily, none of the crew was injured. The war ended not long after his last bombing mission. Charlie felt "great" when he heard the war was over. He had enough points to go home, but was sent to Pisa, in northern Italy, where a base was set up to fly planes back and forth to Africa, carrying troops and Japanese prisoners, for three or four months until he could get on a plane heading for home.

Charlie's wife, Mildred, picked him up at Fort MacArthur, where he took a five day leave, then headed home to Lancaster. On September 18, 1945, he was honorably discharged from the 515th Air Service Group at the rank of Tech Sergeant. For his time spent in the Army Air Corps, Charlie received the following awards: the Silver Star; Air Medal with two Oak Leaf Clusters; Purple Heart Medal; American Campaign Medal; European-African-Middle Eastern Campaign Medal; Presidential Unit Citation; World War II Victory Medal; Good Conduct Medal.

Charlie and Mildred had two children together; two sons, Charles D. and Mark R. Rader. After the war, Charlie went to work for Bank of America for a short time. Shell Oil Company offered him a better deal, so he went to work for them as a salesman. At age 40, he made another career change. His wife had been involved with the automobile dealerships in the Valley and had urged him to get involved in the industry. He initially worked at Lancaster Ford from 1960-1966, then moved to a sales manager position with Pioneer Lincoln-Mercury, where his wife was employed. Charlie became a partner in the dealership which later became Pioneer Honda. He sold his partnership in the business and retired in 1993.

Charlie kept in contact with the many men he had met during the war. He joined the 483rd Bombardment Group (H) Association. Charlie and his wife, Mildred, live in Lancaster, California.

B-17's amidst the flak on a bombing mission. Photo courtesy of Charlie Rader.

DONALD D. "DON" RANDLEMAN

Donald R. Randleman was born on November 11, 1915, in Ft. Collins, Larimer Co., Colorado. He was the son of Dale and Eula Rachel (Horner) Randleman, from Nebraska and Colorado, respectively. By 1920, the Randleman family had relocated to Maricopa Co., Arizona, where Dale was a farmer. Don had one younger brother, Jack H., and a sister, Betty Randleman. Around 1923, Dale moved his family further out west to Ventura, California, where he purchased land and had his own walnut ranch.

Don graduated from Ventura High School in 1933, and moved with his family to the Antelope Valley in 1934. They settled on the east side of the Antelope Valley where Dale had an alfalfa farm. In 1935, Don graduated with a class of four students from Antelope Valley Junior College, which was then held at the AVJUHS campus. On October 8, 1938, Don married Winifred H. Nelson in Hollister, California.

Don was visiting his parents on their 200 acre ranch in Rosamond, California, when he heard about the attack on Pearl Harbor. He was drafted into the U.S. Army and inducted at Fort MacArthur, California. In November of 1943, Don was sent to basic training with the 102nd Infantry Division at the newly constructed Camp Swift, near Bastrop, Texas. While there, he endured the heat, humidity and bugs, along with strenuous physical training.

128

After basic training, the 102nd was sent to Fort Dix, near Trenton, New Jersey, with Don assigned for mortar training. Don was attached to Company "D" of the 406th Infantry Regiment. The Division staged at Camp Kilmer, New Jersey, in preparation for their departure from New York on September 12, 1944, bound for Cherbourg, France. They arrived in France on September 23, 1944 and crossed through Belgium October 31, 1944 and into Holland on the same date. The 406th entered into combat attached to the 30th Infantry Division, first at Linnich, Germany, on December 1, 1944, along the Roer River. Through freezing rain and snow, they crossed the Roer River on Febuary 23, 1945, and moved onward to clear Katzem by February 25. As the 406th moved, they were hit with heavy artillery, machine gun and small arms fire, killing and wounding many men along the way.

On March 17, 1945, Don was seriously wounded at Rhinehausen, on the banks of the Rhine River. He was air-lifted to Paris, France and then to a hospital in Coventry, England. Don was at the hospital on V-E Day. He was sent home on a hospital ship to New York Hospital, then by hospital train to Fort Lewis, Washington. He was given a 60 day convalescence furlough while recovering from his wounds. When Japan finally surrendered, he was on a plane going back to Fort Lewis, Washington, returning from his furlough. Don was given a disability discharge from the U.S. Army at the rank of Private, in October, 1945. He received the Purple Heart Medal; European Theater of Operations Campaign Medal with two Battle Stars; Sharpshooter Medal; Good Conduct Medal.

Donald and Winifred had two children together; a daughter, Christina L. and a son, Robert D. Randleman. After his discharge, Donald went back to his home in Santa Ana, California. He worked in Bakersfield for a while, then came back to the Antelope Valley where he went back to his roots, farming in Rosamond. After farming, Don secured at job at Edwards Air Force Base, working in the space industry.

Donald continued to suffer from back pains due to his injury in World War II. He joined the Disabled American Veterans organization and continued to keep in contact with the friends he made during the war. Don passed away February 28, 1962, in Lancaster, California. He is buried at Joshua Memorial Park and Cemetery in Lancaster. Winifred currently lives in Lancaster, and his daughter, Christina, in Rosamond.

JACK HORNER "JACKSON" RANDLEMAN

On February 14, 1917, Jack H. Randleman was born in Ft. Collins, Larimer Co., Colorado, to James Dale and Eula Rachel (Horner) Randleman. After moving to the Antelope Valley in 1934, Jack graduated from Antelope Valley Junior College in 1936.

Jack entered into the Army Air Corps where he was attached to the 376th Bombardment Group (Heavy), 513th Bombardment Squadron. He was stationed at San Pancrazio, Italy during the war. The 376th was stationed in Italy from November 1943 to April 1945.

Jack went through training and was commissioned at Hondo Air Force Base in Hondo, Texas. From there, Jack was sent to March Air Force Base, in Riverside, California, for further training with his crew as a navigator on a B-24 Liberator. The crew then flew to Italy where Jack would spend many hours as a navigator, seeing combat attacks of shipping and harbor installations in Libya, Tunisia, Sicily, and Italy, cutting off the enemy supply lines to Africa.

In 1943, the 376th was recognized as the first to arrive at the Rome Raid, the Ploesti raid, and the first over Wiener-Neustadt. Jack flew the required missions and returned stateside on March 17, 1945.

Jack married Martha "Pat" Pattison on December 19, 1942, in Santa Monica, Los Angeles Co., California. They had four children together; Dale P., Richard, Sue, and Scott Randleman.

Jack received numerous medals during the war including the Air Medal with several Battle Stars. He was discharged at the rank of 1st Lieutenant and returned to live in the Antelope Valley for 25 years working as an alfalfa rancher in Rosamond.

His brother, Donald, was in the Army Infantry during World War II, along with his brother-in-law, Jack Hawke, an Army Air Corps pilot and husband of his sister, Betty (Randleman) Hawke.

Jack passed away on July 3, 2003 in Mariposa, Mariposa Co., California. His wife, Pat, survives him and is currently living in Mariposa.

Jack and Pat Randleman – photo courtesy of Winifred Randleman

RALPH ANDERSON REECE

Ralph Anderson Reece was born November 25, 1921, in Atchison, Atchison Co., Kansas, son of Roy Anderson and Ruth (Harrington) Reece. In 1920, Roy, his wife Ruth, and daughter, Pearl Alice, were living in Atchison, Kansas, where Roy was employed as a clerk at the local bank. By 1930, the Reece family had grown to include three more children including Ralph, Florence Maxine, and Roy Clark Reece. They were living in Oklahoma City, Oklahoma, where Roy was employed as a salesman.

Ralph was employed at a service station in Foss, Oklahoma, when he heard the news about Pearl Harbor. He enlisted in the Army Air Corps with hopes of becoming a fighter pilot. Ralph's first weeks in the service were spent at Fort Sill, in Oklahoma, and Sheppard Field, in Texas. Ralph was sent to Eglin Field, Valparaiso, Florida, where he trained at the Aircraft Mechanics School.

As part of the Air Depot Group, Ralph was assigned to duty at Waller Field, Trinidad, British West Indies. He stayed in contact with his family by mail and saw several U.S.O. shows while stationed at Waller Field. Ralph was in Trinidad when he heard that the war had ended.

After his discharge from the Army Air Corps at the rank of Corporal, Ralph went to work in Hot Springs Arkansas. On August 1, 1945, he married Flora Belle Smith, a former Women's Air Service Pilot during World War II. They were married in Oklahoma City, Oklahoma. Together, they had three children; Connie Kay, Cheryl Suzanne and Russell Alan Reece. In 1946, Ralph and Flora Belle moved to California. Ralph and Flora Belle currently live in Lancaster, where Ralph retired after working for many years in the plumbing business.

CHARLES EDWARD ROGERS

On October 30, 1923, Charles Edward Rogers was born in Glendora, Los Angeles, Co., California, the second son born to Alonzo Harrison and Etta May (Testerman) Rogers, both from Missouri. The Rogers family moved to the Antelope Valley in 1936 from the Azusa area of Los Angeles Co., California. Charles had two older siblings; a brother, William, and sister, Ercell Rogers, a 1939 graduate of AVJUHS.

Charles graduated from AVJUHS in 1941 and attended Antelope Valley Junior College. While attending AVJUHS, Charles was hired to drive a school bus [due to a shortage of bus drivers] to pick up all the students in the Redmond area of the Antelope Valley, go to class, and then return the children home.

Charles was inducted into the Army Air Corps on November 1, 1943, and entered into active service on December 3, 1943. He was stationed at Hondo Army Air Field in Hondo, Texas, attached to the 2523rd Army Air Force Bomber Unit. On February 26, 1944, Charles held the rank of Staff Sergeant, when he was selected to attend Washington State College, in Pullman, Washington prior to an appointment as an Aviation Cadet in the Army Air Forces Flying Command. During that time he studied numerous academic subjects and received elementary flight training.

Charles was discharged as an Aviation Cadet on June 8, 1945, to accept the Commission of 2nd Lieutenant in the Army Air Corps. On June 9, 1945, Charles held the position of Navigator after completing his studies at Washington State College and navigation training at Williams Field in Higley, Arizona.

On November 20, 1948, Charles married Georgette Olive Farland in Pasadena, Los Angeles Co., California. They had two children together; Melvin and Karen Rogers.

After his discharge from the Army Air Corps, Charles completed his education at the University of Southern California School of Pharmacy, where he graduated with a pharmaceutical degree. He worked in the San Fernando Valley, California, for several years before moving to Dinuba, Tulare Co., California, where he had a farm and also worked as a pharmacist.

Charles passed away in Visalia, Tulare Co., California on June 17, 1993, at the age of 69. He was interred at Visalia District Cemetery in Tulare Co., California on June 21, 1993.

WILLIAM ALONZO "BILL" ROGERS

William A. Rogers was born in Los Angeles, California on August 26, 1918, the first born son of Alonzo Harrison and Etta May (Testerman) Rogers, both from Missouri. The Rogers family lived in the Azusa area of Los Angeles County where Alonzo was a citrus farmer. The family moved to the Antelope Valley in 1936 where Bill attended AVJUHS, graduating with the class of 1938. He also attended San Luis Obispo State College.

On his 24th birthday in 1942, Bill was inducted into the Army Air Corps, in Los Angeles, California. He was sent to Keesler Field in Biloxi, Mississippi, for 19 weeks of aircraft mechanics training, then on to Chanute Airfield for electrical training. On December 13, 1943, Bill was sent overseas, first to Cerignola, Italy, then to Lucera, Italy, attached to the 301st Bombardment Group (H), 32nd Bomb Squadron, 15th Air Force.

The 301st directed most of their attacks on oil centers, communications, and industrial areas in Italy, France, Germany, Poland, Czechoslovakia, Austria, Hungary, Yugoslavia and Greece. They received a Distinguished Unit Citation for a mission to Germany on February 25, 1944, bombing aircraft production centers at Regensberg. The 301st flew missions in support of ground forces in the Anzio and Cassio areas while supporting the invasion of Southern France, knocking out targets to assist the Russians in the Balkans, and aided the Allied forces in the drive through Po Valley.

Bill returned to the U.S. on July 25, 1945 and was discharged at Fort MacArthur, California on September 10, 1945. He had attained the rank of Staff Sergeant while working as an Airplane Electrical Specialist on a B-17 crew. He received the following awards for his service: the European-African-Middle Eastern Campaign Medal, with 8 Stars for Naples-Foggia, Northern France, Southern France, Air Combat-Balkans, North Appennines, Po Valley, Rhineland-Germany, Rome Arno; Presidential Distinguished Unit Badge for "outstanding performance of duty in armed conflict with the enemy." He received one for the bombing at Regensburg, Germany, and one for an attack on the aircraft factories at Wiener Neustadt, Austria. This award was the nation's highest organization award; Good Conduct Medal.

On September 4, 1946, Bill married Harriet Nordman in Los Angeles, California. Two daughters were born from this union; Linda Sue and Pamela Gail Rogers. After the war, Bill was employed at several electronic companies, and was working for Lockheed Aircraft Corporation in Palmdale, California, when he passed away. He was on his way to work at the Lockheed Plant, going through the gate on March 11, 1972, when he died of a sudden heart attack at the young age of fifty-three. Bill had previously worked at Lockheed in Burbank, California and had transferred to Palmdale in 1970. He was interred at Eternal Valley Memorial Park in Newhall, Los Angeles Co., California.

On April 21, 1925, Walter Emory Scates, Jr., was born in Santa Rosa, Sonoma Co., California. His parents were Walter Emory and Nellie Katherine (Kee) Scates, born in Topeka, Shawnee Co., Kansas and Bodega Bay, Sonoma Co., California, respectively. The Scates family moved from Sonoma Co. to the Antelope Valley around 1931. Walter had one sibling, a sister, Florence Elizabeth Scates.

Walter attended AVJUHS, and while a Junior at the high school, in May of 1943, barely 18 years old, he enlisted in the U.S. Army. He was sent to Camp Roberts, in California, for basic training, then on to Fort Ord, California, where he was deployed to the South Pacific attached to the 32nd Infantry "Red Arrow" Division, 126th Infantry Regiment, Co. D. He was a rifleman and heavy equipment operator. Walter received the Rifle Marksmanship badge, along with several qualification bars, for his training and expertise with several weapons.

Walter was sent straight into the heart of the Pacific war, soon crawling through the jungles of New Guinea, fighting the Japanese forces, trying to stop them from advancing and reaching Australia. On February 21, 1944, two months before his 19th birthday, Walter was killed in action at Saidor on the island of New Guinea. He was awarded the Purple Heart Medal.

Four and a half years later, Walter's body was brought back to the United States. On July 19, 1948, he was buried at the Golden Gate Cemetery in San Bruno, California. His sister, Florence (Scates) Pickelheimer lives in Mineola, Texas.

Purple Heart Medal

On May 12, 1920, Milton Schwartz was born in New York, New York, to Harry and Shirley (Blier) Schwartz. Milt had two siblings; a sister, Estelle, and a brother, Eugene Schwartz. The Schwartz family settled in California in 1923 and moved to the Antelope Valley in 1925. By 1930, Harry was employed as a livestock dealer, with the family living on Date Avenue in Lancaster.

Milt attended Lancaster Grammar School and graduated from AVJUHS in 1938. He graduated from AVJC in 1940. Milt was attending the University of California, Berkeley, when he heard the news about the attack on Pearl Harbor. Milt enlisted in the U.S. Army under the stipulation that he would be allowed to graduate from college before being inducted.

In March of 1943, Milt entered the Army Air Corps and was sent to Lincoln, Nebraska for basic pre-flight training. The recruits were taken to a firing range for rifle training in 21° below zero weather – freezing, with snow covering the ground all around them. While there, he learned to fly a small airplane before he was sent to Santa Ana, California to be a pilot.

In 1944, Milt was stationed at Fort Campbell, Kentucky. He had previously met his future wife, Betty Ehlers, while at a dance in Des Moines, Iowa, in 1943. The couple were married on November 16, 1944 at Fort Campbell, before Milt was sent overseas to the European Theater of Operations. In January, 1945 Milt was sent to Camp Myles Standish, a staging area near Boston, Massachusetts. He was assigned duty as a Liaison Officer for the 220th Armored Engineer Battalion, 20th Armored Division. The 20th Armored Division was one of the most traveled Divisions in Europe during World War II, and were known as the "Liberators" on their shoulder patch. The patch included a tank track, cannon, and a bolt of lightening.

The Division departed on February 6, 1945, arriving at Le Havre, France, on February 18th. After several weeks of preparation, the orders came through late in March, for the 20th Division to move. The troops encountered combat activity near the Rhine River in Germany in April of 1945. They swept across Southern Germany led by General Patton, and liberated the Concentration Camp of Dachau, near Munich, on April 29, 1945. The next day, the 20th attacked German Secret Service installations near Munich. In one day, they had moved over 50 miles, encountering resistance along the way, crossing three rivers, and capturing 1,200 prisoners.

Milt was in Salzburg, Germany when the 20th Division duties were completed in Europe. Along the way he was entertained by U.S.O. shows with Eddie Cantor, Bob Hope, and many more celebrities. Milt's diet consisted mainly of rations, as the mess kitchens were not set up in many of the areas during combat. He was in Lompoc, California, at Camp Cooke, preparing to leave for the invasion of Japan, when he heard the war was over. The Division was set to hit Japan on D-Day + 3.

In October, 1946, after four years of service, Milt was honorably discharged at the rank of 2nd Lieutenant. He was awarded the following decorations: European-African-Middle Eastern Theater Campaign Medal; Rhineland Campaign Ribbon; World War II Victory Medal; Good Conduct Medal.

After the war, Milt went back to school at U.C. Berkeley, where he graduated with a B.S. degree in Civil Engineering. He worked for the state of California as a Civil Engineer building bridges in northern California for seven years, then became a highway, bridge, and dam contractor for the next 50 years.

Milt and his wife, Betty, had two children together; two daughters, Cathleen and Carin Schwartz. Betty and Milt reside in Belmont, California, where they have lived for over 50 years.

Milt Schwartz, in doorway, opens PX #12, with enlisted men in Chemun area of Germany – May 1945.

ROBERT DALE "SCOTTY" SCOTT

Robert Dale Scott was born August 19, 1924 in Missouri, the son of Everett C. and Irene (Hood) Scott. The Scott family moved to the Antelope Valley between 1924 and 1930, where Everett earned a living as a farmer.

Dale graduated from AVJUHS with the class of 1942. Friend and classmate, Paul Wheeler, remembered Dale joining up with the Army Air Corps and training as a P-38 fighter pilot, attached to the 8th Air Force. He was transferred to the 9th Tactical Air Force where he piloted a P-47 aircraft.

When Eleanor Roosevelt visited Dale's P-38 base in France, the group commander selected Dale to fly Mrs. Roosevelt in a P-38 "piggy back." This special P-38 contained a bubble canopy located directly behind the main canopy, which allowed the passenger to ride along in place of the radio gear. She wanted to fly east to the U.S. Army front line, but the commander instructed Dale to only fly to within five miles of the combat zone, hoping the First Lady would not know the difference. Everything went well and Dale was very impressed with Mrs. Roosevelt and proud of the experience.

In 1945, while stationed in France, Dale met up with his high school friend, Cris Eliopulos. Cris was in Paris, in the Army, when he spotted his friend. They had a great time reminiscing about home while enjoying a drink on the Champs-Elysées, in Paris.

1st Lieutenant Robert Dale Scott passed away in Los Angeles Co., California on February 21, 1987. He is buried at the Riverside National Cemetery in Riverside Co., California.

On November 6, 1921, Robert Eugene Settle was born in Lancaster, California, the son of William Benjamin and Marian Ruth (Allen) Settle. Robert was the tenth of eleven children born to the couple. He attended Lancaster Grammar School and graduated from AVJUHS with the class of 1938. After graduating from high school, Robert attended Antelope Valley Junior College.

Robert enlisted in the Army Air Corps, early in 1941, before the attack on Pearl Harbor. He went through training at March Field, in Riverside, California, with actor Jimmy Stewart as his drill corporal. He was then sent to Mather Air Field in Sacramento, California, a center for pilot, navigation, and bombardier training. Robert graduated at Mather with Class 43B, as a navigator, with the rank of Lieutenant.

After graduating at Mather, Robert was sent to Davis-Monthan Army Air Field in Tucson, Arizona, an operational training base for B-18, B-24 and B-29 aircraft. In 1943, Robert was in Marietta, Georgia, getting ready to take the first B-29 "Superfortress" overseas, as the navigator. Bell-Atlanta Aircraft in Marietta was one of four corporations specified by the Army to produce the B-29's.

Robert was on his way to England with the B-29, then on to India, for duty in the China-Burma-India Theater of Operations. He flew to China with a troop carrier group attached to the 14th Air Force, nicknamed the "Flying Tigers." In May 1943, President Roosevelt ordered the original American Volunteer Group Flying Tigers organization constituted as the 14th Air Force. General Claire Chennault was recalled to active duty at the rank of Brigadier General, as commanding officer of the "China Air Task Force." Robert assumed the post of co-pilot on one memorable flight with Chennault piloting the aircraft.

The 14th Air Force conducted fighter and bomber operations along a five mile front from Chunking and Cheng Tu in the western part of China, to Indo China in the south. From the Tibetan Plateau in Burma and on to the China Sea and Formosa in eastern China, the Flying Tigers eventually halted the Japanese Air Force operations as World War II came to an end.

Robert went back to the United States near the end of 1945 and was assigned to the Pentagon as Protocol Officer for General Henry "Hap" Arnold, commander of the Army Air Forces. In 1948, Robert was sent to Army Language School at the Presidio of Monterey in California, to study the Russian language. In 1948 and 1949, he was at Fairchild Air Force Base in Spokane, Washington. While there, Robert was sent to Yokoda, Japan for the Korean War. During the Korean War he was a navigator on a B-36 bomber and also taught Russian to the B-36 crews.

The Air Force would be Robert's life for over 22 years, beginning in 1941 and ending with his retirement, at the rank of Lt. Colonel, as a Russian Analyst to the National Security Agency at Fort George G. Meade in Maryland, in 1963. From 1963 to 1976, Robert was employed as a civilian, with the Department of Defense, as an intelligence officer. During this time, he was sent to Okinawa, Japan, from 1967 to 1968. Robert served with the United States Government for over 36 years.

During the war, Robert met his wife, June Senkbeil, in Sacramento. Together they had three children; two daughters, Sandy and Roberta; and one son, Bruce Allen Settle. Bruce served in Vietnam with the U.S. Marine Corps where he received two Purple Heart Medals. Robert moved back to the Antelope Valley in 1986, to Rosamond, to be near his family. He was active in the Kern-Antelope Historical Society, along with his brother, Glen. Robert and June were also active in the Lancaster United Methodist Church and with the Rosamond Senior Citizens group.

Robert passed away on November 20, 1992 at the age of 71. He is interred at Joshua Memorial Park and Cemetery in Lancaster, California.

Robert Settle – Flying Tigers

LEWIS LONNIE "LUKE" SHOEMAKER

Lewis Lonnie Shoemaker was born July 18, 1923, in Kirksville, Adair Co., Missouri, the son of Oren W. and Mildred F. Shoemaker, both from Missouri. Lewis was working in St. Louis, Missouri, when he heard the news about the attack on Pearl Harbor.

Lewis was drafted into the U.S. Army in November, 1942, and sent to Jefferson Barracks in St. Louis Co., Missouri, for basic training. During basic training, Lewis remembered many long hours of orientation and assignments, along with regimented training, turning young men into soldiers. After basic training, Lewis was sent to Camp Phillips, near Salina, Kansas, for advanced training in the Army Infantry. After training in Kansas, he was sent to Murfreesboro, Tennessee, near Nashville, then to Fort Dix, New Jersey, and ultimately, to Camp Kilmer, New Jersey, for staging in preparation for overseas assignment.

Lewis shipped off to Europe onboard the *Queen Elizabeth I* troopship and landed in Glasgow, Scotland, where he boarded a troop train to a large replacement depot just outside of London. There, he was assigned to the 1st Army, Infantry Division, (known as the "Big Red One") with Company E, and sent to Swanage, Dorset, a coastal village in the south of England. In Swanage, the troops were billeted at the Grand Hotel. During their stay at the hotel, the troops were in training for the coastal landing assaults at Normandy, France, that they would be making in the upcoming weeks.

Lewis was a part of the D-Day invasion of Normandy by the Allies on June 6, 1944. His unit landed on Omaha Beach, which was the landing point where the most intense combat took place. This was the beach immortalized in the movie, "Saving Private Ryan". As Lewis expressed it, "Combat was hell".

On July 5, 1944, Lewis was injured in combat when he was hit by shrapnel. After a short recovery time due to his injuries, he was sent back to his unit. The 1st Infantry Division moved through Normandy, liberating Liege, Belgium, and pushed on to the German border, crossing through the Siegfried Line. During this time Lewis was promoted to Sergeant. They attacked the city of Aachen, Germany, and after several days of bitter fighting, the German commander surrendered on October 21, 1944. Lewis was severely injured in combat on November 11, 1944. He was hit by machine gun fire, resulting in a major leg injury, while in a battle just outside Cologne, Germany. He was evacuated back to England for surgery, then back to the United States for another ten months of hospitalization and rehabilitation.

Lewis was continuing to recover at the military hospital at Camp Carson, Colorado Springs, Colorado, when he heard the war was over. He was honorably discharged in September 1945, at Camp Carson. Lewis received the Purple Heart Medal, among other honors, for his service during the war.

After his discharge, Lewis returned to his parents home, continuing his recovery in addition to entering college in Kirksville, Missouri. On December 22, 1946, Lewis married Mary G. Fritsinger in Kirksville, Adair Co., Missouri. He completed his Bachelors Degree at Northeast Missouri State Teachers College [now Truman University], and graduated in May 1949.

Lewis, with Mary and two-year old son Paul, then headed immediately to California to look for a teaching job. He landed his first teaching job in Barstow, San Bernardino Co., California, where he stayed for five years. In June 1955, he accepted a position with the Antelope Valley Joint Union High School District and moved to Lancaster, Los Angeles Co., California. His second son, Mark, was born in Lancaster. Lewis taught at Antelope Valley High School first, then changed to Quartz Hill High School when it opened in 1964. There, he taught Boys Physical Education and Geography, and was an outstanding athletic coach.

Lewis joined the American Legion and the Disabled American Veterans organizations after the war. He thought that his time in the service gave him a "good, positive outlook on life and that discipline, respect, and patriotism were reinforced." However, the combat injury he suffered during the war, still affects his health and activities to this day. Lewis retired from teaching at Quartz Hill High School in June, 1983. Lewis and his wife, Mary, live in Lancaster, California.

FLORA BELLE SMITH

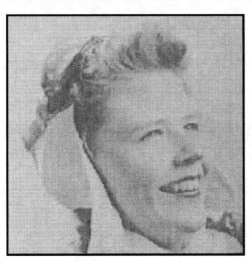

On October 21, 1924, in Sayre, Beckham Co., Oklahoma, Flora Belle Smith was born to Robert Jessie and Agnes (Duncan) Smith. Robert was born in Port, Washita Co., Oklahoma, and Agnes was born in Decatur, Wise Co., Texas. In 1930, the Smith family was living in Washita, Custer Co., Oklahoma. The family included one son, James Evan, and three daughters, Mary Lea, Flora Belle, and Agnes LaWanda Smith.

Flora Belle had always dreamed of flying, and she realized her dream by joining the Women's Air Service Pilots (WASP) in 1943. "Jackie Cochran put an ad in the newspaper requesting young women who were interested in flying, to sign up and help with the war effort," Flora Belle recalled. At this point, she had never flown and needed at least 35 hours to qualify for pilot training.

Flora Belle's brother, James, loaned her the money to pay for flying lessons and started her on the road to Sweetwater, Texas for WASP training.

At Avenger Field in Sweetwater, Texas, Flora Belle entered into Class 44-W-4. Out of the 98 women in her class who began the training, only 51 graduated. Fifty percent washed out of the program due to the rigorous physical training. For some, it was extremely tough waking up at 4:30 a.m. to be on the flight line, with marching, ground school, "white glove" inspections, and finally, the stress of flying.

Flora Belle soloed in a Fairchild PT-19 trainer. She had about six hours of flight time when she switched to the Stearman PT-17 biplane trainer. Next, Flora Belle flew the North American AT-6 fighter trainer [her favorite "sweet flying" airplane]. The training in the Vultee BT-13 was her least favorite time. The airplane vibrated and shook more than the other planes. It was used in instrument training for the pilots. After the BT-13 training, it was back to the AT-6, and in May of 1944, Flora Belle earned her wings.

After basic flight training, Flora Belle was sent to Foster Field in Victoria, Texas for her first assignment. At Foster Field, she was assigned to the Operations group, where she flew non-flying personnel to and from assignments. Next, Flora Belle was sent to Harlington, Texas. At Harlington, she learned to fly the Martin B-26 Marauder, towing artillery targets for gunnery school training. At Enid Air Base, in Enid, Oklahoma, Flora Belle's job included flying airplanes that had just been repaired. "We flew what they told us to fly, and did what they needed us to do, taking on the role of our nation's pilots at home, while they were overseas fighting the war."

Flora Belle concluded her military service with over 500 flight hours in several different airplanes. She was glad when the war came to an end, but saddened when the WASP were deactivated in 1944, and not militarized. On August 1, 1945, Flora Belle married Ralph Anderson Reece in Oklahoma City, Oklahoma. Together they had three children; Connie Kay, Cheryl Suzanne, and Russell Alan Reece. Ralph was a Colonel in the Army Air Corps stationed at Waller Field, Trinidad in the British West Indies during the war.

In 1946, Flora Belle and Ralph moved to California. She joined the WASP Fifinella group after the war, to keep in touch with her fellow pilots, and remains in contact with the many friends she made while in service. Fifinella, a spunky female gremlin, was the mascot logo designed by Walt Disney Studios and used by the WASP. Flora Belle remembered Jackie Cochran telling the WASP, "You have to be better than the men to keep in competition, but always be a lady."

Flora Belle and her husband, Ralph, are both retired and live in Lancaster, California.

ROY CLIFTON "CLIFF" SMITH, JR.

On October 14, 1922, Roy Clifton Smith, Jr. was born to Roy Clifton and Arva M. (Reetz) Smith, Sr. in Los Angeles, Los Angeles Co., California. In 1930, the family was living in Covina, Los Angeles Co., California, with Roy, Sr. employed as a foreman on a ranch. Along with Roy, Jr., the family included daughter, Shirley M. Smith, who would marry Navy veteran Charles "Cece" Ellison.

In 1938, Roy moved to the Antelope Valley and was living in Lancaster when he heard about the attack on Pearl Harbor. He enlisted in the Army Air Corps in 1942 and was a member of the Special Services Branch, putting on shows as a musician and drummer, entertaining the nation's troops.

Roy served at Muroc Army Air Field, (now Edwards Air Force Base), England, and other areas across Europe during World War II. He was overseas when the war ended.

After serving in the Army Air Corps for three years, Roy was honorably discharged in 1945. After the war, he worked for his father in the amusement and vending machine business and was married to Jean Rollo. They had one child together, a daughter, Lyndy Lane Smith.

Roy passed away in January, 1965, in Reno, Washoe Co., Nevada. He was buried at Oakdale Cemetery in Covina, Los Angeles Co., California.

SAMUEL QUINN "SAM" SMITH

Samuel Quinn Smith was born December 11, 1923 in Toledo, Lucas Co., Ohio, the son of John W. and Amy D. (Ball) Smith. John was born in New York, and Amy was a native of Ohio. In 1930, the Smith family was living in Toledo with John employed as an accountant. Sam had two younger sisters; Amy D. and Martha S. Smith.

Sam was in Toledo, Ohio, attending high school, when he heard the news about the bombing of Pearl Harbor. He was drafted into the U.S. Army and reported for induction on July 24, 1943. Sam was sent to Fort Benning, Georgia for Infantry training. After basic training, he was chosen to attend Eastern Kentucky Teachers College as part of the Army Specialized Training Program (ASTP). During World War II, the U.S. Army established the ASTP at colleges and universities in order to train soldiers in needed skills such as engineering, medicine, and languages. Sam studied engineering while in the ASTP until the program was cancelled.

Sam was assigned to the 62nd Armored Infantry Battalion, 14th Armored Division, known as the "Liberator," as a 60mm Mortar Gunner. The Division landed at La Malle, France on October 29, 1944. They spent nearly five months in France,

cutting off German escape routes while under attack. The 14th moved into Germany in March of 1945, entering into combat, then assigned to defensive positions. Back into combat, they crossed the Rhine River in April, proceeding under heavy German fire. Sam remembered his combat experience, behind enemy lines in Germany, as "a different world."

LIBERATOR

Sam was a patient at a hospital in Nancy, France, when he heard the war was over. He was honorably discharged at the rank of Private, 1ˢᵗ Class, in April, 1946. After the war, Sam attended the University of Toledo, in Ohio, supported by the G.I. Bill. He moved to California in 1950, where he secured a job as a Flight Test computer programmer with the U.S. Air Force, Civil Service.

Sam retired as a computer programmer in 1983, and currently lives at home in Lancaster, California.

App. not Req.

Prepare in Duplicate

Local Board No. 14   88
Lucas County   095
    JUL 14 1943   012
630 Main Street
Toledo, Ohio

(LOCAL BOARD DATE STAMP WITH CODE)

July 14, 1943
(Date of mailing)

ORDER TO REPORT FOR INDUCTION

The President of the United States,

To ____ SAMUEL _____ QUIN _____ SMITH ____
        (First name)   (Middle name)   (Last name)

Order No. 11118

GREETING:

Having submitted yourself to a local board composed of your neighbors for the purpose of determining your availability for training and service in the land or naval forces of the United States, you are hereby notified that you have now been selected for training and service therein.

You will, therefore, report to the local board named above at 630 Main St., Toledo, Ohio
                                                              (Place of reporting)

at 8:30 A. m., on the ____ 24th ____ day of ____ July ____, 193

(Hour of reporting)

BRING YOUR REGISTRATION AND CLASSIFICATION CARDS

This local board will furnish transportation to an induction station. You will there be examined, and, if accepted for training and service, you will then be inducted into the land or naval forces.

Persons reporting to the induction station in some instances may be rejected for physical or other reasons. It is well to keep this in mind in arranging your affairs, to prevent any undue hardship if you are rejected at the induction station. If you are employed, you should advise your employer of this notice and of the possibility that you may not be accepted at the induction station. Your employer can then be prepared to replace you if you are accepted, or to continue your employment if you are rejected.

Willful failure to report promptly to this local board at the hour and on the day named in this notice is a violation of the Selective Training and Service Act of 1940, as amended, and subjects the violator to fine and imprisonment.

If you are so far removed from your own local board that reporting in compliance with this order will be a serious hardship and you desire to report to a local board in the area of which you are now located, go immediately to that local board and make written request for transfer of your delivery for induction, taking this order with you.

H. A. Lederhaus
Member or clerk of the local board.

D. S. S. Form 150
(Revised 1-15-43)

U. S. GOVERNMENT PRINTING OFFICE   16—40871-2

Order to report for Induction

CARL EDWIN "COCKY/COWBOY" SNIDER

Carl Edwin Snider was born September 27, 1921 in Wapakoneta, Auglaize Co., Ohio, the son of Luther O. and Ethel E. (Lowry) Snider. Carl had two siblings; a brother, Glen W., and sister, Katharyn O. Snider.

Carl was drafted into the U.S. Army in June 1942, and inducted at Fort Hayes, Columbus, Ohio. He was sent to Fort Leonard Wood, Rolla, Missouri, where he trained to serve in the Army Corps of Engineers. In World War II, the engineering combat regiments and battalions supported the maneuvering forces by constructing roads and bridges, and also helped with mine warfare.

After training, Carl was on his way to the San Francisco Port of Embarkation, Fort McDowell, at Angel Island, where more than 300,000 soldiers were shipped to the Pacific Theater of Operations. Carl was attached to the 6th Infantry, 28th Battalion, Company B, 4th Platoon. The Battalion was deployed to Brisbane, Australia in support of the Southwest Pacific Expedition.

While in Australia, Carl became ill and was sent back to the United States. He was a patient at Hoff General Hospital, one of the leading Army hospitals in the United States, in Santa Barbara, California, when he received a medical discharge from the Army in September of 1943. Carl was discharged at the rank of Private, 1st Class. Among the awards he received was the Asiatic-Pacific Theater Campaign Medal.

Carl was married to Kathryn E. LaRue on April 16, 1942, just before he was drafted into the Army. They were married in Marion, Grant Co., Indiana. Together, they had three children; a son, Keith A., and two daughters, Kathy A. and Melanie S. Snider. In 1953, Carl and Kathryn sold nearly all of their possessions, loaded up the kids in the car, and started out from Criderville, Ohio, on an "adventure" in search of a better place to live and work. They headed to Florida, then South Dakota, to Washington, and then down the Pacific coast to the Los Angeles, California area. Carl was looking for a job in the aircraft industry when they settled in the Hawthorne area of Los Angeles County. Carl worked for several aircraft companies including Douglas Aircraft, where he was trained as a jig and fixture builder, Rohr, Northrop and Lockheed. Kathryn was employed by North American until she took a voluntary lay-off. Later, she secured a job with the Los Angeles County Probation Department, where she remained until retiring in 1991.

In 1969, Carl was transferred to the Antelope Valley with Lockheed Aircraft. After over twenty-five years with Lockheed and thirty-two years in the aerospace industry, Carl was almost ready for retirement when he passed away on October 22, 1985. He is buried at the Joshua Memorial Park and Cemetery in Lancaster. His wife, Kathryn, lives in Quartz Hill, California.

EGBERT G. "BERT" STANFORTH, JR.

Egbert G. "Bert" Stanforth was born January 28, 1920 in Philadelphia, Philadelphia Co., Pennsylvania, the son of Egbert G. and Ferol Stanforth. By 1930, the Stanforth family was living in Wabash, Tippecanoe Co., Indiana, with elder Egbert employed as an investment agent. Bert had one sister, Hilda Lena Stanforth.

Bert married Georgia on September 14, 1940 in St. Louis, Missouri. They had two children together; Michael and Jeffrey Stanforth. Bert joined the Army Air Corps and was stationed at Adak, Alaska. Adak was one of the most populated of the Aleutian Islands during World War II. Bert was honorably discharged from the Army Air Corps at the rank of Staff Sergeant.

Bert and his family moved to California in 1952. He passed away in Lancaster, California on February 1, 2000. He is buried at the Joshua Memorial Park and Cemetery in Lancaster.

On June 11, 1921, O. Milton "Milt" Stark was born in Goldthwaite, Mills Co., Texas, the son of Nile Westley and Charlotte M. (Ince) Stark, both from Texas. The Stark family moved to California in 1923, settling in the Wilsona area of the Antelope Valley. Milt had two siblings; a sister, Zanita, and brother, Norman Eugene Stark. Milt graduated from AVJUHS with the class of 1938, and attended Antelope Valley Junior College, graduating in 1940. He worked for Lockheed Aircraft building the P-38 after graduating from college.

Milt was at his parent's home in east Palmdale, when the news about the attack on Pearl Harbor was announced. He enlisted in the Army Air Corps rather than taking a chance on being drafted. Milt rode a troop train from Los Angeles, California, to Sheppard Field in Wichita, Texas, in a bunk that was too small for his extremely tall stature. During basic training, he stayed in barracks with men who were mainly from the Southern California area. Milt recalled the first few weeks of basic training; learning to put on the Army lace-up leggings, his first set of long underwear, many miles of marching, and hours of training at the rifle range.

After basic training, he was stationed at the University of Nevada as an aviation student, then went on to Santa Ana Preflight School and Hondo Navigation School where he graduated as a 2nd Lieutenant Navigator. He was then sent to Amarillo, Texas and Lowery Field, Colorado where he became a B-29 Flight Engineer. At Randolph Field, Texas he flew with his pilot and co-pilot in B-29 transition. They were scheduled to pick up the rest of their B-29 crew and be in the South Pacific in less than a month when the atom bomb was dropped which ended the war. He was placed on inactive duty in February 1946.

"In the Air Corps we were in many accelerated programs, only to sit down and wait for the next training program. During one of these periods of waiting, we were sent down to Camp Pendleton from pre-flight at Santa Ana to be extras in a movie called 'Winged Victory.' After the shoot, we were allowed to swim in the ocean. I was caught in a riptide, and except for a couple of cadets rescuing me, I would have drowned!"

Upon returning to his home in Lancaster, Milt found employment as a Correctional Officer at the California Vocational Institution (now Mira Loma). He took educational leaves to attend the University of Southern California (USC), receiving a BA degree. In 1949, he was accepted in the Los Angeles County Probation Department as a Probation Trainee, under the GI bill, for on the job training. In this department he worked in Adult Investigations, Adult Supervision and then as a Supervising Deputy Probation Officer in juvenile work and probation camps. He was a Probation Director as the administrative head of four different probation camps for 20 years, retiring in 1979 after 30 years of service.

On August 8, 1948 Milt married Susan Rhine of Thornton, Arkansas who he had met at USC. Together they raised four children; Amy, Mary, John and Nita Stark, living in Leona Valley for most of the time while they were growing up. Milt served on the Westside Union School Board for 12 ½ years. Board meetings were held in the building which was previously the Esperanza Grammar School where Milt had gone to school from the 1st through 5th grade. Because of this, and together with his service to the community while on the Board, the building was named the 'O. Milton Stark Administrative Building.' He has been active in the Wildflower Preservation Committee, the State Parks Advisory Committee, the Sierra Club, and the West Antelope Valley Historical Society. Milt helped reactivate this organization in 1980 and for the past 13 years has been the editor of their newsletter. In 2000, he was elected president of the Poppy Reserve/Mojave Desert Interpretive Association. He has photographed Antelope Valley wildflowers since 1969. In 1991 he published his first book, *A FLOWER-WATCHER'S GUIDE to*

Antelope Valley Wildflowers and in 2000, published an update of this book entitled *A FLOWER-WATCHER'S GUIDE to Wildflowers of the Western Mojave Desert.* He continues to be very active leading wildflower tours during the Spring, and giving talks to schools, churches and service clubs on wildflowers and various historical subjects.

JOHN ARTHUR "JOHNNIE/TRIGGER" STEGE

John Arthur Stege was born in Los Angeles, California on October 26, 1920, the only son of two children born to Arthur and Clemis Stege. The Stege family moved from St. Louis, Missouri to Los Angeles, California, then to Lancaster in 1923 where Arthur owned and managed the local butcher shop.

John attended grade school in Lancaster and graduated from AVJUHS in 1938. John was very active in sports playing football and baseball in high school. He attended Compton Junior College in 1938-1939. Then, while attending Antelope Valley Junior College, John participated in the Civilian Pilot Training program.

With a discussion about the war in Europe, John and his father had decided that it would be a good idea to try and become a pilot in the service instead of letting the draft decide the future for him. John was accepted into the Army Air Corps. He started training in the Cadet program in Glendale, California. During training, John was sent to Oxnard and Bakersfield in California, and Luke Field in Phoenix, Arizona, where he graduated at the rank of 2nd Lieutenant in December 1941.

After graduation, John was assigned to the 48th Pursuit Squadron, 14th Pursuit Group at March Field, California. He was checked out to fly the P-40, P-66 and P-43 airplanes. The 48th moved to North Island Naval Air Station in San Diego, California, in February 1942. In March of 1942, John was checked out in the P-38. This airplane would be the "love" of his military life – pulling him through many dangerous situations during the war.

The squadron was assigned brand new Lockheed P-38F Lightning aircraft in June of 1942, assigned to Bradley Field, Connecticut, then routed across the North Atlantic Ocean to England, via Goose Bay, Newfoundland; Reykjavik, Iceland, and Scotland. This flight started July 25, 1942 and ended on August 3, 1942. While in England, the 48th Squadron was stationed for a short time at Atcham, England, about 150 miles north of London. At Atcham, the pilots of the 48th received additional training which included simulator attacks on bomber formation, high altitude rendezvous exercises, gunnery training off the English coast, and instruction in British operation and intelligence procedures.

John's first combat mission was October 13, 1942, out of Tangmere, England. John recalled seeing "Nothing but clouds. My P-38F, the one I flew from March Field, was still hooked to my fanny - the same P-38. It's saved my life so far. By now my time in this machine is 200 hours. On the date of November 11, 1942, we took off from England and went to the Rock of Gibraltar and then over to North Africa – Maison Blanche, Algiers – and up to Youks les Bains, just a grain field, and here is where we went into real combat fighting with the Germans – 109's and 190's. We didn't do so good – they had the experience. All this flying was done in a formation of four. My flight leader was Captain R. Watson. I was his wingman." In North Africa, John flew over 30 combat missions, participating in aerial combat missions as bomber escort protecting against the German Messerschmidt 109's and Focke-Wulf 190's.

On November 20, 1942 the flight leader, Captain Watson, informed the pilots of their next mission - strafe tanks and trucks – so off they went. "We departed late in the afternoon and we found our targets, we strafed them, then turned for our base at Youks les Bains. We flew for about one hour, heading for Youks, when all of a sudden, Watson said, "We're going to belly in on the desert." John recalled, "This is my P-38F and I'm going to have to do this. I could not believe it, but we all did it, and not one of us got a scratch. This was at sundown, and there we were. The P-38 saved my life!" It had become too late to return all the way to Youks before nightfall and since the base had no landing lights, the desert was the only option. John's P-38 as well as the three others, were ruined.

They ended up on the edge of the Sahara Desert and were now surrounded by three members of the
French Camel Corps and about 30 Arabs. "They took us
back to their oasis and there we slept, ate chicken and dates,
and had a little wine for seven days, thinking someone
would come and get us – no phones! We found an old
French auto, put fuel in it from one of the P-38's and seven
days later, we were back in Youks – the gas in the P-38
saved me again!"

John returned to the states in February 1943 where he
trained P-38 pilots at Muroc (now Edwards Air Force
Base), Salinas, and Santa Maria, California. He returned to
"active" duty with the Air Force in 1944. John had become
bored instructing and wanted to return to his love – flying.
He and another pilot friend volunteered to go to the Pacific.

John returned to combat and served in the Pacific
Theater with the 13th Fighter Command of the 347th Fighter
Group, 68th Fighter Squadron. John flew 70 missions while
in the Pacific. He was a P-38 Fighter Squadron
Commander in New Guinea and the Philippines.

During his military career, John flew 135 missions,
1,500 flying hours, with 525 combat hours. He was
proficient as a pilot of single and twin engine aircraft
having flown the P-38; P-40; P-39; P-51, P-47; P-66; A-29
and C-45.

John received the Distinguished Flying Cross (DFC) and
Air Medal with one Silver Oak Leaf Cluster. The DFC was
awarded by direction of the President in 1945 for "extraordinary achievement while participating in an
aerial flight to Tarakan, Borneo, on 18 November, 1944. These officers were members of a formation of
twenty-six P-38 aircraft which took off for an incendiary bombing and strafing mission against oil fields at
this Japanese base. After flying 600 miles, the formation dropped to an altitude of 200 feet. As they
approached the target,, some of the aircraft made minimum-altitude runs over assigned targets while others
flew top-cover. In the face of intense anti-aircraft fire a successful attack was made which set fire to
numerous tanks, three merchant vessels, a tanker, three small vessels under construction, nine or ten barges
and small boats in the harbor, a pumping station and other installations. Flames and smoke rose to the
height of 17,000 feet, and fires and explosions were in evidence for three days. The outstanding courage
and devotion to duty displayed by these officers in the partial destruction of this vital enemy oil source are
worthy of the highest commendation."

John was honorably discharged at the rank
of Major in January 1946. On November 17,
1949, John married his sweetheart, Charlene
Mertes. They had five children together -
John, Jr.; Lorraine; Roseann; Marylynn; and
Sally Stege. John went into the retail liquor
business and is now semi-retired after twenty-
five years of working. He joined the
American Legion, Post 291, in Newport
Beach, California where he enjoys the
camaraderie and activities. John currently
lives at home in Newport Beach.

*"The P-38 was a good plane to fly. We used to say, 0
to 50 hours – anything could happen; 50 to 100 hours –
you were a better pilot; 100 to 500 hours – you were over
confident and cocky; after 500 hours – no one could tell
you how to fly it!" John Stege*

146

On October 14, 1921, Irma "Babe" Story was born in Burbank, Los Angeles Co., California, the daughter of Nathaniel and Irma (Spofford) Story. Nathaniel was born in Michigan and moved to California in 1899 to work for his uncle, Tom Story. Irma Spofford was born in New Hampshire and moved to Burbank around 1907, where she met and married Nathaniel in January, 1908. Babe had three older siblings; two brothers, Alan and Thomas; and one sister, Esther (Story) Lee.

The Story family moved to the Antelope Valley in 1922, where Nathaniel worked for the Union Oil Company. Babe remembered that she always wanted to learn how to fly after spending time with her brother at the old Lancaster airport on Avenue I and 10th Street West. He was learning to become a mechanic at the time, and Babe would tag along, running errands for some of the pilots in exchange for airplane rides.

Babe attended Lancaster Grammar School and graduated from AVJUHS in 1938. After three years of schooling at Antelope Valley Junior College, Babe heard the Civilian Pilot Training Program (CPT) was starting up. Aviatrix and businesswoman, Pancho Barnes, owned a flight school in Palmdale and was recruiting potential students, of which ten percent could be women. They had to fill the quota with qualified men, first, so Babe missed out on the first two groups as they were full. She was the number two girl on the list for the third group, with another girl signed up ahead of her. Unfortunately for the other girl, she had an eye injury and could not pass the physical, so Babe jumped to the top spot, and in the spring of 1941, it was her turn to fly. She was one of only two women trained in the CPT Program, along with Meg Castle, both in the same class.

In June of 1941, Babe earned her private pilot's license in a 65 horsepower Porterfield, while under the instruction of John Barnes (no relation to Pancho). She went to work for Vega (part of Lockheed Aircraft) in September, 1941, as a riveter - not exactly what she had wanted to do. In September of 1942, the Air Transport Command issued orders authorizing the employment of women flyers, with the need for pilots to fly new planes from factories to the military air fields, and for other training purposes. With World War II in full swing, the men were needed for combat related duties overseas. With the help of aviatrix, Jacqueline "Jackie" Cochran and Nancy Love, the Women's Air Service Pilots (WASP) were born.

News of the opportunity for women to fly, sparked women all over the United States to apply to the WASP. Babe filled out the paperwork needed to join, but her supervisors at Vega Aircraft, did not want to let her go. Babe received a telegram from General Henry "Hap" Arnold, telling her to report for an interview in Los Angeles, if the interview was successful, she was to report to Long Beach for an Air Corps physical. If she passed the physical, she was to report for training at Sweetwater, Texas. Babe passed the interview and the physical, and Vega had to let her go.

In April, Babe reported for training at Avenger Field, in Sweetwater. Ahead, was six months of primary, basic and advanced training, with two months in each phase of ground school and flight school, with single and multi-engine aircraft training. One month prior to graduation, twenty-five students in Babe's class, along with twenty-five members from the preceding class, were picked to be sent on "special assignment." When the women received their orders, they were divided by height with the taller ones assigned to fly the B-17's, those of middle height went to the C-60's, and the shortest, which Babe was, went to the B-26 "Widow-maker." The women were being trained to fly in the Ferrying Command. Two days after she earned her wings, Babe was off flying, with no break after training, as the women were needed to fly due to the severe shortage of men. No uniforms were issued, so the women in Babe's group flew to Dodge City, Kansas in civilian clothes, to be trained on the B-26. The training was experimental at that time, to see if the women could fly the big airplanes, including the B-26 bomber, which many of the men had refused to fly due to the numerous training accidents during take-off and landings.

After two months of training in Kansas, Babe graduated from B-26 school, number one in her class, along with 10 other women. After the women soloed in the B-26, a telegram was sent to Washington informing them of what the women had done. A reply was sent back stating, "No man could refuse to fly the B-26 anymore, and not lose their wings." Babe was allowed to go home, on leave, for a few days before her next stop at Harlington Army Air Base, in Texas.

Babe stayed with the B-26 at Harlington, towing targets at the Aerial Gunnery School, while being fired at and making difficult maneuvers at over 300 miles an hour. She was at Harlington for about a year, until Congress disbanded the WASP program in December, 1944.

After taking some time off and several different jobs later, Babe was a flight instructor until 1949, then went into the crop dusting business as part-owner of Antelope Valley Pest Control, along with veteran Army Air Corps fighter pilot, Charles Dungan. In 1950, the WASP were offered a commission by the Air Force. Babe applied into the Reserves, but finally had to resign because she couldn't get enough points in while flying for Antelope Valley Pest Control. She retired at the rank of Major in the U.S. Air Force Reserves. After World War II, Babe was a member of the Los Angeles chapter of the Ninety-Nines, an international organization of women pilots. Babe flew for over twenty-one years for a living, and worked for Santa Fe Engineers as her final job before retirement.

It wasn't until 1977, when a special legislation was passed giving the WASP some military benefits. Babe joined the San Fernando Valley Chapter of the Ninety-Nines and keeps busy speaking to groups about her time with the WASP.

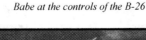

Babe at the controls of the B-26

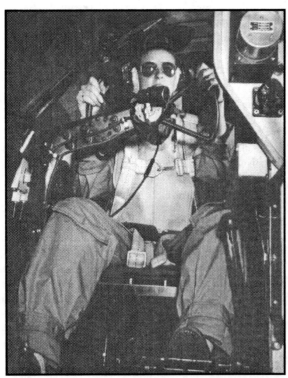

Pancho Barnes, Pheobe Omlie, and Babe Story, September 1949.

ROY RAYMOND STOUDT

Roy Raymond Stoudt was born March 21, 1920 in Emaus, Lehigh Co., Pennsylvania, the son of Raymond Victor and Marie Elizabeth (Kaufmann) Stoudt. In 1921, the Stoudt family packed all their possessions in suitcases, leaving all their furniture and large items behind, and boarded a train headed for Los Angeles, California. Roy's parents were divorced when he was nine years old. Marie married Griffin Sheldrake in the 1930's, then she was married to Robert Clyde Primmer on March 26, 1956. Roy had two siblings; a sister, Margaretha Marie (Stoudt) Moore; a brother, Layard Philip Stoudt; and a step-brother, Walter Primmer.

The family moved to Lancaster in 1936, when Roy's step-father was called back to work at Southern California Edison. Roy graduated from AVJUHS in 1939 where he played football, basketball and baseball. He was student body president in his senior year. Roy attended AVJC for two years where he played football and basketball. During his second year of college he enrolled in the Civilian Pilot Training Program. He flew 60 hours in a Piper Cub, passed his flight test and a written exam, and received his private pilot's license. Roy graduated from college in 1941.

Immediately after graduation, Roy and his mother drove to Van Nuys, California to enlist in the Army and Navy Air Corps. In October of 1941, Roy received orders from the Army Air Corps to report to Rankin Aero Academy in Tulare, California for primary training. He was sent as a replacement for a cadet who had just "washed out." Roy was studying and listening to the radio when he heard about the attack on Pearl Harbor.

After completion of primary training, Roy was sent to basic training at Merced, California. There, he flew the Consolidated-Vultee BT-13 trainer. After basic training, Roy was sent to Luke Field in Phoenix, Arizona for advanced training. Luke Field was a military base and for the first time, Roy was living in a barracks. At Luke Field, the men were taught aerobatic maneuvers, formation, navigation, instrument and

149

night flying and gunnery. On graduation day, the cadets were called forward and given their orders to their next duty station and their commission as 2nd Lieutenants. Roy recalled, "There were six or eight of us who had not been called. We thought for a while that we had not graduated! Then they called us forward, one at a time, and our orders were to report to instructors school, there at Luke Field. That really stuck a pin in my balloon. Instructor was not even on the list. When we left primary training, they gave us a list of planes to choose which ones we wanted to fly. My first choice was the Douglas A-20. I did as I was ordered and reported to instructors school. Several of my classmates did fly A-20s, were sent to North Africa and not many of them came home." Roy was in class 42-E when he completed instructors school. He basically did the same training as a cadet, only this time from the back of an AT-6 Texan, instead of the front seat.

Roy had been dating Maxine Hazel Bates during his time at Antelope Valley Junior College. They were thinking about getting married, and in-between his second and third class, he was able to get a leave. They were married in Lancaster on August 23, 1942.

In May of 1943, Roy was promoted to 1st Lieutenant. He was transferred to the P-40 Training Unit where he trained Chinese officers to fly the aircraft. "These were the cream of the crop officers from China," Roy recalled, "they had all been through what would be our West Point. Each instructor would receive three students; one could speak some English; one, very little; and the third, hardly at all. We also had an interpreter available to us. We used lots of hand signals while in the air!"

P-40s in formation – Roy Stoudt, fifth plane down, over Luke Field

"One day, when operating off of an auxiliary field, my students and I were waiting for our planes to return from the flight previous to ours. We waited quite a while, then all three students arrived, but no Lt. Scott. I finally found one of the students and inquired about Lt. Scott. He told me, 'Him o.k., bail out,

Roy with three of his Chinese students at Luke Field - 1943

other side of White Tank Mountains.' I took another plane to see what was going on and Lt. Scott was not far from his crashed P-40. They were flying tactical formation and the student slid under, to the inside of the turn and cut Lt. Scott's tail off. Sort of combat duty after all!"

Roy was transferred, along with six other instructors, to George Air Force Base, Victorville, California to start-up a P-39 Training Unit for newly graduated American 2nd Lieutenants. Roy was only there about six months when he was transferred to Pinellas, Florida to attend a P-51 Training Unit. While he was in Florida, George Air Force Base P-39 school had closed. Roy had to report back to Luke Field to train the American 2nd Lieutenants in the P-38 aircraft.

After his assignment at Luke Field was completed, Roy was transferred to Fort Collins, Colorado, to attend Garrison School. After completing the course, he was sent to Buckley Field, Aurora, Colorado. His next orders were to a Replacement Center in South Carolina. From there, Roy boarded a troop train headed for Pittsburg, California. After two weeks in Pittsburg, the troops were loaded onto a Sherman Class ship and sailed under the Golden Gate Bridge in San Francisco, bound for Fort McKinley, Manila and Luzon Island in the Philippines.

Roy was assigned as an adjunct of an Aircraft Control and Warning Squadron. He did not like the non-flying job, and after almost a year, he had plenty of points to be separated from the service. He returned to the United States and was placed on inactive duty in Marysville, California and promoted to Captain.

In 1947, Roy returned to Lancaster where he went to work for Southern California Edison. He attended inactive duty reserve meetings in Lancaster. In the early 1950's, Roy was called up to active reserve duty with the 452nd Photo Reconnaissance Group flying P-51s. "I was in Long Beach, California – a weekend warrior – one weekend per month and two weeks training each year. After about three years, they phased out the 452nd and gave our P-51s to the National Guard. I was promoted to Major at that time."

Roy was back on inactive reserve duty status at home in Lancaster. In 1960, he received a promotion with the Edison Company and moved to Covina, California. He was transferred to an inactive reserve unit in Ontario, California and was assigned as Air Force Academy Liaison Officer and promoted to Lieutenant Colonel. In 1963, Roy was promoted again by Edison and moved to Tulare, California. He was also transferred to an inactive Air Force reserve unit in the area. While in Tulare, Roy completed over twenty years of service in the Air Force and retired at the rank of Lieutenant Colonel.

Republic of China Commendation Award - 1946

Primary training at Rankin Aero Academy – Roy, far left

In 1964, Roy moved back to Covina, California. His wife, Maxine, passed away in 1984. They had two children together; two sons, James Raymond and Richard Roy Stoudt. James is a Vietnam veteran born in Phoenix, Arizona, and Richard was born in Lancaster, California at Dr. Sensman's hospital on Lancaster Boulevard. Roy has two step-children; Michele and Michael Finn. After being a widower for five years, Roy met Anita Faye (Poindexter) Harper. They were married in Kauai, Hawaii, in 1989. Anita passed away in 2002. Both Maxine and Anita graduated from AVJUHS.

Roy is retired from the Southern California Edison Company and the Air Force, and currently lives in San Bernardino, California.

P-51 Training Unit, Luke Field, Arizona. Flight instructors and Chinese students - Roy Stoudt, front row, 4th from right

DONALD RAYMOND "DON" STOUT

Donald Raymond Stout was born January 12, 1918 in Lebanon, Warren Co., Ohio, the second son born to Isaac Marshall and Flora (Thayer) Stout. Isaac was born in Ohio, and Flora was born in New York. The Stout family moved to California in 1920, and to the Antelope Valley in 1925, where Isaac was a teacher and principal at Lancaster Grammar School. Don had one sibling, a brother, Lawrence T. Stout.

In 1934, Don graduated from AVJUHS. He attended AVJC and then went to Chaffee Jr. College, where he received his AA degree in 1936. Don graduated from the University of California at Berkeley in 1940.

Don enlisted in the Army Air Corps and was inducted in Los Angeles, California in October of 1941. He went through six weeks of training in San Antonio, Texas - up at 6 a.m., with classes, shots, marching and rifle training. He missed his home in Lancaster and his fiancé, Ercell Rogers.

After pre-flight training, Don was sent to Primary Flying School in Tulsa, Oklahoma, where he spent 60 hours training in the Fairchild PT-19 aircraft. After further flight training and ground school, Don flew overseas to England, as co-pilot on a B-17F, with the 8th Air Force, 305th Bombardment Group (H), 366th Bombardment Squadron, which was under the command of Colonel Curtis E. LeMay.

The 305th was stationed at Chelveston, England on January 27, 1943, when Don participated in the first air raid over Germany. He recalled, "We were flying B-17 Flying Fortresses with no nose turrets. They could be hit head on at 12:00 o'clock. There were 54 bombers with no escort and because of bad weather, we had to hit our secondary target, Wilhelmshaven.

We were at 27,000 feet when we were hit by flak. Five ME-109's then jumped us. The five crewmen in the back were killed. We had lost two engines and the remaining five crewmen jumped at 19,000 feet.

It was very quiet after the noise in the aircraft. I opened my chute at about 3,500 feet as the fighters made two passes at me and hit my parachute. They put two holes in my parachute, but I was not hit. I knew then I would always be a Christian. I landed in a plowed field where a German farmer met me with a shotgun. He didn't speak English and I didn't speak German, but I knew what he meant. We were put in solitary for four days."

Don had seen his B-17 crash, and he knew some of his crewmates were onboard. Of the ten crewmembers, the Germans had killed two of the men while they came down in their parachutes. One was killed after striking the ground - his parachute had been shot to pieces. Others were shot when they landed on the ground, or had been killed in the airplane. Don, along with four of his crewmates, were taken prisoner when they hit the ground in the field.

Don's fiancé, Ercell Rogers, was working at Lancaster Radio Store when she received a telegram from his parents saying he had been captured. She recalled, "This was early in the war and I rushed into Whit Carter's office to tell him. By chance, the National Representative of the American Red Cross was in the office at the time. He went to the regional office in San Francisco and had them send me maps and information on prison camps available through the Red Cross."

On the fifth day of his imprisonment, Don recalled, "I met Hanns Scharff. He was the German who interrogated all Allied air prisoners. He was tall and handsome in his uniform and black boots. He spoke fluent English. I could only give my name, rank and serial number, and I was shocked to see he already had a scrapbook with pictures of the crew, where they graduated from flight school, and where they had been stationed. Ours was the first plane shot down over Germany and they wanted to discover our primary target and how we got to England. We flew our own planes across the north Atlantic. He volunteered that he had been living in Southern California and had been working at North American in Inglewood. He was visiting his ill mother and could not leave when the war began."

Don was now a Prisoner of War, No. 149 at Stalag Luft 3, a "Kriegsgefangenen" at a prison camp in

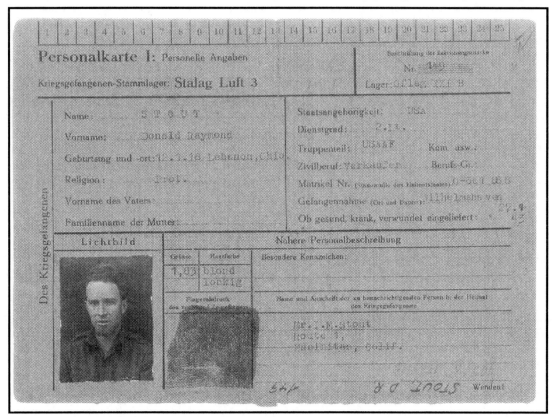

Schubin, Poland, along with the Royal Air Force prisoners. "This camp was in an old private school, and it soon filled up, so we were sent to another camp, Stalag 111, in Sagan, Germany, which was ninety miles south of Berlin."

"We could keep our uniforms and I was given wooden shoes by a Dutch man. At first, I thought they would be cold, but found they insulated the feet and were good in the mud. We alternated between American, British, and Canadian food parcels, but we were always hungry. I will always support the Red Cross. We made utensils from "Kilm" cans that were in the Canadian food parcels. "Kilm" is milk spelled backwards.

It was our duty to help with escape activities and distract the enemy. A radio was built secretly – guards were bribed or parts were made. The men had many skills. They made escape food, clothing, and maps, forged documents, dug tunnels and dispersed the sand from those tunnels. That was my job and we were called penguins. They made suspenders with bags attached to wear under our clothing. When we got to the volleyball area, we would mix with the players, pull the pin in each sack and shuffle around to disperse the sand. The volleyball court raised more than a foot! We had to give up bedboards to shore up the tunnels. All those things were done in secret. There were three tunnels – Tom, Dick and Harry. After the Americans were moved to the South camp, Harry was completed. 75 got out, but only three made good on their escape. 50 were executed by the Gestapo. We stopped escape activities after 50 urns with their ashes were brought back to camp.

There was a small library, furnished by the Y.M.C.A. We spent time in bed in the winter to keep warmer, so it was a good time to read. A very popular book was 'The Robe' by Lloyd C. Douglas. There was a long waiting list for that book. A Scot named Padre Murdo MacDonald was our chaplain. He was a paratrooper and was captured in Africa. He was a pastor, professor, mountain climber and a favorite of all the men in the camp. Everyone ran to get a seat at his Sunday service. Many others crowded on the floor. He gave us inspiration and hope. He was a Professor Emeritas of the University of Glasgow, and an author. Padre traveled to America for our reunions and gave the sermon at the Sunday morning prayer breakfasts."

The POW's were allowed to write four postcards and three V-Mail letters per month. There was no limit on incoming letters. On November 11, 1944, Don wrote a letter to the Antelope Valley Ledger-Gazette, printed in the February 22, 1945, Thursday edition, "Letters from Servicemen". The letter was written from Stalag Luft 3 in Germany:

"This letter will have to be written by proxy, but I feel that as I have so many friends there in Lancaster, they may like to know a little of what has happened to me. I am on my third year as a P.O.W. and as I wrote the above date, I wished that it might prove to be a second Armistice Day. That is the first thing for which we are all waiting – PEACE – then comes our mail, and next in interest is meal time. I have been cooking for a bunch of twelve men, and it helps to fill up the weary hours. Of course, that means no other duties such as getting hot water, sweeping or WASHING DISHES. In October, I went on Kreigie seniority and had my first parole walk, and I can assure you, it was great to be OUTSIDE the wire! Our time is mostly spent indoors now, as winter has set in and we are hoping it will not be too severe. In the summer we have all kinds of sports which tend to make the time pass more quickly. Right now I am taking a course in College Algebra and studying Math of Finance on the side. We have a very good reference library here and also a general one.

We were all so optimistic on June 6th, but after feeling we would be home for Christmas, have now made up our minds we shall still have to wait a while – but we can dream and hope and pray for the day when we shall be able to return to our homes.

Only four letters received in September, but October brought two parcels, May and July, fifty letters and my cigarette parcels. So far this month I have had forty three and I want to take this opportunity to thank my many friends in that locality who have been so faithful in writing me even though I have been unable to answer. After living there for fifteen years, Lancaster is HOME to me."

(Signed) Your old friend,
Don Stout

On January 27, 1945, after having been a prisoner for two years, Don recalled a "celebration" of sorts, "We were having a little celebration (if you can call it that). We made a cake using ground hardtack biscuits from the Red Cross parcels. We used ground ascorbic acid tablets and tooth powder, and it raised about a quarter of an inch. Our celebration was cut short when the Russians were twenty-five kilometers to the east, and the Germans decided to put us on the march to another camp. We marched five nights in snow and a minus 20 degree blizzard, slept in barns and tried to keep warm. They then put us in '40 & 8' cattle cars. They were for 40 men or 8 horses, but they crowded sixty men in each car. We were cold and tired and decided half would stand while the other half tried to sleep on the floor.

Our destination was 'Hell Camp' in Moosburg, Bavaria. The camp had bed bugs, lice, and no food parcels, and people were sick. There was mud, rain and filth, and the men tried to stay warm by staying in bed. My usual weight before the war was 175 pounds and it went down to 129 pounds.

On April 29, 1945, General George Patton liberated the camp, the flag was raised, and we got food which made us sick again. We were taken to Camp Lucky Strike in Belgium where we were de-loused and given uniforms. We finally boarded Liberty Ships and headed for home. The Statue of Liberty was the most beautiful sight anyone could imagine. I thank God I came home and that I have had all these years with my wonderful family. Of course, the real heroes are the ones who were not lucky enough to come home."

The following is from the diary of a fellow prisoner - interred at the same camp - Vernon L. Burda. Don did not know Vernon at the camp, but met him at a reunion, many years after the war.

"Finally, spring came and the renewed offensive of the Allies started pushing the Germans back. One day in the latter part of April, we saw fighter planes scouting our camp and on April 29th we were ordered inside the barracks as we could hear the big guns, rifles and machine guns. Peering through cracks in the wall, we could see Allied infantrymen advancing through the fields and pushing toward the town of Moosburg. Almost immediately thereafter, we all heard the most pleasant sound we had heard for a long time – the sound, the rumble of American tanks. And when those tanks rolled into the prison compound, they looked as big as battleships. The Kriegies spilled out of the barracks, unmindful of the live bullets still whistling through the air, and cheered the troops and gobbled those K-rations which the American soldiers threw to us – just as though those K-rations were candy.

Then, suddenly for no apparent reason, a hush fell over the compound, and all eyes turned toward the town in which stood two high church steeples. Over 20,000 eyes saw machine gun bullets splatter against the steeples, a period of quiet, and then it occurred, a scene, the happening of which brought tears streaming down the face of every single American prisoner-of-war there, and a sob from every throat – we saw the greatest sight, the most emotional minute that we would ever witness – raised before our eyes and flying defiantly above one of the church steeples was the symbol of our beloved land – THE AMERICAN FLAG.

As one great mass, all felt emotion that one who has not been deprived of freedom, who has not suffered behind barbed wire for months without adequate food, clothes, heat or word of loved ones and of home, could not possibly feel. Yes, the tears flowed from over ten thousand faces that day – over ten thousand unashamed faces, as that Flag shocked us back with memories of the place we all held most dear – OUR BELOVED LAND, OUR HOME."

Shortly after his return home to Lancaster, Don married his sweetheart, Ercell Mae Rogers, July 14, 1945, in Glendale, Los Angeles Co., California. Ercell graduated from AVJUHS in 1939. Don and Ercell were engaged before he entered the service, and she waited for him the entire 3 ½ years while he was gone. They had three children together; Judy, Gary, and Nancy Stout.

Don was honorably discharged in January 1946 at the rank of 1st Lieutenant. Among other service awards, he received the Air Medal with 1 Oak Leaf Cluster, and the Prisoner of War Medal. Don was employed in the retail business after the war, working at J.C. Penny in Lancaster, Compton, and Burbank, until 1958. He retired from Bullock's Department Store in Canoga Park, California, in 1986.

Don joined the Disabled American Veterans group and keeps in contact with the many friends he made during the war. He speaks at local high school History and Civics classes, telling of his experiences as a POW. People have heard Don's inspirational story told on Veterans Day through programs at lodges, churches, and many other gatherings.

In retrospect Don related, "I respect the military very much. Their mission is to protect our freedoms, which we cherish. The military impressed upon me that freedom is not free – many men sacrificed everything, so that we may live in a free country and do as we want." Don was one of those men who made that sacrifice.

Don and Ercell are retired and live in Simi Valley, California, but make frequent trips to the Antelope Valley to visit friends and attend local reunions.

FRANK WALLACE STUBBINGS

William E. Stubbings and Ann Marshall were married around 1914 in Ontario, Canada. They emigrated to Detroit, Wayne Co., Michigan in 1916 with their two sons, Douglas and Harold. After settling in Detroit, William and Ann had two more children, sons Frank and Kenneth.

Frank Wallace Stubbings was born October 23, 1917 in Detroit, Wayne Co., Michigan. At age 22, Frank remembers hearing about the attack on Pearl Harbor and in 1943, went to enlist "to get the Nazis", but was not accepted due to a medical problem. About a year later, on February 25, 1944, Frank was called back and inducted into the Army Air Corps.

After basic training, Frank was sent to Daniel Field in Augusta, Georgia. His first job assignment was as a K.P. (Kitchen Police) "Pusher". While in Augusta, Frank met and married Madeline Pouliot in 1944.

His next assignment was mechanics school in Sacramento, California, where he spent four months in training. Frank was then sent to Cook, Nebraska in preparation for Cadet School. All his plans changed when he was sent to the Army Infantry instead, due to his skills in

handling a rifle. Frank was off again, this time to Oklahoma City, Oklahoma, then to Texas for Infantry training. While in Texas, Frank recalled saving a young soldiers life during a training exercise, "We were being shot at over our heads when the man next to me starts to panic, hysterically, and wants to stand up and run. I grabbed him and held him down, yelling for them to stop firing. I was afraid I wouldn't be able to hold him down much longer." The firing finally stopped and they removed the young man from the exercise.

Frank's next assignment would be a journey overseas, to the heart of the war, in France and Germany. He took hundreds of photographs during his time in the service, and wrote home quite frequently. They usually had good food, because they cooked it themselves. Frank spent time in Regensburg, near the Rhine River, in Germany, and stayed there until the war ended. They didn't hear the war was over until the next day, and there they were, right in the middle of it.

Frank was assigned to the U.S. Army 120th Station Hospital in Bayreuth, Bavaria, Germany, on the German/Russian border. He stayed there until his discharge at the rank of Corporal in March, 1946. During the war, Frank was quite the entrepreneur among his fellow officers. He always seemed to have an abundant stock of cigarettes and beer to make some extra money. Another way that Frank made extra money to send back home to his wife, was with a

Always the "prankster", Frank dressed in German uniform with Nazi flag.

little trading – selling Bavarian china. He would send other servicemen's wives the dishes, and they would send his wife $35.00 in return. Frank also enjoyed pulling pranks on the other servicemen – all in good fun.

For his time in the service, Frank was awarded the American Campaign Medal; European Theater Medal with one Bronze Star; World War II Victory Medal; Good Conduct Medal.

After the war, Frank and his wife moved back to Detroit, Michigan. Frank set up a business to make some quick money by operating a basketball and archery concession at a lake near Detroit. Later, in 1946, Frank and Madeline headed for California, with plans to go to San Diego, but they settled in Los Angeles instead. They had two sons together, Ross and Alan Stubbings. Frank went to work for Vance's Photo Shop. He sold photo coupons for $3.50 a piece, and had a quota of 11 per day. With Frank's persuasive personality, he met his quota in no time.

Frank and Madeline moved up to the Antelope Valley in late 1946, where he would go from ranch to ranch, taking family portraits. They lived on a ranch on 70th West and Avenue I. In 1947, Frank opened a Photo Studio on Lancaster Blvd. in Lancaster, California, where he stayed for 40 years. He moved into a house on the corner of Beech and Jackman in 1949. In 1968, Frank was married a second time to Betty Jane (Whitney) Doerr, in Big Bear, California. In the late 1980's, Frank moved his photo business to Beech Avenue, in Lancaster, which he still runs today. Over the years, Frank was responsible for taking many of the wonderful aerial photographs of the Antelope Valley, along with group photographs at the Old Timers Barbeque every year, and hundreds of other people and scenes from the area. He has watched many of the babies he took photos of starting in the late 1940's, grow up and bring their business back to him by taking photographs of their children.

Frank joined the service to fight for his country. He made many close friendships during that time, but has lost touch with most of them. His military experience changed his way of thinking about war. He believes that war should be the last alternative.

Cheers!

157

Bob Hope with Frank Stubbings - 1945

Frank Stubbings – self portrait

ARLYNN HORACE "BILL" SWENSON

Arlynn Horace "Bill" Swenson was born August 24, 1926 in Allamakee Co., Iowa, the son of Jacob and Thenora (Megorden) Swenson. Jacob and Thenora were both born in Iowa, with Jacob's parents born in Norway. Bill had three siblings; a brother, Vernon, and two sisters, Lillian and Clarice Swenson. The Swenson family lived in Center Township in Allamakee Co., where Jacob earned a living as a farmer.

Bill was living in Iowa when he heard the news about the attack on Pearl Harbor. He was drafted into the U.S. Army in 1945 and went through accelerated basic training in southern Louisiana and in California. Bill was attached to the 8th Army and left for Yokohama, Japan to join the Army of Occupation. He was assigned duty as part of the Quartermaster Graves Registration Service (GRS) personnel while in Yokohama.

According to the U.S. Army of Military History, one of the "soberest and yet one of the most imperative missions held by any unit is the Graves Registration Section of the Quartermaster Company. The GRS is charged with commencing the somber journey of the remains of American soldiers killed or who died in Japan, back to final repatriation in their homeland."

The war was over when Bill was in Japan. He was a Sergeant for one year in the Army before he took over the same job in GRS, holding the same position as a civilian. Bill was discharged in 1947 and settled in California in 1948. During his service in Japan, Bill was awarded a citation for climbing Mount Fuji, Japan's highest peak, in the middle of winter, to recover bodies from an air crash.

Bill met his wife, Irene Moore, a 1937 graduate of AVJUHS, while serving in Yokohama. Her family moved to the Antelope Valley in 1929 where her father owned the "Squeeze Inn" on Sierra Highway. Irene was a civilian employee working for the Quartermaster while Bill was a Sergeant in the Army. They were married on July 7, 1948, at St. Paul's Cathedral in Los Angeles, California. Bill and Irene had two children; a daughter, Karen Joy, and son, Kurt Warren Swenson. After Bill was discharged from the Army, he went to work for the U.S. Post Office. The Swenson family moved to the Antelope Valley in 1956, where Bill attended Antelope Valley Junior College. He was employed in Civil Service at Edwards Air Force Base, in the Instrumentation field.

Bill recalled that the war "changed my life. I met my wife and moved to California." On September 25, 2001, Bill passed away in Lancaster, California. He was taken back to Iowa where he was buried at the Old East Paint Creek Cemetery, in Waterville, in a 100-year old family plot.

1946 – Yokohama, Japan

GLEN E. THOMAS

Glen E. Thomas, the son of Walter J. and Zella Rachel (Mathis) Thomas, was born about 1918 in California. In 1930, the Thomas family was living in Taft, Kern Co., California, where Walter was employed as an oil worker in the oil fields. Glen had two siblings, a brother, Calvin K., and a sister, Donna M. Thomas.

The family moved to Rosamond, in the northern area of the Antelope Valley, where Glen was a teacher and basketball coach at the Rosamond Grammar School. In 1941, his basketball squad won the championship, with one of the players, future World War II Army mortarman, Alec Cecil Burton. Glen also played on a basketball team with future Army Air Corps veteran John Stege, and was coached by U.S. Navy veteran, Glen Settle.

Glen enlisted in the Army Air Corps and was an aviation cadet at Luke Field, in Arizona. He went through B-26 bomber training at Barksdale Air Base near Shreveport, Louisiana, and from there, went on to Georgia where he picked up his "own" B-26-C.

The following is a letter written to Ercell (Rogers) Stout, dated June 1, 1943. She met Glen when he and John Stege came into Lancaster Radio where Ercell was working. At the time the letter was written, Glen was a Lieutenant.

Dear Ercell,

This is the little old letter I was talking about when we met in Lancaster. Many gallons of water has gone under the bridge since.

I finished what training they were giving me at Shreveport, La. From there I went to Georgia and got myself a beautiful B-26-C. We test flew it there. It was then loaded and we went to our embarkation point. I have been out of the U.S.A. about a week. At present, I'm somewhere in South America.

My trip has been just like a moving picture show. We have seen plantations that look more like a movie set than the real McCoy. We are in the midst of a jungle that has real tigers, how about that? It looks awful thick to walk through. Sure wouldn't much like to walk out of about 100 miles of it.

We are leaving here tomorrow. We aren't too far from where our final destination is located. Getting anxious to get there but having an awful good time while we go over there.

I must close now or I will be telling military secrets or something.

Glen

Second Lieutenant Glen E. Thomas died while in service to his country, in Africa, when he was killed in a plane crash – a non-battle related accident. His parents lived in San Bernardino Co., California, where they both passed away in the early 1980's. Glen's brother, Calvin, died in Oregon, in 2000. Of the many friends and students who knew Glen, they all said he was "a great guy."

Kurt F. Ullman was born March 30, 1921, in Schoenbeck, on the Elbe River, in Germany, the only child born to Fritz H. and Frieda (Mors) Ullman. The Ullman family emigrated from Germany to the United States through Ellis Island, New York, in 1923. After processing through Ellis Island, the Ullman family boarded a train and headed to the Antelope Valley. Fritz had an uncle, Theodore K. Ullman, who owned a ranch in the Leona Valley area of the Antelope Valley. Kurt grew up in the Del Sur area of Lancaster, attended Del Sur Grammar School, and graduated from AVJUHS in 1939, where he enjoyed playing football.

On December 7, 1941, Kurt was in Chase Hall at Cal Poly, San Luis Obispo, attending school, when he heard about the attack on Pearl Harbor. He enlisted in the Army Air Corps in 1942, in the Cadet program, as he wanted to become a pilot. The laws on enlisting had changed and Kurt was drafted into the Army and instead, sent to the Infantry. He was angry when they sent him to the Infantry when he wanted to be in, and was qualified for, the Army Air Corps. The Cadet Board wrote a letter attesting to the fact that Kurt was qualified, but the draft board would not release him.

Kurt went through Infantry basic training at Camp Wolters, Texas. He thought it was interesting and actually enjoyed it, except for the fact that he wanted to fly. After training, Kurt was sent to Aviation Cadet School in San Antonio, Texas, then on to Fort Stockton and San Angelo, Texas. He graduated as a pilot and commissioned 2nd Lieutenant at Lubbock, Texas.

Kurt's first assignment was as a pilot onboard a C-47-A troop carrier with the 9th Air Force, 440th Troop Carrier Group, 97th Squadron. On February 24, 1944, the air echelon from the 440th departed Morrison Field, Florida, bound for Preswick, Scotland, via South America, Ascension Island and Africa. They arrived at Prestwick on March 8th. They set up their base at Army Air Field Station No. 481, in Bottesford, Nottingham, England. In April, they transferred to Station No. 463, in Exeter, Devon, England.

On June 7, 1944, D-Day + 1, Kurt recalled, "On the morning of June 7, we hit the coast at first light on a re-supply mission [the mission was called MEMPHIS] . On June 6, about six hours before the Normandy landing, the 440th Troop Carrier took the 101st Airborne in and dropped them behind the lines. As we approached the coast, the sky turned red with their greetings. I thought for sure this was it, but I made it through, I believe without a hit. When we got to the drop zone and dropped, we made a steep left hand turn to get out of there, as they were also sending up live ammo. It was in this turn that I got clobbered! It sounded like hail on a tin roof. Immediately, my co-pilot said, "There's fire coming out of the right engine." I called for the fire extinguisher and he pulled the lever, but said the fire wasn't completely out. At the same time, I cut the right engine and increased power on the left. At this point, the rest of the formation was pulling ahead of me –fast! We hit the coast and at the same time I realized the left engine had lost oil pressure and was exceeding the red line for RPM. At this instant I knew we were all through as far as going home that day. The time interval was very short - only seconds - and both engines were dead.

The only option was to ditch in the English Channel. As water landings go, we made it o.k., especially as I was later told that my wheels were also down as the hydraulic system apparently was also hit. In a short while, a Navy P.T. boat came over, but would not approach closer than about a hundred yards. We managed to get our raft and cross to the boat. A few minutes later, the airplane sank. After we got on the P.T. boat, a sailor asked me about my leg as it had blood all over it. This was the first I knew that I had been hit. As the hours went by, my wound made itself known.

The boat took us to the cruiser, *Tuscaloosa*, where we stayed most of the day. It would shell the shore every so often. That evening, we were all moved to the cruiser, *Quincey*, which was headed for England and re-supply. There was quite a group of us placed in a survivor center that night and then returned to our units."

161

Kurt, along with the 440th Troop Carrier Group, received the Distinguished Unit Badge for his efforts on July 5, 6, and 7, 1944, along with the Purple Heart Medal. The citations reads:

"...For outstanding performance of duty in action against the enemy of 5, 6 and 7 June 1944. On these dates, members of Group Headquarters and of the 95th, 96th, 97th and 98th Troop Carrier Squadrons of the 440th Troop Carrier Group carried out 108 sorties and dropped formations of paratroops on critical objectives as part of the Troop Carrier mission to provide the vanguard for the invasion of the European continent. Despite discouraging weather conditions, this group flew their unarmed and unarmored aircraft at minimum altitudes and air speeds, over water and through intense enemy anti-aircraft fire to accomplish their vital task which was of inestimable importance to the success of the initial phases of the invasion of Normandy. The officers and enlisted men of the 440th Troop Carrier Group displayed imperturbable coolness and unswerving devotion to duty in rendering a most distinguished service which is conspicuously outstanding in the record of accomplishment of our Air Forces."

Between March 1944 and October 1945, Kurt would take part in six more crucial battle campaigns, from southern France, to the Rhineland in Germany, and central Europe, surviving a forced emergency landing in a small field near the town of Partadown, in northern Ireland, on a return trip from Marrakech, Morocco. No crew members were hurt, but the aircraft was badly damaged.

Kurt was in France when he heard the news of the war ending in Europe. He was a student at Redding University, in England, when the war ended in the Pacific. On December 28, 1945, Kurt was honorably discharged from active duty, at Camp Beale Separation Center, California. For his service in the Army Air Corps he received the following awards: Purple Heart Medal; Air Medal with 2 Oak Leaf Clusters; Distinguished Unit Badge; European-African-Middle Eastern Service Medal with 7 Bronze Stars for campaigns in Rhineland, Central Europe, Rome-Arno, Ardennes, Southern France, Normandy, Northern France; American Theater Service Medal. He held the rank of Lieutenant Colonel.

On February 22, 1947, Kurt married Dorothy Westbrook in Lancaster, California. Together they had four children; Dana Marie, Gary Dennis, Julie Ann, and Paul Steven Ullman. After the war, Kurt attended Cal Poly, San Luis Obispo, supported by the G.I. Bill. He went into several different fields of employment with ranching, banking, real estate and a trust deed business among them. Kurt is retired and lives in Quartz Hill, California, where he commented, "I have great respect for the military. My service in the war defined my life and I believe we all matured."

97th Combat Crew – Kurt Ullman, sixth man from right, back row.
Photo courtesy of the 440th Troop Carrier Group History Project, 2003.

162

On May 15, 1923, Stanley Clinton Washburn was born, the second son of George S. and Harriet (Kallakowsky) Washburn in Stockton, San Joaquin Co., California. Stanley had one sibling, a brother, George A. Washburn. The Washburn family moved from Stockton to the Wilsona area of the Antelope Valley in 1931. Stanley graduated from AVJUHS in 1942, where he played on the Varsity basketball team along with future World War II sailor, Paul Wheeler; Merchant Marine, George Bones; and Army Air Corps pilot, Jack Cozad.

In January of 1943, Stanley was drafted into the Army Air Corps. He was inducted at Fort MacArthur, California then sent for basic training in Fresno, California. His first few days in the service were filled with confusion and getting used to the military routine. While in basic training, Stanley spent hours marching, drilling and training in basic firearms use.

After basic training, Stanley was sent to Lowry Field in Denver, Colorado, where he attended Cook and Baker School. His next stop was in Savannah, Georgia for more training, then back to California in preparation for overseas deployment.

Stanley's duty assignment was as Mess Sergeant, attached to the 133rd Army Air Force Base Unit, when he was shipped overseas to the China-Burma-India Theater of Operations. Stanley recalled his experience on the journey over to India. "The first 31 days were spent on a troop ship, to finally arrive in Bombay, India. We then spent 36 hours with 250 troops on an English ship bound for Karachi – then, another 21 days on a troop train to Assam, India."

The duties of the Mess Sergeant included supervising the mess hall, and requisitioning, purchasing and preparing food and supplies for the troops. This was accomplished while enduring the "oppressive heat and monsoon seasons." Stanley remembered, "Although our camp in Assam Province did not have any engagement with the enemy, we were directly involved with troops by flying supplies and fuel to the United States and Chinese troops. The flights were made over "The Hump" [the Himalayan Mountains] into China. A memorable moment was when we were visited by General Joe Stillwell." General Stillwell, known as "Vinegar Joe", was the Allied Commander of the China-Burma-India Theater during the start of the Pacific phase of the war.

While in India, Stanley and the troops were entertained by the classic actress, Paulette Goddard, along with other U.S.O. entertainment troops. He stayed in contact with his family by V-Mail and letters while in service of his country for over three years. Stanley was in a camp, in India, when he heard that the war had ended. "We were all so excited, we burned down the latrines!"

Stanley was discharged from the Army Air Corps in January 1946, at the rank of Staff Sergeant. He was decorated with the following awards: Asiatic-Pacific Campaign Medal; Distinguished Unit Badge; World War II Victory Medal.

On March 8, 1951, Stanley married Marion R. Wall in Lancaster, California. They had one child, a daughter, Elaine H. Washburn. After the war, Stanley was employed as a salesman with Antelope Valley Distributing Company in Lancaster. Stanley is retired and lives in Lebanon, Missouri.

In retrospect, Stanley thought that "the military did much for young, unmarried men. It made me think about the importance of family and friends. It strengthened my patriotism and pride in my country."

Arthur Allen Weaver was born February 11, 1924, in Huntington Park, Los Angeles Co., California, the son of Allen Arthur and Mabel (Dunningan) Weaver. Allen and Mabel were both born in Canada and emigrated to the United States in 1923. Arthur had two sisters; Jeanne, born in Canada, and Beth, his twin sister, born in California. The Weaver family moved to the Antelope Valley soon after Arthur was born. Allen worked for the Southern California Edison Company, while Mabel taught lessons in music and piano.

Arthur lived on Cedar Avenue, in Lancaster, while growing up and attended the Lancaster Grammar School nearby. He graduated from AVJUHS with the class of 1941.

When duty called, Arthur enlisted in the U.S. Army in March of 1943. He was inducted at Fort MacArthur in Los Angeles, then shipped to Camp Roberts, California, for basic training. After less than a month of training, Arthur was sent to Stanford University for testing to enter the Army Specialized Training Program (ASTP). After testing at Stanford, he was transferred to Santa Clara University as an ASTP student of engineering. After 18 months at Santa Clara, the program was cancelled due to a shortage of replacement troops needed in Europe.

Arthur trained with the 11th Armored Division at Camp Cooke, California, then, less than a month later, he was sent to Jackson, South Carolina to join the 26th Infantry Division, nicknamed the "Yankee Division", 101st Combat Engineers. One month later he was on a Liberty Ship bound for France. Arthur was attached to a service company that secured and delivered supplies to the companies of the 101st Combat Engineers. These supplies consisted of demolitions, ordnance needs, ammunition, food rations, and any other requests that were received. Arthur was the only one who knew how to type, so a great deal of his time was spent in preparing various orders or notices needed by those in command.

"Our unit, the 26th Infantry Division, sailed from New York on August 26, 1944," Arthur recalled, "arriving in Cherbourg, France on September 7, 1944. This was the first convoy to go directly to France. All others before went to England. The first four days aboard the Liberty Ship were beautiful, and we all spent our time standing in a chow line. On the fifth day, we hit rough weather that lasted for the rest of the trip. This meant that after the fifth day, you could get all you wanted to eat at any time of the day!

We assembled at the Normandy Hedgerows and prepared to move eastward. The first stop was an area near Fontainebleau, France, and then on to Nancy. We were now with General Patton's 3rd Army. We were moving 20 to 30 miles a day. That lasted until the Red Ball Express, who delivered gasoline, had problems and practically shut the war effort down.

The battles continued in Athieville, then Arracourt. Still in France, we were in Bezange La Grande and the Saar Union, and finally in Germany at a place called Achen. Our next move was to Metz, arriving on Christmas day. We were looking forward to this break from action when the next day, orders came down to move out and meet the enemy. We were to move north through Belgium and then to Luxembourg. There is one thing we will always remember – it was freezing cold. By the time we made it to Wiltz and Bastogne, the forces ahead of us, our Infantry and the 4th Armored, had broken through the German lines and they were retreating. Furthermore, for the first part of the battle, there were weather conditions that kept our Air Force grounded, but when the weather cleared and our planes were in the air, this signaled the beginning of the end of the Battle of the Bulge.

Our next move was to Saar Lautern, Germany. On March 25, 1945, we crossed the Rhine and were moving rapidly towards Berlin. We moved through Darmstadt and Fulda, and then moved south to Husenic, Czechoslovakia where we celebrated VE Day on May 7th, 1945. I will always remember the speed in which we moved across Europe with General Patton, and the respect he received from those he commanded."

After moving through Europe so rapidly, the troops were now stopped, awaiting orders for what to do next. Many activities were organized to keep the soldiers busy. Arthur remembered, "We had baseball and other sports. I played on the baseball team for our company and for some reason developed a painful thigh. They sent me to an area First Aid Station but they were unable to find the cause of the pain. Finally, I was transported by air to an Army hospital in Nancy, France. After several examinations, they concluded that I should be sent back to the States. This was all well and good to go home, however, all my belongings (clothes, letters, photos, notes, etc.) were back in Husenic. I tried to have someone send them to me, but it just didn't happen.

I was moved to Cherbourg, France and put aboard the U.S. Army Transport ship, *Edmund B. Alexander* that sailed on July 24, 1945 to New York. From there, I went by train to an Army hospital in Auburn, California for further treatment. I was then moved to the Army Presidio in San Francisco, California."

On January 20, 1945, Major General Willard S. Paul, commander of the "Yankee Division" added the following to a letter written by General Patton, speaking directly to the men of the 26th Infantry:

"When you initially attacked for seven days and nights without halting for rest, you met and defeated more than twice your own number. Your advance required the enemy to turn fresh divisions against you, and you, in turn, hacked them to pieces as you ruthlessly cut your way deep into the flank of the 'Bulge'. Your feats of daring and endurance in the sub-freezing weather and snow-clad mountains and gorges of Luxembourg are legion; your contribution to the relief of Bastogne was immeasurable. It was particularly fitting that the elimination of the 'Bulge' should find the Yankee Division seizing and holding firmly on the same line held by our own forces prior to the breakthrough.

I am proud of this feat by you as well as those you performed earlier. We shall advance on Berlin together."

Arthur was discharged on January 13, 1946, at the rank of Corporal. He received the American Campaign Medal; European-Africa-Middle Eastern Campaign Medal; World War II Victory Medal; Good Conduct Medal.

After arriving home, Arthur began his search for a college to attend, and at the suggestion of David Roach, Dean of AVJC in Lancaster, he applied and was accepted at Stanford University. In 1947, he graduated with a bachelor of arts degree, majoring in Economics. After completing college, Arthur was employed in the business of paper manufacturing and later, in paper recycling.

On March 31, 1951, Arthur married Lucy Ludlow in Carmel, Monterey Co., California. Together they had four children; Fred Arthur, Carrie Louise, Allen Arthur and Henry Allen Weaver. Arthur and Lucy are retired and live in the city of Orange, Orange Co., California.

Arthur stated his thoughts on how the military and war changed his life. "It must be used when necessary to preserve our freedom. It gave me a better view of our world after spending the first 18 years in Lancaster, and not going any further than Los Angeles. I was able to see the many avenues available in the life ahead."

On October 8, 1919, Lawrence Alfred Wheeler was born to William M. and Nora May (Fultz) Wheeler, in Acton, Los Angeles Co., California. He had two siblings; a brother, Paul Ernest, and sister, Thelma Wheeler. Larry graduated from AVJUHS with the class of 1937, and attended AVJC in 1938.

In June 1941, Larry was selected as an alternate chosen on the 12th draft call conducted in Lancaster. He was drafted into the U.S. Army Infantry soon after the draft call in 1941, and served in the Anti-Tank Company, assigned to the 3rd Infantry Division.

In 1943, Larry received an unexpected visit from Lancaster friend, Lt. Dave Brown. Dave was an armament officer in the Army Air Corps stationed in Tunisia and flew to Sicily, Italy, to deliver supplies. He received information from his mother that his high school buddy, Larry Wheeler, was with the 3rd Division. The soldiers of the 3rd Division were on R & R, resting, after the major battle in Sicily was near an end.

The airfield where Dave landed was a few miles away from the 3rd Division camp, so he borrowed a Jeep and was able to find the bivouacked area where Larry's anti-tank group was located. Larry was surprised when he discovered Dave standing at his tent. The two of them had about an hour to spend catching up on the good old days in Lancaster.

Larry's tour of duty ended about two months after they broke out of the beachhead at Anzio, Italy. In an Italian farmhouse where Larry's squad was observing German troop movement, they came under fire from a German 88 field gun. As the shells screamed in, the soldiers ran for their foxholes, out in the yard of the farmhouse. Larry dove into a Dutch oven, which received a direct hit from an 88 shell. When the skirmish ended, the medics dug Larry from the rubble, discovering that he had suffered a concussion. He was taken to a rear field hospital, also suffering from yellow jaundice and malaria. Larry was sent back to the United States in June 1944. He was discharged in Texas, in 1945.

Larry was discharged at the rank of Private, 1st Class. Among the awards he received for his time in the service were; the European-African-Middle Eastern Campaign Medal with four Bronze Battle Stars; American Defense Service Medal.

After the war, Larry was employed by AVJUHS District as the garage foreman in the transportation department. On April 8, 1965, Larry married Myrtle Faye (Whitaker) Sullins in Las Vegas, Clark Co., Nevada. Larry passed away on October 7, 1990, in Fresno Co., California. He is buried at the Lancaster Cemetery in Lancaster, Los Angeles Co., California.

Lawrence Wheeler, on left, with Sergeant in Italy

166

JAMES FREDERICK "JIM" WITTE

James Frederick Witte was born November 9, 1920 in Lancaster, Los Angeles Co., California, at Cedar Avenue and Lancaster Blvd. as the bank on Lancaster Blvd. was being robbed. Jim was the only child of Fred H. and Margaret (Schwaeble) Witte, both of German descent. In 1880, Jim's grandfather, John Witte, homesteaded 300 acres on 90th Street West between Avenues J and K. Jim's father, Fred, later owned and operated the alfalfa ranch.

In September 1942, Jim was drafted into the Army Air Corps. After basic training at Camp Kerns, Utah, Jim served at various duty stations in Nevada, California, Texas and Illinois before he was honorably discharged at the rank of Corporal in December 1945. While in the service he received the Good Conduct Medal and the Sharp Shooter badge.

After his discharge, Jim returned to work on the family alfalfa ranch and taught under the G.I. Bill. On September 28, 1946, Fred married Violet Austin of Mattoon, Illinois, in Hollywood, Los Angeles Co., California. They had one child, a son, Jeffrey F. Witte.

Jim was employed for many years by Lockheed Aircraft in Palmdale, California, as a supervisor in Flight Test Engineering. He was also a Lieutenant with the Los Angeles County Sheriff's Reserves for 17 years after graduating from the Police Officer Standards and Training academy. He is now retired and lives in Clovis, California with his wife, Violet, a retired elementary school teacher.

PETER J. "PETE" ZARO

Peter J. Zaro was born April 5, 1919, in Los Angeles, Los Angeles Co., California, the son of Gregorio and Desideria (Diez) Zaro, both from the Basque region of Spain. Gregorio emigrated from San Martin in 1910, and Desideria in 1912, via Le Havre, France. Pete had one sibling, a sister, Marie F. Zaro. The Zaro family moved from Los Angeles to the Fairmont area of the Antelope Valley where Gregorio owned an alfalfa ranch. Pete graduated from AVJUHS with the class of 1936.

On November 12, 1941, Pete was drafted into the U.S. Coast Artillery and inducted at Fort MacArthur, in California. He was sent to Galveston, Texas as part of the harbor defense with the Searchlight Battalion. He spent four years with the Coast Artillery and was honorably discharged at the rank of Staff Sergeant on December 11, 1945. Pete received the American Defense Medal; American Theater of Operations Medal; Good Conduct Medal.

After the war, Pete continued alfalfa farming and on November 11, 1947, he married Lilly Landa in Las Vegas, Clark Co., Nevada. They had two children; sons Pete, Jr. and Steve Zaro.

Pete passed away on June 28, 2003 in Pasco, Washington, at the age of 84. He and his wife, Lilly, had lived in Pasco, farming alfalfa since 1968. Lilly lives in Pasco near their son Pete, Jr. and his wife, Sabra, son Steve and wife, Jannette, along with several grandchildren.

Pete at home in Lancaster, California

Pete Zaro, left, with John Almandoz

Kenneth Wayne Zink was born March 19, 1925 in Breckenridge, Stevens Co., Texas, to James Boyd Zink, Sr., born about 1903 in Kansas, and Cecil Beatrice Jolly, born about 1912 in Texas. Ken had three siblings; two sisters, Marguerite Olive and Lalah Lea; and one brother, James B. Zink, Junior. James, Sr., a World War I veteran, had spent about a year in Long Beach and the Huntington Park area of Southern California as the proprietor of a restaurant near Huntington Park City. Ken's family moved to Littlerock, California in the Antelope Valley, shortly after 1930.

Ken was a student at AVJUHS in 1941 when he heard about the attack on Pearl Harbor. At the time, he was in the barn at his father's farm, milking a cow. Ken had wanted to become a soldier at a very young age and one month after he turned 18, he was voluntarily inducted into the U.S. Army.

His first days in the service were lonely, and he was scared, confused and resistant to taking orders. Basic training began at Fort Haan, near Riverside, California. Ken was assigned to the 864th Anti-Aircraft Artillery Battalion. After basic training, the Battalion was sent to Fort Irwin, near Barstow, California to train with small arms, machine guns and anti-aircraft anti-tank weapons. For practice, they fired at tank targets and socks pulled by aircraft. The troops lived in pup tents, and were allowed one shower per week. They dug in and guarded the cement battleship on the Dry Lake at Muroc (now Edwards Air Force Base) for a few weeks during training. The men kept themselves entertained by staging boxing matches and having "beer busts" about once a month. Ken volunteered for the accelerated glider training program, but the program was subsequently cancelled.

In October 1943, Ken shipped out for Hawaii assigned to the Hawaiian Anti-Aircraft Command, then to Saipan in May of 1944. In Saipan, Ken wasn't afraid to go ashore, but seeing all the bodies floating in the water bothered him. The movies "Saving Private Ryan" and "Snow Falling on Cedars" resurrected all those feelings. Ken's duty in Saipan was to locate supply dumps and then notify the unit to whom they belonged. He received a commendation for this mission.

Ken at Camp Irwin "tent city" - 1943

The worst memory he has of the war was when the Japanese made a Banzai attack using 5,000 troops – it was so bad it sounded like 50,000 were attacking. "It was their [the Japanese] last hurrah! Before attacking Tinian, there was a 72 hour barrage over our beach camp and it stopped about midnight. Everyone woke up wondering what was happening. I guess that's where the saying 'the sound of silence' comes from."

While on Saipan, another duty assignment Ken had was to update maps and charts for the General Staff. He was promoted to Staff Sergeant and later to Senior Master Sergeant, Chief of Data Control at Edwards Air Force Base.

While away from home, Ken kept in touch with his family through V-Mail and letters. At first they survived on C-rations, then later the troops were provided with a mess hall. Ken recalled a humorous moment in the mess hall. "While there, I remembered seeing a green turkey – it even smelled green!" He saw several U.S.O. shows and was entertained by several movie and music stars, including comedian, Bob Hope.

After the war, Ken enlisted into the active Army Reserves and was recalled to duty January 5, 1948. His duties included escorting deceased World War II soldiers to their home of record. He helped with the funeral arrangements, met with the soldiers families and presented a flag to the next of kin during the funeral services. Usually, this tour of duty was for six months, but the commanding officer asked Ken to stay for eleven months. He worked out of Van Nuys Airport during his reserve duty.

In December 1948, Ken reenlisted in the Air Force serving three separate tours in Japan. He was stationed in Japan from December 1948-1952, 1954-1958, and 1961-1963. While stationed in Japan, Ken married Toyoko May Yoshida on August 30, 1954. They were married by the American Consulate in Fukuoka. Ken then transferred to Edwards Air Force Base where he retired as a Senior Master Sergeant on February 2, 1970, with twenty-seven years of service.

For his service in the Army and the Air Force, Ken received the Air Force Commendation Medal; Air Force Good Conduct Medal with two Oak Leaf Clusters; Army Good Conduct Medal; Air Force Longevity Service Award with five Oak Leaf Clusters; National Defense Service Medal; Occupation Medal, Japan; Asiatic-Pacific Medal with one Battle Star; World War II Victory Medal; Meritorious Unit Award; Korean Service Medal; United Nations Service Medal; United Nations-Korean Medal; Republic of Korea War Service Medal; Outstanding Unit Award; Certificate of Commendation.

After retiring from the military, Ken settled in Littlerock, California. He needed about 40 units to complete a bachelor of arts and teaching credential, so he used the G.I. Bill. He majored in Anthropology and attended Antelope Valley Junior College, the University of Maryland and California State University at San Bernardino. Ken then taught math and science at Almondale Middle School for 13 years, along with owning and operating a fruit orchard. He was a member of the American Legion, South Antelope Valley Post #401, serving in most of the officer positions – Adjutant, Commander and Chaplain; President of the Pearblossom Kiwanis; and an Elder in the Littlerock Community Presbyterian Church.

Ken and Toyoko had three children; Lori, Wayne and Rick Zink. Ken is still living in Littlerock, California, where he is enjoying retirement. They have traveled to New Zealand, Australia, Canada, Hawaii, Japan, Jordan, and all throughout the United States.

Reflecting on his time in the military, Ken stated, "I think the service time affected my life in most ways. It taught me discipline, patience, caring for others feelings. Mostly, I learned the value of life and how it can be gone in a blink. After my outfit moved up to Mt. Tapacho, Saipan, we knew there were some Japanese in a cave on a cliff above us. The island was not secure and we knew they would ultimately starve or come out. The orders were to not climb the cliff and we obeyed. A new recruit came into the outfit and ignored the warning. He climbed, and as his head rose above the ledge, a shot rang out and a bullet went through his neck. The next day, the Japanese waved a white flag and surrendered. They came down with dignity, were all cleaned up, and the Lieutenant in their charge rode in a separate vehicle from the four enlisted men."

Saipan, Japan 1944 – Ken, U.S. Army, with brother, Jim Zink, Military Air Transport.

March 1945 Ledger-Gazette ad: H.W. "Hank" Hunter, founded his Dodge business in Lancaster in 1944. After the war, H.W. Hunter hired many of the returning veterans, including Army veteran, Al Coltzau, an employee for 37 years, Coast Guard veteran, David Batz, and Army Air Corps pilot, Charles Dungan. Today, grandsons Tom Fuller, Jr. and Tim Fuller, handle the business with a personal touch – a family tradition - currently in its third generation. "Since the founding in 1944, involvement in the community was stressed." – Tim Fuller.

H.W. HUNTER DODGE-CRYSLER-JEEP is currently located at
1130 Auto Mall Drive, Lancaster, California

U.S. NAVY, COAST GUARD & MERCHANT MARINE

173

Henry Aldrich was born at home on February 26, 1918, in Putnam, Dewey Co., Oklahoma, son of Fred Howard and Emillia Mae (Park) Aldrich. By 1920, the family had moved to Colorado. Henry had two sisters; Leta and Della, and two brothers; Harold and Samuel Aldrich.

Coming from a poor, migrant farming family, Henry decided he would be better off joining the service. He enlisted in the Navy when recruiters told him they had the best food of all the other services. After entering the Navy at Denver, Colorado May 15, 1937 at age 19, Henry later attended Submarine School at New London, Connecticut in 1940. Upon graduation in 1941 he was assigned duty aboard the submarine *U.S.S. Spearfish*.

The *Spearfish* operated between Hawaii and the west coast until October 1941 when the crew departed Pearl Harbor and headed for Manila in the Philippine Islands. They conducted training operations there from November 1941 until the outbreak of war on December 8, 1941. It was at that time the *Spearfish* was assigned her first war patrol.

This mission took Henry to the South China Sea, near Saigon and Camranh Bay, French Indochina, and Borneo. On December 20, 1941 the *Spearfish* encountered a Japanese submarine and made a submerged attack. Four torpedoes were fired, but all missed the target. In February, 1942 the second mission began with patrolling in Java and Flores Seas where they made several unsuccessful torpedo attacks on two Japanese cruiser task forces. In March they took on twelve members of the Commander of the Submarines of the Asiatic Fleet staff in Java, for transportation to Australia.

From March to May, 1941 the third war patrol took the *Spearfish* to the Sulu Sea and the Lingayen Gulf. In April they sank an enemy cargo ship and sank a large Japanese freighter. On May 3, 1941, the *Spearfish* silently slipped into Manila Bay and picked up 27 passengers from Corregidor to evacuate them to Fremantle, Australia. From June to August the submarine crew scoured the South China Sea looking for enemy ships, ending up in Luzon where they encountered and damaged two enemy freighters.

In May of 1943 the *Spearfish* returned to Pearl Harbor to begin their seventh war patrol. In June

U.S.S. Spearfish

they patrolled the Truk Island area doing photographic reconnaissance of Eniwetok Atoll, then cruised near Marcus Island, close to the Japanese installations located there.

Henry's daughter, Judi, recalled one of her father's most vivid recollections of the war. In September 1943, the *Spearfish* made a submerged torpedo attack on a convoy of seven Japanese freighters escorted by one destroyer and two torpedo boats. The submarine fired torpedoes at four of the ships and damaged two. For the next 23 hours, the submerged *Spearfish* was depth charged by the Japanese ships. Large canisters filled with TNT explosives were dropped off the ships where the enemy crew estimated the submarine was located. Henry was on the bridge of the *Spearfish*, as Chief Navigator, standing in ankle deep water, rocked by the depth charges coming at them from above. The air in the submarine was beginning to get stale and poisoned, and eventually they were forced to surface only to find they were in the middle of a squall. Luckily, the convoy of seven ships were forced to depart due to the heavy seas.

On February 25, 1947, Henry married Billie Beatrice Spencer in Tampa, Florida. They had two daughters, Henry's adopted step-daughter, Sydney, and the couple's natural child, Judith Kay Aldrich. Henry was in Tampa after being transferred in 1946 as a recruiter for the Navy.

Henry spent most of World War II aboard the *Spearfish* and another submarine, the *U.S.S. Pilotfish*. Henry Aldrich made eleven war patrols with these two units. He told his family and fellow servicemen that his time in the submarine service and the end of World War II were the highlights of his Naval career. His favorite liberty point was in Shanghai, China.

He was discharged from the regular Navy on November 26, 1956, and entered the Fleet Reserve at that time. Upon completing almost twenty years in the Navy, Aldrich said, "It doesn't seem that long. In fact, it seems like only yesterday when I came in." He professed that one of the finest benefits a person acquires in the Navy is the education gained by meeting people and getting along with them.

Henry received the American Defense Medal; American Campaign Medal; Asiatic-Pacific Campaign Medal; World War II Victory Medal; United Nations Service Medal; National Defense Service Medal; and the Good Conduct Medal.

On the lighter side of Henry's service days was a stint in the movies. Henry was an "extra" in a series of Hollywood submarine photoplays. His handsome face also adorned Hollywood movie posters for "*Submarine Command*," and advertising popular war related films of the 1950's. The photo below shows Henry about to "get powdered" before a location shot in a Navy movie sequence filmed in San Diego, California.

Henry Aldrich, QMC, SubRon 3, 2nd from right, before a movie location shot filmed in San Diego, California.

In 1957 Henry Aldrich, QMQC (SS), USNFR, Quartermaster on the Submarine Flotilla ONE Staff, was transferred to the Administrative Command, Naval Training Center, San Diego, California, where he served for two years as an active duty fleet reservist.

After his retirement from the Navy, Henry moved his family to Lancaster, California where he started the FedMart store chain with co-owner, Saul Price. In November 1966, the first Lancaster FedMart opened for business. Henry became the franchise owner of the FedMart at 20th St. West and Ave. J in Lancaster in 1967, but later sold the store back to the corporation in 1973.

Henry died May 21, 1991, in Lancaster, California, and is interred at the Desert Lawn Cemetery, in Palmdale, California.

David James Batz was born June 9, 1924, in Riverside, Riverside Co., California. He was the sixth of eight children. His father, Arthur Francis Batz, was born December 20, 1886 in St. Cloud, Minnesota. His mother, Etta Louise (Kowalski) Batz, was born on July 15, 1887, in Brownsville, Texas. The family moved from Riverside to a ranch on the east side of the Antelope Valley in 1932. Dave attended Redmond Grammar School, and graduated from Antelope Valley High School in June 1942.

Dave enlisted in the United States Coast Guard Reserve in November 1942 and served in the Pacific during World War II. He was part of the Okinawa invasion onboard a Landing Ship, Troop (LST). The contribution of the men on these vessels was an invaluable part of the Allied offensives in the Pacific Theater. The Coast Guard was called upon by the Navy to use these landing craft to ferry the soldiers ashore on the enemy beaches. The LST crews came under fire in the course of almost every invasion..

While in the Pacific, Dave's brother, Tony, serving in the U.S. Marines, was wounded on Okinawa and was hospitalized on Guam. The Captain of the ship that Dave was on arranged to have Dave flown to Guam to be there overnight with his brother. Coincidentally, when Dave landed on Okinawa for the first time, his brother, Tony, also landed within one mile on the same beach. They didn't know this at the time, and didn't find out until sometime later.

After his honorable discharge from the Coast Guard in April 1946, Dave attended Antelope Valley Junior College. He was elected President of the Student Body in the spring of 1947. Dave played football for the college where he broke his leg in the last game of the 1947 season. At that time, there were only three doctors in the valley and none were available to see him that night. His sister, Mary (Batz) Godde, took him to her house and fed him aspirin all night until they could see a doctor the next morning.

After the war, Dave worked for Challenge Dairy and later owned the Antelope Valley distributorship for the Carnation company.

Dave married Diane Rueckheim, October 25, 1959, in Lancaster, California. They owned Batz Liquors, located at the corner of 15th St. West and Ave. I in Lancaster, from 1966 – 1984. Dave then worked for H.W. Hunter, an automotive dealer in Lancaster, until he retired.

Dave Batz back row, 2nd from left

Dave and Diane were involved with quarter horse breeding and racing. They were involved in the Antelope Valley Fair for many years with the horse shows. The Batz brothers competed for many years in the hay loading contests at the Rural Olympics at the Antelope Valley Fair. Dave was also a well-renowned barbeque chef, famous for his deep-pit barbeque meat, cooking at the Old Timer's Barbeque for 30 years. In addition to local barbequing, he once prepared a feast for the former President, Ronald Reagan, during his tenure as Governor of California.

Dave passed away on September 27, 1998, in Lancaster, California, and is interred at the Good Shepherd Cemetery on the west side of Lancaster. He is survived by two daughters; Denise (Batz) Tyler and Donna (Batz) Childs.

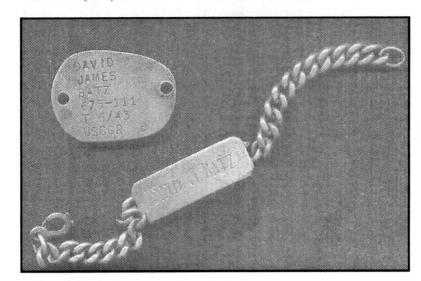

Dave Batz's Coast Guard dog tag and identification bracelet

ROBERT VANCE "DINK" BENNETT

On November 13, 1922, Robert Vance Bennett was born in Runnels Co., Texas, the son of Charles Jackson and Modesta Lea (Barnett) Bennett, both from Texas. The Bennett family was living in Runnels County in 1920 with eight children. In 1930, the family was still living in Texas, with Charles self employed as the proprietor of a filling station in Runnels County.

In 1932, Robert moved to the Antelope Valley, where he graduated from AVJUHS in 1939, at the age of 16. He attended San Angelo College in Texas, for two years, then entered the United States Naval Reserves in 1941. Robert went through training at Corpus Christi, Texas, graduating with Flight Class 8A in 1942.

On March 7, 1943, Robert married Cora Belle Padgett. While he was stationed away from home, Cora lived with Robert's sister in Texas.

On September 19, 1943, while assigned to an aircraft carrier as a fighter pilot in the North Atlantic Ocean, Ensign Robert V. Bennett was killed in a flight deck catapult accident, with his aircraft lost at sea. His name is listed on the Tablets of the Missing, Battery Park, New York City, New York. He is also

recognized on a memorial plaque in San Angelo, Texas which reads, "This memorial grove of oak trees and this tablet of bronze are affectionately dedicated to the memory of the patriotic ex-students of San Angelo College who lost their lives in World War II."

Donald Raymond Bones was born March 24, 1918 in Duarte, Los Angeles Co., California. Donald was the first son of three children born to George Raymond and Jessie Mae (Vosburgh) Bones, Senior. He had two brothers; Jack S. Bones and George Raymond Bones, Jr. The Bones family were well known pioneers in the south Antelope Valley since 1908, when Louis Bones began the "Bones Fruit Empire" in Littlerock. They ran several successful pear and peach packing houses located on Pearblossom Highway, exporting over 200,000 crates of fruit each year.

George Raymond Bones, Sr. moved to Littlerock from Baldwin Park in January of 1919, along with his bride of three years and infant son Don. They cultivated and watched their pear orchards thrive with the fruit becoming famous all around the world.

Donald was a Lieutenant in the United States Navy, serving in India, Normandy, France and Okinawa, Japan. After the war, Donald continued working in the fruit orchard business in Littlerock, owning the Don Bones Packing House. He married Marylea Stone in 1944. They had two children; Donna Lea and Dorothy May Bones. In 1966 he married Rosanell (Burhus) Schuster in Riverside Co., California.

Donald passed away December 30, 1987 in Littlerock, Los Angeles Co., California. He is interred at Desert Lawn Cemetery in Palmdale, California. Don is survived by his two daughters Donna (Bones) Sheppard and Dorothy Bones.

Bones brothers, l to r; Donald, Jack and George, Jr. with parents,
George and Jessie Bones – 50th wedding anniversary, 1966

179

GEORGE RAYMOND BONES, JR.

George Raymond Bones, Jr. was born July 22, 1925 in Littlerock, Los Angeles Co., California, the last of three sons born to George Raymond and Jessie Mae (Vosburgh) Bones, Senior. George attended grade school at Littlerock Elementary School, part of the Keppel Union School District. He attended Antelope Valley High School in Lancaster until 1942.

In 1943, George started sailing with the United States Merchant Marines, part of the U.S. Maritime Service. George spent his first weeks in boot camp in Avalon on Catalina Island, California. After training, George was sent to the Pacific Rim with the rank of Ordinary Seaman.

The Merchant Marines were first established under the U.S. Coast Guard and later supervised by U.S. Navy officers. The ships were built to transport supplies and personnel, with fleets of freighters, tankers, and transports, to bases all over the world for U.S. and Allied forces.

While on leave, June 4, 1944, George married Dorothy Zink, in Littlerock, California. On December 14, 1944, while at Avalon, George wrote the following to his wife, Dorothy:

My Darling Sugar,

I haven't got much time tonight so I won't be able to say much, as I got extra duty for having my peacoat laying on my bed besides loading a ship tonight. In fact I've got to close right now dearest, but I'll try and write more in a few minutes or hours. I love you dearest.

Well Sugar it's been 3 hours, we unloaded and loaded the boat which carries the goods for this outfit from the mainland, then we had to go on this so called extra duty, it consisted of sweeping out all the Heads and mopping them. I've got to go back on tonight at 10:00 o'clock, till, I don't know what time. It's really not so bad though as it may sound.

Today dearest, was about our easiest day for me, for one reason, there was no swimming, that is the hardest for me because they don't try and teach a guy to swim they just make him jump 20 ft. off the dock in a life jacket, about all they teach you here is about getting off a sinking ship. It's all along this line. The way they teach you is really terrific too.

Sugar, this old life of a sailor is terrible. The most terrible part about it is just being away from you, even when I would give my left arm to be with you, I can't. But I guess we are lucky to be this close, for we will be able to be again together one of these days...

Just a few lines to let you know what's over here. In the first and only place, there is nothing. You can't have a beer or nothing else other than coke and ice cream, also just the same old faces every day. I would give a million dollars to see your face right this minute even if only for a minute. My heart is in Littlerock just as yours is in Avalon, with me.

Your loving husband
Butch

Soon after this letter was written, the crew departed for Hawaii, then on to the Philippine Islands, a place George was not fond of. In his letters George said he wouldn't buy anything for himself while on shore leave as he never wanted to be reminded of that place. He described his shore leave as "hot and dusty and not even a place to get a drink of water." After walking around for about an hour, George went to the United Seaman's Club where he stood in line for "two solid hours to get five packages of gum and two bottles of beer."

On a lighter note, while ashore on the Philippines, one of George's friends bought a monkey for 20 pesos (about $10.00). After he brought it back aboard the ship, the monkey got loose and his friend was described as going up and down the masts chasing the monkey. After three hours they still hadn't caught it.

The monkey was later caught, but two days later, the ship's Chief ordered him to get rid of it. The monkey was sold at loss for $8.00.

In March, 1945, George volunteered for a daring rescue while onboard the *S.S. John Howard Payne*. In complete darkness, with rough seas, the ship's chief mate, along with George and five other men, were lowered in a lifeboat and proceeded to rescue two survivors of a crashed Army plane. George received the Meritorious Service Medal along with the following citation:

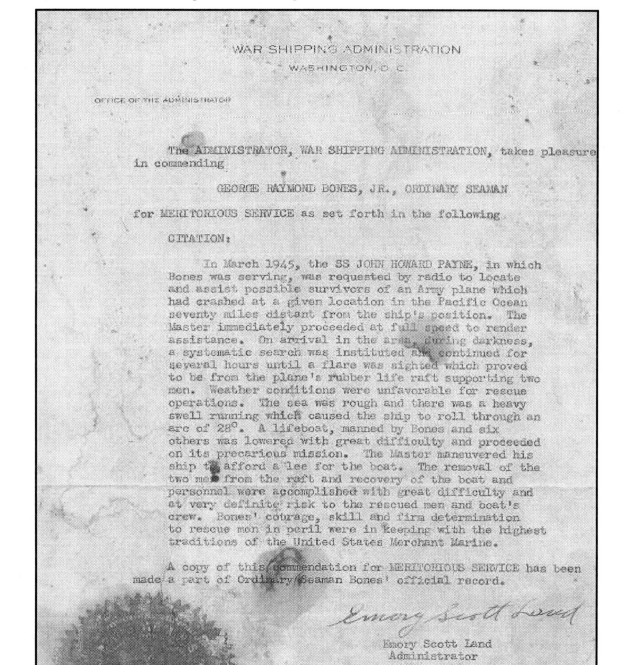

WAR SHIPPING ADMINISTRATION

WASHINGTON, D. C.

OFFICE OF THE ADMINISTRATOR

The ADMINISTRATOR, WAR SHIPPING ADMINISTRATION, takes pleasure in commending

GEORGE RAYMOND BONES, JR., ORDINARY SEAMAN

for MERITORIOUS SERVICE as set forth in the following

CITATION:

In March 1945, the SS JOHN HOWARD PAYNE, in which Bones was serving, was requested by radio to locate and assist possible survivors of an Army plane which had crashed at a given location in the Pacific Ocean seventy miles distant from the ship's position. The Master immediately proceeded at full speed to render assistance. On arrival in the area, during darkness, a systematic search was instituted and continued for several hours until a flare was sighted which proved to be from the plane's rubber life raft supporting two men. Weather conditions were unfavorable for rescue operations. The sea was rough and there was a heavy swell running which caused the ship to roll through an arc of 28°. A lifeboat, manned by Bones and six others was lowered with great difficulty and proceeded on its precarious mission. The Master maneuvered his ship to afford a lee for the boat. The removal of the two men from the raft and recovery of the boat and personnel were accomplished with great difficulty and at very definite risk to the rescued men and boat's crew. Bones' courage, skill and firm determination to rescue men in peril were in keeping with the highest traditions of the United States Merchant Marine.

A copy of this commendation for MERITORIOUS SERVICE has been made a part of Ordinary Seaman Bones' official record.

Emory Scott Land
Administrator

January 8, 1946

George passed the time while at sea by listening to music and reading old Reader's Digests. The Navy gun crew had an old phonograph player onboard and the crew joined in on "sing-a longs" with the records

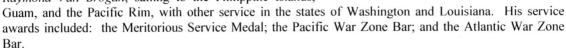

to keep them occupied while not on duty. Some of the favorite tunes were "Always" and "I'll Walk Alone." The First Engineer on the ship also played the guitar with two other men playing harmonicas, and one fellow played the saxophone to take the "gloominess" out of the nights.

George wrote letters daily, sometimes writing two or three letters per day to his wife, Dorothy. In a letter dated July 29, 1945, George wrote, "I have been hoping to get some mail started and on it's way to you before too many days, but it looks as though I may have twenty-five or thirty piled up before I can mail them, so I have decided to put two or three letters in each envelope. It will not only save stamps but they will also be a lot easier to handle when they go ashore."

While on tour with the Merchant Marines, George saw duty onboard the *S.S. John Howard Payne* and the *S.S. Raymond Van Brogan*, sailing to the Philippine Islands, Guam, and the Pacific Rim, with other service in the states of Washington and Louisiana. His service awards included: the Meritorious Service Medal; the Pacific War Zone Bar; and the Atlantic War Zone Bar.

George was in the Philippine Islands where he heard the war was over in Germany. On August 15, 1945 he was at sea, near the Marshall Islands, when he heard the war was over. It was a bittersweet day as George had just heard that Dorothy's father had passed away. One month after the war was over, he arrived at San Pedro, California, then immediately shipped out to New Orleans, Louisiana via the Panama Canal.

In the days and weeks that followed, George finally reunited with Dorothy. They celebrated the end of the war in San Francisco, California. George headed back to Littlerock where he attended classes and earned his high school diploma. He continued working on the family farm and eventually took charge of his own fruit packing plant in Littlerock. George was the last of the Bones brothers to continue in the farming business.

George and Dorothy had three children; two sons, Bradley J. Bones, Sr., and Douglas George Bones; and a daughter, Denece (Bones) Parsons. George passed away on November 30, 1995 in his hometown of Littlerock, California. He is interred at Desert Lawn Cemetery, Palmdale, California.

WILLIAM "BILL" BRADY, JR.

William Brady, Jr. was born June 14, 1921 in Easthampton, Hampshire Co., Massachusetts, the first son of William and Alice Elvira (Cross) Brady, Senior. Bill had seven siblings; four brothers – Joseph, Eugene, Erwin, and Warren; and three sisters – Marge, Alice, and Gloria. His four brothers also served in World War II. Joseph served in the Navy aboard the *U.S.S. Helena*; Eugene was an Army Ranger; Erwin and Warren both served in the Army as paratroopers.

Bill joined the Navy in April 1941, wanting to "see the world." He enjoyed his first days in the service with 16 weeks of basic training in Rhode Island as a Seaman, 1st Class. His recollection of the training was learning drills, tying knots, and sleeping in hammocks. After basic training, Bill was sent to A & E school in Detroit, Michigan. His first job assignment was as an aviation mechanic.

Bill arrived for duty in Honolulu, Hawaii, on November 2, 1941. He was stationed on Ford Island in Pearl Harbor on that Sunday morning of December 7, 1941. Bill and service mate, Bob Borger, were enjoying the morning sun out at the ball field, playing catch, when they witnessed the *U.S.S. Arizona* blowing up. All of a sudden, the Japanese planes were overhead, strafing them. In the next hours and days, "pure chaos" was what happened as Bill described, "Over the loudspeaker it was announced that everyone was to return to their duty stations. We were temporarily assigned from our squadron into the mess hall. We knew where that was, so we went down there to try and put the fires out. They called us again, after we got that taken care of, then they called us to sick bay to help with the injured. We then went down to the beach where all the ships were coming in and we started swimming out to help them. That went on for the next three of four days."

Only an unusual turn of events had saved Bill and his friend Bob, from being one of the thousands killed or injured on the *U.S.S. Arizona*. Bill was supposed to have gone to a "Battle of the Bands" on the *Arizona*, by motor launch, the night before, but a problem with one of their friends kept them back at the barracks on Ford Island. Bob's father was not so lucky – he was one of the crew who perished that day, trapped inside the hull of the *Arizona*. This would be one of the worst events Bill would witness during his 13 years of service with the Navy.

Bill was involved in six major sea battles during the war. Beginning at Pearl Harbor, Bill moved on to New Guinea and the Battle of the Coral Sea. Next, he would enter the Battle of Midway, then on to Guadalcanal for the Battle of the Solomon's, the Philippines, then up to Okinawa, Japan. Bill was in many different squadrons; VP-21, 82, and 204; VB-128 and VB-772. The VP squadrons were aviation patrol duty, with the VB squadrons, bombers. Most of his time was spent in the Lockheed Ventura airplane, a twin-engine bomber, where he was positioned back in the tail section, laying on his stomach with a K-20 camera.

Lockheed Ventura

While on a mission, striking over Borneo, Bill's airplane was shot down by the Japanese. The pilot headed out to sea to ditch the airplane in the water. He made as smooth a landing as he could in the ocean, given the circumstances. The five man crew used one three man raft and one seven man raft to make their escape. They tied the two rafts together and spent the next five days at sea, hoping to be rescued. With only a few cans of fresh water and hardtack to eat, their situation looked hopeless.

Of the five men that went down with the airplane, one man – the radioman – got his leg stuck when they crashed. He contracted gangrene, became delirious and died while in the raft. The men gave him a burial at sea. After he died, the remainder of the crew went into the seven man raft and towed the other raft behind them. The days were extremely hot and the nights were very cold. Sharks were approaching the rafts so they used what shark repellent they had. After the fifth day they were spotted by a DC-3 airplane which was circling and circling above the rafts. A day or two later, they were picked up by the U.S.S. Yukon, a refrigerator ship. While onboard, the ship's doctor only allowed them to eat crackers for the first day, then after that, they could eat all they wanted. Since the ship was a refrigerator ship, they had all the meat they could eat!

The Silver Star was awarded to Bill after he broke radio silence to alert the crews of 18 B-24's from the Air Corps, about a Japanese anti-aircraft cruiser they had detected during a strike on Singapore. Bill's squadron had 15 airplanes, loaded with 500 pound bombs. They were aiming at 20 major cargo ships in the harbor. They went in at an altitude of 500 feet, and to their surprise an undetected Japanese anti-aircraft cruiser appeared as the squadron made their approach.

Bill's group was the third group to go in. The anti-aircraft fire had downed the first groups going in for the strike and the Japanese fighters were now attacking their group. They shot down three of the Japanese fighters as they dropped their bombs and quickly headed out of the area, short on fuel and under fire. They alerted the Lt. Colonel in charge of the Air Corps and directed him to come in on another approach to avoid the anti-aircraft cruiser. As Bill's group was departing Singapore, they saw the B-24's drop their 1,000 pound bombs and leave the area.

When they returned to the Navy base, Bill began counting airplanes to see who made it back and who didn't. That night the squadron lost 12 of the 15 airplanes. Soon after they had landed, Bill recalled seeing a B-24 coming in on the Naval landing strip. This was unusual as the Navy and the Army Air Corps had separate landing strips. He wondered what was wrong, then someone said, "He's probably going to get us for breaking radio silence." The B-24 pilot landed and wanted to know who was with the squadron that just came in. He said out of the 18 B-24's that went in, they only lost two, thanks to the warning from the Navy squadron. He praised the group and invited them back to the Air Corps area.

A few weeks later, the Air Corps sent a messenger over to Bill's group, inviting them over to their ready room. As they walked in, the crew gave them a big cheer, and the Lieutenant Colonel informed them the General in charge had recommended Bill and the pilot for the Silver Star. Another crew member received the Distinguished Flying Cross, while the radioman and the co-pilot received an Air Medal.

During his service with the Navy, Bill was awarded the Silver Star; three Distinguished Flying Crosses (Borneo, Guadalcanal and the Battle of Midway); six Navy Air Medals; two Presidential Unit Citations; and a Navy Unit Citation.

After World War II, Bill continued his service in the Naval Reserve until 1948. On October 2, 1948, he married Florence Edna Wilkinson in Northampton, Hampshire Co., Massachusetts. Four children were born from this union; one son and three daughters.

Bill was recalled in 1951 to serve his country during the Korean War. He was honorably discharged from the Navy in 1954. He worked for Douglas Aircraft in El Segundo, California, after the war. The family settled in the Antelope Valley in 1954 where Bill worked for Lockheed as a flight line mechanic for 30 years. He retired from Lockheed in 1984.

Bill continues to participate in the community with the Veterans of Foreign Wars and the American Legion. He is also a member of the Pearl Harbor Survivor's Association. He frequently speaks at local middle schools and high schools about his experiences during World War II. Bill and his wife, Florence, currently live in Palmdale, California.

Bill Brady, standing at far right, with Navy buddies

CLIFFORD GREENLEAF "CLIFF" BURTON

On January 25, 1925, Clifford Greenleaf Burton was born in Bakersfield, Kern Co., California, the son of H. Clifford and Alice E. (Greenleaf) Burton. H. Clifford immigrated to the Antelope Valley from England in 1900. His wife Alice, was born in Bakersfield, California.

The Burton family lived near the Tropico Gold Mine, five miles west of Rosamond, Kern Co., California, where Cliff's father was the mine superintendent at the Tropico Mining and Milling Company.

Cliff graduated from AVJUHS with the class of 1941. He heard about the attack on Pearl Harbor on his car radio while driving to Newport Beach, California. He enlisted in the U.S. Navy in Los Angeles, then was sent on a long train ride to the Great Lakes for boot camp training.

After boot camp, Cliff was sent to a pre-electronics school in Chicago, Illinois. He went on to electronics school in Gulfport, Mississippi and then to Treasure Island in San Francisco, California. The Navy was in need of electronics (radar) repairmen at that time.

Cliff was in San Francisco at Treasure Island, when the war in Europe ended. He remembers the celebrations on Market Street, San Francisco, with people celebrating in the streets. Soon after, Cliff was onboard a troop ship for 30 days, heading from San Francisco, passing Iwo Jima, and anchoring at Okinawa where the bay was full of ships loaded for the invasion of Japan. Many of the ships were wrecked and onshore due to a recent typhoon. The survivors from the storm were taken onboard Cliff's troop ship.

The troop ship sailed again to Sasebo, Japan, where Cliff was transferred to a repair ship, the *U.S.S. Beaver*. He went from port to port in Japan doing repair work on other ships. From Japan, the *Beaver* went to Shanghai, China. There, Cliff was transferred ashore to shore patrol duty, a job that would last for several months. In 1946, Cliff was finally sent home, where he was glad to return safely to his family.

After his return home, Cliff renewed old friendships and returned to school. He attended the University of California, Berkeley, where he earned his Bachelor's degree in Mining Engineering. On April 8, 1950, Cliff married Alice Harper in Westwood, Los Angeles, Co., California. Together they had two children; a son, John Clifford, and a daughter, Wendy Elizabeth Burton. Cliff continued in the footsteps of his father as a mining engineer, and now lives in La Mesa, San Diego Co., California.

From his time in the service, Cliff has "great memories of meeting with Japanese families. It gave me increased respect for people of other nationalities, race, and ethnic back-grounds."

Cliff, left, with Japanese friends and shipmate, Marty Alves, far right. Nagoya, Japan – 1945.

185

On March 11, 1922, Stanley Paul Butchart was born in New Orleans, Plaquemines Parish, Louisiana, the son of James Paul and Nellie Eva (Jacker) Butchart. James was born in the state of Washington and Nellie was born in Chicago, Illinois.

In the fall of 1940, after graduating from high school in Spokane, Washington, Stan entered Spokane Junior College where he took part in the Civilian Pilot Training (CPT) program. He completed both primary and secondary CPT in 1941. His goal was to become a naval aviator.

Stan enlisted in the U.S. Navy in July 1942 as a Seaman 2nd Class, which was soon changed to Aviation Cadet (V-5 Pre-Flight program). He spent ten weeks in pre-flight school at St. Mary's College in Moraga, California, then three months at Pasco, Washington for primary flight training. He was then transferred to Corpus Cristi, Texas for three months of advanced flight training. Stan received his Navy wings on July 3, 1943. After eight carrier landings on a make-shift carrier on Lake Michigan, he was assigned to Torpedo Squadron 51 (VT-51).

While assigned to VT-51, Stan flew the Eastern (GM) TBM Avenger, a torpedo bomber, onboard the *U.S.S. San Jacinto*, in the South Pacific. In June, 1944, the *Jacinto* would take part in the Marianas operation and in the Battle of the Philippine Sea. The bombers struck targets in Palaus, the Bonins and the Carolines. In October of 1944, they participated in raids on Okinawa, Formosa, the Philippines and in the Battle of Leyte Gulf.

On October 10, 1944, Stan was sent into action against the Japanese fleet. Stan recalled when "a surface anti-aircraft round blew a large hole through the right wing of my TBM torpedo bomber. I still made it back aboard my carrier, the *San Jacinto*. I was hit several other times, but not as bad."

On January 5, 1945, Stan married Miriam Alma Young, in Salisbury, Wicomico Co., Maryland.

Stan was on the island of Maui, in a swimming pool, relaxing while preparing for his second tour to the Pacific, when he heard the war was over. When he heard the news he was "damned happy!" Stan was discharged in November 1945, in Seattle, Washington at the rank of Lieutenant. The Distinguished Flying Cross and a Presidential Unit Citation were among the many medals and citations Stan received for his service during World War II.

After his discharge, Stan flew back to Maryland to reunite with his wife, Miriam. While in Maryland, he bought a car, a 1940 Plymouth, and drove back to Spokane, Washington. In January 1946, Stan enrolled in school at the University of Washington, where he would obtain a Bachelor's degree in Aeronautical Engineering. He graduated in June of 1949. From September 1949 – June 1950, he was back at the University of Washington to secure a Bachelor's degree in Mechanical Engineering. After graduation, Stan went to work for Boeing Aircraft as a junior design engineer.

Stan and Miriam had four children together; Deborah Ann, Dean Stanley, Deidre Kay, and Dale Paul Butchart. The Butchart family moved to the Antelope Valley on May 10, 1951, in time for Stan to start his new career as a research pilot with Dryden, then called the High-Speed Flight Research Station. Stan made flight test history by launching rocket-powered planes early on in the 1950's at Edwards Air Force Base. While piloting the B-29 and P2B, he launched the rocket-powered X-1A, X-1B, X-1E, and the D-558-II. By 1966, he was head of the Research Pilots Branch and later became the acting chief of Flight Operations. Stan retired from NASA/Dryden on February 27, 1976, as director of Flight Operations.

Stan joined the Society of Experimental Test Pilots and became one of 65 Charter Members. He was elected a Fellow of the Society and became the Society president in 1980. He was selected for the Aerospace Walk of Honor in Lancaster, California where a granite monument stands in his honor. Stan keeps in touch with the friends he made while in the Navy, including former U.S. President, George H.W. Bush, also a pilot in Torpedo Squadron VT-51. Stan still calls Lancaster his home where he has resided for over 52 years.

Future wife, Miriam Young and Stan Butchart
Salisbury, Maryland - March 1944

Stan Butchart – November 1943
Salisbury, Maryland

Torpedo Squadron VT-51 group photo taken at Chincoteague, Virginia, 1943
Front row, kneeling, 3rd from left, Ensign Stan Butchart; Back row, 5th from left, Ensign George H.W. Bush

Gordon L. Campbell was born April 6, 1926 in Lancaster, Los Angeles Co., California, the fourth of four sons born to George M. and Adna Fern (Cheney) Campbell, Sr. The Campbell family moved from Bakersfield to the Antelope Valley where George was employed as a salesman for an oil company. Gordon graduated from AVJUHS in the class of 1944. Gordon's three older brothers also served in the military during World War II; George, Jr., served with the Marine Corps while Paul and John served in the Navy.

Gordon enlisted in the U.S. Navy and was inducted in 1944 at the Los Angeles Induction Center. His first days in boot camp were filled with confusion and learning how to live communally in large barracks with hundreds of people he didn't know. After boot camp, Gordon was sent to the Amphibious Training Center on Coronado Island, San Diego, for three months training in amphibious operations. His first assignment was as a deckhand/coxswain on a LCVP (Landing Craft, Vehicle, Personnel) on the *U.S.S. Mellette*, APA-156.

Gordon saw combat in several landings during WWII, including Iwo Jima, Okinawa and Tokyo Bay at the war's end. While onboard the LCVP delivering the Marines to the beachhead at Iwo Jima, Gordon recalled this harrowing story:

"At Iwo Jima, after delivering our cargo of 1,500 Marines to the beachhead on mid afternoon, February 19, 1945, an injured Marine climbed up the ramp of our LCVP. We took him out to an Aid Station set up on a barge out of range of the Jap artillery. The Aid Station then gave us about 10 or 15 severely wounded Marines to transport out to the *U.S.S. General Stuart Heintzelman* (APA-159), several miles distant. After locating the ship and unloading the wounded Marines, it was late in the day – nearly dinner time – so we hurried back to our ship in the little LCVP. Instead of dinner, we got loaded down with a communications Jeep and trailer with orders to unload it and return to the ship as soon as possible as they were under orders to unload their cargo and depart the area as soon as possible.

On reaching the control boat for our segment of the beach, the officer in charge took one look at our cargo, pointed to a nearby portable, floating dock, and told us we could not unload the Jeep until morning. The officer said to tie our boat up, in the meantime, and get some rest. There were a couple of other boats from the *Mellette* there and the crews were surprised, and relived, to see us. They thought we'd been lost on the beach to shellfire.

We spent much of the night watching the "fireworks" on the island. At one point, an LCVP from the *U.S.S. Bayfield* (APA-33) our squadron flagship, came by with a worried crew and two cargo nets full of land mines aboard. Three of the crewmen wandered off, down the dock, while the fourth disappeared down amongst the land mines for a while. Sometime later, someone noticed that their boat was riding very low in the water. All four of its crewmen were gone now, somewhere among the dozens of boats. Their boat was obviously sinking now so I untied it from the dock and gave it a push. The ocean currents caught it and away it went, never to be seen again. Later, someone claimed to have heard the crew talking about scuttling their boat to keep from having to land such a hazardous cargo on the beach which was heavily under Japanese shellfire.

On D (battle day) +1, we were again denied the beach, this time because the seas were too rough and we would surely lose both the Jeep and our boat if we tried to land. This didn't seem to bother the Marine Sergeant who came with the Jeep. Every hour or so, throughout the day, he would crank up the generator powering his radio, mutter a few coded words into it, shut it off, then crawl into a corner somewhere to sleep. D+2 and D+3 were the same. We had only some C-rations to eat (cookie shaped biscuits, somewhat like hardtack).

On D+4, we went back to our ship and asked them to *please* take the Jeep back and reload it onto some larger vessel which *could* get to the beach. They wouldn't even allow us a few minutes aboard to get something to eat. We were told, "The ship must be unloaded and ready to depart by noon of the next day, so get to it." By lunch time, Phillips, our boat's Coxswain, decided to take drastic measures. We set out for the U.S.S. Bayfield for help. It was mid-afternoon before we found it. The ship's Captain, when apprised of our situation, called down to the deck officer, "Hoist that Jeep aboard. If I have to, I'll take it home with me!" We were allowed, two at a time, to go aboard for a hot meal. Phillips and I went first. We ate quickly in order to allow our other two crewmen time to eat.

After the two crewmen went onboard the Bayfield, the seas began to rise. Soon after, the sun began setting. It seemed the other two crewmen were staying forever! Finally, well after dark, the deck officers signaled us back alongside to pick up our two wayward crewmen. We didn't realize until we were back alongside the ship, just how high the seas were running. One moment we would be only five or ten feet below the ship's deck, only to plunge down to about 20 fee below the deck the next moment. After a couple of tries, our two crewmen realized it was entirely too risky to try further. The ship had been ordered back out to sea and was already getting underway. Phillip yelled at them to stay onboard until morning when we would pick them up.

Blue Beach, Iwo Jima, D-Day + 1 or 2, February 20/21, 1945, with amphibious ducks at water's edge. Photo Copyright Nadine Whalen, widow of Lt. Howard Whalen, Boat Group Commander, U.S.S. Sanborn, APA-193.

Phillips and I quickly found ourselves alone, many miles from the island, in pitch blackness and rough seas. Iwo was visible on the horizon, sporadically illuminated by flares or shell bursts. Phillips had the wheel and steered for the island at about eight knots – fast enough to send salt spray over the boat with each wave we encountered. I was perched on the bow, keeping an eye out for 'whatever', since the person steering a Higgins Boat (nickname for a LCVP) cannot see directly ahead. With each passing wave (and there were many waves) I got drenched with salt water. Finally, I think about midnight, Phillips was too exhausted and sick (he claimed) to continue, so he turned the wheel over to me and crawled down in to the cargo space, under a tarp, to rest.

I continued at the same speed until I was reasonably sure that he was asleep. The ocean spray was still whipping into my face, so I cut our speed about half, around four knots. Some time later I could make out the outline of a destroyer, some distance ahead, firing one of its forward guns every minute or two. I picked a course which would bring us close to her port side. It seemed to take forever at our slow pace to come up on the destroyer. We had a system of identification signals in place: a lamp with a red lens was to be waved horizontally on even-numbered nights, and vertically on odd-numbered nights – or was it visa-versa? Coincidentally, the red lens on our flashlight had been broken a night or two back. Someone had scrounged up a red cloth as a substitute, so as we neared the ship, I began groping about for the flashlight and the rag. I called Phillips for help, but he was beyond hearing. Finally I found both the flashlight and the rag, and laid them down within easy reach, just as we came astern of the ship. Inching along passed it, I watched anxiously – maybe they wouldn't see us – maybe they wouldn't care about us – Geez, was it an even night or odd?? We were about mid-ship now. Suddenly, a small white light flashed from the deck, just below the superstructure. I had to assume they were signaling me, so I grabbed the light. Even or odd? Hell, I didn't know, so I gave them both – let them decide! Well, they didn't blow us out of the water. No one hailed us, no one signaled, they just totally ignored us!

LCVP or Higgins Boat, approx. 36' in length x 10' 10" wide, capacity: 36 men.

Dawn was breaking when we finally got within sight of our floating dock. Phillips roused himself then, looking a little sheepish on realizing that he'd slept through the entire night. The transport ships were returning to anchorage now, and we, spotting the *Bayfield*, set out for it. After recovering our other two crewmen, we struck out for our own ship, the *Mellette*, joining the group of Higgins Boats circling behind it, waiting for another load to take to the beach.

We were signaled to come along side. Lt. Mackay, one of our Boat Group officers, called down and told us to go to the Mess Hall for breakfast. While eating, Lt. Mackay heard about our "adventure" and sent us off to our quarters to rest. Some hours later, we were abruptly awakened by a huge commotion up on deck. It was a terrible racket, which we finally realized were the ships guns being fired. I scrambled up to see what was going on, getting there just in time to see a small airplane, several miles off, trailing a cloud of smoke as it slowly went down and crashed into the sea. (We had never been below decks before, during gunnery drills, so the sound and vibration from all the guns was new to us) Twelve 40mm cannons, a bunch of 20mm's, plus one five inch cannon, can create quite a racket when all fired at once!

A short time later, they called our boats in and began hoisting them back aboard ship. After five days, our part of the Iwo Jima campaign was over. I feel a bit guilty now, so many years later, to have gotten out of that one so easily, compared to what the Marines went through in order to take the island. Guilty, but fortunate."

Gordon was onboard ship, leaving the harbor at Guam and on his way to San Francisco, when he heard the war was over. The ship was called back and rerouted to Japan instead, where they were part of the Allied ship force present in Tokyo Bay during the surrender ceremony, September 2, 1945. Gordon spent two years in the Navy, from 1944 to May 1946, when he was honorably discharged at Camp Shoemaker at the rank of Seaman, 2nd Class. After he was discharged, Gordon hitchhiked to Lancaster where he renewed

190

acquaintances with his old friends. He attended Antelope Valley Junior College and then continued his education at the University of Redlands in California. Gordon spent five years employed in Engineering Surveying; eleven years in Engineering Materials testing; and fifteen years as a Geologist.

Gordon and Harriet Mae Wethy were married June 29, 1961 in Miami, Dade Co., Florida. Gordon is retired and currently lives in Ormond Beach, Volusia Co., Florida.

U.S.S. Mellette (APA-156), Amphibious Attack Transport Ship - Gordon Campbell's home during World War II. Photo courtesy of Gordon L. Campbell.

John William Campbell was born October 11, 1924, in Bakersfield, Kern Co., California, the third of four sons born to George Montgomery and Adna Fern (Cheney) Campbell, Sr. John attended AVJUHS until he enlisted in the Navy in August 1942, two months before his 18th birthday. He was proud to join the Navy to serve his country and protect his family during wartime.

John's first day at boot camp in San Diego, California was a breeze. They served cornbread and beans for breakfast – John thought it was great, while most of the other recruits hated it. After boot camp John was sent to Machinist Mate School, then after completion of the training, shipped out to Pearl Harbor. While at Pearl Harbor, he worked on the recovery of the U.S.S. Oklahoma while waiting for his assignment to a ship.

His first assignment was onboard the *U.S.S. Monongahela* (AO-42) as a deckhand. John enjoyed standing watch in the crow's nest. It was a thrilling climb for him with an impressive view of the ocean at the top.

John's next ship assignment was onboard the *U.S.S. De Grasse* (AK-223, formerly AP-164) where he celebrated his twentieth birthday on October 11, 1944, dry-docked at Pearl Harbor. On November 11, 1944, the *De Grasse* steamed in a convoy from Pearl Harbor to Eniwetok Atoll, Marshall Islands, anchoring in Eniwetok Lagoon on November 22, 1944. After two days, they were underway again, this time bound for Saipan Island, Marianas. Early morning on November 30, they raised anchor, en route for a short distance to Tinian, Marianas, where they anchored a few hours later. The next day, the troops were allowed to disembark while the cargo was discharged. On December 7, 1944 general quarters were called to repel against Japanese air attacks.

With the supplies unloaded, the *De Grasse* was back at sea, headed for Pearl Harbor; Hilo, Hawaii, and Honolulu, Oahu, where the ship was moored for a short time. On February 13, 1944, they were on their way again, this time to Guam via Eniwetok Atoll, Marshall Islands. Many of the days were spent with the routine duties onboard ship, exercising the crew at general drills, firing practice, and loading/unloading troops and equipment at their battle destinations in the South Pacific.

The *De Grasse* carried troops from Eniwetok, Guam, Saipan, and Majuro, to Ulithi, the staging point for the Okinawa operation. In April 1945 the *De Grasse* arrived off Okinawa unloading men and supplies at Ie Shima, Ryuku Islands. Due to nightly air raids, the crew was forced to stop unloading and go to a place of shelter. Continuously receiving the "Flash Red" alert, "all hell broke loose." Fifty Japanese planes were reported overhead one night – "The air was rent with the roar of machine gun fire and the sky was filled with tracers. Low flying planes were diving across the heavy concentration of ships in the harbor. We learned later, from a reliable source, that this was the heaviest concentration of fire ever put up in the Pacific until this time."

While anchored off of Okinawa, a Japanese Kamikaze almost hit the *De Grasse*, crashing into a ship anchored next to it. None of the crew was injured on the *De Grasse*, but the adjacent ship suffered considerable damage and crew injuries. The crew also experienced a typhoon while in the harbor at Okinawa. A warning was issued, sending the ship out to sea to ride it out. John recalled this as one of his most harrowing experiences.

John was at sea, in the South Pacific, en route from Saipan, Marianas Islands to San Francisco, California, when he heard the news that the war was over. He was thankful that we won the war and he was finally going home. He was also very grateful that his three brothers were also going home unscathed. John was discharged March 16, 1946. He received the Asiatic/Pacific Medal with three Battle Stars; the American Area and Victory Medals. John returned home to Lancaster to spend time with his family and friends. He ate all the foods he couldn't get at sea, especially fresh fruit and vegetables. He went to work at Aven's Furniture Company and Standard Oil Company in Lancaster, for a short time after returning home. He attended Antelope Valley Junior College in 1947. John married Lucille Helen Wethy, October 2, 1948, in San Francisco, California, then spent three years at Charron-Williams Commercial College in Miami, Florida. He chose the Accounting/Auditing field for his career after attending college.

John enjoyed the camaraderie of his fellow shipmates and joined the American Legion, Post 98, in Coral Gables, Florida. He was a member of the Guadalcanal Campaign Veterans Association and the *U.S.S. De Grasse* Reunion Club. John and Lucille attended the *De Grasse* annual reunions every year until his death on February 22, 2001. His widow, Lucille, still attends the reunions in memory of her husband, John. John passed away in Miami, Dade Co., Florida and is buried in the Lancaster Cemetery District, Lancaster, California.

Photo left: John Campbell, left; center Bob Cook, AVHS buddy; and right, unknown shipmate. Photo right: Navy memorabilia collected by John Campbell during World War II. Top – "The Borders" Fleet Recreation activity center program, Waikiki, Oahu..."swimming; good eats and drinks; reading and writing; library with newspapers; games and gadgets; fun and frolic every minute." Middle: Joe DiMaggio's Yacht Club, circa 1945 table card – a favorite watering hole for servicemen in San Francisco, California. Below: U.S.S. De Grasse, U.S. Navy photo. All photos courtesy of Lucille Campbell.

Howard Max Crane was born February 14, 1918 in Pratt, Pratt Co., Kansas, the son of William, from Indiana, and Emily (Roy) Crane, from California.

William and Emily were married in Fallon, Nevada, in 1913 and crossed the Nevada desert by horse and wagon to Oregon, where Howard's older brother was born. Later the family traveled to Kansas where Howard was born. In 1929, the family decided to move to Fair Oaks, California so Emily could be closer to her family.

From 1940 through 1941, Howard attended Sacramento Junior College where he took courses in Aeronautics. In 1941, Lockheed Aircraft Company offered Howard a job in Burbank, California, where he worked until entering the U.S. Navy on November 6, 1942.

Howard was sent to the U.S. Naval Air Station at North Island in San Diego, California, where he was trained to work on the aircraft coming back from the Pacific war zone. His group was part of the Emergency Repair and Patrol Division.

Howard flew the occasional patrol and repair checkout flights onboard the aircraft in accordance with the Navy rule – if you worked on the aircraft, you had to fly in it to fix the problems, if possible. Howard worked on the following aircraft: Consolidated's PBY-2 & PBY-4; North American SNJ; Curtiss SB2C; Grumman F6F, F4F, TBF, TBM, and other Navy aircraft coming in from repair depots and U.S. factories to be delivered to Navy Squadron Groups overseas.

In February 1946, Howard was discharged from the Navy at the rank of Aviation Machinist's Mate, First Class, at San Pedro, California. During his service he received the World War II Victory Medal; American Area and the Good Conduct Medal. After serving almost four years in the Navy, Howard returned to work at Lockheed Aircraft Corporation.

On December 31, 1947, Howard married Betty Mueller in Pasadena, California. They had two daughters; Laura and Gale Crane. Betty passed away in 1970, and on December 26, 1971, Howard married Cora Belle Walburn in Lancaster. She had two sons, Mitch and Glenn Miller, from a previous marriage.

Howard continued working at Lockheed, mostly in their Experimental Engineering Division on flight testing of airplanes in Burbank and Palmdale, California. He worked on the Lockheed Hudson Bomber, P-38; B-17; PV-2; F-94; F-104; T-33; U-2; SR-71; and the F-117 Stealth aircraft. Howard retired from Lockheed in 1983.

Howard and Cora Belle currently live in Palmdale, California, where they enjoy time spent researching their family history.

KENNETH RAYMOND "KEN" CREESE

Kenneth Raymond Creese was born April 7, 1924, in San Diego, California, the son of Arthur Raymond, a WWI veteran born in Pennsylvania, and Daisy Bull (Marginson) Creese, from England. Ken had two sisters; Gladys and Irene Creese. In 1930, Arthur worked as a welder for the Gas Co. in San Diego, living with his wife and three children.

Arthur passed away during the Depression when Ken was only 12 years old. Daisy worked as a dental nurse, trying to support three children by herself. Ken attended school at Hoover High in San Diego, where he played football and was a member of the band as a trumpet player.

Ken was 17 on April 7, 1941. On the 21st of April, he joined the U.S. Navy, underage, and not yet finished with high school. With the depression still ongoing, (and the dislike of English Literature in high school) Ken felt the need to join the service to take some of the financial burden away from his widowed mother.

Ken went through boot camp in San Diego then was assigned special duty as a telephone operator at the main gate, where he stayed for another two months. Ken shipped out to Pearl Harbor onboard the *U.S.S. Wharton*. After arriving at Pearl Harbor, he went to berth on the receiving ship, the *U.S.S. Dixie*. Ken was then assigned to the 1st Division onboard the *U.S.S. Detroit*, a light, 4-stack cruiser.

While assigned to the *Detroit*, the crew went to sea from Pearl Harbor every two weeks for training which lasted through the latter part of November 1941, and into the first few days of December. Approximately two weeks before the Pearl Harbor attack, the *Detroit* went into the floating dry dock for repairs and scraping the bottom of the ship. Ken said "It was one of the hardest jobs I had to do while in the Navy. (It was all hands over the sides until the job was completed) We tried to get an extension to stay in the dock for a few more days, but the request was denied." The *Detroit* left the floating dry dock on Tuesday, December 2, for trial runs at sea. They returned to Pearl Harbor on the Friday afternoon of December 5, 1941. The *Detroit* was sitting high in the water, as they hadn't taken on any fuel or stores after the trial runs.

On Sunday, December 7, the *Detroit* was tied up to Fox F-13, next to Ford Island, just in front of the *U.S.S. Raleigh*, and directly across from the *U.S.S. Arizona* which was on Battleship Row. Ken was getting ready to take a trip around the island. He'd been there since August 1941 and had never gone around it. He was planning to take liberty and go site seeing around the island, relax and take a break from his duties. Ken wouldn't get to make the trip until 1971.

The first sense of something wrong was the sound of the bugle call. The first call sounded was for fire and rescue. Ken's station was on the fo'c'sle [pronounced *fok-sul*], on the forward part of the ship. When he arrived at his station, Ken saw smoke coming from Ford Island. Just about that time they sounded General Quarters. A ladder ran from the forward deck to the upper gun deck where Ken's position on the 6" gun battery was, which was on the port side of the ship. They couldn't fire the main battery in the harbor, so they took the crews from the port and starboard batteries and started passing 3" ammunition up to use on the 3" gun instead.

Pearl Harbor, December 7, 1941

195

Japanese torpedo planes attacked the ships *Detroit*, *Raleigh*, and *Utah*. Six torpedoes were dropped hitting the *Raleigh* and *Utah*. One torpedo passed under the *Detroit's* fantail and ran up on Ford Island. Ken had a view of the *Utah*, which was right behind the *Raleigh*, capsizing. One Japanese plane under fire from the *Detroit* was set on fire and crashed on the *U.S.S. Curtiss*.

Ken recalled one of the Japanese planes coming down between the *Detroit* and Ford Island, "It was machine-gunning the guys who had abandoned ship from the *Utah*, swimming to shore. We were very fortunate because we'd been to sea and we were sitting high in the water. The torpedo went right under our fantail – that's the one they discovered on the beach. It had fins on it to make it run shallow. We had a cluster of bombs miss our port bow. During the second wave, we had a cluster of about 8-10 bombs. It looked like it was going to hit us directly, but at the last second, they veered off to the port side and hit about 100' off our port bow."

The *Detroit* received orders to get underway and rounded the north end of Ford Island, then turned south, passing the beached *U.S.S. Nevada* off Hospital Point. The bright orange and red flames were visible as they left the harbor. Billows of black smoke were so dense it was impossible to see all the devastation. "We were very lucky – *our* ship." said Ken. "We didn't get hit, except for a few machine gun bullets in the stack. One of my shipmates was wounded in the ankle from the shrapnel that hit one of the stacks and received the Purple Heart. We really didn't see the devastation until we came back from sea after three days. The battleships and everything else had been hit and sunk."

After the attack on Pearl Harbor, the crew of the *Detroit* spent time escorting the *S.S. Matsonia* and *S.S. Lurline* converted luxury liners back to the U.S. The ships were carrying the wounded and military families back home. They made three runs from Pearl Harbor to the U.S. between December 1941 to April 1942.

Ken's longest sea tour was based out of Adak, the largest Army/Navy base for the fleet in the Aleutian Islands, Alaska. They had some tough times with the icy weather in the Bering Sea. The waves at times were 60 – 80 feet high. Ken was also involved in the Battle of Attu and Kiska. When they went to take Kiska, the crew thought they would have a huge battle on their hands. The only things they found on the island were abandoned houses and a lone dog, left by the Japanese. The Japanese had evacuated almost 10,000 troops off the island, leaving the place deserted.

Ken recalled listening to Tokyo Rose, "Telling us we were getting our butts kicked and that we were homesick. Most of us probably were, but not THAT homesick. Sometimes it was just hilarious. We heard her on the radio almost every night. We left the radio on all night. That was one of the things they did to pep up the shipmates and the troops – to listen to her – because we all knew she was telling lies, that we were getting our butts kicked all over the world – but we knew it wasn't true."

Ken Creese, on trumpet, change of command in the Aleutian Islands

In 1944, Ken left the *U.S.S. Detroit* in San Francisco Bay and was sent to San Diego, California, to the radio tower at the Naval Air Station on North Island. He finished the war out in San Diego, and on October 10, 1945, Ken was given one dime to get home on. He hopped on the street car, right across from the harbor, and headed home. "That was my ship out pay – one dime to get home! No other pay except my final paycheck. No shipping home money, no per diem, no expense money for eating or anything else!" Ken was discharged at the rank of Radioman, 3rd Class. He received the American Defense Medal with one Bronze Clasp and the World War II Victory Medal.

After his discharge, Ken spent time enjoying the sun at Mission Beach in San Diego, playing volleyball and running around with former schoolmates. In 1946 and again in 1948, he drove a Yellow Cab in San Diego. In 1948, Ken attended the Radio Broadcasting School in Hollywood, California.

On June 3, 1950, Ken married Mary Anne Walsh in Reno, Nevada. They had seven children; Gary, Pamela, Paula, Bradley, Karen, Kendra and Gwendolyn Creese. He went to work for Douglas Aircraft [later named McDonnell-Douglas] in Santa Monica, California, and was transferred to Lancaster in 1956 to the rocket site at Edwards Air Force Base. Ken later worked for the Northrop Corporation and retired from the aerospace industry after 39 years. He is a member of the American Legion Post 311 in Lancaster, the VFW Post 3000 in Quartz Hill, and the past Commander of VFW Post 7283 in Lancaster. He was also the past National President of the Pearl Harbor Survivors Association.

Ken and his wife, Mary Anne, currently live in Lancaster. "I was only 17 when Pearl Harbor was attacked. I grew up real fast on that day of infamy. It made me respect my fellow man and appreciate life."

CRAIG BOWEN "DOC" CROCKARD

Craig was born July 1, 1909 in Douglas, Ward Co., North Dakota, the only son born to Clarence and Edna Crockard. Craig had one sister, Collette. He moved to the Antelope Valley in the 1930's, to the area now known as Quartz Hill. From October of 1940 to October 1942, he was employed at the Garrett Supply Company in Vernon, California. Craig had completed two years of college, focusing on pre-med classes, before enlisting in the Navy.

Craig enlisted in the U.S. Navy in October 1942. He went through basic training at the Naval Training Center in San Diego, California. He completed 13 weeks of training as a Physical Therapy Technician at the U.S. Naval Hospital, also in San Diego.

During the war, Craig was stationed on Tinian Island, in the Philippines. He was in charge of the pharmacy, "mixing up trouble," his buddies recalled. Craig spent many long days and nights at the pharmacy, making sure the medicine was dispensed correctly.

In October 1945, Craig received an honorable discharge from the Navy at the rank of Pharmacist's Mate, First Class. He was discharged at the U.S.N. Personnel Separation Center in San Pedro, California. Craig received the Asiatic Pacific Medal with one star; the Philippine Liberation Medal; the American Theater Medal; and the Good Conduct Medal.

Craig's interests varied after the war – He was a drummer in a big band orchestra, a newspaper editor, an equestrian stable owner, and a polo player. Craig was also the owner of Antelope Country Hardware store in Quartz Hill. He finally found his niche as a doctor of Chiropractic medicine. He graduated from California State University, Berkeley and from Los Angeles Chiropractic College. "Doc" Crockard was a well loved Chiropractor in Quartz Hill for over 40 years, where he retired in 1984. Craig also served as a Reserve with the Los Angeles County Sheriff's Department in the Sheriff's Posse, where he participated in search and rescue missions on horseback. He was a member of the Lancaster Elks Lodge 1625, American Legion Post 311, and Mason's Lodge 43.

Craig had four children from his second marriage to Pilar; Bruce, Jim, Linda, and Jeff. On January 25, 1992, Craig married Alma Elmer. Craig passed away on August 29, 2001. His ashes were spread over the Pacific Ocean, just off the coast near San Diego, California. His wife, Alma, currently lives in Quartz Hill.

Doc Crockard at work, "mixing up trouble" in the pharmacy on Tinian Island, Philippines

ROBERT WILLIAM "BOB" DE BRY

Robert William DeBry was born January 11, 1927 in Salt Lake City, Utah, the son of Dutch immigrants Gerrit and Pieternella (Stuurman) DeBry. He was the tenth of eleven children born to the couple. The family moved to the Los Angeles area from Salt Lake City in the early 1930's with Gerrit working as a house painter to support his large family.

On August 23, 1944, at the age of 17, Bob enlisted in the U.S. Navy. He reported for active duty October 5, 1944, in San Diego, California. After boot camp, Bob entered the Class "A" Cook and Baker School at the Naval Training Center in San Diego, California. After completing school, he was shipped via train to San Francisco, California, where he was assigned to a minesweeper, the *U.S.S. Observer*.

Just prior to the war ending, Bob was sent to Portland, Oregon, where he was assigned to a new Liberty Ship, the *U.S.S. Bronx* (APA 236), a troop carrier. He made three trips across the Pacific Ocean to pick up troops and bring them home. His first trip was to Corregidor and Manila, in the Philippines. On the islands, Bob encountered many signs and warnings about the unexploded bombs and booby traps set up by the Japanese.

The second trip was to Okinawa where the ship was caught in a typhoon. Several ships were sunk. They went on to Shanghai, China for more troops, then back home to San Francisco, California. The third trip across the Pacific was to Tokyo, Japan. Each of the trips took about 30 days, each way. Occasionally they would see mines that had broken loose and were floating – a huge danger to ocean travelers. They used

198

their guns to explode the mines.

Bob was honorably discharged on July 22, 1946 at San Pedro, California, with the rank of Ship's Cook, 3rd Class.

On November 7, 1947, Bob married Irene Shimek, the daughter of Joseph and Josephine (Perchal) Shimek, in Los Angeles, California. They had three children; two sons, Michael William and Steve Mitchell, and one daughter, Marlene DeBry.

In July 1954, Bob graduated from the Sheriff's Academy in Los Angeles, California. He worked as a Deputy in the Los Angeles area until 1961, when he was transferred to the Lancaster Sheriff's Department in the Antelope Valley. After 27 years on the Department, Bob retired in July, 1981.

Bob and his family lived in the Quartz Hill/Lancaster area for over 35 years. Irene worked as a secretary for the Antelope Valley Union High School District for 20 years before retiring from Quartz Hill High School. All three children graduated from Quartz Hill High School with their son, Michael, being a member of the first Quartz Hill High School graduation, class of 1967.

Bob and Irene currently call St. George, Utah their home, moving there recently after many years in the Antelope Valley.

U.S.S. Bronx (APA-236)

Bob with an unexploded booby trap on Corregidor

Sign on Corrigidor: "Attention! Souvenir Hunters – For a quick death pick up ammunition on this island."

Donald Norman Duncan was born in Glen Ellyn, Du Page Co., Illinois on April 14, 1920 to Alexander Cameron, Jr. and Pearl Ann (Boyd) Duncan. He had two brothers, Alexander Cameron, Jr. and Bruce Minor Duncan.

Don attended elementary and high school in Glen Ellyn and also attended college at Naperville North Central College in Naperville, Illinois, majoring in Business Engineering. While still in high school, Don swept out hangars at an airfield close to Glen Ellyn in exchange for flying lessons. When Don was in his second year of college, he decided he wanted to choose which branch of the service he would serve in. On August 1, 1941 Don enlisted in the U.S. Navy in Chicago, Illinois.

When the Japanese struck at Pearl Harbor, Don was stationed at the Jacksonville Naval Air Station in Florida. He attended Flight School and graduated in May of 1942, as an Ensign, in just three months due to his previous civilian pilot training. Don was being checked out on a primary training plane when the instructor had him make three or four landings. It was then that the instructor inquired regarding any previous flying, and asked Don if he had ever flown before. Don replied, "I had over 200 hours of flight time prior to enlistment."

After Flight School, Don was sent to San Juan, Puerto Rico to fly sea planes. He was "inshore" patrol for six months, flying off of ships. Don had the opportunity to fly multi-engine aircraft and was assigned to VP-128 Squadron which patrolled both the Atlantic and Pacific Ocean. He was first assigned to Iceland, then to the Pacific Theater. While patrolling the Pacific, Don flew in numerous combat missions. Along with the VP-128, Don was assigned to Patrol Squadrons VP-126 and VR-3, Airborne Early Warning (AEW) Squadron and later, the Naval Air Facility at Andrews Air Force Base in Washington, D.C.

Don remembered several memorable experiences during his World War II service. The first happened at Midway Island when he was flying the Lockheed PV-1 Ventura. Prior to take-off, he told the co-pilot not to take off until he had reached 100 knots. An engine failed, and at 50 feet above the water, Don dropped the bomb cargo. When he landed, he found the armaments were all still onboard the aircraft. The bomb release had failed! In the Pacific Theater, Don participated in combat while flying the PV-1. One incident that stands out in his mind is the time he was attacked by Japanese gunfire. His plane had been hit, but he was able to fly it back to base. When Don examined the plane upon his return he found it had been struck in the fuselage.

When Don heard that the war was over he was onboard a ship returning to San Francisco. As the ship entered San Francisco Bay, he saw his brother on the deck of an outbound ship. Needless to say, he waved and thought what a coincidence that was to have both been there, passing each other, right at the same time.

After the war ended, Don continued his service in the Navy and was stationed at the Naval Air Station at Patuxent River, Maryland. While there, he flew the VR-3 from Washington, D.C. to Moffett Field, California. The VR-3 provided support for the Berlin Airlift while based on the East Coast. Because the transport planes could not span the Atlantic in one "jump," Don began flying the C-54 aircraft from Washington, D.C. to Rhein-Main Airport in Frankfort, Germany in support of the planes based at Rhein-Main. He flew the C-54 over the Atlantic for many long hours without incident.

Don retired from the U.S. Navy in July 1962, at the rank of Lieutenant Commander, after 21 years of service. For his service during World War II, he received the following awards: the Distinguished Flying Cross; 3 Air Medals; European, Pacific, American Theater Medals; Philippine Liberation Medal. After his retirement from the Navy, Don went to work for Lockheed Aircraft in Burbank, California as a general engineer for Aircraft Support Equipment, building flight simulators for the airlines.

In March 1943, Don married Shirley M. St. Francis in Deland, Illinois. They had one daughter, Marsha Jean, and two sons, Donald Norman, Jr. and David Neal Duncan. In July 1975, Shirley passed away after suffering a heart attack. Don married Lila Mae (Cummings) Bonner on July 2, 1977 in Lake View Terrace, Los Angeles Co., California. They moved to Quartz Hill in 1981 to be closer to Lila's daughter, Carol.

Don is a member of the American Legion and keeps in touch with several World War II service buddies from the VP-128 Squadron.

Moffett Field, California – June 29, 1948 – Don Duncan, left.

"Camp Kwitcherbelliaken" – Iceland, 1942
John Sable, Swede Larson and Don Duncan

CHARLES BERNARD "CECE" ELLISON

Charles Bernard Ellison was born April 19, 1921, in LaMoure, LaMoure Co., North Dakota. He was the second son of Oscar, from North Dakota, and Anna (Barrett) Ellison, from Ohio. Cece's father, Oscar, passed away when Cece was only four years old. His mother, Anne, an English teacher, moved the boys to Southern California to raise them after her husbands death. Being a single, working mother of two young boys in the 1920's was not an easy job, and teachers in California were paid a higher salary than the teachers in North Dakota.

The Ellison family moved to Lancaster in the late 1920's. Cece attended grade school at Lancaster Grammar School, through high school to college in Lancaster, graduating from AVJUHS in 1938, and Antelope Valley Junior College in 1941.

Cece was at home on Fig Street in Lancaster, when he heard the news about Pearl Harbor. He enlisted in the U.S. Navy, and was anxious to start his assignment to do his part in the war. While waiting to be called up for service, Cece attended a three week Oxy-acetylene school in San Pedro, California. This class helped him secure a job working in a shipyard. In July 1942, he married his sweetheart, Shirley M. Smith.

Finally, in September 1942, after overcoming a vision problem that held him back from joining the service, he was accepted into the Navy. Instead of being assigned to boot camp in San Diego, California, he was sent to brand new facility in Sandpoint, Idaho – Farragut Naval Training Station - near the Canadian border. Farragut was built as a direct result of the Japanese attack on Pearl Harbor. The site was picked for safety reasons. Unlike San Diego, which was possibly not safe from coastal bombings, the site was far from any coast, and was next to Lake Pend Oreille which provided an inland "ocean" on which to train the troops.

Cece went though boot camp at Farragut with his best friend from school, Walter Primmer. They both left in November, greeted by plenty of snow on their arrival at the training facility. After boot camp, Cece was assigned to the Great Lakes Training Base in North Chicago, with his barracks right on Lake Michigan. Cece's first job assignment was as an Oxy-acetylene Operator. Due to his specialized schooling and experience at the shipyard before he entered the Navy, Cece received a higher pay rate instead of a helper's rate.

After spending 13 months in the South Atlantic, he left for duties in the South Pacific. On October 5, 1944, he was assigned to the ship *U.S.S. Montauk* (LSV-6). assigned to damage control – repairing and fire fighting duties. The job was not a pleasant one at first. Cece had to wear a heavy asbestos suit – in the hot and humid weather of the Pacific. This lasted only a few days, as the heat was unbearable when wearing the suit. Cece told the Chief that it was too hot and if he had to help someone, he just couldn't do it wearing the constrictive asbestos suit. They gave him a pair of extra long gloves instead, to help protect him from the flame of the torch.

On April 1, 1945, Easter Sunday, the invasion of Okinawa began. At 6:00 a.m., the crew of the Landing Ship Vehicle, *Montauk,* began offloading 1,400 Army troops. Cece kept a diary during his time spent on the *Montauk.*

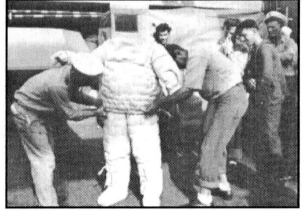

Asbestos suit being fitted on a Naval fireman. Photo courtesy of the U.S.S. Salt Lake City (CA25) Association Memorabilia collection; Sandy Askew, Historian.

The following is a vivid account taken from that diary:

"*April 1ˢᵗ (Easter)* Accompanied 'fake' landing force in. Were joined by 30 more troop ships, escorts and cruisers.

6:30 A.M. We broke off to proceed to main landing area. LST and PA burning off starboard bern save air cover and one DE with us. At 7:05 the fake landing started. Heavy shelling from ships being returned on shore. We are to rendezvous at 1000 with the *Eldorado* at the main landing area on south west side. We are alone at this time.

1200 We are laying off beach awaiting orders, 8 battleships ahead of us shelling landing area. Sporadic raids among us. LST astern hit. At 1800 we moved closer ashore, about one mile away. Two battleships and one cruiser around us. Ship to shore firing has stopped for the present. No enemy air attacks. We are on the west side of the island.

7:05 P.M. We are undergoing quite severe air attacks. Terrific barrage from ships. One seen to fall. One suicide plane rams *U.S.S. West Virginia,* slight damage. GQ (General Quarters) all night and at 4:30 A.M. we are again under air attack, two knocked out. We are with GC-11(*Eldorado*) flagship of amphib fleet. Vice Admiral Turner aboard. Are acting as assistant communication ship for these operations. The rest of *April 2ⁿᵈ* Comparatively quiet.

April 3ʳᵈ at GQ from 1:05 A.M. until 7:30 A.M. Enemy planes in vicinity but no attack came.

2100 Another attack, 7 planes overhead, all shot down by night fighters.

April 4ᵗʰ Adverse weather, no alerts.

April 5ᵗʰ Bad weather, no raids.

April 6ᵗʰ Heavy air attack commencing at 1515 – ending 2015. Total of 67 planes shot down over and around us. No fun. We got one. Two U.S. planes shot down by our ships.

April 7ᵗʰ Started unloading. One more U.S. plane downed by our ships. Later 2 Japs downed.

April 8ᵗʰ One alert. Unloading continuing.

April 9ᵗʰ One attack, 10 Japs overhead – 4 shot down. One destroyer disabled.

April 10ᵗʰ Unloading continued. Very nasty weather. No alerts.

April 11ᵗʰ Unloading ceased because of weather. Just standing by. This island is 67 miles long and from 3 to 10 miles wide. Population of over 400,000. Produce sugar.

April 12ᵗʰ Another red letter day. Violent air battles all afternoon commencing at 1300 and ending at 1700. We got 71 Japs that we know of. Mostly by our fighter planes. Marine based Corsairs and fighters from *Essex, Belleau Wood, Esormet, Tulagi,* a British carrier, (and) *Intrepid.* Lost one destroyer, on DD and another "can" hit. British can HMS-27 hit but got 4 Japs. Ready to leave here.

April 13ᵗʰ Unloading continues. Five attacks taking six (6) bombers downed around us. More out at sea.

April 14ᵗʰ Three attacks – several "splashed".

April 15ᵗʰ Unloading stopped – all troops disembarked. Heavy air attacks starting at 1800 and ending at 2245. We were strafed for the first time. Bombs close by. One casualty. Believe we got one plane, not confirmed yet.

April 16ᵗʰ GQ at 0230 ending 0630. Bombers overhead. Left Okinawa at 0900. Attacked again while underway. Bound for Saipan in 16 ship convoy and 9 escorts. Used over 3500 gals. Of smoke oil at Okinawa."

Cece kept a diary every day while at sea, for 13 months. If there wasn't anything happening, he wouldn't write anything down, only an arrival, departure, or anything out of the ordinary. After Saipan, the ship left for Guam and the Eniwetok Atoll, in the Marshall Islands. Cece was on a 72 hour leave in August 1945, in San Francisco, when he got word that "the bomb" was dropped. He hitchhiked from San Francisco to Los Angeles, only to get stuck in Los Banos at midnight. He hitched a ride with a truck driver the following day, who took him into Los Angeles. After visiting with his mother and his family, Cece headed back for San Francisco, this time on a train. He was honorably discharged at Terminal Island in October 1945, at the rank of Ship Fitter, 2ⁿᵈ Class.

Cece and Shirley Ellison had three children; two sons, Jon C. and Mark D. Ellision; and one daughter, Kristi Anne. When he returned home, he went into business for himself, setting up automatic vending machines and amusements at Muroc, now Edwards Air Force Base, in November 1945. He is semi-retired, helping his son run the same business started over 58 years ago. Cece is active in the American Legion and Veterans of Foreign Wars, and is the past Exalted Ruler of the local B.P.O. Elks. He still keeps up his old friendships with school and Navy buddies Walt Primmer, Jack Reynolds and schoolmate, John Stege. He is also an avid University of Southern California football fan and travels to several games each season.

Shirley and Cece Ellison at Bob Murphy's Restaurant in La Cienega, California.

ROBERT BARRETT "BOB" ELLISON

Robert Barrett Ellison, the first son of Oscar and Anna (Barrett) Ellison, was born February 4, 1920, in LaMoure, LaMoure Co., North Dakota. Bob grew up in Lancaster where he attended Lancaster Grammar School and graduated from AVJUHS in 1938. He graduated from Antelope Valley Jr. College in 1940.

Bob worked for the Southern California Telephone Company (Bell Systems) in Palmdale, before the war, as a Line Foreman.

Bob enlisted in the U.S. Coast Guard in 1941, inducted at Port Townsend, Washington, where he also went through boot camp. After boot camp he was sent to Radar School in New London, Connecticut. He graduated with the first group of Coast Guard personnel to go through the Radar School.

He served on the *U.S.S.* (CG Cutter) *Tampa* (WPG-48), escorting merchant ships to England during the war. The German U-Boats were on the prowl, searching for ships to attack and sink in the North Atlantic. The *Tampa* traveled though the icy waters of Greenland, out of Boston from 1941 – 1944.

Bob also served on the *U.S.S* (CG) *Orange* and the *U.S.S.* (CG) *Blackthorn*. The *Blackthorn*, a buoy tender, operated out of San Pedro, California, servicing aids to navigation. Bob's duty stations included the Port Townsend Training Station; Seattle; San Diego, California Air Station; New York Receiving Station; Coast Guard Receiving Station in Alameda, California; Coast Guard Receiving Station, San Francisco; and the Coast Guard Training Station in Groton, Connecticut.

Bob was honorably discharged on May 17, 1946, due to a hardship case. His mother was living alone, ill with cancer, when Bob requested the discharge. He attained the rank of Radar man, 1st Class (Regular).

During his time in the Coast Guard he received the following awards and ribbons: American Theater of Operations ribbon; World War II Victory ribbon; Asiatic-Pacific Theater of Operations ribbon with two Stars; Philippine Liberation ribbon with one Star; American Defense ribbon; European-African-Middle Eastern Campaign ribbon; and the Good Conduct ribbon.

Bob married Grace Bonnell on October 5, 1950, in Las Vegas, Nevada. They had three children; two sons, Michael Barnett and Thomas Robert Ellison; and one daughter, Bonnell "Bonnie" Marie Ellison.

Bob was employed for over 44 years with the Southern California Pacific Telephone Company in the Lancaster/Palmdale area. He continued to keep in contact with the men he made close friendships with during the war. He was also a member of the Veterans of Foreign Wars.

On June 13, 1986, Bob passed away in Lancaster, California. He is buried at the Lancaster Cemetery in Lancaster, Los Angeles Co., California.

EDWARD HENKEL

Edward Henkel entered the U.S. Navy from California. He was onboard the *U.S.S. Hull* from the Third Fleet, caught in a typhoon between December 17-18, 1944. During the typhoon, the wind reached a velocity of 131 mph, and as a result, the *U.S.S. Hull* (DD-350) capsized and sunk. Three other destroyers were capsized with a loss of 778 lives. Only 13 survivors from the *Hull* were recovered and six from the *Monaghan* (DD-354). No survivors from the *Spence* (DD-512) were found.

Edward Henkel lost his life on December 18, 1944 when the *Hull* sank. His body was never recovered. At the time of his death he had attained the rank of Machinist's Mate, 1st Class. His name is among those on the Tables of the Missing at the Manila American Cemetery, in Manila, Philippines.

U.S.S. Hull photo contributed by Fred Weiss, NavSource Naval History

MARY BEATRICE HUTCHINSON

Mary Beatrice Hutchinson was born December 27, 1922 in Alhambra, Los Angeles Co., California. She was the daughter of Edgar C., a cabinet maker from England, and Lydia Morton (Lutgerding) Hutchinson, from Arizona. She had one brother, Edgar Charles Hutchinson, Jr.; and two sisters, Lydia June and Roberta May Hutchinson, all born in California.

Mary enlisted in the U.S. Navy in 1944 in order to serve her country and further her education. She traveled by train to Hunter College in New York, enthusiastic about starting her new life in the military. When she arrived at Hunter College, Mary was impressed with what she saw. This was her first trip outside of California.

Her first experiences in the Navy were marching from one building to another, in ranks. The training she received was to be more mental than physical as time went on. After boot camp she was sent to Cedar Falls, Iowa, for Yeoman training. After eight weeks she was sent to the North

Island Naval Air Station in San Diego, California, assigned to Com Fleet West.

Mary's first assignment was Yeoman to five Landing Signal Officers – four Naval and one Marine. Her first responsibility was to set up files according to the newly-learned Navy filing system. This job made her indispensable as the officers could no longer find their files!

When Mary was off duty, she enjoyed singing in the Protestant Church Choir. The choir made an appearance at a church in Coronado, near San Diego. She kept in communication with her family through letters and telephone calls, with a few trips home to Pasadena, California by train or car. She enjoyed her time in service to her country and saw it as a learning experience. She got to visit new areas of the country and felt her knowledge was broadened by her training in the military school.

Mary was discharged from the Navy in May 1946, at the rank of Yeoman, 3rd Class. During her service she was attached to the Headquarters, Squadron 14-1, Fleet Air Wing 14. She received the American Area Campaign Medal and the World War II Victory Medal.

In the weeks following her discharge, Mary was busy planning her upcoming wedding. She was married to Murray Pond, a Fireman in the U.S. Navy, on June 2, 1946, in Pasadena, California. Mary went to work at the Social Security Administration in Pasadena, where she was an Administrative Assistant. She and Murray had three children; two daughters, Kathleen Suzanne and Sharon Kay Pond; and one son, Lawrence Charles Pond.

The family moved to the Antelope Valley in 1954 where Mary continued to keep in touch with a service pal/bridesmaid for several years. The Ponds currently live in the Quartz Hill area of the Antelope Valley.

RONALD JAMES "RON" KNAPP

Ronald James Knapp was born May 11, 1926 in Chamberlain, Brule Co., South Dakota, the son of Roy A. and Winnafred (Mills) Knapp. He had one brother, Richard S. Knapp. The Knapp family moved to California in 1930, settling in the Antelope Valley in 1934. Ron attended grammar school in Lancaster and graduated from AVJUHS in 1943. Ron's father was a well loved principal at AVJUHS during the pre-war years and continuing well after the war was over.

On Sunday, December 7, 1941, Ron was participating in a stage set at AVJUHS when the news of Pearl Harbor was announced. He was in his junior year at high school. Ron graduated in 1943, during the middle period of the war. At that time it was the "thing we all wanted to do – join the service." Ron enlisted in the Navy at barely 17 years of age. He was selected for officer training as part of the V-12 program.

The V-12 program, newly implemented in July 1943, allowed the student to attend a college university along with active duty in the Navy. They skipped basic training, but still went through marching, drills, and obstacle courses along with intense Engineering courses at the University of Wisconsin at Madison, and the University of Notre Dame in South Bend, Indiana. Ron remembered that the "real pressure was from the college curriculum, not Navy drills."

After eight semesters of college, three per year, Ron completed the V-12 program. At the completion of the program he was given an officers commission as an Ensign, and assigned to the Naval Air Transport Service first at Moffett Field, California, then at Rogers Field in Hawaii. By this time, the war was over. Ron's first job assignment was as an Air Transport Officer. This was during the period when tremendous amounts of air traffic was flying to and from the Pacific. Thousands of Naval personnel were returning from the Pacific in early 1946. Ron commented that "had the war lasted longer, we were slated to serve on aircraft carriers."

While Ron was attending college at Notre Dame, he saw Bob Hope and Bing Crosby perform. It was planned only as a Bob Hope show, but Bing was traveling across the U.S. and stopped off to surprise Bob Hope. Onboard a troop transport ship from Hawaii to San Francisco, Ron ran into a friend from Lancaster, Blas Gorrindo. Blas was returning from Pacific duty in the Navy. He ran into Sterling Rinear, also from Lancaster, while he was in Hawaii.

Ron served three years in the Navy and was discharged in July 1946. He went back home to Lancaster on July 4, where he celebrated his "independence" from the Navy. Ron vacationed at Yellowstone Park and several other places in the Northwest. He hired on as a Jr. Engineer at North American Aviation in Inglewood, California by August 1946. A year later he would go back to school at the University of Michigan. He spent five years as an Aeronautical/Aerospace Engineer with NASA, and 35 years with Lockheed.

On August 3, 1952, Ron married Patricia R. Andrews in South Pasadena, Los Angeles Co., California. Together they had five children; Stephen, David, Diana, Paul and Julia Anne Knapp. Ron continues to keep in contact with members of the V-12 group of Aeronautical Engineering students. They have a reunion every year and a half. In March 2003, ten couples involved with the V-12 group met in Tucson, Arizona.

In retrospect, Ron remarked that "While my service wasn't as momentous as those who were in harms way, it nevertheless built character, and certainly the training I received served me well throughout my working life. I still have a high respect for the military and always support our servicemen. We need a strong military to protect our country. With strength we can best avoid war."

Ron currently calls Ashland, Oregon his home.

Ron's father, Dr. Roy Knapp, was Chairman of the Antelope Valley war-time Red Cross Fund Drive. He had plenty of volunteer help, and each year the goal was exceeded. Dr. Knapp was also Superintendent of AVJUHS and AVJC from 1933 through 1962. The photo was taken in 1943 with Dr. Knapp in the center, on the left, Mrs. Julia Hurst, and to the right, Mrs. Marie Griffith. Photo courtesy of Ron Knapp.

Alberto Llarena was born in El Sereno, Los Angeles Co., California on November 20, 1921, the son of Tomas and Romalda (Aizpurrutia) Llarena, both immigrants from Spain. Albert moved with his family to the Antelope Valley in 1926 where they began alfalfa farming on the southwest corner of Avenue H and 90th Street West. He had two half-brothers, Joe and John Almandoz.

Al graduated from Del Sur Elementary School in 1935 and graduated from AVJUHS with the class of 1939. He was deer hunting in Bishop, California when he heard about the attack on Pearl Harbor in 1941. After high school, he continued farming and raising sheep until 1943 when he enlisted in the Merchant Marines.

Boot camp training was spent on Catalina Island. Every Thursday night they held boxing events. If you won the boxing match, you received a weekend pass. Al's future wife, Lois, recalled his fine boxing skills and every Friday night she drove to Wilmington to pick him up for his weekend visit won in the boxing ring.

After boot camp Al was sent to Wilmington to serve onboard a freighter, the *U.S.S. Christopher Gayle*, as a cook. "Our first trip out we hauled pallet boards to the Philippines. We were in New Guinea when the war ended. We were ordered to Australia to pick up food and head for Yokohama, Japan to feed the people that were starving there. We were then ordered to head home to Seattle, Washington, but hit a typhoon so was ordered to dock in San Francisco. Before we arrived the ship was diverted again to San Pedro, where we took on bunkers and headed for Panama. Sat there for a couple of days, then sailed for Atlanta, Georgia where we left the ship, boarded a train and came home to Los Angeles."

"I had to have 36 months of sea duty before I could be discharged so I served aboard several ships that ran from Seattle to the north and down into the Mexican waters to the south. Every three months aboard I got 30 days leave. I was serving aboard the *U.S.S. McKay* and we were in the Wilmington harbor where it was being loaded with 350,000 barrels of lighter fluid when it blew up, killing the two men who were working aboard. We were to spend the night there so I called the next morning to find out what time I was to return and found out what happened. It was a good ship and I really enjoyed serving on it."

Al was honorably discharged in 1946 after three years of service with the Merchant Marines. He made many lasting friendships while in the service and kept in contact with them over the years. After the war he went home to Lancaster where he continued farming. On January 16, 1950, he married his high school sweetheart, Lois Beery, in Reno, Nevada. They had five children: Marlene, Tom, Francine, Jeanette, and Rick Llarena.

Al was a member of the Quartz Hill VFW, Post 3000, the American Legion, Post 311, and the Lancaster Elks. He coached Little League and Pony League at Quartz Hill. Al enjoyed hunting, sporting events and spending time with his children and grandchildren. Al passed away on September 23, 1994 in Lancaster, California and is buried at Lancaster Cemetery in Lancaster.

Catalina Island – 1943

Louis Ramirez Perez was born June 10, 1925 in Los Angeles, California, the son of Miguel C. and Rosa (Ramirez) Perez. Miguel and Rosa emigrated to the United States in 1919 from Mexico. Louis had two siblings; one brother, Michael, and a sister, Henrietta Perez.

Louis enlisted in the U.S. Navy in June of 1943 in Los Angeles. With his mother crying as he left, Louis boarded a Greyhound bus and went to boot camp training at the U.S. Naval Training Center in San Diego, California. Everyone was given a series of different tests including underwater sound, Morse code, semaphore, and other to determine their placement in the Navy. After boot camp, he was sent to the Destroyer Base for Amphibious Training, located in San Diego. While attending school, Louis trained at Coronado Island, familiarizing himself with Landing Craft Vehicles (LCVP).

On September 1, 1943 Louis left San Diego, on a train bound for San Francisco. He arrived at Camp Pleasanton where he stayed for three days, in preparation for boarding the Amphibious Attack Transport ship, the *U.S.S. Sheridan* (APA-51). Louis was first assigned to the ship's crew - rigging, splicing wires, and ship maintenance.

After loading her cargo, the *Sheridan* got underway, sailing for the Western Pacific on October 1, 1943. The first stop was Nouméa, New Caledonia, to deliver the cargo, then on October 25, they arrived at Wellington, New Zealand. On November 1, the ship stopped at Efate Island where the crew underwent amphibious training. From Efate Island, the *Sheridan* sailed to the Gilbert Islands with the 2nd Division Marines onboard, in support of the invasion of Tarawa and in the company of the battleship *U.S.S. Maryland* and attack transport *U.S.S. Monrovia*.

On November 14, 1943, a letter was written to the crew of the *U.S.S. Sheridan* by John J. Mockrish, Commander, D-M, USNR:

To all the officers and men of the United States Navy, and United States Marine Corps on board the U.S.S. Sheridan.

As we are now entering the final stage of our operation and soon will be in the combat zone, I take this opportunity to advise all hands that we are about to enter into the biggest offensive yet undertaken by any of our forces, the taking of the Gilbert Island group. We are a chosen and privileged group.

Our government and our people have indicated their confidence in our ability, by choosing us to perform this task. That confidence must and will be fulfilled by the successful accomplishment of the task we are about to undertake.

I know each and everyone of us will prove ourselves worthy of that confidence because we firmly believe in the principles of democracy for which we are fighting.

In this and other of our future assignments we must always have before our minds that our enemy is a strong and wily foe, that no quarter will be asked nor given. We must also remember that in successfully accomplishing our mission we are avenging the loss of our shipmates in past actions. This is not a one man job, each and everyone of us must know and do their job. There is no luck in this work, but plain hard work, hard fighting, common sense, and carrying our share of the load. Our load is a big one, but our lives, the lives of our shipmates around us and the lives of our dear ones at home, makes that load worthy of everything we have to put into the effort to make this a successful venture. Therefore let us be alert and make no mistakes. Mistakes cost lives and lives cannot be replaced.

I want to thank you for your cooperation in the past, you have done a fine job. In the coming event, I know you will do much better because it will not be play, but a matter of life and death and we want life.

I am proud to command you. We have a job to do, a big one. Lets go – plenty of success and may God bless you and give you the strength to carry out our mission.

Louis arrived off Tarawa Atoll (Betio Island) in the early morning of November 20, 1943. The day began with debarking troops for the third wave to go to Red Beach 3. Visible to the starboard side could be seen a Japanese transport who had partially sunk and destroyed on the previous day of the invasion. As the LCM hit the beach, the Marines rushed off. Several of them were shot while they were still inside the LCM. After debarking the Marines, Louis raised the ramp. On the portside of Louis' LCM was an LCVP who got a direct hit by the Japanese. Four sailors jumped off the LCVP and were yelling at Louis to pick them up. Louis dropped the ramp so they could come onboard. These sailors had already experienced combat at Guadalcanal so they immediately began to take care of the wounded inside the LCM. They administered morphine and marked a cross on their forehead with lipstick, which they had in a canister. While the sailors were attending the wounded, Louis tried to raise the ramp automatically, but it failed to rise. He then went down to the engine room to help the Motor Mac to manually raise the ramp. With that accomplished, they went back to the Sheridan to drop off the wounded and the four sailors who had come on board.

On the fourth trip, Louis went to the same Red Beach 3 to deliver his cargo of rolls of heavy gauge wire and pre-fabricated material for making airstrips. After he unloaded the cargo, he proceeded to back up the LCM and hit the coral reef. They were stuck. No one was able to pull them off. Louis recalled, "Snipers from the sunken Japanese transport were shooting at any landing craft within their shooting range, including us. After the invasion, we were accused of going for a short swim to cool off since there was nothing else to do." The sun was setting when the men noticed that all the Task Force in the horizon were leaving. The men could not believe it. They were being abandoned. They yelled and cursed – even the Motor Mac came above to watch the departure. They settled down for the night and established a "watch". Louis remembered that while stranded, a Japanese airplane, which the men nicknamed "Washing Machine Charlie" [due to the clunking noise], flew overhead twice that night. He didn't fire at them so he was probably looking over the situation from above.

The crew had been cold all night so they were awake at the crack of dawn. They were searching the horizon when they saw all the ships returning. They all cheered, and by this time they decided to restart the engines to see if they could break away, which they did. They cheered again and headed towards the incoming ships.

The crew endured three days of landing approximately 1,200 personnel and about 400 tons of equipment from the 8th Regiment, 2nd Marine Division, onto Red Beach 3. On the November 24, 1943, at approximately 11:00 a.m., Task Force 53 was ordered to notify all their beach parties to return to their ships due to a sudden change of orders. Although Louis was fortunate to have already been 100 yards from the Sheridan, [who was already traveling about six miles per hour] he was unaware of the orders to leave the island. He told his crew to prepare to be hoisted aboard. He then shifted to full speed ahead to catch the Sheridan. He was waved to come alongside the ship when he saw the boom swing outward to pick them up.

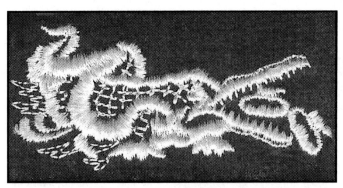

Embroidered patch from Louis's uniform sleeve – alligator with tanks

Amphibious tank logo on a 1944 postcard -
W.R. Thompson & Co., Publishers, Richmond, VA

210

Louis' crew tried three times to put the ring on the hook, but failed. This time they make it and were hoisted aboard.

Due to the sudden change of orders, the *Sheridan's* beach party of eight LCVP boats and crews, plus one officer, were unable to return to the ship. Four officers and forty-three men of the beach part were also unable to return. "Fifty-six years later, my wife and I searched the Internet for shipmates," Louis recalled. "That is when we found Henry Gretzner, the Motor Mac whom I had helped to manually raise the ramp of the LCM at Tarawa." After all these years, Louis had forgotten his name, but Gretzner had not forgotten Louis' name. Gretzner said, "I remember you. I want to thank you for taking care of us." Louis replied, "I didn't take care of you – it was team work. We were just eighteen. We didn't know what we were doing. It was our job and so we did it. A few weeks later we found Milton Miller, a Seaman Second Class, who was also part of my crew." When Louis called him, he was told Miller was taking a nap. A few days later, Louis called again and was told Miller had passed away.

On November 24, 1943 the Sheridan sailed in the company of the *U.S.S. Monrovia, Doyen, Heywood, Biddle* and the *LaSalle*, bound for Pearl Harbor as hospital ships. They arrived at Pearl Harbor on December 2, 1943 and unloaded the wounded Marines who were then sent to local hospitals for treatment. At this time, Lieutenant Edward Albert Heimberger, better known as Eddie Albert, the Hollywood movie star, left the *U.S.S. Sheridan* for other assignments. Admiral Chester W. Nimitz, Vice Admiral Gromly, Rear Admiral Turner and their staffs, came aboard on an inspection trip.

The *Sheridan* was ordered to return stateside, to San Diego, California. They were to replenish their landing crafts, radio equipment, make repairs and replace beach party personnel. On January 13, 1944 the *Sheridan* sailed for Lahaini Roads, Maui, in the Hawaiian Islands. She arrived on January 21 and sailed the following day for Kwajalein with Task Group 53.2. The *Sheridan* arrived at Kwajalein Atoll on January 31. She transferred all troops to LSTs the same day and moved to the transport area for the remainder of the day. The U.S. forces bombarded Kwajalein Atoll all day on January 31. The *Sheridan* served as a temporary hospital ship during the battle at Kwajalein until the hospital ship *U.S.S. Solace* arrived.

On February 8, the *Sheridan* sailed for Pearl Harbor. On February 17, she arrived at Maui, where she unloaded all Marine troops and equipment and sailed for Pearl Harbor. On May 30, 1944 the *Sheridan* sailed with Task Group 52.3 en route to Eniwetok, Marshall Islands. They arrived on June 9, 1944 and she immediately commenced transferring various troop elements to assigned LSTs. On June 15, 1944 the *Sheridan* arrived at Saipan where troops and cargo were offloaded to make room for 245 casualties and the bodies of twelve deceased men, to be buried at sea. From June 20 to September 15, 1944 the *Sheridan* made several trips to and from Pearl Harbor to Eniwetok, loading and unloading troops, cargo, supplies and equipment.

On September 15, 1944 the *Sheridan* was ordered to sail for Eniwetok again. They arrived on October 3 and sailed on October 14 enroute to Leyte Gulf, in the Philippine Islands. They arrived on October 20, in assault with 1,439 personnel and 950 tons of equipment of the 1st Battalion, 383rd Infantry Regiment, 96th Division, U.S. Army, on Beach Orange II. Seventy-eight casualties, of which seven were civilian, were received and cared for onboard. On October 21, on civilian, Mrs. Roberto Cayobit, gave birth to a son who was christened by the ship's Chaplain, Lieutenant J.T. Keown. He was christened Roberto Sheridan Cayobit, the first native child born under the American flag after the re-occupation of the Philippines by American forces.

The *Sheridan* completed her general unloading on October 22. On this day, Louis had completed his duty of unloading hatch #3 and was standing on the electrical compartment when he saw a Japanese airplane take-off from the island and circle away from them. Louis turned around, pointed skyward and yelled to the bridge, as loud as he could, "Enemy aircraft, enemy aircraft," so they would see the airplane also. General Quarters was immediately sounded. By now, the airplane had completed its turn as Louis was running to his battle station while looking skyward at the airplane. That's when Louis saw the torpedo fall from the enemy airplane. Louis hit the deck. He lay there, waiting to hear the explosion, but nothing happened. He heard the airplane fly overhead, so he knew the Sheridan was not the target. The target was the *U.S.S. Honolulu* cruiser. It was hit on the portside, but did not sink; instead, it was beached.

On October 22, 1944 the *Sheridan* was ordered to sail for Hollandia, New Guinea where, upon their arrival, Captain Paul H. Wiedorn relieved Commander Allen H. Guthrie as commanding officer of the *Sheridan*. Between November 5, 1944 and March 27, 1945 the *Sheridan* sailed to Noemfoor Island, Leyte Gulf, Manus Island, Bougainville Island, Lingayen Gulf, and Zambales Province, loading and unloading Army troops and tons of equipment, casualties and survivors, landing in assault thousands of personnel. In Leyte Gulf they experienced heavy enemy air attacks.

On March 27, 1945 the *Sheridan* was underway for Okinawa. On April 1, she arrived at Okinawa, in assault. On April 5, she set sail for Guam and Pearl Harbor where they were ordered stateside. Louis remembered that it was a foggy April 30, 1945 when the *Sheridan* was entering the San Francisco Harbor. She was flying a "Homeward Bound Pennant" which represents a star for every officer onboard, and a foot of flag for every enlisted man onboard. The flag was so long that a weather balloon filled with helium was attached to the end of the banner to keep it from touching the water.

Just as the *Sheridan* was under the Golden Gate Bridge, the fog began to lift. The men were standing shoulder to shoulder, looking up at the bridge where there were people waving flags as a "Welcome Home." It was an emotional moment for the crew. There were also two fireboats, one on each side of the ship, spraying tunnels of water in celebration of their return. The *Sheridan* tied up at Pier 20 and remained there until June 30, 1945. From there, she sailed to San Diego and returned to San Francisco. On July 15 she was underway again for Eniwetok and Leyte. They arrived at Leyte on August 5 and moved to Guiuian, Samar, Philippine Islands where they debarked personnel. On August 14 they left for Zamboanga, Mindinao, Philippine Islands. When the *Sheridan* entered Big Pier Zamboanga, the news was received that World War II was officially declared at an end. She moved to Subic Bay, Luzon on August 26 and sailed the following day for Tokyo Bay in company with Task Group 33.1.

On September 2, 1945 at 9:30 a.m., the *Sheridan* entered Tokyo Harbor. She passed in near vicinity of the *U.S.S. Missouri* during surrender ceremonies. They dropped anchor about 7,000 yards from the *Missouri*. The ship operated off the coast of China, the Philippine Islands and Okinawa during the months of September-November. On December 7, she left Japan and returned to San Diego December 23 with troops of the 5th Marine Division. She sailed from San Diego on January 11, 1946 through the Panama Canal and arrived at Mobile, Alabama on February 1, 1946 for deactivation. The Sheridan was decommissioned on March 5, 1946 and on April 12, was stricken from the Navy list.

Louis was honorably discharged in March of 1946, while holding the rank of Coxswain, Third Class. For his service during the war he was awarded the American Campaign Medal; Asiatic-Pacific Campaign Medal with six Stars; Philippine Liberation Ribbon with two Stars; China Service Medal; Navy Unit Commendation Medal (USN/USMC); World War II Victory Medal.

After his discharge, Louis spent time fishing and relaxing at Mammoth, California and took a year off for a much needed rest. In February 1947, Louis secured a job at North American Aviation in El Segundo, California. On November 2, 1952 Louis married Estela (Stella) Martha Hernandez in Los Angeles, California. They had two children together; Virginia and Michael Perez.

The Perez family moved to the Antelope Valley in 1983. After forty years of service with North American (now North American Rockwell), Louis retired from his position as warehouse supervisor in 1987. During the last four years, Louis and his wife, Stella, have been searching for shipmates from the *U.S.S. Sheridan*. At their home in Palmdale, an entire room of the house, dubbed "The War Room" by Stella, has been devoted to the research, documents and photographs they have acquired during the last four years. They both enjoy attending the *Sheridan* reunions which they have organized. The first reunion was held after fifty-six years since the shipmates had seen each other. It was in the year 2000, in Des Moines, Iowa. Forty-seven shipmates attended and it was the most memorable one for them.

U.S.S. Sheridan – photo courtesy of Louis Perez.

EARL MAURICE PERKINS

Earl Maurice Perkins was born December 14, 1925 in Lancaster, California, the second of six children born to John Alfred and Lillian (Ince) Perkins. Maurice had four brothers; Clarence Alfred, Richard Andre, Charles Lloyd, and John Wendell Perkins; one sister, Barbara Jean Perkins. John A. Perkins moved his family to the Lancaster/Palmdale area in the 1920's, where he was employed as a truck driver for the road department.

Maurice was a Seaman 2nd Class in the U.S. Navy on April 7, 1943. He was onboard the *U.S.S. Aaron Ward* (DD-483), a Navy destroyer, in the South Pacific war zone, part of Task Force 18 in Tulagi Harbor, Solomon Islands.

The *Aaron Ward* departed the harbor hurriedly on April 7, 1943, hoping to avoid a looming large-scale Japanese attack. While covering the LST-449 through Lengo Channel, three enemy planes were spotted. The gunners opened fire, but within minutes three more dive bombers were heading for the ship.

While quickening the speed of the ship, the *Aaron Ward* opened fire on the enemy planes with 20 and 40mm guns. Three bombs released by the first three Japanese planes struck on or near the ship, rocking the *Aaron Ward* violently. Large holes were torn in the side of the ship flooding the forward fireroom, forward engine room and after engine room. All electrical power was lost on the 5-inch and 40mm guns, but the gunners continued firing after switching to local control. Power was lost to the rudder causing the ship to circle helplessly as the second group of dive bombers attacked.

With severe damage suffered from the enemy bombs, the *Aaron Ward* began to list towards the starboard side. Two tugs in the area tied their lines to the ship and with the crew of the *Aaron Ward*, attempted to beach the ship on a nearby Florida Island shoal. During this brave rescue attempt, the bulkheads gave way, causing the ship to sink. The tugs quickly cut their lines, got clear of the ship while it plummeted to the bottom of the sea, forty fathoms below. Twenty-seven of the crew died that day, April 7, 1943; fifty-nine were wounded; seven were missing.

Maurice Perkins was among the crew listed as Missing at Sea. He was presumed dead on April 8, 1944, one year after the sinking of the *Aaron Ward*. Maurice was awarded the Purple Heart; American Defense Service Medal; Asiatic-Pacific Campaign Medal; and the World War II Victory Medal, all posthumously, by the Chief of Naval Personnel in Washington, D.C. Maurice's name is inscribed on the Tablets of the Missing at Manila American Cemetery, Manila, Philippines.

"He stands in the unbroken line of patriots who have dared to die that freedom might live, and grow, and increase its blessings. Freedom lives, and through it he lives – in a way that humbles the undertakings of most men. In grateful memory of Earl Maurice Perkins who died in the service of his country." Taken from a memorial certificate presented to the family of Maurice, signed by Franklin D. Roosevelt, President of the United States.

U.S.S. Aaron Ward (DD-483) – Official U.S. Navy photograph taken 17 August 1942, Solomon Islands.

On December 8, 1924, in Buffalo, Erie Co., New York, Bertha Ann Philipp was born to Joseph and Anna (Scholier) Philipp, both of Austro-Hungarian descent. Joseph immigrated to the United States around 1907, while Anna came over around 1913. Bertha had one older brother, Joseph Philipp. In 1920, the Philipp family was living in Buffalo, New York, where Joseph was employed as a machinist for an automotive plant. By 1930, Anna had remarried, but the family was still living in Buffalo, New York.

Bertha was "shampooing her hair" at her home in Tonawanda, New York, when she heard about the bombing of Pearl Harbor. She felt it was her "patriotic duty to help free up the boys to *active* duty." Bertha enlisted in the WAVES (Women Accepted for Volunteer Emergency Service). The WAVES were a branch of the U.S. Navy, returning to service in August, 1942, after a 23 year absence. Prior to this return, only a small corps of Navy nurses represented the women in the Naval service and they never had any formal officer status. Within a year over 27,000 women were sworn in as WAVES.

Bertha was inducted in Los Angeles, California, then sent to Hunter College, in New York. The first few days of service were both confusing and exciting to her. She was proud to be a part of history. She remembers boot camp training as miles of marching and being taught to identify certain airplanes. After boot camp, Bertha was sent to Camp Elliott in San Diego, California where her first assignment was in the Provost Marshall's office as Yeoman to the Security Officer.

Her desk job consisted of typical office work. Along with other duties, typing and filing was her daily routine. One of her duties was to keep an up-to-date (daily) list of the sailors in the brig. This was how she met her future husband, Millard Ewing, Jr. He would call her office several times a week, trying to locate one of his men – to see if he was listed as being in the brig. They started meeting at the recreation hall to play cards and games. After a few months they fell in love, and on March 23, 1946, they were married in Los Angeles, California.

While in the military, it is customary to wear your uniform when you get married, but Bertha wanted to get married in a wedding dress. She had to write a letter to the Commander at Camp Elliott, requesting permission to wear her dress:

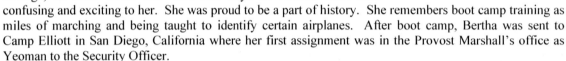

U. S. NAVAL TRAINING AND
DISTRIBUTION CENTER
CAMP ELLIOTT
SAN DIEGO 44, CALIFORNIA

21 March 1946.

To: Commander, TADCEN, Camp Elliott, San Diego 44,
        California.
Via: (1) W. R. Representative.
        (2) Executive Officer.

Subj: Permission to Wear Wedding Gown - Request for.

1. It is requested that I be permitted to wear a wedding gown at my wedding to Lieut(jg) M.F. Ewing, USNR, on Saturday, 23 March 1946. The ceremony will be performed at University Methodist Church, Los Angeles, California.

Bertha Ann PHILIPP, S1c

Permission was granted!

Left to right – Robert Bowman, USNR, Best man; Lt. (j.g.) Millard Ewing, Jr. USNR; Linda Ewing, flower girl; Bertha Philipp; Barbara Wagner, Step-sister, Maid of Honor. University Methodist Church, Los Angeles, California

While in the WAVES, Bertha attained the rank of Seaman, 1st Class. After her time in the service, Bertha traveled and visited her family in Los Angeles. Bertha and Millard had three children together: two daughters, Constance and Carolyn; and one son, William Philipp Ewing.

Bertha currently lives in Littlerock, California and enjoys her retirement dancing with Antelope Valley's Boogie Woogie Mamas, a competition dance group comprised of women over 55, who have fun keeping active by dancing, performing and competing with all age groups.

LEONCE EDMUND "POLLY" POLLARD

Leonce Edmund Pollard was born October 17, 1924, in Clarksdale, Coahoma Co., Mississippi. His parents were Joseph Marion and Helen Ruth (Landry) Pollard. Joseph was born in Tennessee and Helen was from Mississippi. Leonce had one brother, Joseph M. Pollard. Leonce and his family arrived in Lancaster, California in 1941. He graduated from AVJUHS in 1943.

Leonce joined up with the U.S. Navy and was sent to San Diego, California. He was assigned to duty as a Torpedoman aboard the *U.S.S. Laffey*, one of the most famous destroyers of World War II. In June of 1944, the crew of the *Laffey* participated in the Normandy Invasion at Utah Beach. They also supported the Cherbourg, France, bombardment at the end of June, 1944. On November 11, 1944, they were in the Pacific with Admiral Halsey's Third Fleet and rescued a downed Japanese pilot.

By December, the *Laffey* was in the Philippines supporting the

Army's 77th Division near Leyte Island and Army troops on Mindoro Island. In January, 1945, the *Laffey* escorted ships that took Army troops to the Lingayen Gulf for the invasion of Luzon. During the Marine landing on Iwo Jima, the *Laffey* was there again supporting the carrier task force.

On April 16, 1945, while on duty at the Radar Picket Line, Station No. 1, off of Okinawa, the *Laffey* was attacked by 22 Japanese Kamikaze suicide planes. They repeatedly bombed the ship over an 80 minute time period. The *Laffey* gunners shot down nine Japanese planes but five Kamikazes crashed their airplanes into the ship. The ships rudder was bombed so she could only travel around in circles. By the end of the attack, among the rubble and fires on the ship, 32 of her crew were dead, with another 71 wounded. Historians have said that no other ship was hit so hard, for so long, in so short a time, without sinking or being abandoned due to the damage. For this battle, the men of the *U.S.S. Laffey* received the Presidential Unit Citation.

Leonce was honorably discharged from the U.S. Navy on April 22, 1946, at the rank of Torpedoman, 3rd Class. He received the Asiatic-Pacific Area Medal with 4 Battle Stars and the World War II Victory Medal.

On December 21, 1947, Leonce married Silda May Wilson in Long Beach, California. Leonce met Silda when she was teaching at the Belleview School (now Quartz Hill Elementary School) in Quartz Hill. They had three children together: Steven Edmund, Harry David and Amy Sue Pollard. After the war, Leonce was employed as a lineman for the Southern California Edison Company from 1949 to 1967. He managed a ranch for Lancaster resident, Forrest Godde, in Coeur d' Alene, Kootenai Co., Idaho from 1967 to 1985.

Leonce passed away at his home on October 25, 1985 in Coeur d" Alene, Idaho. His wife Silda, is currently living in Idaho and his brother, Joseph Pollard, lives in Grass Valley, California.

U.S.S. Laffey at sea

*U.S.S. Laffey damage from Japanese bombing
at Okinawa – both photos courtesy of Silda Pollard*

216

On December 31, 1923, Murray D. Pond was born in Los Angeles, Los Angeles Co., California, the son of Milan Nathaniel and Eva Mae (Batstone) Pond. The Pond family moved to the Antelope Valley, permanently, in 1939, due to Mrs. Pond's health problems with asthma. The dry, desert air made it easier for her to breathe. They had been making weekend trips from the Los Angeles area to spend time in a cabin near the Soledad Canyon area, just south of Vincent, and had decided a permanent home in the Quartz Hill area would be easier on Eva and the family.

Murray's father established an accounting practice in Lancaster while still attending to his business in Los Angeles. After several moves in the area, the Pond family purchased a 10-acre almond orchard near 56th St. West and M-8 in Quartz Hill.

Murray entered AVJUHS when he was a junior and graduated in 1941. After high school, he worked in Los Angeles until he entered the engineering program in the fall of 1941 at Cal Poly, San Luis Obispo. He enlisted in the U.S. Navy and remained at Cal Poly through the end of the first semester in 1942. He then went to engineering college at Cal Tech in Pasadena, California.

Boot camp training was spent during the cold winter months in Chicago, Illinois. After boot camp, Murray was sent to PT (Patrol) Boat engine school in Detroit, Michigan. His assignment was servicing engines on the PT Squadrons while onboard the *U.S.S. Orestes* stationed in the Philippines and the South Pacific.

Murray was out in the Pacific when he heard the news that the war was over. After the hostilities had ceased, one of his most memorable experiences was stripping down the PT boats to nothing, and then racing them! The ship returned to San Pedro, California and Murray was honorably discharged in 1946 at the rank of Fireman, 1st Class. He was awarded the Asiatic-Pacific Area Medal; American Area Medal; and the World War II Victory Medal.

On June 2, 1946, after his discharge from the Navy, Murray married Mary Beatrice Hutchinson in Pasadena, Los Angeles, Co., California. Mary was a Yeoman, 3rd Class in the Navy from 1944 to May of 1946, attached to Fleet Air Wing 14 in San Diego, California. Murray and Mary had three children; two daughters, Kathleen Suzanne and Sharon Kay Pond; and one son, Lawrence Charles Pond.

Murray worked in Pasadena for a few years following his marriage to Mary, then the family moved back to the Antelope Valley in 1953. They lived in Palmdale where Murray secured a job as the manager of the Palmdale Irrigation District. After many years with the Palmdale Irrigation District, Murray started his own Commercial Real Estate business. Murray and his wife, Mary, currently call Quartz Hill their home.

Walter Clyde Primmer was born April 10, 1920, in Lancaster, California, the son of R. Clyde and Margaret Jane (McFarland) Primmer. Clyde was born in Illinois, of German descent, and Margaret was born in Ireland. Clyde's parents, Rudolph and Esther Primmer, had farmed the land in McHenry Co., Illinois for many years before deciding to head west to California where the winters were less harsh.

They sold the farm, loaded their livestock and farming equipment on a train, and headed to Littlerock in the Antelope Valley. Clyde and his father rode in the boxcar to tend the stock, while Esther and one daughter rode by passenger train. They arrived at the train station in Palmdale on December 21, 1901. The family stayed, on and off, in the Antelope Valley, but moved to Los Angeles around 1904. In 1916, Clyde moved back to Littlerock where he worked in the orchard business. Tired of the orchard job, he opened up his own automotive repair shop, during which time he served in World War I. He retired at the age of 73 after over 46 years in the automotive business.

In 1925, Clyde built a home on Date Ave. in Lancaster, near where Walt would attend Lancaster Grammar School. Walt graduated from AVJUHS in 1938, and from Antelope Valley Junior College in 1940. On August 2, 1942, Walt married his high school sweetheart, Mildred L. "Mickey" Dunham, in Lancaster, California.

When Pearl Harbor was attacked, Walt was working at Lockheed in Burbank, California. He and Cece Ellison enlisted in the U.S. Navy September 30, 1942 to make sure they didn't end up in the Army Infantry. They thought they would be sent to sunny San Diego for boot camp, but instead were shipped off in October to the cold, harsh weather at a new facility under construction at Sandpoint, Idaho – Farragut Naval Training Station - near the Canadian border.

After boot camp, Walt was assigned to Carrier Aircraft Service Unit #1 (CASU) on Ford Island, at Pearl Harbor, and later went to CASU #2 at Barber's Point, Territory of Hawaii. While in the service, he met up with his school friend, Cece Ellison, in Oakland, California, where Walt and Mickey were living. Walt was stationed near there at the Naval Auxiliary Air Station in Oakland, California.

Walt was in Oakland when he heard the news about the end of the war. He was honorably discharged at the rank of Aviation Machinist Mate, First Class, on December 1, 1945. He was awarded the Asiatic-Pacific Campaign Medal; American Campaign Medal; World War II Victory Medal; Good Conduct Medal.

In the days and weeks that followed his discharge, Walt took his wife and new daughter, Judie, and headed for home in Lancaster to live in a cottage behind his parents home on Date Avenue. He went to work at Muroc Army Air Base and also attended school at Polaris Flight Academy, supported by the G.I. Bill, to obtain his Private Pilots license. Walt worked in the jet engine shop at Edwards Air Force Base (formerly Muroc) for almost six years, then was a Jet Engine Representative with Westinghouse for nearly eight years. He was employed with General Electric, also as a Jet Engine Representative, for twenty-four years until his retirement.

Walt and Mickey had two other children; Richard W., and Kenneth R. Primmer, who recently passed away. They enjoy retirement by taking camping trips in their travel trailer and keep busy as members of the West Antelope Valley Historical Society. Walt and Mickey attend many local functions, including the Old Timers Barbeque held annually in October, put on by the Old Timers Association of which Walt was president for three years. Walt, along with friend and Navy veteran Jack Reynolds, joined the local B.P.O. Elks and both are still active in the organization.

Mickey and Walt Primmer with Cece Ellison – May 22, 1945 at the Palace Hotel in San Francisco

TO ALL EX-SERVICE MEN, AND THOSE OF YOU WHO HAVE NOT BEEN DISCHARGED:

Lancaster Lodge No. 1625, The Benevolent and Protective Order of Elks of the United States of America, send greetings and salutations.

The Citizens of Antelope Valley are deeply grateful to you and the hundreds of other service men who have served their Country, and who are responsible for bringing World War II to a glorious climax.

The Officers and Members of this Order wish in some way to express the thanks we all have in our hearts.

Therefore we, the members of Lancaster Lodge, cordially invite you to be our guest Tuesday evening, March fifth, nineteen hundred forty-six at 6:30. We will meet at the Elks Club House, 1323 Sierra Highway, Lancaster, Calif., and after a short welcome, will adjourn to the Lancaster Federal Building, 13th and Fig St., for a Buffet Supper, to be followed by an outstanding program of entertainment.

THIS IS YOUR PROGRAM: we hope you will make a special effort to be with us. It will give us an opportunity to thank you for your service to us and your Country.

Sincerely yours,

H. W. Hunter

P. S. The enclosed postal card is for your convenience. Please indicate in the proper place if you will be able to attend, so we will know how many to plan for.

Invitation received by Walt Primmer from local car dealer, H.W. Hunter and the Lancaster Elks Lodge, No. 1625, acknowledging the servicemen of WW II

On October 6, 1924, William John Pritchard was born in Lancaster, Los Angeles Co., California, the son of William John and Gertrude M. (Strong) Pritchard, Sr. William Pritchard, Sr., was born in California, with both parents of English descent, while Gertrude was born in Iowa. Her father was also born in Iowa and her mother was from Germany.

In 1930, the Pritchard family was living in the Antelope Valley with William, Sr. self employed as an alfalfa farmer. The family had grown to include four children; William, Jr., Marjorie L., James F., and Ida L. Pritchard. Another daughter, Ellen H. Pritchard was born in 1932.

Bill graduated from AVJUHS and enlisted in the U.S. Navy in 1942. Before his Naval career was in full swing, he married Polline McGowan on March 3, 1943, in Seattle, King Co., Washington. Together they would have four children; William John Pritchard, III, who died at birth in 1946; Michael W., died from polio in 1959; Cecilia P. and Patrick J. Pritchard.

Throughout his Naval career, Bill would engage in many battles and campaigns, the first being the New Georgia Group Operations located in the central Solomon Islands of the South Pacific in mid-1943. The next campaign would take him in support of the Treasury-Bougainville Operations near the close of 1943. Early in 1944, Bill took part in the Bismarck-Archipelago Operations with invasion support for Green Island and Rabaul. In April, 1944 the Naval operations shifted to Hollandia, in Dutch New Guinea, in support of clearing the island of Japanese troops. In mid-June of 1944, the Marianas Operation took place in support of the capture and occupation of Saipan. The Japanese Navy sailed to the area to battle the Pacific Fleet, but after losing more than 400 planes in a massive air battle, left in defeat.

The Leyte Landing Operation would take place in October of 1944, with Naval Admiral Halsey in command. The sea battle would last for four days, and in the end, the Japanese fleet was almost completely destroyed, leaving the Allied ships in complete control of the surface in the Pacific. After the Leyte Landing Operation support, Bill sailed on to the Manila Bay in support of the invasion of Mindoro in December, 1944 to February, 1945. Through April and May of 1945, Bill arrived at Mindanao Island in support of the Consolidation of the Southern Solomon Islands in the Philippines and was at the assault and occupation of Okinawa.

After World War II was over, Bill was sent to Advanced Fire Control School, then in 1950, he attended Fire Control Technician School. Bill was sent to Korea in April – July, 1951, for the First United Nations Counter Offense attack and the Communist China Spring Offensive Operations strike. In July – November, 1951, he would take part in the United Nations Fall Offensive in Korea. A second strike would take place, the Second Korean Winter Offensive in November, 1951, through April of 1952.

On July 2, 1958, working his way up through the ranks the hard way, Bill was commissioned an Ensign in the U.S. Navy. On July 9, 1960, Bill would get married for the second time to Myrtle Sullivan in Honolulu, Hawaii. In 1961, Bill would attended ComCruDesPac (Commander of Cruisers and Destroyers, Pacific Fleet) Engineering Officers School.

As the conflict in Vietnam heated up, a combined U.S. Navy and South Vietnamese Navy effort was set up to stop the flow of supplies from North Vietnam into South Vietnam. Bill was a Lieutenant Commander onboard the *U.S.S. Dynamic* (MSO-432), a minesweeper, just outside Da Nang, Vietnam, on May 5, 1968, when he died following a massive heart attack.

Bill was awarded the following campaign and service medals for his service during World War II, the Korean War, and Vietnam: Good Conduct Medal with six Stars; American Defense Medal; American Area Medal; Asiatic-Pacific Medal with nine Stars; World War II Victory Medal; China Service Medal; Japan Occupation Medal; Philippine Occupation Medal with two Stars; United Nations Service Medal; the Korean Service Medal with four Stars; National Defense Medal with one Star; Armed Forces

Expeditionary Medal Matsu-Quemoy Islands; Vietnam Service Medal with two Stars; Vietnam Campaign Medal.

Lieutenant Commander William J. Pritchard, Jr. was buried at Joshua Memorial Park in Lancaster, California. His sister, Ellen (Pritchard) Rosas currently lives in Lancaster.

JACK DANIEL REYNOLDS

On June 19, 1920, Jack Daniel Reynolds was born in Los Angeles, California, to Walter P. and Janet (Kunz) Reynolds. In January of 1920, Walter and Janet were living in Los Angeles with Walter employed as a bookkeeper for a local wholesale grocery company. Walter was born in Illinois and Janet was born in Ohio. By 1930, the Reynolds family had grown to include two children; Jack D. and Barbara Reynolds. They were living in Beverly Hills with Walter employed as the owner of a retail shoe store.

Walter moved his family to the Antelope Valley in 1936 where Jack graduated from AVJUHS in 1938, and from Antelope Valley Junior College in 1941. Jack enlisted in the U.S. Navy in 1942 and was sent to boot camp for training. After boot camp he was sent to Columbia University in New York to officer's candidate school. The program was cancelled before Jack graduated.

Jack was assigned to the *U.S.S. Medusa* (AR-1), a fleet repair ship. In mid-January 1945, after seeing combat at New Hebrides, and repairing ships en route to New Guinea, the ship departed for Hollandia where they joined up with a convoy bound for San Pedro Bay. There, they serviced ships engaged in the capture of Luzon and other islands in the Philippines until July. At the end of August, 1945, with the hostilities ended in the Pacific, the *Medusa* sailed for Manila.

Jack met up with high school buddy, Cece Ellison, at Manila Bay, just after the war. Cece took a Liberty Ship to the *Medusa*, where they had a dinner of "beans and weenies" together onboard the ship. From Manila, Jack sailed back to the United States and reported to the base at Terminal Island in San Francisco, California.

In January of 1946, Jack was honorably discharged at the rank of Quarter Master, Second Class. On September 27, 1947, he married Barbara Godde. They had one child together, a daughter, Kimberly Reynolds. After the war, Jack was part owner of a company in the Antelope Valley. Also, after the war, Jack joined the B.P.O. Elks and became the Exalted Ruler. He is now the Senior Past Exalted Ruler of the local organization. Jack still keeps in close contact with his high school and Navy buddies, Cece Ellison and Walt Primmer.

U.S.S. Medusa (AR-1) – Photo courtesy of the U.S. National Archives

221

Willard L. Ritchie was born January 22, 1927 in Dinuba, Tulare Co., California, the son of Willard L. and Mamie Baird (O'Neal) Ritchie, Sr., both born in Missouri. In 1930, the Ritchie family was living in Cutler, Orosi Township, Tulare Co., California. The family included children Dorothy, Willard Jr., and William Ritchie, all born in California. Willard, Sr. was earning a living working on a farm.

Willard entered the Naval Service through the Recruiting Station at Merced, California on January 21, 1944. He was sworn in at the railroad station in Fresno, California before boarding the San Joaquin daylight train to Oakland. He changed trains to the Shasta daylight and went on to Spokane, Washington. Then, he was off on another train to Coeur d' Alene, Idaho where Farragut Naval Training Center was located.

Willard was assigned to Camp Ward, Company 117. Boot camp was "very cold for a 17 year old kid from the San Joaquin Valley in California." After boot camp training, he was transferred to Treasure Island, San Francisco to await new construction of the *U.S.S. General S.D. Sturgis* (AP-137). While waiting for the ship to be completed, he went to school for fire fighting, small boat handling, seamanship, and 20mm and 5"-38 gun training at Point Montera, California.

The *U.S.S. General S.D. Sturgis* was put in commission on April 24, 1944, and Willard sailed with a small crew to Swan Island shipyard in Portland, Oregon on May 13, 1944. Willard arrived in Portland on May 15, 1944. The ship was decommissioned on May 25, 1944, for conversion to a troop transport. Willard remained in Portland to work with the older crewmembers in getting the ship in shape for commissioning. He went to work with the storekeeper's striker due to the fact that he could type. They needed people to fill out requisitions for supplies, so Willard fit the bill for the job.

The ship came with spare parts for just about everything you could think of, from the engine room to the bridge. As a storekeeper, Willard helped inventory some of these spares and mark the boxes for identification. The ship was put back into commission at Saint Johns, Oregon on July 15, 1944. They sailed for San Francisco, California on July 16, 1944. The ship traveled down the Columbia River to the Pacific Ocean and arrived in San Francisco on July 18, to finish outfitting the ship.

Willard left for San Pedro, California on July 27, 1944, onboard the *Sturgis*. The *Sturgis* anchored in the Los Angeles harbor and began to make daily shakedown cruises with people from the Naval shipyard aboard as observers, and with a Destroyer Escort to watch over them. After the shakedown was completed, the crew of the *Sturgis* was underway, once again, bound for Seattle, Washington, on August 7, 1944.

General S.D. Sturgis (AP-137) – National Archives photo

222

After arriving in Seattle, they commenced loading civilian and military passengers.

The *Sturgis* sailed out again, bound for Honolulu, Hawaii, where they arrived on August 24, 1944. They docked at Pier 1 under the Aloha Tower in downtown Honolulu to unload civilian passengers. Most of the passengers were Navy WAVES and civilian women sent to work at Pearl Harbor. When the women were all safely off the ship, the *Sturgis* sailed around the point to Pearl Harbor. Willard recalled, "We saw lots of damage still there from December 7, 1941. I was in a whaleboat going to the supply depot and we went around the Arizona where she lay on the bottom."

They made three round trips carrying both civilian and military passengers from San Francisco to Pearl Harbor and returning with like passengers between August 28, 1944 and October 9, 1944. On November 16, 1944, Willard and the crew of the *Sturgis*, were underway, in a convoy, bound for Eniwetok Atoll, Marshall Islands, and arrived at Eniwetok on December 4, 1944. On December 5, they left for Ulithi, and arrived on December 9. The *U.S.S. General S.D. Sturgis* was officially designated as a receiving ship for the Third Fleet on December 14, 1944. While anchored on January 12, 1945, the ship was under submarine attack.

Underway again on January 27, 1945, this time to moor on the starboard side of the U.S.S. New Jersey, to receive aboard Admiral Halsey's Third Fleet staff, en route to Pearl Harbor. Admiral Halsey's flag secretary, Commander Harold Stassen, was onboard as part of the Third Fleet staff. They debarked Halsey's personnel at Pearl Harbor on February 10, 1945, then on their way again when they had to turn around due to engine trouble. The repairs were made and they were underway, bound for San Francisco. They received diversionary orders to change course for Seattle, Washington. After arriving in Seattle on February 19, the ship entered Todd Pacific Shipyard for an overhaul. After the overhaul, the *Sturgis*, left once again, for San Francisco.

Willard was transferred to Camp Shoemaker Receiving Station in Pleasanton, California. From Camp Shoemaker, he was assigned to the *U.S.S. LCT-1430* (Landing Craft Tank), at Hunter's Point Naval Shipyard, San Francisco. He worked to get the LCT ready, but the assignment was cancelled. He was then assigned back to Camp Shoemaker aboard the *U.S.S. Trapper* (ACM-9). This ship was a Chimo class, Auxiliary Mine Layer. Willard was off to the Pacific again on the *Trapper*, with three Yard Mine Sweepers (YMS).

When the war was over, Willard was at the Kwajalein Atoll in the Marshall Islands, where he left the ship, *Trapper*. He flew back to Pearl Harbor (Hickam Field) and caught the *U.S.S. Saratoga*, as a passenger, back to San Francisco, then back to Camp Shoemaker for reassignment. There, he was assigned to the *U.S.S. Haven* (AH-12). The *Haven* ferried Navy wives whose husbands were stationed on Guam and Saipan. This was the first group of dependents to go to where their husbands were stationed. The ship had chicken wire all along the rails to keep the small children onboard. Willard made two trips with this type of passenger load.

The *Haven* was then assigned to "Operation Crossroads" for the Atomic Bomb tests at Bikini Atoll in the Marshall Islands. Willard recalled what transpired while on the ship. "The Haven was the radiological survey ship which carried several scientists aboard from the Atomic Energy Commission, Bureau of Standards, and the Fish and Wildlife Commission. They cataloged all species of fish. The atomic energy people played "hide and seek" with a block of lead containing a radioactive source inside. They would find it with a Geiger counters. Dr. Condon, from the Bureau of Standards; Dr. Stafford Warren, from the Atomic Energy Commission; Senator Saltonstall of Massachusetts, and many other dignitaries from other nations were onboard. The *U.S.S. Mount McKinley*, with Admiral W.H.P Blandy commanding, was the flagship.

The first bomb was dropped from a B-29 – lots of smoke, fire, and major damage to the ships in the target area. The height of the detonation was unknown to me. The number two bomb was lowered down through a caisson under the *U.S.S. LSM-60* (Landing Ship Material). The detonation raised a wall of water ¾ of a mile across and ¼ mile high. We saw the battleship *Arkansas* standing on end, then no more. Lots of ships were sunk in this blast. We were only twelve miles from the underwater blast and they expected a tidal wave, but by the time it got to us, it was about three feet high.

We went back into the lagoon that afternoon. We went to Pearl Harbor and then onto San Diego for decontamination of all our water systems. I only had six months left on my enlistment and was let off the *Haven* in San Diego."

Willard was reassigned from the Receiving Station at the Naval Station in San Diego, to the *U.S.S. LSMR-401* (Landing Ship Medium Rocket). He spent the last six months of his enlistment sailing each

Monday morning to San Clemente Island where they fired rockets at the range on the island. They would sail on Monday, arrive that evening, do dry runs all day Tuesday, then one "hot" run and all the rockets onboard were expended. Back to San Diego on Wednesday, Thursday and Friday to take on fuel, stores, and lots of rockets. Liberty was on Saturday and Sunday, then back to San Clemente on Monday to start all over again.

Willard was honorably discharged from the U.S. Navy on November 20, 1947. He joined the reserves at the time he was discharged, as the Navy had promised him one cruise each year. This never happened until he was recalled during August of 1950. Willard was stationed at the Receiving Station, Naval Station, San Diego, California, where he was a Storekeeper, 2nd Class. His duty at the receiving station was to issue clothing to the incoming people who were being recalled for the Korean War. He was assigned to his own clothing store in the Reserve Fleet area of the Naval Station.

Willard was released from active duty on December 13, 1951. He was honorably discharged, for the last time, on December 20, 1952. He received the American Campaign Medal; Asiatic-Pacific Campaign Medal with 1 Star; Philippine Liberation Medal with 1 Star; World War II Victory Medal; National Defense Service Medal, 1950-1954; Navy Good Conduct Medal.

In 1956, Willard moved to the Antelope Valley where he worked in Civil Service for both the Navy and the Air Force. He joined the American Legion and the Veterans of Foreign Wars organizations. On December 26, 1959, Willard married Marion Mae Parkhurst in Las Vegas, Clark Co., Nevada. Together they had one daughter, Karen Joyce Ritchie. Willard also had a step-daughter, Gail Ann Mitchell.

RICHARD MERRILL "RICH" ROWELL

Richard Merrill Rowell, first son of Maurice and Agnes (Merrill) Rowell, was born in Sonoma, California on August 6, 1916. The Rowell family moved to the Antelope Valley in the early 1920's where Maurice was the principal of AVJUHS from 1924, until his death in 1928, at age forty-four. Agnes Rowell was a highly respected English and Algebra teacher at AVJUHS for over twenty-five years. Maurice and Agnes had three children, all boys – Richard Merrill, Homer Adams and Robert Benson Rowell.

After graduating from Antelope Valley Joint Union High School in 1933, Richard attended Antelope Valley Junior College for a year. In 1934, he enrolled at the California Institute of Technology, graduating with a BS degree in 1938.

Richard enlisted in the Naval Reserve on August 8, 1939 and was commissioned Ensign on August 20, 1940. In November of 1940, he joined the Fighting Squadron led by Lt. Edward "Butch" O'Hare. In December 1941, Ensign Rowell was assigned with VF-3 Squadron of fighter pilots on board the carrier *U.S.S. Lexington* (CV-2).

The role of a fighter pilot aboard an aircraft carrier at sea was to win and hold control of the air, just as a fighter pilot does with a land base. Ensign Rowell continuously put his life on the line when he escorted dozens of torpedo bombers to safely drop their loads on the Japanese ships.

To be a successful fighter pilot, he had to master more tasks than any single man in World War II. He had to be exceptionally good at handling a fighter plane; ready and alert with extreme eye and hand coordination with split-second timing. Hundreds of hours of training went into learning complex mechanical systems, electronics, navigation, radio and operational procedures. All of this required an extreme amount of personal judgment, skill and courage.

During the battle off the coast of Bougainville in the South Pacific, Ensign Rowell received the Distinguished Flying Cross. On February 20, 1942 he received credit for two bomber assists. As described in the book "The First Team" by John B. Lundstrom, "Five pilots, 'Scoop' Vorse, Bob Morgan, Howard Johnson, John Lackey, and Richard Rowell, swarmed after the (Japanese) bombers, disposing of cripples already shot up by the 3rd Division and cutting out of formation one of the four surviving bombers by means of slashing low runs…The Fighting Three had done it's part to wreck the bomb run…" The citation related that he "made vigorous and determined attacks in the face of combined enemy machine gun and cannon fire against a formation of enemy bombers."

On May 8, 1942 Ensign Rowell was assigned to the Fighting Two Squadron VF-2, commanded by Lt. Noel Gayler. The *Lexington* strike group was divided into three tactical groups, each with a fighter escort. Lt. Gayler had orders to "attack any incoming enemy strike airplanes and harass them all the way back…" Lt. Gayler's group consisted of four fighter pilots all escorting torpedo bombers en route to bomb the Japanese carriers.

The four pilots, Lt. Gayler, Ens. Peterson, Lt. (jg) Clark, and Ens. Rowell, had worked their way up to 6,000 feet, joining the torpedo planes in the air over the Coral Sea. Two fighter pilots were on either side of the torpedo planes. Ensign Rowell was flying as wingman for Lt. Clark when, without warning, "several Zeros tumbled out of nearly clouds and confronted Gayler and his wingman, Dale Peterson. At first Gayler hoped to draw the enemy's attention to keep the Zeros away from the vulnerable torpedo bombers, but in this he was too successful. The Zeros were just too fast, knifing in and out with their slashing hit-and-run attacks which shattered the cohesiveness of the escorts." Also contributing to the difficulty was the fact that they had been flying at 105 knots along with the slower torpedo bombers they were escorting. They had no time to accelerate to combat speed before the enemy was upon them. The F4F Wildcat had to have a speed of at least 130 knots to maneuver it properly in a combat fight.

"Soon it was every man for himself. Gayler glimpsed Clark and his wingman, Richard Rowell, disappear into a cloud – Zeros right on their tails. As for Peterson, he was no longer in sight. The Japanese may have gotten him on his first pass." Lt. Gayler was the only pilot left from the four man escort. He fought off the remaining Zeros. "The sacrifice of the torpedo escort crew drew four Zeros away from the torpedo bombers allowing the attack of the Japanese carriers to go on unimpeded."

Ensign Richard Rowell was listed as Missing in Action on May 8, 1942 after failing to return from his mission. He was declared dead one year later in May, 1943. For his courage in the Battle of the Coral Sea he was awarded a Gold Star in lieu of a second Distinguished Flying Cross, "he zealously engaged enemy Japanese aircraft contributing materially to the defense of our forces. In this action he gallantly gave up his life in the service of his country." He was also awarded the Purple Heart medal. The U.S. Navy destroyer escort *U.S.S. Richard M. Rowell* (DE-403) was named in his honor, sponsored by his mother, Agnes Rowell. The ship was launched on November 17, 1942 only six months after Richard's disappearance.

Richard's name is inscribed on the Tablets of the Missing at Manila American Cemetery, Manila, Philippines. His brother, Robert, currently lives in Alaska with his children. Richard's sister-in-law, Marguerite (Powers) Rowell, wife of Dr. Homer Rowell (deceased), lives in Lancaster, California with her daughter, Susan.

March 5, 1942, U.S.S. Lexington VF-3 – Ensign Richard M. Rowell, kneeling, far right. Seated to the left of Ensign Rowell is Lt. Edward H. "Butch" O'Hare, first U.S. Navy Ace; Seated fourth from the left is Lt. Cmdr. John "Jimmy" Thatch.
Photo courtesy of the United States Navy

ESTELLE SCHWARTZ

Estelle Schwartz was born September 11, 1919, in Newport News, Virginia, the daughter of Harry and Shirley (Blier) Schwartz. Harry immigrated to the U.S. from Czechoslovakia and Shirley, from Romania. Estelle had two younger brothers, Milton and Eugene Schwartz. The Schwartz family moved to California in 1923, coming to the Antelope Valley in 1925. Harry was employed as a livestock dealer in 1930, with the family living on Date Avenue in Lancaster.

Estelle graduated from AVJUHS in 1936 and enlisted in the Coast Guard SPARS in 1943. President Franklin Roosevelt signed a law on November 23, 1942, creating the Woman's Reserve of the Coast Guard. The SPARS name came from the Coast Guard Latin motto: *Semper Paratus – Always Ready.* The purpose of the SPARS was to free up the men from shore duty so they would be available to serve at sea. The SPARS were modeled after the Navy Reserve WAVES.

Most of the two years Estelle spent in the Coast Guard were in Ketchican, Alaska, near Juneau. She was honorably discharged in 1945, and in September of 1950, she married William Walsh in Lancaster, California. They had three children together; Shelley, Michael and Jeoffrey Walsh. After the war she was employed in the social services field.

Estelle died on July 4, 1994, at Yosemite National Park. Her ashes were scattered in the park - one of her favorite places to visit.

GLEN ALLEN SETTLE

William Benjamin Settle, the first born son of Newton and Martha (Titchenal) Settle, married Marian Ruth Allen on November 20, 1900, in Santa Paula, Ventura Co., California. They had eleven children together; Ruth, Maude, William, Earle, Irving, Glen, Mildred, Marcus, Aileen, Robert, and Jack Settle. William was working for the Southern Pacific Railroad in Castaic and Piru, California, then moved with the company to the Antelope Valley. Their sixth child, Glen, was born September 27, 1911, in Palmdale, Los Angeles Co., California.

Glen grew up in the Antelope Valley where he attended the Palmdale School, a two story brick building near the west side of the railroad tracks. The Settle family left Palmdale in 1919 when Glen was in third grade. They moved to Lancaster where Glen attended Lancaster Grammar School, and graduated from AVJUHS in 1929. He was active in sports, excelling in football, basketball, baseball, track and swimming. Glen won letters in each of those Varsity sports while attending AVJUHS. After high school, Glen attended Antelope Valley Junior College where he helped form their first basketball team.

In 1929, Glen and his brother, Irving, along with two school friends, Don Hatfield and Jerry Matay, ventured off to college at Texas A. & I. in Kingsville, Texas, where they had been awarded athletic scholarships and recruited to play on the Varsity football team. By the end of the school term, the depression had hit hard and the college had to cut back on their athletic programs.

226

With no funds to continue, the boys headed back to Lancaster. Glen worked for Bill and Whit Carter at the A.V. Produce grocery store until 1932, when he obtained another athletic scholarship, this time to Ripon College in Wisconsin. At the end of the football season, Glen decided it was too cold for him in Wisconsin, so he and his friends headed back for Lancaster. Glen attended Fresno State College along with his brother, Mark. Bill and Whit Carter offered Glen a partnership in their A.V. Produce Company, which he accepted. In 1933, Glen married Sue Miller. After their marriage, she helped Glen run the A.V. Produce Company Store No. 2, in Rosamond. The marriage would last eleven years and would end in 1943, about a year after Glen enlisted in the U.S. Navy.

Glen was at the Rosamond Bowling Alley when he heard the news about Pearl Harbor. He could not believe it was happening, and was glued to the radio, waiting for any updates. Glen enlisted in the U.S. Navy on October 9, 1942. He had read in the Los Angeles papers that former heavyweight boxing champ, Gene Tunney, now a commander in the Navy, and his aide, would be interviewing athletic instructors and coaches from the Southern California area. If accepted after the interview, they would become U.S. Navy Physical Instructors. Glen was one of fifteen selected out of over 100 applicants. He was assigned the rank of Chief Specialist (A) in the U.S. Navy.

On October 23, 1942, Glen was sent to Norfolk, Virginia for basic recruit training. He wrote many letters home and took several trips to Michigan to visit his sister, Ruth, while on leave. After basic training, Glen was assigned to the Physical Instructors Training School. He had been receiving the Ledger-Gazette, the Antelope Valley newspaper, by mail, as a courtesy to the servicemen. He wrote a letter in November 1942, which was placed in the paper for all to read. He was pleased with the ten pounds he had lost during all his hard training. Glen went on to tell the readers what one full day consisted of:

"Up at 4:45 a.m. every day and do conditional calisthenics exercises for an hour; eat and then we drill for two hours; go to the Pistol Range or Whale Boats whatever it may be; eat again, then start in again with about two more hours of drills; after this, we go to a lecture, and again to another lecture after we eat, and to bed by 9:00 p.m."

U.S.N. Chiefs – Len Roberts, Glen Settle and Frank Miller – 1942
On top of the Empire State Building in New York

227

Glen also wrote that *"all Americans were a dime a dozen."* He had come across some big name athletes of the time while going through training - *"Bob Feller, Cleveland's great young pitcher; Tom Drake, Brooklyn Dodger pitcher; Ace Parker, great football star; Fred Appostoli and Amard Emanuel of the boxing world. I could go on and on and name them for hours. It is very interesting to talk and mingle with all the greats of the sporting world."*

Glen was sent to San Diego, California, to the Naval Training Station (NTS) to train new recruits. Next, he was assigned to gunnery school. From there he went to the NTS in Bainbridge, Maryland. While stationed there, Glen was assigned to transfer Navy personnel to various Navy bases and ships throughout the United States. During this time he made ten trips from the east coast to the west coast.

In August of 1944, Glen was assigned to the *U.S.S. Purdy* in Boston, Massachusetts. He spent approximately six months onboard the *Purdy*. Next, he was off to Williamsburg, Virginia for six months at Camp Peary. From there, Glen was ordered to "Fleet City" (Shoemaker Navy Training Center) near Hayward, in Northern California. After another move to Treasure Island Naval Base, in the middle of the San Francisco Bay, Glen was shipped out to the Pacific. He was on his way to the Philippine Islands to spend time on Samar and Leyte Island.

The SeaBees had already cleared out the island when Glen arrived in 1945. He remembered eating coconuts, bananas and lamb stew, which he never ate again after his discharge from the military. Glen was in the Philippines when he heard that the war was over. He had asked to be discharged on the east coast so he could go through Detroit and pick up a new car. Disappointing news on purchasing a new car – you had to have a "high priority" need to buy one, so his brother-in-law, Olen Forquer, located a used Dodge for him.

Glen Settle front left, Philippines – 1945

Glen was honorably discharged at the rank of Chief Specialist (A) (PA), at Lido Beach, New York USN Personnel Separation Center on December 3, 1945. He received the American Theater Campaign Medal and the Good Conduct Medal. Glen returned to the Antelope Valley and resumed working again with A.V. Distributing Company. Before the war, A.V. Produce Company had sold out their interest in the retail grocery business and started A.V. Distributing Company, dealing more in the wholesale line of beverages, ice cream, and frozen foods. A.V. Distributing Company was the first business to own refrigerated trucks in the Antelope Valley.

In 1948, Glen married Dorene Burton, daughter of H. Clifford Burton and Alice E. Greenleaf. They helped run Burton's Tropico Gold Mine in Rosamond from 1948 – 1956. In 1956, the Tropico closed. It was one of the last large California gold mines to cease operations. On January 15, 1958, Tropico was reopened and renamed the Tropico Gold Camp Museum. Glen and Dorene ran the museum along with escorting visitors on guided tours of the mine, for the next 22 years.

Following their idea, Glen and Dorene were in attendance at the first organizational meeting of the Kern-Antelope Historical Society in May of 1959. Glen was elected President in December 1959. They both became charter members and were very active in establishing the Society. Glen served as President of the Rosamond Chamber of Commerce in 1960-1961; member of the Edwards Air Force Base Civilian Advisory Committee 1960-1961; Director of the Antelope Valley Progress Association 1960-1963; elected member of the Board of Trustees for Antelope Valley Junior College, representing Rosamond; appointed to the California State Historical Landmarks Committee by Governor Ronald Reagan, in 1967.

Although his eyesight is failing him, Glen is still active in the Antelope Valley community as a lifetime member of the Rosamond V.F.W., a charter member of Lancaster Elks 1625, and a member of Kern-Antelope Valley Historical Society and Antelope Valley Genealogical Society. He spends time with school pal and World War II veteran, Glen Ralphs, along with many other "old timers" in the Valley. He lives in Lancaster where he shares his home with his brother Robert's son, Bruce Settle.

JACK HURST SETTLE

Jack Hurst Settle was born February 6, 1925 in Lancaster, California, the eleventh child born to William Benjamin and Marian Ruth (Allen) Settle. Jack attended Lancaster Grammar School and AVJUHS. In 1942, at the age of 17, while in his junior year at high school, Jack enlisted in the U.S. Navy.

After only three weeks of training in San Diego, California at the Naval Training Center, Jack was sent to the Pacific on a destroyer. He spent four years in the Navy and was honorably discharged near the end of 1945. He was awarded the Asiatic-Pacific Campaign Medal and the World War II Victory Medal.

Jack was employed with the border patrol near Temecula, in San Diego County, California after his discharge from the Navy. He later went to work for the Y.M.C.A., and moved to Grand Junction, Mesa Co., Colorado. Jack was killed in a car accident, near Denver, in May of 1977.

Brothers Glen and Robert Settle, standing in back row.
Jack Settle, front left, nephew William Settle, on right

Jack Settle – Lancaster, California
1942

229

ROBERT E. "BOB" SHERLOCK

On March 8, 1911, Robert E. Sherlock was born in Chicago, Cook Co., Illinois, the son of John Joseph and Marie (Wiegers) Sherlock. John was born in Ireland and Marie was from Canada. Bob had three siblings; John, Thomas, and Mary Sherlock. In 1920, the Sherlock family was living in Bakersfield, Kern Co., California, and by 1930, they had moved to Beverly Hills, Los Angeles Co., California. Soon after 1930, the Sherlock family moved to the Antelope Valley.

Bob enlisted in the U.S. Navy in 1941, and was at sea, onboard the *U.S.S. Enterprise* (CV-6), just north of Pearl Harbor, when the Japanese attacked. The *Enterprise* engaged in World War II when her scout planes encountered Japanese squadrons attacking Pearl Harbor. The *Enterprise* would become the most decorated ship of World War II.

Bob's first assignment in the Navy was as a photographer. He would continue serving as a photographer on the *Enterprise* surviving 17 battles including; Pearl Harbor; the Pacific raids on the Marshall-Gilbert Islands, Wake Island, and Marcus Island; Battle of Midway; Battle of Guadalcanal; Capture and Defense of Guadalcanal; Eastern Solomons; Santa Cruz; Naval Battle of Guadalcanal; Rennell Island; Gilbert Islands; Marshall Islands Operations; the Asiatic-Pacific raids on the Truk Islands, Palau, Yap, Ulithi, Woleai; Hollandia (New Guinea); Mariana Island Operations; Battle of the Philippine Sea 1 & 2; Battle of Stewart Islands.

Bob was honorably discharged at the rank of Chief Petty Officer in 1944. He received the following awards for his service; Asiatic-Pacific Area Medal with 17 Battle Stars; Presidential Unit Citation with 2 Stars, with one for the *Enterprise* participation in the Doolittle raid on Tokyo. The *Enterprise* was part of Vice Admiral William Halsey's Task Force 16, providing air cover during the air attack approach; American Defense Medal with 1 Star; American Area Medal; World War II Victory Medal; Good Conduct Medal.

After the war, Bob continued in the photography business. He was a newspaper reporter and went on to be a newspaper executive. On May 5, 1950, Bob married Elisabeth Smith in San Gabriel, California. They had two children together; a daughter Mary, and son, Joe Sherlock. Bob passed away in Alhambra, California on July 31, 2002. He is buried at the Resurrection Cemetery, Monterey Park, California.

The U.S.S. Enterprise photo crew – Robert Sherlock, standing at far right

230

Everett J. "Jim" Slaton was born May 28, 1920, in Valient, Creek Co., Oklahoma, the son of Isaac Newton and Myrtle Elisabeth (White) Slaton. He had two brothers; Eldon and Harvey Clay Slaton; and one half brother, George Andrew Clark. In 1930, Myrtle and her two sons were living in Sutton, Muskogee Co., Oklahoma.

Jim had already enlisted in the U.S. Navy and was onboard the *U.S.S. Helena* at Pearl Harbor when the Japanese attacked. The *Helena* was tied up alongside 1010 dock at the Pearl Harbor Navy Yard, on the east side of the harbor, when she was hit with a single torpedo during the raid, flooding an engine room and boiler room.

Prior to the attack on Pearl Harbor, Jim had gone through basic training and was sent to the Naval Training Center at North Island, San Diego, California. He received training in flying the Curtiss SOC-3 "Seagull" Scout-Observation plane, and also in radio communications, then attached to Task Force 54, Carrier Aircraft Service Unit (CASU). Jim would later receive further training at the Annapolis Naval Academy in Washington, D.C.

Jim recalled a narrow escape on February 23, 1942. "I was on a SOC-3 plane out of San Francisco, California, searching for submarines, when our plane went down. The pilot drowned. I suffered a broken back, but was rescued and taken to Mare Island Hospital on Mare Island. After this, I was not allowed to fly anymore and became a part of the regular Navy."

While with the CASU, Jim was stationed on the *U.S.S. Wasp* and the *U.S.S. Enterprise*. After his recovery from the SOC-3 accident, Jim was assigned to several ships and went through many battles during World War II. He was assigned to the *U.S.S. Prince William* on Wake Island and Guam; *U.S.S. Yorktown* in the Coral Sea, Battle of the Philippines at Eniwetok; *U.S.S. Franklin* at Kwajalien, Okinawa. Earlier, he had served on the *U.S.S. Kenmore* which took him from Washington, D.C. through the Panama Canal.

Two humorous events Jim recalled were when "an inebriated sailor returned to the ship after a night in San Francisco. He hid a prized coal scuttle in the radio room. When the officer of the day stumbled over it, he expressed many expletives and told him to get rid of it. Another time, a sailor brought a piano down the gangplank, but they wouldn't let him bring it aboard. I wondered where he stole it from and how he was able to roll it down the sidewalks without being apprehended!"

In December of 1944, Jim returned to the U.S. and was sent to Dallas, Texas Naval Station where he taught navigations and communications. On July 1, 1945, Jim married Francys Jane Friesen, in Alameda, Oakland Co., California. Jim was back in Texas when he heard the news of the war ending. He was honorably discharged at the rank of First Class Radioman in May, 1946, at Norman, Oklahoma. Jim received the following awards for his service: Asiatic-Pacific Campaign Medal with three Stars; American Campaign Medal; World War II Victory Medal; Defense Service Medal; Philippine Liberation Campaign Medal; Good Conduct Medal.

Jim left Oklahoma for Nebraska to pick up his wife, Francys, then headed to California. After arriving in California, Jim worked for Douglas Aircraft. He also attended BIOLA College (Bible Institute of Los Angeles) in Los Angeles, California. He became a Baptist Minister and also worked for Boeing and Lockheed. In his later years he worked as a custodian for the Lancaster School District.

Jim and Francys had five children together; Elisabeth Ann, James Philip, Barbara Lynn, Mary Francys, and David Everett Slaton.

Reflecting on his time in the Navy, Jim stated that he "appreciated the benefits for servicemen such as the G.I. Bill for schooling and housing, but while in the service, I became convinced that I should not kill. I had it written in my service record that I would not take up a gun. I could have been court marshaled for this action, but I was not."

HAROLD DANIEL SMITH

Harold Daniel Smith was born June 18, 1926 in Miami, Gila Co., Arizona, the second son born to Leslie Calvin and Mattie Katherine (McKelvey) Smith. Harold had three siblings; two brothers, Henry and Marion; and one sister, Shirley Smith. The Smith family moved to Rosamond, Kern Co., California in 1937, where Leslie was working at the Silver Queen Mine. Harold graduated from Rosamond Grammar School in 1940.

Harold enlisted in the U.S. Navy at the age of 17, while attending AVJUHS, following in the footsteps of his older brother, Henry H. Smith. Harold served on an aircraft carrier during World War II and was rated as an AOM-3, Aviation Ordnanceman. He was responsible for keeping naval aircraft power plants, armament and ordnance systems in top condition along with loading aviation ordnance including bombs, mines, and torpedoes.

Harold was injured in 1944 when a 350 pound bomb fell out of the rack, striking him on his head causing a severe injury. He was in and out of the hospital many times, until his death in Los Angeles, on November 3, 1960. He was buried at Union Cemetery, Bakersfield, Kern Co., California.

HENRY HARVEY "HARVEY" SMITH

On October 18, 1923, Henry Harvey Smith was born in Arizona, the first son born to Leslie Calvin and Mattie Katherine (McKelvey) Smith. Harvey lived with his parents and siblings in Rosamond, Kern Co., California from 1937 – 1941.

Harvey enlisted in the U.S. Navy in 1941, while he was a student at AVJUHS. His duty assignment included serving onboard the submarine, *U.S.S. Bluefish.* Harvey was stationed in Cuba for a time, then was sent to the Pacific where he participated in several battles during World War II.

Harvey married Betty Lundy in Bakersfield, Kern Co., California. They had two children; Rebecca and Steven Smith, both born in Bakersfield. Harvey passed away on July 14, 1990 in Bakersfield, and is buried at Union Cemetery, along with his brother, Harold.

WAYNE S. SQUIRE, SR.

Wayne S. Squire, Sr., was born October 11, 1927 in Seattle, King Co., Washington, the only child born to Stanley Alfred and Lillian Olive (Garvey) Squire. Stanley was born in New York, and Lillian was born in Washington. In 1930, the Squire family was living in Seattle, with Stanley employed as a painter in an automobile plant.

Wayne recalled the times before and after enlisting in the U.S. Navy in 1944, starting off with basic training at San Diego Naval Training Station, California. "As the war in Europe gradually ground-down, Japan and the Pacific Islands came more into focus. As a 17 year old, I could not wait to join the Navy. During the World War II era, just about everyone went to war. If too young for the Armed Forces, then, along with your younger brothers, sisters, and parents, you joined one of the three shifts at the ship yards, aircraft factory, or munitions plants. In my neighborhood there were no anti-war demonstrations. Draft cards were not burned. I never knew a draft dodger. Just about every able bodied man or woman joined-up and went to war or work in some war related activity. It was a total effort!

I noticed after joining the Navy and boarding my first ship, it appeared that much of the crew was made up of 17 year olds. 18 was considered as getting along, and 19 was definitely 'over the hill'. It seemed to me that much of the World War II Navy was manned by teenagers aboard ships blasting out "Praise the Lord and Pass the Ammunition" on the ships loud speakers, while at sea!

Before boarding my ship at Treasure Island, San Francisco, I was somewhat perplexed to see that we were issued foul weather, or Arctic type clothing. Fur lined parkas, hats and boots.....Nothing I could expect to wear in the hot, humid tropics of the South Pacific. We looked more like combat Marines than Naval personnel. As to where we were going – the reply was, 'Don't ask!; Top Secret, again; Loose Lips Sink Ships'. I guessed Alaska. As we sailed beneath the Golden Gate Bridge, I looked up to see the bridge rail above lined with crowds waving farewell. In fact, I wondered if it was a patriotic gesture or final farewell, forever keeping in mind the gold stars in our neighbors windows at home, honoring many a soldier, Marine, or sailor who never returned home.

As we approached the Faralon Islands, I expected that surely the ship would turn to a northerly heading, or Alaska. Why else were we equipped with Arctic type foul weather gear? The ship didn't turn north. We just continued on west for days, passing Guam and the Philippines. Eventually, we landed at White Beach, Okinawa. My remembrance of Okinawa was of having gone through a typhoon. Ashore, I lay down in a rice paddy and hung on to saw grass to keep from being tumbled over. Later, we were told that the wind reached 168 miles per hour. Sometime thereafter, the Japanese were requested to surrender, but refused. Then, two atom bombs were dropped and the war came to an abrupt end.

We learned that our mission at Okinawa had been to form up a landing boat pool, headed for an expected land invasion of the Japanese home islands. Our target was the northern most island of Hokido, thus the foul weather gear and equipment. We were later told that 90% of our group would not have survived the landing. We were to drive the landing boats at Hokido, transporting the Marines ashore for the expected invasion. Had the land invasion of Japan gone forward, thousands of lives, both American and Japanese, would have been lost. The dropping of the bomb saved my life. I probably would not have lived through the invasion of Japan.

After Okinawa and the wars end, we were shipped north, up the Yellow Sea, to north China. At Tsingtao, we found ourselves about to become embroiled in a Chinese civil war between the Nationalists and the Communists. As we went further north, up the Yellow Sea to Taku, near Beijing, (Peking) things really began to heat up. After brief liberties in Tiensin, word came to pull out as soon as possible. Bullets began to fly between the feuding Chinese civil war factions. Our purpose in China had been to remove the surrendered Japanese soldiers who had been occupying much of China since

233

1937, and return them to Japan. In that as a Navy man, I had not been assigned to a ship, so I was told to go down to the Taku harbor and find a ship – any ship headed back to the U.S. The war was over – go home.

The only thing I could hook a ride on was a very old and dilapidated LST (Landing Ship, Tank) that may or may not make it back to the U.S. The Chinese junks nearby, on the Yellow Sea, looked like luxury liners next to the old LST which was judged only marginally sea worthy. It was decided that the LST could not make it across 6,000 miles of ocean to New Orleans, so we were sent to Korea for demolition. The Koreans decided they were much too busy and didn't want the job. Our only option was to head the LST toward the open South China Sea and hope for the best.

Then came three months of numerous engine failures, out of fuel episodes, leaks and near disasters. We wiled away the evening hours on the ships stern (fantail) shooting at following sharks. The days of 'political and ecological correctness' had not, as yet, arrived. I wondered if the following sharks were waiting for us to sink or after the meat scraps from the galley, tossed overboard.

Upon leaving China, we picked up a number of Marines for transport back to the U.S. I noted that many had spent the entire duration of the war, i.e., four years on duty stations and ships throughout the Pacific. Many had not been home in four years. A six month deployment was rare, if ever, and e-mail did not exist yet. Eventually, we made it to New Orleans where the ship nearly sank in the Mississippi River."

While in the Navy, Wayne was a Coxswain attached to GROPAC 13, a group formed for the invasion of Japan. He was honorably discharged in August, 1946. Wayne was awarded the following medals for his service in the Navy: Asiatic-Pacific Campaign Medal; American Campaign Medal; China Service Medal; Navy Occupation Service Medal; World War II Victory Medal.

Wayne was glad when the war ended and was excited to go back home. He finished high school upon his return home, then in 1953, he earned a bachelor's degree in Social Sciences from Stanford University, California. On November 1, 1958 Wayne married Mary Gonzalez in Santa Barbara, California. Together they had two children; Linda Marie Squire and Wayne Stanley Squire, Jr. The Squire family moved to Quartz Hill, California, in 1968. Wayne was employed with the Atlantic-Richfield Company and the Richfield Oil Company, as a Marketing Representative for 28 years, retiring in 1985. Wayne and his wife, Mary, are retired and live in Quartz Hill.

On his time in the service, Wayne stated, "My contribution was miniscule to the Greatest Generation, however, I walked the walk and talked the talk. I was proud to have served, and I'd do it again. The real credit goes to those who never came home."

On April 9, 1921, Richard E. Stambook was born in Lancaster, Los Angeles Co., California, the son of William and Hazel (Brockman) Stambook. William was born in California, of French descent, and Hazel was born in Colorado. In 1930, the Stambook family was living in Willow Springs, Kern Co., California, where William was employed as an engineer in the oil business. The children in the family at that time, included three sons; Donald, Richard and Robert.

Richard attended Bakersfield College in Kern Co., where he completed the Civilian Pilot Training (CPT) Program. He enlisted in the U.S. Navy on June 12, 1941 as an aviation cadet. He earned his wings as a Naval Aviator and was commissioned an Ensign on January 9, 1942, in Pensacola, Florida.

Richard served in a Composite Scouting Squadron at Pearl Harbor until March of 1942. He spent the next four months assigned to Scouting Squadron 3-D14, then was transferred again, this time joining up with VF-6 aboard the *U.S.S. Enterprise* (CV-6). Richard served on the *Enterprise*, flying F4F Wildcats, for the next eight months at sea, and at New Caledonia, Guadalcanal.

Next, Richard joined VF-27 aboard the *U.S.S. Princeton*, this time flying the Grumman F6F-3 Hellcat. He saw combat from May to October 1944. On June 11, 1944, he shot down his first Japanese airplane, a "Betty," the Allied reporting name for the Japanese Mitsubishi G4-M bomber. Richard shot the bomber down three miles south of Kagman Point, Saipan, while on combat air patrol. Just eight days later, he was involved in the "Great Marianas Turkey Shoot," where he downed three "Zekes," the Japanese A6M Zero fighters, and a "Judy," the D4Y Suisei dive bomber. With these "kills" Richard would become the Antelope Valley's only Ace fighter pilot.

On September 21, 1944, in the Manila Bay area of the Philippines, Richard shot down two "Tonys," the Japanese Kawasaki Ki-61 fighter, and one "Zeke." On October 13, he and his wingman each shot down a "Tojo," near Tainan. Five days later, Richard shot down one more airplane, a "Nick." On October 24, 1944, the *Princeton* was severely damaged by a Japanese dive-bomber attack. The bomb crashed through the flight deck and hangar, then exploded. Efforts to save the ship proved futile, and after the remaining personnel were taken off, the ship was sunk with a torpedoes from the *U.S.S. Reno*.

Richard was transferred to VBF-98 in November, 1944, and he served with that unit until the end of the war. He was released from active duty on October 18, 1945, with a total of 10 confirmed enemy aircraft shot down, and one unconfirmed. Among the awards for his service during World War II, Richard received the Silver Star; Distinguished Flying Cross with one Gold Star; and the Air Medal with two Gold Stars. He retired from the Naval Reserve as a Lieutenant Commander on April 21, 1959. While remaining in the Naval Reserve, Richard flew with Trans World Airlines (TWA) for thirty years until his retirement in 1985. He flew many types of aircraft, including the DC-3 and the Lockheed L-1011.

On August 5, 1945, Richard married Nettie Allen. They had four children together; Randy, Candace, Trudy and Sheila Stambook. Richard and Nettie lived in San Diego, California from 1975 until his death on April 12, 2000. He is buried at El Camino Memorial Park in San Diego, California.

His family recalled one of Richard's fondest memories - the joy of flying his first airplane, the Piper J-3 Cub over the Mojave Desert in the Antelope Valley as a teenager.

DEAN LEROY "STEB" STEBBINS

Dean LeRoy Stebbins was born April 25, 1923, in Farnam, Dawson Co., Nebraska, the son of Orrie and Lila (Hicks) Stebbins. The Stebbins family moved to the Antelope Valley in 1929 from Nebraska. Dean had an older sister, LaVon, and a younger brother, Gilbert Darrell Stebbins, who also served during WWII in the Army. Dean attended Lancaster Grammar School and graduated from AVJUHS in 1941.

In 1942, Dean enlisted in the U.S. Navy. He served in the Pacific area on the submarines *U.S.S. Pickerel, U.S.S. Dolphin* (SS-169), and the *U.S.S. Cutlass* (SS-478). Dean was honorably discharged at the rank of Electrician's Mate, 3rd Class, and received the following awards for his service during World War II: Asiatic-Pacific Area Medal; American Area Medal; World War II Victory Medal; Good Conduct Medal.

After the war, Dean worked for Southern California Edison Company, and retired after 36 years of service. On September 20, 1952, he married Bette Schein in Las Vegas, Nevada. They had one daughter together, Peggy Sue Stebbins. Dean passed away on July 14, 1996, in Lancaster, Los Angeles Co., California.

ROY DUANE STOUT

On June 7, 1924, Roy Duane Stout was born in the Highland Park area of Los Angeles, Los Angeles Co., California, the only child of Carl Thadish and Mary Lydia (Buddemeyer) Stout. Carl and Mary divorced when Roy was five years old. He attended grammar schools in California, and also in Missouri, where his grandmother lived.

Roy's mother met and married Henry Chester "Blackie" Hoekstra. Henry was stationed in the U.S. Navy in San Pedro, California, where Roy attended Richard Henry Dana Junior High School. In 1938, Roy's stepfather, Blackie, was transferred to the Asiatic Fleet, which meant another move, this time to Tsingtao, China. While there, Roy learned that Japan was occupying China, and he saw first hand, the atrocities of war. One time, a Japanese soldier put a bayonet up to Roy's body, telling him he was not allowed to go any farther in a certain direction. Roy recalled, "At night, the Japanese tanks would patrol the streets, firing at nothing in particular, just to remind people that there was a curfew."

Roy spent time in Shanghai, then moved to Manila in the Philippine Islands. He attended high school for a year before the U.S. Navy evacuated the family back to the United States. The family ended up in Long Beach, California, where Roy attended high school and worked on the Long Beach Pike in an amusement zone, running various change games for a dollar per shift. He continued working at several different jobs until December 7, 1941.

While returning from a vacation in Missouri, Roy was on the Arizona border with his parents when he heard the news about the attack on Pearl Harbor. "Of course, I wanted to join the Navy, but with my stepfather in the Navy, Mother didn't want me to sign up. However, when the draft was getting close, I joined the Seabees, which had an attractive sound. When they sent me to Camp Bradford, Norfolk, Virginia, for boot camp training in 1943, I saw the first casualties, returnees of the Pacific War. I didn't want to be a Marine! The Navy appealed to me, and as they were recruiting men, I joined the regular Navy for six years, and so I became a 'real' sailor.

We were sent to Bainbridge, Maryland to do our 'second' boot camp training. As we were old salts, I became the company drill master. We would put on a show for the new recruits for about 10 to 15 minutes of close-order drill, and then stand at rest for the rest of the time watching them try to learn close-order drill, as the instructors had them watch us. After boot camp, I was assigned to Signalman School because of my semaphore and light training in the Boy Scouts.

The Navy needed Signalmen in the newly organized part of its Beach Battalion structure in the amphibious forces. Of course, they sent me right back to Camp Bradford, Virginia, for marine assault training, in addition to learning what a beach battalion did. I was assigned to the 7th Naval Beach Battalion, a new battalion formed from the earlier ones and the new comers, fitting us all in.

A beach battalion was made up of about 450 men, divided by a company staff which was headed by the Beach Master, assistant BMG Doctor, all officers, and nine platoons. Each platoon had about 42 men, including a Hydrographic section, a boat repair section, and a communication section made up of four radiomen and four signalmen (I was a Signalman, 3rd Class, in platoon B-2). We also had a medical section of eight men."

After a short leave, Roy was transferred to Lido Beach, Long Island, New York, a staging area, before being shipped overseas. In early 1944, he sailed for Green Rock, Ireland aboard the former Cunard liner, *HMS Acquitania*. After landing at Green Rock, the battalion boarded a train bound for southern England. Their destination was Salcombe, in Devon, England, which would be their home base. While traveling to Salcombe, passing through the small towns, people would be lined up on the streets, waving flags and giving the "V" for Victory sign. In return, the Navy men tossed candy and chewing gum to the children.

In the Spring of 1944, Roy went through extensive training in and around Salcombe, including the Slapton Sands, where a German submarine and the ships' landing troops had an "incident". This incident was kept secret for many years, but is now being told. In May of 1944, Roy was transferred to several staging areas around southern England. He left Southampton, England, just prior to the invasion of France.

"My platoon was supposed to have landed in the third wave on Omaha Beach on D-Day, the 6th of June 1944, but due to bad weather and confusion on the beach with the fierce battle going on, most of the Battalion did not land on D-Day. Most of the 7th Beach Battalion landed on D-Day + 1 (my 20th birthday) and was on the beach for 21 days. I, along with about 20 others, volunteered to stay for another 72 days.

My first days on the beach, when not signaling and standing watch, were taken up by carrying the fallen soldiers to the first cemetery on Normandy, which was just yards from our bivouac. We were attached to an Engineering Company of the Army, but they never claimed us. As we had no cooks, there was no need of a kitchen, so we were left to our own ideas. We soon developed our ideas! As we signaled the ships and boats where to land, we always asked what they were carrying. If it was food, then our food larder, too, became well stocked. In other words, we stole or begged for our food until the Beach Battalion returned to England. Then, plans were made for the volunteers to be fed by the Engineering Company for which we were doing the communications. There wasn't too much time for site-seeing, so you might say we just spent the summer of 1944 on the beach of France.

Upon my return to England, I was transferred to Oceanside, California, for leave and more training. On March 17, 1945, Betty Scott and I were married. Shortly thereafter, my group was sent to Hawaii to form beach party teams for the invasion of Japan. While waiting for the time of the invasion, we were stationed in the Philippines. The U.S. dropped the Big Bomb on Japan in 1945. After peace was declared, we landed on the beach of Wakayama, Japan. Some landing of troops and supplies was directed by our beach group.

Our unit was sent to the Port of Nagoya, where we set up a Port Director's office and opened the port to U.S. ships. After a few weeks, I was transferred to the *U.S.S. Blue Ridge* (AGC/LCC-19), an Amphibious Flagship. We proceeded to Shanghai, China, to repatriate the Koreans back to Korea. Later, I returned to San Diego aboard the *U.S.S. Mount McKinley* (AGC/LCC-7), another Flagship.

With a growing family, Roy was interested in better wages, so in 1949, he put in for submarine duty and was sent to New London, Connecticut for training. Eventually, he was sent back to San Diego and assigned to the *U.S.S. Charr* (SS-328), a diesel submarine. Following a short assignment on the *Charr*, Roy was assigned to the *U.S.S. Perch* (SS-313), a submarine designed for amphibious landing of troops.

"We were known as the *'Pregnant Perch'*, as a large tank was attached to the submarine behind the tail. In the tank, they experimented with carrying various types of vehicles from airplanes to rubber boats and motor boats. We were sent to the Alaskan waters off Point Barrow, on the north coast of Alaska, to test ice swimming clothes in pancake ice seas. The Marines were the testers. A photo of the icy *Perch* made the front page of the New York Daily News on May 29, 1952. The photo showed our superstructure fully covered with ice, which made for an unusual time. We tried to submerge, but we couldn't. We would only go under a few feet. We didn't know why until the 'bells rang' and we heard, 'Oh, the ice is keeping us up.' We flooded all the ballast tanks and waited until the ice broke loose from the hull. It was a very quick ride to the deep, when the ice broke loose! Then, it was a flurry to blow all the water out of the ballast tanks to compensate.

After this, we were sent to Japan and trained British Royal Marines to submarine life for their loading and unloading of rubber boats with their equipment and explosives, for a landing above the 38th Parallel on Korean shores."

After his assignment on the *Perch*, Roy was transferred to Vanderbilt University as an Assistant Instructor in Navigation. He was stationed at Vanderbilt for three years, then returned to Pearl Harbor aboard the *U.S.S. Gudgeon* (SS-211) for another tour on submarines. In July of 1957, he left Yokosuka, Japan for a Cold War spy run off the coast of Russia, near Vladivostok. In the second chapter of the book, "Blind Man's Bluff", written in 1998, the events surrounding the *Gudgeon's* part in the Cold War were described.

Roy recounted his part in the patrol run, "We had been patrolling for some days when, for whatever reason, the Soviets spotted our periscope, on a sweep. We submerged for what would be almost 72 hours. We were submerged without fresh air, and unable to charge the batteries. Four Soviet Escort ships had spotted us and we were in a battle of wits to outmaneuver the Russians and escape out to sea, away from the ships. An outer door of the garbage ejector jammed which prevented us from going down beyond 200 feet to look for temperature layers so we could hide from sonar detectors. We had what we called 'Spooks' aboard who recorded and deciphered Russian ships noise to identify them by other subs. 'Spooks' put all the secret papers in canvas bags and weighted the bags, so they would sink when we surfaced. The word was, 'We will sink the sub before being captured'. Luckily that didn't happen!

When we did surface, I, being the senior Quartermaster/Signalman aboard, had the duty of being the first one out of the hatch to the bridge. I reported what I saw to the officer of the deck, who was immediately behind me. Closely following was the Captain. We immediately started communication with the Russians, identifying each other as 'U.S. ship' and 'Russian' by flashing a light which I had brought to the bridge with me upon surfacing. Again, by Morse code, we told them we were on the way to Japan. They flashed back, 'Thanks for the ASW (Anti-Submarine Warfare) exercise'.

What the book [Blind Man's Bluff] never really said was that, as we were surfacing, the radioman had sent a message to our Admiral in charge, as to what and where we were. The Admiral happened to be eating dinner, but immediately informed the Air Force that we were under attack. Within about ten minutes, as we were still doing our thing with flashing light, three U.S. planes were flying overhead."

The *U.S.S. Gudgeon* proceeded back to Yokosuka, Japan, where they were "rewarded" with a trip to Pakistan. Eventually, the *Gudgeon* was the first U.S. submarine to circumnavigate the world, going through the Suez Canal, the Mediterranean Sea, eight countries, and the Panama Canal. When they arrived back at Pearl Harbor, their steaming time was 80 days. Roy was transferred to Submarine Squadron One Flag and retired in 1962 at the rank of Chief Petty Officer, after 20 years of service. Among the many awards he received for his service were; in World War II, the French Croix de Guerre (War Cross) for bravery in liberating the French people; and the Submarine Combat Patrol Award in the Korean War.

In 1957, while in the Navy, Roy had begun officiating basketball, baseball, and softball games. After retiring from the Navy, he attended Al Somer's Baseball Umpiring School, followed by a year in the Minor Leagues. He officiated at professional basketball games in the American Basketball League, and also baseball games, until July, 1965, when he joined the Los Angeles County Sheriffs Department as a Corrections Officer.

In August, 1994, Roy's wife, Betty, died after 49 years of marriage. Together they had four children; Fred Duane, Jeanne Roi Ann, Donald Scott, and Mary Suzanne Stout. They also adopted a son, Sean McCarthy. On February 14, 1997, Roy married Helen Keeton. They live in Lake Elizabeth, California, where Roy continues to umpire fast-pitch softball, a hobby he dearly enjoys.

DONALD STANLEY ULMANEK

On July 25, 1921 Donald Stanley Ulmanek was born to Frank and Anne (Broton) Ulmanek in Bothell, King Co., Washington. Frank was serving in the U.S. Navy at the Bremerton Shipyards in Washington when he was selected to be a Navy recruiter. He was transferred to San Francisco, then to Long Beach, California. Don had three sisters; Anne (Basko), Barbara (Little), and Patricia (Choumas) Ulmanek; and two brothers, Frank S., Jr. (1933-1953), and Wesley Ulmanek.

Don attended school in the Long Beach area and graduated from Wilson High School in 1939. Immediately after graduating, he joined the Civilian Conservation Corps, serving for two years.

Don was married to Virginia Bulen before he enlisted in the Navy. After enlisting in the U.S. Navy Reserves he was sent to Farragut Naval Center, Idaho's inland Naval base, for basic training and was assigned to serve onboard the destroyer, *U.S.S. Hoel* (DD-533) as a Quartermaster, 3rd Class.

The *U.S.S. Hoel* departed Mare Island, Vallejo, near San Francisco, California on October 26, 1943, bound for Pearl Harbor as part of a convoy. The convoy, which included three other destroyers, one minesweeper, and three escort carriers, departed Pearl Harbor on November 10, 1943. The *Hoel* arrived at the Little Makin Atoll in the Gilbert Island chain where they witnessed an attack by the Japanese on the escort carrier, *U.S.S. Liscome Bay*. The destroyers were able to rescue 272 survivors, but 642 were lost with the ship.

The *Hoel* conducted screening duties in the area through November, then sailed back to Pearl Harbor arriving in mid-December. In January of 1944, the *Hoel* crewmembers began training for the invasion of the Marshall Islands. They departed Pearl Harbor on January 23, 1944 and arrived at the Kwajalein Atoll on January 31 to begin escort and support duties. In February, the *Hoel* attacked the Parry and Japtan Islands. The month of March included patrol duties in Cape Botiangen, New Hanover. In April, the *Hoel* returned to Purvis Bay to screen a convoy carrying troops and supplies to Emirau Island.

In the summer of 1944, the *Hoel* was assigned to Cruiser Division 12 and was kept active with training exercises and convoy duty. In August, the *Hoel* was assigned to the Third Amphibious Force preparing for the invasion of the Palau Islands. They screened ships and rescued a pilot and passenger from a plane. In the month of October, the *Hoel* was assigned to task unit Taffy III in preparation for the invasion of the Philippines.

On the morning of October 25, 1944 the *Hoel* was sunk while fighting a much larger Japanese force. The fearless crew drew enemy fire to the ship and away from the other U.S. carriers in the Leyte Gulf. The *Hoel* suffered over 40 hits from the enemy ships. The Japanese continued to fire, finally sinking her in 4,000 fathoms.

Only 86 of the *Hoel's* crew survived, while 253 officers and men died with their ship. Along with the *U.S.S. Johnston* (DD-557) and the *U.S.S. Samuel B. Roberts* (DE-413), the *Hoel* was sunk on October 25, 1944. Quartermaster, 3rd Class and "Plank Holder" [original crew member], Donald Stanley Ulmanek was among the brave crewmembers lost when the *U.S.S. Hoel* went down. His name is inscribed on the Tablets of the Missing at Manila American Cemetery, Manila, Philippines. He is honored on a beautiful monument located at the Fort Rosecrans National Cemetery, Point Loma, San Diego Co., California. The memorial is dedicated to the officers and men of the *U.S.S. Hoel, U.S.S. Johnston* and *U.S.S. Samuel B. Roberts.*

The memorial reads:

IN EVERLASTING MEMORY

INSCRIBED HERE ARE THE NAMES OF 525 MEN WHO DIED
IN THE BATTLE OF LEYTE GULF DURING THE LIBERATION
OF THE PHILIPPINE ISLANDS ON 25 OCT 44. THEIR
SHIPS, THE DESTROYERS USS JOHNSTON DD-557 AND
USS HOEL DD-533 AND DESTROYER ESCORT USS
SAMUEL B. ROBERTS DE-413, WERE SUNK WHILE
FIGHTING A VASTLY SUPERIOR ENEMY FORCE OF FOUR
BATTLESHIPS, EIGHT CRUISERS AND ELEVEN DESTROYERS
IN WHAT WAS TO BE THE LAST AND LONGEST SURFACE
BATTLE OF WORLD WAR II.

MAY THE NAMES AND SACRIFICE OF THESE BRAVE MEN MADE
BE FOREVER REMEMBERED. THEIR FAMILIES, SHIPMATES
AND FRIENDS GRATEFULLY AND LOVINGLY DEDICATE THIS
MEMORIAL IN THEIR HONOR.

WE WON'T FORGET

U.S.S. Hoel off San Francisco August 3, 1943. U.S. Navy official photograph #NH 97895, courtesy of the Naval Historical Center, Washington, D.C. The Hoel received a Presidential Unit Citation and five Battle Stars.

Don received the following awards while serving onboard the *U.S.S. Hoel*: Purple Heart Medal; Presidential Unit Citation with one Bronze Star; American Campaign Medal; Asiatic-Pacific Campaign Medal with five Battle Stars; World War II Victory Medal; Philippine Republic Presidential Unit Citation; Philippine Liberation Medal with two Battle Stars; Plank Owner Certificate for Original Commissioning Crew; Combat Action Medal [a new medal, recently awarded].

Don's sister, Barbara (Ulmanek) Little, former Mayor of Lancaster, is the current manager of the Lancaster Cemetery District, Lancaster, California, where a memorial for all veterans is planned to be built in the near future.

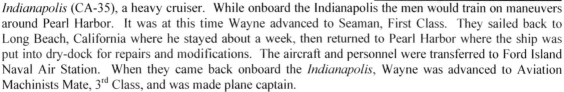

In 1920, Wayne Gray Watson was born in Glendale, Los Angeles Co., California, the son of Thomas William and Annabelle "Belle" Samantha (Helm) Watson. Thomas was the second and the fourth mayor of Glendale and city manager from 1914 to 1921. He resigned from the city and joined the real estate business, then moved his family to Montrose, California. When the depression hit in 1929, Thomas had put all of his finances in developing real estate in North Glendale. He lost it all, including his home and cars. During the time from 1929 until Wayne joined the Navy, the family moved several times.

Wayne graduated from Glendale High School in 1939 and joined the Navy on May 15, 1940 in Los Angeles, California. He was twenty-years old at that time. Wayne was sworn in and boarded a train bound for San Diego. While at boot camp, he belonged to Company 4030. After three months of boot camp, Wayne was sent to North Island, San Diego for training at Aviation Machinist's School.

After graduation in November, 1940, Wayne was assigned to the *U.S.S. Platte*, an oil tanker. There, he was reassigned to the *U.S.S. Indianapolis* (CA-35), a heavy cruiser. While onboard the Indianapolis the men would train on maneuvers around Pearl Harbor. It was at this time Wayne advanced to Seaman, First Class. They sailed back to Long Beach, California where he stayed about a week, then returned to Pearl Harbor where the ship was put into dry-dock for repairs and modifications. The aircraft and personnel were transferred to Ford Island Naval Air Station. When they came back onboard the *Indianapolis*, Wayne was advanced to Aviation Machinists Mate, 3rd Class, and was made plane captain.

Wayne recalled, "December 5, 1941 we were told we were going to sea in the early afternoon. We headed out to sea under wartime watches, with the *Lexington* (an aircraft carrier), another heavy cruiser, *Chicago*, and four destroyers. The next day (December 7) we were by ourselves and headed for Johnson Island. On December 7, we could see Johnson Island in the distance and received word that Pearl Harbor had been attacked. We then headed back to Pearl Harbor to join up with our Task Force. As we entered the waters to go into the harbor on December 11, we thought we saw a submarine, so we circled and waited for the channel to be cleared with depth charges. We then docked at the submarine base to re-supply. We had an airplane crash at sea, so we had to repair the plane.

We left Pearl Harbor with the *Lexington* Task Force to search in the area for Japanese ships. Then we headed for the Coral Sea and Bougainville. There, we were raided by sixteen Jap bombers. We shot them all down. Lieutenant O'Hare of the *Lexington* shot down five of them, and made Ace. We turned once and missed three bombs. This was in February-March of 1942."

From there, the *Indianapolis* headed for New Guinea with a large Task Force, including the carriers *Lexington* and *Yorktown*. "They launched all of their planes, formed in the air, and then flew to the other

U.S.S. Indianapolis – photo courtesy of Wayne Watson

side of New Guinea," Wayne remembered, "to bomb the ports of Salamaua and Lae. They sunk or damaged twenty-nine ships. We then went back to Pearl Harbor around April 1, 1942, after being at sea for fifty-four days."

"We then went to San Francisco where we stayed for twelve days. At the end of April, we picked up eight troops ships with 10,000 troops and headed for Australia. We were outfitted with depth charges. An unexpected storm in the channel broke up the Task Force and it took three days to regroup."

"While in the Coral Sea, we were about 200 miles from the Battle of the Coral Sea. We arrived at Melbourne for refueling, about the middle of May 1942. We stayed at Melbourne for three days, then left for Pearl Harbor. I stayed aboard the Indianapolis when it came into Pearl Harbor from Australia on May 22, 1942. After a short stay at Pearl Harbor, we left for the Aleutian Islands with a new captain, M.L. Deyo, replacing Captain F.W. Hanson.

Shortly after we left Pearl Harbor, on July 3, we were recovering one of our planes with a 'dog recovery' in open sea. The plane was coming up on our port side to land in the sea where we would retrieve it without a sea sled. The plane went into a bank to land on the starboard side of the ship. He lost airspeed and slipped into the water – starboard wing first. The plane disappeared. When we got to the crash site, all we found was one flying glove. Lost were Lt. (jg) Billings and William Kyde, Radioman, First Class.

We arrived at Dutch Harbor a few days after the Japanese had shelled the place as a decoy for the Midway Battle. Two of our aircraft with Lieutenant O'Neill and Lieutenant Hunker were in the air to assist in the shelling of Attu. Other ships were also shelling Attu from the other side of the island. Lieutenant O'Neill made a bombing run with two 100-pound bombs, which were reported to hit on the target area. Then, they resumed their position as scout observation planes for the other ships. There wasn't much damage to Jap buildings onshore.

On August 8, 1942 we had a Task Force consisting of the Indianapolis, two light cruisers and about four destroyers. We catapulted two scout observation crafts (SOCs) to observe our shelling of Kiska. During the shelling, a Japanese destroyer came out of the harbor shooting towards the stern of the Indianapolis and their main battery. One of the light cruisers astern of us threw a 6-gun salvo at them. A second salvo hit the ship and it sank immediately. Our planes reported all the craft in the harbor were damaged. They could see no personnel on the ground as they were entrenched.

Lieutenant O'Neill's plane was badly damaged when it returned to the ship. He reported a Japanese fighter did the damage. He saw Ensign Segeser's plane heading for a cloud with a Jap Zero chasing him. Segeser and his radioman, Bobby Crawford, Aviation Radioman, First Class, never returned.

During the next several weeks we lost our last two planes due to rough weather. This caused us to return to Pearl Harbor to get more planes, modifications of the bridge, and to get another commanding officer, Captain Nicholas Vytlacil. While in Pearl Harbor, we were told to 'send our cold weather gear home,' since we would be heading out to the South Pacific. To our surprise, we headed back north with warm weather clothing! It was about two weeks before we were re-issued cold weather gear."

In the heart of winter, they started patrolling in the rough seas between Kiska and Japan, searching for Japanese supply ships. At one time they had been at sea for seventy-eight days. During their time in the Aleutians, the men had the opportunity to take liberty ashore at Dutch Harbor and Kodiak .

"We had four lockers and four bunks on the mezzanine deck in the hangar," Wayne remembered. "We, and others, used the Head on the fantail of the ship. The fantail also was where we bathed and washed our clothes out of a bucket. Our Title B underwear was dried by hanging them up in the hangar, letting them freeze, shaking them out, and then doing final drying by a steam pipe!

On February 20, 1943 at about 2300, they sounded General Quarters. I went to the quarterdeck and saw the blinker light sending a recognition signal about two points off the port bow. I went up on the deck and saw a large black image of a ship. About that time, I saw six balls of fire heading toward us. I turned and headed back toward the quarterdeck and looked over my shoulder. I saw what they had fired fell short into the water. About that time we fired our 8-inch cannons at them. Every one was a direct hit. The ship blew up and started burning immediately so we circled for a while, looking for survivors and watched the ship. We sensed there might be submarines in the area, so we departed before the ship sank.

We couldn't fly much due to the short days and rough seas. The *Indianapolis* had a lot of damage from the rough seas. At one point, we took a wave over the port side that literally stopped the ship. You could feel it stop and shiver, then go ahead again. The wave smashed the belly of a plane sitting on the catapult, sixty-eight feet above the water line. The wave also smashed the door on the port hangar up against the overhead and washed all of our spare control surfaces into the sea."

In March 1943 the *Indianapolis* headed into Mare Island, San Francisco for repairs. Wayne was transferred off the *Indianapolis* in May 1943. After a short stay at Alameda Naval Air Station, he volunteered for duty with PATSU 110, maintaining PBY (patrol bombers) aircraft, "Black Cats," in the New Guinea area. First, Wayne traveled to Brisbane, Australia. While stationed at Brisbane, they stayed at a Seabee camp and worked with the Seabees who were building a hospital. The men were also called to work at an air station, in Brisbane, to work on the aircraft there. The next stop was Samari, New Guinea aboard the *San Pablo*, a seaplane tender. Wayne was stationed in New Guinea until November 1943. He left New Guinea on a PBY airplane bound for Palm Island. The island was forty miles off the coast of Australia, near Townsville.

PBY Black Cat maintenance crew, Palm Island, 1944. Wayne Watson third row, 5th from right.

While stationed at Palm Island, Wayne removed and replaced both engines on the PBY's. He flew as a flight engineer on five-hour test hops after finishing work on each plane. In April 1944 the Palm Island base was closed and the crew was sent back to Samari, New Guinea on another seaplane tender.

"I had not had any leave for four years, so in May 1944 I was sent back to Alameda Naval Air Station, near San Francisco, after taking a thirty-day leave. During this leave I took a bus to Spokane, Washington and got dumped by my girlfriend. Little did I know, but she had a replacement in mind and introduced me to Lois (Loie) Marie Felgenhauer. At that time I didn't know what a BIG favor she did for me! Before I left Spokane I proposed marriage to Loie and went back to Alameda. One month later I sent an engagement ring to her and she accepted my proposal. We were married March 11, 1945 in Fairfield, Washington."

Wayne was the engine crew leader with Squadron VR-2 based at Alameda Naval Air Station. The squadron was made up of PB2-Y's, 4-engine seaplanes. In August 1945, Wayne was promoted to Chief Petty Officer and worked in the engineering department. Shortly thereafter, World War II came to an end. The squadron was disbanded and he was transferred to another duty station.

He was stationed at Moffett Field, near San Jose, California, for a few months. Another transfer to Alameda Naval Air Station included security and shore patrol duty. Loie was pregnant with their first child at that time, Patricia Anne Watson, born February 19, 1946. "I shipped over (re-enlisted) in May 1946. I went on a thirty-day leave, and after returning, went into A&R (complete overhaul of aircraft). My specialty was working on water-injected carburetors for fighter planes. During this time I went to Oakland Hospital for eye surgery and was off work for thirty days."

"Next, I was told I would be transferred to sea. We moved from our Alameda apartment to a Quonset hut for a month. I was sent to

Moffett Field for two weeks, then flew out to Pearl Harbor on the Mars, a large 4-engine seaplane. After a three month assignment in Kaneoe, Oahu, in the summer of 1947, I returned to Los Angeles. We lived in a Quonset hut for several months until Loie was eight months pregnant with our son, Robert. We moved to naval housing at Long Beach, California. I was assigned to recruiting duties, first out of Los Angeles, then out of Burbank. We didn't like moving around so much with a family. I had seven duty stations in two years, and I really didn't like the recruiting job, so I requested a discharge. The discharge was granted and I left the Navy in July 1948 as an Aviation Chief Machinists Mate ADC."

During his career in the Navy, Wayne received the Asiatic-Pacific Medal with three Stars; Good Conduct Medal with one Star; American Defense Medal with one Star; American Theater Medal; World War II Victory Medal.

After his discharge from the Navy, Wayne answered an ad in the newspaper for a job with Standard stations. He landed the job and worked out of Long Beach. The weather was too damp for one of his children so the family moved to Sunland, California. In 1950, Wayne leased a Shell station in Glendale, California, which he later sold for a busier station in Burbank. After eighteen years, he sold the business and went to work for a Buick agency doing all of their service work.

During this time period Wayne was active in the American Legion, Sunland Post No. 736 for fifteen years. He spent four years as an Assistant Scoutmaster and Camping Chairman. He also spent twelve years in the Sheriff's Department as a reserve deputy with the Sylmar Mountain Rescue Team. He retired from the reserves in 1977. In 1978, Wayne began thinking about retirement and started building a house on property in Lancaster purchased from the Bureau of Land Management. He retired from Walter Rueff Buick in 1980.

Wayne is a life member of the U.S. Navy Cruiser Sailors Association; a life member of American Legion Post 311, Antelope Valley; a member of the B.P.O. Elks Lodge No. 2027 in Palmdale; and a member of the Loyal Order of Moose, Lodge No. 507, in Palmdale. In the last twenty-four years, Wayne and his wife, Loie, have enjoyed traveling in their R.V. in various places around the United States.

Medium Seaplane Squadron VR-3 – Wayne Watson, back row, seventh from right.

Ivan Ayers Westerfield was born about 1920 in Illinois, the son of Sara A. Westerfield, also born in Illinois. In 1930, Sara was employed as a matron at the McKinley Boys Industrial Home in Los Angeles, California, where she and Ivan also resided. Sara was a widow at that time, but would later marry George Dougherty. Ivan graduated from AVJUHS with the class of 1938.

Ivan entered the United States Navy from California, before the attack on Pearl Harbor. He was a Seaman, 1st Class, onboard the *U.S.S. Arizona* when the Japanese attacked. Ivan lost his life at Pearl Harbor, and was the first war casualty from the Antelope Valley, missing from the *U.S.S. Arizona*.

Ivan A. Westerfield received the Purple Heart Medal from the U.S. Navy. His name is among those inscribed on the Tablets of the Missing at Honolulu Memorial, Honolulu, Hawaii, and also on the *U.S.S. Arizona* Memorial at Pearl Harbor, along with over 1,000 sailors, marines and civilians who died on the *Arizona*, on December 7, 1941, while defending their country.

U.S.S. Arizona, Pearl Harbor December 7, 1941. Photo courtesy of the National Archives, photo NA 80-G-32414.

245

On January 14, 1923, Paul Ernest Wheeler was born to William M. and Nora May (Fultz) Wheeler, in Lancaster, Los Angeles Co., California. Paul had two siblings; a brother, Lawrence, and sister, Thelma Wheeler. Paul graduated from AVJUHS with the class of 1941. He was active in several sports while at school including football and basketball. He was also president of the student body.

Paul enlisted in the U.S. Coast Guard in June of 1942 and was called to service in February 1943. He joined the Boat Division as a Coxswain on a LCVP, (Landing Craft, Vehicle Personnel) hauling soldiers back and forth to the Pacific Islands, from ship-to-shore.

One of Paul's most memorable recollections was while onboard the *U.S.S. Arthur Middleton* (APA-25). " We were in a convoy with between 60-80 ships, in the middle of the ocean with extremely rough seas. We began refueling an APD class, 4-stacker 'tin can' WWI era ship en route to the Philippine Islands. They put the boom out and dropped the line to refuel when the *Middleton* got a head of the ship and the line tightened up, pulling us toward them. A sailor aboard the destroyer chopped the fuel line clear, but the bow wake from our ship pulled the destroyer, crashing it into our side. The collision crushed four of their landing barges, dislodging their depth charges without any explosion. The destroyer pivoted across our bow as we rammed it several times, tearing off their radar mast. Their ship was knocked out of commission and had to be towed back into port. After this, the joke aboard ship was to paint a destroyer on our bridge to indicate 'one destroyer killed'."

The crew of the *Middleton* successfully delivered men and machines to the beaches for the invasions of Saipan, Leyte, Lingayen Gulf and Okinawa. Paul took part in the Saipan invasion June 15-20, 1944 and returned to Pearl Harbor on July 9th. They arrived at Manus, Admiralty Islands on October 3 for the Leyte landings and remained there until October 24th. In January 1945, they arrived off Lingayen Gulf, in time to send troops ashore while under Japanese air attack. Fifteen crew members were wounded from shrapnel caused by other ships firing at Japanese aircraft. During February and March, 1945 the *Middleton* participated in training exercises off Guadalcanal, then readied for the invasion of Okinawa in April 1945.

Paul recalled the day when a celebrity came onboard, "In March of 1945, my ship, along with hundreds of others, was on our way for the invasion of Okinawa. The amphibious task force we were assigned to, was going to be staging at Ulith Atoll, Western Caroline Islands, before the D-Day landing.

While anchored in the harbor, the ship's crew was surprised – Lieutenant Commander Jack Dempsey came onboard. Lieutenant Commander Dempsey was an Information and Morale Officer. He showed his fight movies of becoming World Heavy Weight Champion. The crew had a great time talking to him on a one to one basis.

On April 1, 1945, our landing boats put combat Army infantry in the first wave on the beaches of Okinawa. On D-Day + 1, Lieutenant Commander Dempsey was on the beach."

Paul also had the good fortune to be stationed on Oahu for nine months before going south on his ship. He recalled, "Dr. Savage was a local doctor in Lancaster. His son, Ed, was a manager for the Y.M.C.A. in Honolulu, Hawaii. He was in contact with the Ledger-Gazette [newspaper] and was able to know the locations of all of the Antelope Valley guys in the Pacific Area. All we had to do was call Ed every so often, and he would give the whereabouts of the A.V. men. Using this method, I was able to see the following servicemen: Lieutenant Linton Parker; Lieutenant Harry DuBois; Dean Stebbins - I was able to visit on his submarine while berthed at Pearl Harbor; Bob Sherlock and Gil Craton – I went onboard their ship, the *U.S.S. Enterprise*, at Pearl Harbor as well; Lee Shelton; Wes Mumaw; Paul Potter; Kenny McCablie; and Walt Primmer."

Paul was at Pacific Beach, near San Diego, California attending gunnery school, when he heard the war was over. He was discharged in October 1945, at the rank of Seaman, 1st Class. Among other awards, he received four Battle Stars for the invasions of Saipan, Leyte, Lingayen and Okinawa.

Before and after the war, Paul was employed with the Southern California Edison Company (SCE). He left the Valley in 1958 with SCE and moved to Santa Monica. On December 20, 1958, Paul married Virginia M. Jacobsen in Lancaster, Los Angeles Co., California. They had one child together, a son, Bradley Wheeler. Paul retired from SCE in 1985 after 44 years of service. Paul currently lives in Santa Monica, California, where he enjoys his position as the South West Area Membership Chairman for the Coast Guard Combat Veterans Association.

Paul Wheeler, far right, with LCVP boat crew

U.S.S. Arthur Middleton, 1945 – U.S. Navy Photo No. 339869

John Anthony Batz was born March 23, 1926 in Riverside, San Bernardino Co., California, the seventh child of Arthur Francis Batz and Etta Louise (Kowalski) Batz, and the fourth son to serve his country during World War II. The family moved to a ranch on the east side of the Antelope Valley in December 1932. Anthony had seven siblings; five brothers, Louis, Francis, Robert, David and Raymond; and two sisters, Mary and Amelia Batz.

Anthony attended Redmond Grammar school and graduated from AVJUHS in 1943, where he earned letters in basketball and track. In the fall of 1944, Anthony entered the United States Marine Corps and began boot camp training in San Diego, California. He wrote to his sister and brother-in-law, Mary and Francis Godde, about his training:

"Received your letter today, and was glad to hear from you. Received a box of nuts from Mother yesterday. They really tasted swell. I finished up the last of the cupcakes on Thursday. The last one was just as good and fresh as the first one. I'm looking forward to the next ones.

Today was the second day of firing the M1. I did fairly well. If I can improve a little, I might make Expert. I sure hope so, although Expert calls for 306 points out of a possible 340.

We got paid today. The huge sum of $35.00. One kid owed the government $6.00. We got together and took up a small collection for him. We also took up a collection for one of our D.I.'s (Drill Instructor). He is only a P.F.C., and is going to be a father soon. We raised about $65.00. He is really a good sport and a swell guy. He said that if the whole platoon qualifies on record day, he will get a G.I. haircut, and carry everybody's gear and sea-bags out to the truck on the day we leave here.

A bunch of the fellows and I have been singing. We had some pretty good harmony. I'm all sung out now. It's about time for taps, so will close now."

In February 1945, Anthony wrote to Mary and Francis Godde telling them he was getting "tired of Spam and Vienna sausage… and would give anything for a barbequed steak." By April 1945, he was on the island of Okinawa when he was wounded after being hit by shrapnel during the invasion. His brother, Dave, who was in the Navy, landed within one mile from where Anthony was stationed on Okinawa. The Captain of the ship Dave was on arranged to have Dave flown to Guam to be there overnight with Anthony when he was injured.

Anthony wrote the following letter from Okinawa on April 29, 1945, before he was injured, to Mary and Francis Godde:

"Well, I guess it's about time I was answering some of your letters, but I've been kind of busy. I don't know how long this letter will be, but I'll do my best.

It doesn't seem possible, but we've been on this island almost a month now. This Easter is one I will always remember because it marked my first campaign. I'm sure thankful that it turned out as easy for us as it did. We met no resistance on the beach but there was scattered resistance all through the hills. The terrain is very rough and the Nips could have had better defenses than they did.

I lost a little weight, but I am gaining it back now. I took part in a couple of fights. The first day I shot a pig to more or less test-fire my rifle. In about a day and a half we moved close to forty miles. Everybody really had sore feet when we got through. I was carrying my rifle, over 200 rounds of ammo, pack, grenades, and two canteens of water. All that stuff gets pretty damn heavy.

There are quite a few horses on the island. The natives use them and I think there must have been a Nip

Calvary outfit here. Most of the horses are quite small. It's quite common to see a big Marine astride a shaggy little horse. Some of the guys used them to carry packs, but they put a stop to that. The natives are quite friendly. They are not Japs, but a mixture of several oriental races. Every time we'd pass a bunch of them, they would bow down. It makes a guy feel kind of foolish. They really grow some wonderful looking vegetables. There isn't much level country, but they really make use of what there is. They even shove out ledges on the hillsides and cultivate them.

Say, I want to thank you for sending those news clippings. I really enjoy reading it and all. The fellows in my squad ask for it.

Well, I guess this is about all for now."

Love,
Anthony

The invasion of Okinawa began on April 1, 1945 when 60,000 troops, including two Marine and two Army divisions, landed on the island. The Marine Corps 1st and 6th Divisions went north to secure the mountain areas of the island. They would participate in the one of the bloodiest battles fought in the Pacific. Allied Naval Fleet Admiral Chester Nimitz stated, "It was the worst fighting of the Pacific war, its sustained intensity surpassing even the brutal combats of Tarawa, Peleliu, and Iwo Jima. Uncommon valor was a common virtue."

After the war, Anthony continued working in the farming business. On November 17, 1951, Anthony married Delores Peltzer. They had five children together; Robert Matthew, Mark Jonathan, Anne Marie, Daniel Thomas and Mary Catherine Batz. Anthony worked for his father-in-law, Mr. Peltzer, for a while and developed an alfalfa ranch near Lovejoy Springs, in east Antelope Valley, on property owned by a friend of the Peltzer family. When the western television series, "Rawhide" (1959-1965) starring Clint Eastwood was in production, Anthony built a corral on his property to keep the cattle in that were used for the show. Anthony's brother, Army veteran Francis Batz, remembered the time when he rounded up chickens for the series. He and his friend, veteran Glen Ralphs, took chickens from Glen's fathers place and sold them at $5.00 a piece to use in scenes for Rawhide!

When Anthony returned from the war, he chose not to talk about his service with his family. His son, Mark, said he asked his Dad many times about the war, but he didn't want to discuss any part of the war with his boys. The family moved to Salem, Polk Co., Oregon, where Anthony passed away on June 2, 1994. He is buried in the Batz family plot in Salem.

GEORGE MONTGOMERY "GMC" CAMPBELL, JR.

George M. Campbell, Jr. was born March 7, 1922 in Bakersfield, Kern Co., California, the first of four sons born to George M., from Tennessee (a veteran of World War I), and Adna (Cheney) Campbell, a native of Oregon. The Campbell family moved to the Antelope Valley from Bakersfield in 1926 where George's father was employed as a salesman for an oil company. George's three brothers also served in the military during World War II; Paul C., John W., and Gordon L. all served in the Navy in the Pacific area.

George was a varsity football letterman at AVJUHS during his high school years. He enlisted in the U.S. Marine Corps in July 1942 in order to meet the national emergency and serve his country.

After rigorous physical training in boot camp, George was sent to Camp Elliott, near El Cajon, California, for advanced training in the Infantry. After training, he was deployed to the South Pacific with the First Fleet Marine Force Pacific. His primary duty was as an Infantry line man. Other assignments included working as a crane and fork lift operator. George also repaired typewriters and watches on occasion.

As part of the 3rd Battalion, 5th Regiment, 1st Division of the Marine Corps, George saw several battlefields including the Solomon Islands, Guadalcanal, the Russell Islands and Okinawa, Japan. During the Guadalcanal conflict, a Japanese troop transporting vessel bringing in troop reinforcements, struck a rock or a coral reef. After receiving several shell hits, instead of sinking entirely, about half of the ship was sticking up out of the water. When the area had been secured – a few days later – George and a couple of his buddies who were good swimmers, swam out to the half sunken ship, looking for souvenirs. After swimming through shark infested waters, all they found were items made in the United States – nothing from Japan! Even the decks of the ship were stamped "U.S. Steel Corp."

Japanese ship sinking in Guadalcanal waters

George was on Okinawa preparing for the invasion of Japan when he heard the war was over. He was discharged in January 1946, after 41 months in the service, with 38 of those months spent in the Pacific. He traveled home to Lancaster where he married his high school sweetheart, Dorothy L. (Smith) Morten. They had three children - two daughters; Melody (Campbell) Cook and Cindy (Campbell) Worley. George has seven grandchildren and two great-grandsons (twins). Son, George Mike Campbell, followed his father's footsteps and joined the Marine Corps in the 1970's.

George went to work at a relative's jewelry store in Oakland, California, then returned to Los Angeles County where he attended a watch repair and instrument repair school in Burbank. He quit after a short time when he found out that the school instructor knew less than George had already been taught by his grandfather.

George continued his friendships with a few of his Marine Corps buddies over the years. He joined the Veterans of Foreign Wars and the American Legion. George spent a good portion of his life self-employed, once owning a watch repair shop, a gas station/auto shop, and a poultry and hog farming business. He claims to be a "Jack of all trades, master of few!" George spent 25 years as a California Peace Officer - most of the time working as a Correctional Counselor. He also spent many years volunteering as a Boy Scout Scoutmaster.

In 1980 George married his second wife, Felomina "Inday" Capendit. He drew the plans and built a cement block house with sand and gravel gathered from the beach, with the help of a few Filipino tradesmen. George and Inday live in this home in San Juan, a beach community in Palompon, Leyte, Philippines, where they both enjoy the laid-back lifestyle of the islands.

V-J Day on Okinawa – "Plenty of casualties – what goes up, must come down. How would you like to make it through the war without getting wounded or killed, and then be killed or wounded by something this stupid?" George M. Campbell, Jr.

From a 1940's V.F.W. magazine article about George's father and his sons in the service: *"George Campbell, Lancaster, was a Lieutenant in the First World War. George believed, as did the rest of us, that that was the War to end all Wars. He therefore considered it safe to produce sons and raise them NOT to be soldiers. George now has three sons in service, all of who have seen active duty. The boys couldn't bear to see all of the old man's plans spoiled so none of them entered the Army and became soldiers. George Jr., is with the Marines somewhere in the South Pacific theater. Paul has just been assigned to the Naval Base at Alameda after having spent nine months on active sea duty in the South Pacific. John is on a ship somewhere in the South Pacific. Maybe the boys have something lined up down there? George has one son (Gordon) still at home who is a senior in High School. He too plans to enter the Navy as soon as possible. This will make George the undisputed champion Father of Sons in the Service."*

Leny Ross, left and George M. Campbell, Jr. on the island of New Caledonia in the South Pacific

254

THOMAS HORTEN "TOM" FARLEY

Thomas Horten Farley was born May 3, 1924 in San Diego, San Diego Co., California, the son of Thomas Horten and Kathryn (Bloche) Farley, Jr. In 1930, the Farley family lived in Oro Grande, San Bernardino Co., California, where the elder Thomas worked on a farm. Tom had two siblings; a brother, Kenneth, and a sister, Mildred Farley.

Tom enlisted in the United States Marine Corps because he wanted to work on airplanes. At the time, if you waited for the draft, most draftees were taken into the Army, and Tom wanted to join the Marines. Boot camp training memories for Tom included, "a bald head, rough clothes, big shoes, misty rain and tents. Your weapon was not a gun or a rifle – it was your sweetheart, sister or mother. Nothing you did was good enough, and you had to say everything in a LOUD voice." Boot camp was filled with inspections – rifle inspection, field strip inspection, sea bag inspection. "Your blanket had to be tight on your bed, and your clothing displayed on the blanket 'just so'."

After boot camp, Tom was sent to El Toro, California, then on to Pearl Harbor where he was attached to the Third Marine Aircraft Wing at Barbers Point. His first job assignment was covering fabric aircraft parts. Tom recalled his "mouth" getting him into trouble, which led to mess and latrine duty quite often. The next stop for Tom was Midway Island. On Christmas day, Tom saw a U.S.O. show featuring Bob Hope. "He told us he had heard Midway wasn't having Christmas. He told off-colored jokes and reminded us that it was the girls we were fighting for." Tom was also stationed at the Marine Corps Air Station at Cherry Point, North Carolina.

Tom was glad when he heard the war had ended. "Three days after V-J Day, I received my mustering out pay and a ticket to Los Angeles. I found a job as a street car conductor." Tom was discharged at the rank of Private, 1st Class.

He had received a "Dear John" letter while overseas serving with the Marines, but after the war was over, he married Hazel, the writer of the letter, in Huntington Beach, California. They had three children together; Thomas, Steven and James Farley. Tom later secured a job as a factory mechanic on a high-speed production line.

Tom passed away on January 5, 2004 in Lancaster, California.

JAMES ARTHUR "JIM" LOTT, JR.

On February 13, 1905 James Arthur Lott, Jr. was born to James Arthur and Carney Elizabeth (Lauvierre) Lott in Independence, Topeka Co., Kansas. He had five siblings; Max, Bernice, Winnie, Jack and Marjory Lott. Jim's father purchased 300 acres of land in Green Valley near San Frascisquito Road in the early 1920's. After his mother, Carney, died in Oklahoma, Jim moved to California in the early 1930's. He married Rosalia Eleanora Krzyzewski on December 20, 1937 in Los Angeles, California. They had three children together; Carnie Antoinette "Tink", James Arthur and Walter Rexford Allen Lott.

Jim was serving overseas in the military before the United States entered into the war. Before he joined the Marines, he had worked as a lumber grader for fifteen years, then as a record press man at the Allied Recording Co. in Hollywood, California, owned by his brother-in-law, Jim Perkins.

In 1944, Jim was a Drill Instructor in San Diego, California, on his second enlistment, and was attached to the 2nd Marine Division, 534 Platoon, Special Services. Drill Instructor was a job that Jim didn't especially like. His specialty was in carpentry, which was his principal duty in this enlistment with the Marine Corps. Jim was also a boxing coach to the men in his platoon, a special job he enjoyed very much.

In September 1944, Jim was onboard the *U.S.S. General C.G. Morton* when he became a member of the Order of the Trident, for passing over the equator. The *Morton* was heading for the Russell Islands in the Solomons. After embarking troops, they proceeded to Espiritu Santo, New Hebrides, and then to Noumea, New Caledonia, and on to San Francisco and San Diego. Jim saw duty in the Philippine Islands and Japan. The following is a partial undated letter written by Jim on American Red Cross paper, to his father, probably written after April 1945, as Jim asks how his father likes the new President, which would be Harry Truman [12 April 1945-20 January 1953] :

"I received your letter just the other day and this is my first chance to answer it....Jack [Jim's brother] is sure lucky to be in the states, because the guys out here probably won't get home for another two years. A dam 'Jap' just shot six times right over my head with a machine gun. He is across the river from me, but I sure as hell don't want to go look for him. He just shot one of my buddies in the foot. They are going to take him to a hospital somewhere. There is a pile of rocks in back of me so I'm pretty sure he can't hit me. Someone will kill him pretty quick, a patrol has gone out already. I wrote to Bernice [Jim's sister] a long time ago, but she never has answered. Something is wrong, about the mail. I used to get five or six letters a week, now I get two or three a month. Maybe everyone has quit writing to me. Well pop, I'm about to run out of anything to write about so I'll close now.

(Signed) Your boy Jimmie

P.S. How do you like the new president?

Jim's daughter, Carnie "Tink" Freeman, recalled her father telling the children about combat, "It was awful. Men were being killed to the right and left of him and he didn't want to remember 'it' or talk about 'it'." He kept in touch with the family through the Red Cross. Jim was gone so long during both enlistments in the Marines, that his children didn't recognize him when he came home. Daughter, Tink, emotionally remembered one of those times when he arrived home. "My brothers and I were guessing what Dad looked like, because we couldn't remember him. We were protecting Mom, so one time when Dad came home, we didn't let him in. He sat on the front porch and cried. We didn't mean to hurt him – we loved him and Mom, but we couldn't remember him....dark hair-yellow-blue eyes or brown?? It was too long."

Near the end of the war, while in the Pacific, Jim was wounded in combat and had also contracted jungle rot and malaria. After some recovery time while overseas, his health declined. He was shipped to Sawtell Hospital in Sepulveda, California, to recover and receive proper care for his wounds. His wife, Rosalia, a nurse, was living with their three children in Chicago, Illinois at that time. She packed up her belongings and came out to Los Angeles, leaving her children in the care of her parents in Chicago, so she could hire on at the hospital where Jim was recovering.

Jim was discharged from the U.S. Marine Corps on December 15, 1945, and among the awards he received was the Purple Heart Medal and a Rifle Marksman badge.

After his recovery, the Lott family moved from Chicago to Hollywood, California in September 1947. Jim secured a job at Security Building Materials in Hollywood. They purchased a home in the San Fernando Valley in January 1950. From 1955-1958, Jim owned his own business, Jim Lott Building Materials, on Burbank Blvd. in Burbank, California. In 1958, after suffering a heart attack, he had to sell his business. In the early 1960's he moved to Leona Valley to help his friend, George Jones, start up a horse boarding ranch. In 1971, Jim bought a ranch for his daughter, "Tink" (Lott) Freeman, in Leona Valley, California. She and her family moved in and named the property the "4 C Ranch."

Jim had been involved with the start-up of semi-pro football in Southern California, beginning in the 1920's. For over six decades he was Commissioner for the High Desert semi-pro football league in Southern California. Palmdale Highland High School coach, Lin Parker, was a player in the semi-pro league and a friend to Jim. Jim joined the Veterans of Foreign Wars and the American Legion organizations. He enjoyed cattle ranching and also wrote poetry about the war and became a cowboy poet in his later years.

On June 27, 1993, Jim passed away in Lancaster, Los Angeles Co., California. He is buried at the Riverside National Cemetery in Riverside, Riverside Co., California.

Jim Lott, far right in uniform, boxing coach onboard the U.S.S. C.G. Morton - 1944

Robert Albert Specht was born December 5, 1923 in Fairmont, Los Angeles Co., California, the son of Henry Philip and Grace Louise (Nicholson) Specht. Henry's family moved to the Antelope Valley about 1884, near the Del Sur area, and settled in to farm the land. Bob had five siblings; three brothers, John, Charles and Clinton, and two sisters, Evelyn and Audrey Specht.

Bob joined the U.S. Marine Corps in August 1940. He and a friend, Willard Hosier, had taken a trip to San Diego, California and decided while they were there to join the Navy. When they went to the recruiting office to take entrance exams, Willard did not pass the color blindness test. Next stop was the Marine recruiter which Bob recalled, "They were very glad to have us – no waiting!"

After enlisting in the Marine Corps, Bob went through boot camp training in San Diego. On February 1, 1941 he was assigned to Company E, 2nd Battalion, 6th Regiment and stationed at Camp Elliot in San Diego Co., California. At that time, the 2nd Marine Division was being reformed and Bob's group was the start of the "rebirth" of the Division. Camp Elliot at that time, was a "tent city."

From March to May 1941, Bob was sent on several sea maneuvers off the coast of California, down through Panama, and on to Charleston, South Carolina. While docked in Charleston, they loaded supplies, not knowing when or where they were going next. Bob remembered the soldiers talking amongst themselves, trying to figure out where they were headed. "The scuttlebutt went wild – last night we loaded mosquito nets!" They left Charleston and arrived at New Foundland on June 28, 1941, then headed for Reykjavík, Iceland, arriving there on July 7, 1941. They unloaded all the supplies and cargo into a Higgins boat, hauled it on to the shore and loaded into trucks for transport to their camps.

The Marines were sent to Iceland to protect the island from any German invasion and to relieve the British and Canadian troops who had previously occupied the island. In the fall of 1941, British Prime Minister, Winston Churchill passed through Iceland and the Marines marched in review for him.

In January of 1942, Bob was transferred to Company M, 3rd Battalion, and sent to Camp Alafoss, Iceland. On February 2, the Marines were sent to sea onboard the *U.S.S. Munargo* and left Reykjavík Harbor for "the roughest seven day crossing to New York." Bob stated, "I felt sure they set sail on the eve of a terrific storm because of the German U-Boat presence in the North Atlantic. I had heard stories of standing on deck and looking way up to see the top of the water. We were not even out of the harbor and were standing on the fantail for roll call, and there we were, looking way up to the top of the waves – kind of scary. After standing watch, they would always have hot coffee and soup for us. After standing up there (on deck) for four hours in that lousy weather, and it was so dark at night and so rough and wet and cold, I really don't know what would have happened if we had been called upon to defend ourselves. There were three of us on duty at one time – one to man the 20mm, one to load, and one to handle the ammo canisters out of the storage. I was always placed on the aft starboard side gun. Guess it just worked out that way. Same deal on our trips in the Pacific."

After debarking in New York, Bob was sent on a troop train back to Camp Elliot, California and was given a 30 day leave. After returning to Camp Elliot, the troops were transferred to new Battalions and started in on "months and months of training and maneuvers." In late fall of 1942, Bob packed up again and boarded a ship sailing from San Diego to join a convoy bound for the Pacific Theater. Traveling along in the convoy was the *U.S.S. Matsonia*. "It was quite a trip across the Pacific. We normally would have classes on some combat subject, such as stripping and reassembling a certain weapon, blind-folded, or hand to hand combat, judo, or something else to take up time. We had salt water only to use for bathing and they supplied us with salt water soap.

A couple of days out of Wellington, New Zealand, the ships engines conked out. It so happened we were in those close-to-land, BIG rolling waves. The ship rolled from side to side and everything in the galley went over. I was on gun watch and we spotted an airplane on the horizon – fortunately it was friendly, because rolling like that, I don't think anyone could have fired a shot other than into the water!"

They arrived at Wellington, New Zealand near the middle of November 1942. In December, they packed up again, this time onboard the *U.S.S. President Adams,* and began their trip in support of the campaign at Guadalcanal. On January 3, 1943 Bob arrived at Guadalcanal with the entire 2nd Marine Division on hand. The 2nd and 8th Regiments had arrived on the beachhead in August 1942. Bob's Regiment arrived to relieve them and took over the front lines shortly after landing. First, they had to unload all the supplies brought on three transport ships, once again by Higgins boats. "There were no docks there and come late afternoon, the transports weighed anchor and took out of there. They didn't want to be caught in shallow water should there be an air raid. It was really tough to be on that island and stand there, watching your only way off the island heading out to sea without you.

The front lines were a ways on up the island from where we landed. Soon, we were at the front and had relieved the troops that had done so well before us. They were pretty well worn out and riddled with malaria and other jungle diseases. Guadalcanal, I think, was the worst place for living conditions. Most all of it was jungle and mud, and all that goes with it.

Sometime before they called the island 'secured', and we were getting close to wiping out the enemy, the 3rd Battalion, 6th Regiment that I was with, was assigned to the area from the waters edge (ocean), and inland. One day, around mid-morning, a Japanese airplane got through the defenses. He came in at tree-top level. They had a gunner in back of what looked like a Grumman Avenger airplane. They made two passes at us, firing their 50 caliber machine guns, both coming and going at us. On the last pass through, they banked out over the water and one of our P-38 aircraft made one pass at him and knocked him down. In the next day or two, the bodies floated up."

The Specht brothers, Robert, Marines; Charles, Navy; Clinton, Army – 1944

In February 1943, the Marines had pushed the Japanese Army off the island and it was considered secured. Bob was headed back to New Zealand on the transport ship *Adams* once again. In October 1943, the 3rd Battalion, 6th Regiment boarded the *U.S.S. Harris.* They stopped at Nouméa, New Caledonia, then out to sea where they met up with the *U.S.S. Maryland.* "We stayed in Nouméa for about five days awaiting the loading of other ships and sometimes followed the '*Mary*' out to sea for gunnery practice. Every morning when I went topside there were more ships added to the convoy. It wasn't long before they almost stretched to the horizon, heading for the Gilbert Islands."

"To the disappointment of every man in the 6th Regiment, we were designated as Corps Reserve. I don't really think disappointment is a bad enough word for what we felt. We felt we were really let down. The word came out from 'High Command' that the Navy was going to bombard the island with so much shell power, and the Air Force was going to come over and bomb them, and by the time they got through, all there would be left for us would be a few groggy Japanese, wandering around haphazardly. It would just be a 'mop-up' operation for us. As it happened, we were needed on Tarawa and were used there instead.

The Army was hitting an island called Makin (Atoll) about 100 miles north of Tarawa at the same time. We could have been used either place, as needed, but the going got very touchy on Tarawa, so we landed on Green Beach." According to U.S. Army historians, "Tarawa was the most heavily defended atoll that would ever be invaded by Allied forces in the Pacific."

"On the morning of November 20th, we, being held in reserve, did not have to 'harness up' and get ready to go over the side into the landing craft. Although the ship was kept in a water tight condition, some of us did get topside to watch the shelling of the island that early morning. It was merciless. I don't know how they (Japanese) survived it other than, as on Guadalcanal, most all of the reinforcements they had were made out of coconut logs. These logs are not the same as hardwood logs. They don't split or chip or anything like that – they just don't break up." The Japanese had built their defenses on the island with the native coconut logs braced with angle irons. The roofs on the shelters were about six feet thick and covered with the logs, sand and corrugated iron, making them almost impossible to destroy.

After Tarawa, by mid-December 1943, Bob arrived at Hilo, Hawaii, where the Marine Base, 'Camp Tarawa,' had been built on the Parker Ranch property. By April 1944, troop replacements had been trained and were getting ready to ship out for the next campaign. Any soldier who had malaria or any other tropical disease since returning to the island was transferred out and replaced. Bob was one of those soldiers transferred out. He was sent to the island of Maui where the Marines had another camp. In November, Bob was sent stateside and with a few other soldiers, flew back to San Francisco, then was granted a 30 day leave. After taking his leave, Bob reported to Camp Pendleton, California.

Bob was assigned to a Military Police Battalion at the camp as Sergeant of the Guard. "It was during this time that the best thing in life happened to me – I met my wife-to-be, Mary Robinson who was living in Lancaster at that time. We were married on March 12, 1945 in Las Vegas, Nevada."

In June 1945, Bob received word to pack up again. The Battalion boarded the *U.S.S. Appling* on June 16, and set sail for the Marshall Islands, then continued on to Guam. On July 6, 1945 the troops arrived at Agana, Guam. Bob was Sergeant of the Guard assigned to the area of Island Command. Sentries were posted at the Naval Supply Depot and throughout the command area. "They had a large Japanese Prisoner of War (POW) compound there, and on one of our days off, we were assigned as guards to take the prisoners on work details. I always got assigned this certain prisoner. He was a large man, ornery, and did not like to take orders. I had to threaten him quite a few times, and rather than get into a real mess, I just refused to take him anymore. Shortly thereafter, the war ended. To make sure the Japanese prisoners could listen to Hirohito's surrender speech, they had speakers set up on the tall poles all around the POW compound. It caused a real fuss, so we were kept on alert, just in case."

In June 1946, after nearly a year on Guam, Bob packed his bags again to catch a Naval Air Transport flight to San Francisco, California. His wife, Mary, had moved to Minnesota to live with her parents while Bob was gone. After a 30 day leave, he was sent to the Great Lakes Naval Training Center near Chicago, and his wife, to serve out the rest of his time in the Marine Corps.

After six years in the Marine Corps, Bob was honorably discharged in August 1945, at the rank of Sergeant. He and Mary stayed in Minnesota for a few years then moved back to the west coast and settled in Oregon. They had three children together; a daughter, Laura, and two sons, John and Steven Specht. After moving to Oregon, Bob attended school where he studied accounting and received his Certified Public Accounting degree.

"Every five years the Second Marine Division Association heads back to New Zealand to meet old friends and make new ones. In 1993, Mary and I joined them for a trip to celebrate the 50th year anniversary of our arrival there. It was a great trip – the people were just the same as in 1942. It was great!"

James Joseph Stegman was born August 23, 1920, in Offerle, Edwards Co., Kansas, one of *eighteen* children born to Alexander and Frances (Kisner) Stegman. James was raised on his parent's wheat farm in southwest Kansas, but a farmers life for him was not to be.

One day, during the Depression years, Jim saw something in a nearby field and the fascination with airplanes began. Filled with excitement, he rode his Shetland pony over to a pilot who was tinkering with a two-cylinder Aeronca airplane. He proceeded to assist the man, and when the plane was ready to fly, the pilot took him for the flight that would hook Jim on flying for the rest of his life.

Jim graduated from Plains High School in 1938 and enlisted in the Marine Corps in October 1940, making $21 a month. He proceeded to go through a rigorous and demanding six weeks of training. After boot camp he was sent to Radio Operators school, then on to the Marine Air Detachment at North Island Naval Air Station in San Diego, California. His first job assignment was as a Radio Operator and Link Trainer Instrument Instructor.

Jim was selected for flight training and graduated in Pensacola, Florida, as an A.P. with the rank of Technical Sergeant in June 1943. He was assigned on a tour of combat duty in the South Pacific, where he flew the SBD Douglas dive-bomber. While in the South Pacific, James logged over 150 hours of combat flying, with 33 successful missions, including strikes against Japanese ground installations on Rabaul, New Britain, and Kavieng, New Ireland. Although he frequently flew through heavy anti-aircraft fire, his plane was never damaged by the enemy.

Jim earned a field commission as a 2nd Lieutenant while overseas in January 1944, at Efate in the New Hebrides Islands. After combat duty he was sent back state-side where he graduated from Engineering Officer's School and saw duty as an engineering officer and pilot until his release from active duty in 1948.

Jim Stegman, Green Island, South Pacific

Jim married Elinor Irene "Ellie" Allison on September 6, 1943, while he was home on leave. They were married in Golden, Colorado where Ellie stayed with her parents while Jim was overseas. Jim wrote to Ellie almost every day to keep up with the home front news. He learned of the birth of the first of five children, Victoria "Vicki" Irene, via cablegram to the South Pacific. Jim and Ellie had four other children; Margaret "Peggy" (Stegman) Meyer, Diane Stegman, John Stegman and Jeanie (Stegman) Carrafa.

Jim was stationed at the Marine Corps Air Station in Cherry Point, North Carolina, when news came that the war was finally over. His first discharge was in January 1949, released until September 1952, when he was called up to serve his country again during the Korean War. Jim flew a Panther jet fighter-bomber with the First Marine Aircraft Wing in Korea. He flew almost daily combat missions during a four month period over Communist-held North Korea with the "Able Eagles" Squadron of Marine Air Group 33. Jim was released for the second time from the Marine Corps in 1955 with the rank of Major. He was decorated with an Air Medal, with five Bronze Stars, along with many other honors and citations.

Between World War II and the Korean War, Jim was self-employed. He ran a tavern for a while and was a dry wheat farmer on a 2,220 acre farm in Kansas. In July 1955, Jim joined the Douglas Aircraft team as production and delivery pilot flying various experimental aircraft until becoming involved with the Douglas A-4 Skyhawk program. Jim flight tested most of the Skyhawks around today, checking every system in the aircraft and putting it through exhausting maneuvers over the Mojave Desert. He logged over 3,000 hours in the A-4 Skyhawk. Jim retired in 1982 from McDonnell-Douglas after twenty-seven years of service.

Today Jim is a member of the American Legion and the Veterans of Foreign Wars, continuing contact with many friends made during his service in the Marine Corps. Jim and Ellie currently live in Lancaster, California.

Jim & Ellie Stegman on their wedding day, September 6, 1943

2nd Lt. Stegman shown about to take off on a mission in the South Pacific. Photo credit: No. 60112 Dist. CPD Official Marine Corps Photo Div. Pub. Rel. Wash., D.C.

CIVILIAN ON THE
HOME FRONT

A *Handbook* for

AIR RAID
WARDENS

United States

OFFICE OF CIVILIAN DEFENSE

Washington, D. C.

Facings.

(All Facings are executed at the halt.)

To the flank.—The commands are Right (Left) FACE. At the command FACE, slightly raise the left heel and the right toe: Face to the right, turning on the right heel, assisted by a slight pressure on the ball of the left foot. Next, place the left foot beside the right. Exercise Left FACE on the left heel in a corresponding manner.

To the rear.—The commands are: About FACE. At the command FACE, carry the toe of the right foot a half-foot length to the rear and slightly to the left of the left heel without changing

Fig. IV—Executing Right FACE

HENRY CLINTON SPAULDING KEETON

Henry Clinton Spaulding Keeton was born July 23, 1917 in Elmira, New York to Leon Buckle Keeton, Jr. and Henrietta Spaulding. In 1934, Henry moved out west to California. While a student at the University of California, Los Angeles (UCLA), Henry signed up for a commission with the Reserve Officers Training Corps (ROTC) in 1938. Henry passed all the tests except color-blindness, which resulted in his receiving a 4F Selective Service System Classification code, or "not qualified for military service" due to his color-blindness. About this time he decided his future would be as a minister of the Presbyterian Church.

Henry graduated from UCLA in 1940, afterwards entering the San Francisco Theological Seminary in San Francisco, California. During that time, he worked at the Methodist Church in Vallejo, California, where a unit of the National Guard was stationed in the church's gymnasium. Henry also served as chaplain to several service units stationed around the San Francisco area, and as an Air Raid Warden during that time.

On June 17, 1941, Henry married Helen Elizabeth Gailey in Los Angeles, California. They had five children together; Elizabeth, Donna, Henry Jr., Bruce, and David Keeton. Henry graduated from seminary school in 1943 and proceeded to the First United Presbyterian Church of San Francisco, where he stayed until 1946. Servicemen who attended the church services were often invited to have a meal with Henry and his family.

Henry was the organizing pastor for St. Andrews Presbyterian Church of Redondo Beach, California beginning in 1946. In 1950, he was assigned pastor for the Greater Parish of Antelope Valley in Littlerock and Acton, California; pastor for Cypress Park Presbyterian Church in Los Angeles in 1951; and pastor for the church in Lake Hughes, California from 1957 to 1980, when Henry retired after 23 years of service at Lake Hughes. The Keeton family lived in Leona Valley, California since 1964. His wife, Helen, was a school teacher from 1941-1943 and 1958-1983, when she retired. Henry and Helen were both long-time members of the Antelope Valley Genealogical Society.

Reverend Henry C.S. Keeton died, after a battle with cancer, on November 23, 1989. He was cremated. Some of his ashes are in the Memorial Rose Garden adjacent to the Church of the Lakes, Lake Hughes, California. Helen married U.S. Navy veteran Roy Duane Stout on February 14, 1997 in Lancaster, California. They live in Elizabeth Lake, a small community near Leona Valley, California.

Helen recalled her remembrances of wartime: "For a year or more after the Pearl Harbor bombing we, on the Pacific Coast, were quite fearful of the Japanese landing somewhere on our beaches. Also, we kept hearing suspicious airplanes overhead, especially at night, while spotlights crisscrossed the sky, trying to pinpoint an enemy plane. With adrenaline pumping in our veins, we dutifully darkened our house with black-out curtains lest any spark of light give away the city location to the enemy overhead. I remember one night the siren at San Anselmo, California, wailed pulsatingly. Henry donned his Air-Raid Warden outfit and went out with others to scour the area. I gathered up a small table, chair, and the cards and envelopes, and wormed my way into the coat closet in the living room. The house was dark. I surrounded my flashlight with the hanging garments in the closet, and proceeded to address Christmas cards!"

Between 1943 and 1946 Helen remembered, "We did what many other Americans did to live with shortages, (meat, milk, toilet paper, etc.) with blackouts and entertaining servicemen. I recall chickens being on sale one day in the fall of 1943, in my San Francisco neighborhood. I was pregnant and had the help of a cleaning lady who was about my age. I told her I was going out to get a chicken for dinner. She continued with her cleaning. I walked three blocks to the meat market and then had to stand in a long, long line for two hours. My cleaning lady's time had long run out, so I expected her to have gone home when I returned. Lo and behold, when I arrived at the manse on Golden Gate Avenue, here she was – polishing silver! She had kept herself busy while waiting for me, so she hunted out my silver items. She said she wanted to show me how to cut up a whole chicken, as I had earlier mentioned I didn't know how to do it. Bless her heart!"

Bibliography and References

The bibliography/reference section is not listed in alphabetical order by title or source. The references are in order according to the veteran's name listed in brackets. Many other sources were used in locating birth, death, 1920 and 1930 U.S. census records, not listed in the bibliography. The American Battle Monuments Commission and the National Archives and Records Administration State Summary of War Casualties (California) were both used in reference to the soldiers who were killed or missing during World War II. In some cases, AVJUHS yearbooks from the 1930's – 1940's were used obtain photographs of the veterans.

Peebles, Curtis. *The Spoken Word: Recollections of Dryden History, The Early Years – Monographs in Aerospace History, No. 30.* Washington, D.C.: U.S. Government Printing Office, 2003.

Antelope Valley Veterans. "Honor Roll." Antelope Valley Ledger-Gazette newspaper. 10 May 1945. Lancaster Library, Lancaster, California. 19 July 2002.

Navy. U.S. Navy Department Dictionary of American Naval Fighting Ships. Compiled by SUBNET. Online http://www.subnet.com/fleet/ss190.htm. 24 September 2002. [Aldrich]

U.S. National Park Service. U.S. Government History of World War II in the Aleutians. Online <http://www.nps.gov/aleu/WWI_in_the_Aleutians.htm>. 26 March 2003. [Alley]

USAF Museum. Aleutian Campaign WWII Combat Pacific – The Aleutian Campaign 1942-1943. Online http://www.wpafb.af.mil/museum/history/wwii/cp10.htm>. 26 March 2003. [Alley]

Bliven, Bruce Jr. *From Pearl Harbor to Okinawa, The War in the Pacific 1941-1945.* New York: Random House, 1960. [Batz, J.]

Army. Combat Chronicle. 66th Infantry Division. Online <http://www.army.mil.CmhPg/lineage/cc.066id.htm>. 10 March 2003. [Batz, A.]

Batz, Robert. "Mrs. Batz Presented With Air Medal." Antelope Valley Ledger-Gazette newspaper. 22 February 1945, pg. 12. Lancaster Library, Lancaster, California. 19 July 2002. [Batz, R.]

National Archives. Robert Batz Missing Aircrew Report No. 5413. May-June 1944. [Batz, R.]

U.S. Air Force. U.S.A.A.F. Chronology, Mediterranean:1944, Part 1. Online <http://www.milhist.net/usaaf/mto44a.html>. 31 March 2003. [Batz, R.]

Navy. *The Slipstream Mark III, Flight Class 8A.* Texas: Aviation Cadet Regiment, U.S. Naval Air Training Center, Corpus Christi. 1942. Book location: Local History Department, Corpus Christi Public Library, Corpus Christi, TX. [Bennett, R.]

Bennett, Robert. "Killed in Line of Duty Recently." Antelope Valley Ledger-Gazette newspaper. 30 September 1943. Lancaster Library, Lancaster, California. 25 July 2003. [Bennett, R.]

Army. Army Military Museum. California's Own: The History of the 40th Infantry Division. Online http://www.militarymuseum.org/division.html>. 06 April 2003. [Brewer]

Brown, David. *Around the World in Twelve Hundred and Eighty Days, A Travel Story by the Tour Guide.* Undated. [Brown]

McMahon, Gerald. *The Siegfried and Beyond, The Odyssey of a Wartime Infantry Regiment, 1943-1945.* Ohio: 71st Infantry Division Association, 1993. [Burton, A.]

Nichols, George. *U.S.S. DeGrasse, AP164/AK223, World War II Pacific Theater Nov. 1943-March 1946.* Daily Deck Log of the *U.S.S. DeGrasse*, printed 1995. [Campbell, J.]

Air Force. 8th Air Force, 339th Fighter Group Association. Online <http://www.web-birds.com>. 02 December 2003. [Cozad]

Lord, Walter. *Day of Infamy.* New York: Henry Holt & Co., 1957. [Creese]
Army. Army Military Museum. We Aim to Hit: The 251st Coast Artillery Regiment (Anti-Aircraft) in World War II. Online <http://www.militarymuseum.org/251stca2.html>. 23 September 2002. [Culleton]

Air Force. 10th Air Force History. Online <http://www.geocities.com/Pentagon/Quarters/4807/history.html>. 22 October 2003. [Didier]

20th Fighter Group. 20th Fighter Group in WWII. Online <http://web-birds.com/8th/20/20th.htm>. 23 October 2003. [Dungan]

Edwards, Syd. "20th Fighter Group, Charles Dungan." E-mail to author, 24 October 2003. [Dungan]

Randall, Peter. "77th Fighter Squadron, Charles Dungan." E-mail to author, 30 October 2003. [Dungan]

Air Force. 77th Fighter Squadron Roll Call. Online <http://www.geocities.com/pentagon/quarters/6940/rollcall3.html>. 23 October 2003. [Dungan]

U.S. Military. U.S. Military Honors – The U.S. Navy in Idaho – Then and Now. Online <http://www.sid-ss.net/honors/hon-06.htm>. 16 September 2003. [Ellison, C.]

Ellison, Robert. Antelope Valley Ledger-Gazette newspaper. 18 November 1943, No. 46, page 1. Lancaster Library, Lancaster, California. 19 July 2002. [Ellison, R.]

Army. 32nd Division in WWII, part 10, Occupation of Japan. Online <http://members.aol.com/Sarge000tb/32-ww2f.html>. 24 October 2003. [Finck]

Foote, Edward. "Edward G. Foote Now Lieutenant." Antelope Valley Ledger-Gazette newspaper. 23 September 1943. Lancaster Library, Lancaster, California. 01 December 2003. [Foote]

Army. History Merrill's Marauders. Online <http://www.marauder.org/history.htm>. 25 October 2002. [Foote]

Passanisi, Robert. "Soldier 2nd Lt. Edward G. Foote." E-mail to author from Merrill's Marauders Association Historian, 06 December 2002. [Foote]

Heiden, Captain Arthur. 20th Fighter Group Col. R.C. Franklin. Online <http://www.geocities.com/Pentagon/Quarters/6940/franklin.html>. 30 March 2003. [Franklin]

Heiden, Captain Arthur. "R.C. Franklin 20th FG." E-mail and photographs to author, 29 March – 31 March 2003. [Franklin]

Reihmer, Don. "R.C. Franklin 20th FG." E-mail to author via Captain Arthur Heiden, 31 March 2003. [Franklin]

Army Air Forces. History 389th Bombardment (Heavy). Online <http://www.armyairforces.com/dbgroups.asp?Group=210>. 03 June 2003. [Fritz]

Halpert, Sam. World War II 8th Air Force. Online <http://www.b17sam.com>. 30 September 2002. [Godde]

Halpert, Sam. "B-24 Ploesti Photograph." E-mail to author, 12 March 2003. [Godde]

Newby, Leroy. *Target Ploesti, View From a Bombsight.* California: Presidio Press, 1983. [Godde]
Godde, Russell. "Lieutenant Godde Received Award Posthumously." Undated newspaper clipping, c. 1940's, from Antelope Valley Ledger-Gazette. Owned 2003 by Mickey Primmer, Lancaster, California. [Godde]

Hawke, Jack. "Letters from Service Men." Antelope Valley Ledger-Gazette, 14 October 1943. Lancaster Library, Lancaster, California 19 July 2002. [Hawke]

Navy. World War II Ships, Destroyer Escorts, USS Hilbert (DE-742). Online <http://www.usshilbert.org/ship_log.cfm>. 21 May 2003. [Henkel]

Kerley, Robert. *The War! As We Saw It! 1944-1945.* Unpublished booklet, story and journal of the 2nd Platoon, Company C, 328th Engineer Combat Battalion of 103rd Infantry Division. Undated. [Kercher]

Army. Army Nurses in the Pacific Theater. Online <http://www.army.mil/cmh-pg/books/wwii/72-14/72-14.htm>. 05 November 2003. [Kreig]

Navy. History, General U.S.S. Morton (AP-138). Online <http://www.multied.com/../NAVY/ap/GeneralCGMorton.html>. 19 February 2004. [Lott]

Bowden, Ray. "USAAF Nose Art Research Project." E-mail and photograph to author, 01-02 January 2004. [Massari]

Rutherfoord, William de Jarnette. *165 Days, A Story of the 25th Division on Luzon.* September 1945. Copy in the possession of M. Mills, Lancaster, California. September 1945. [Mills]

Loncke, Peter. "WWII Wesel, Germany, E. Patterson." E-mail and photograph to author, 24 June 2003. [Patterson, E.]

National Archives. NARA Microfiche Publication, Missing Air Crew Report #13552. Washington: National Archives M1380 MACR #13552. [Patterson, E.]

Wilson, Andy. Letters written by father, Andy Wilson, 12 July 1944-23 March 1945, to wife Betty during WWII. Original letters and photographs held in 2004 by son, Andy Wilson, Flagstaff, Arizona. [Patterson, E.]

Blue, Allan. History of the 491st (The Ringmasters), 491st Bomb Group Association. E-mail to author, 03 June 2003. [Patterson, E.]

Navy. USN Ships - U.S.S. Aaron Ward (DD-483). Online <http://www.history.navy.mil/photos/sh-usn/usnsh-a/dd483.htm>. 14 May 2003. [Perkins]

Navy. Women & the U.S. Navy – WWII Era WAVES. Online <http://www.history.navy.mil/photos/prs-tpic/females/wave-ww2.htm>. 03 January 2004. [Philipp]

Scorza, Darin. "752nd Bomb Squadron, 458th Bomb Group (H)." E-mail to author, 07 January 2004. [Proteau]

Army. History, 102nd Infantry Division. Online <http://www.ibiblio.org/hyperwar/USA/OOB/102-Division.html>. 08 January 2004. [Randleman, D.]

National Archives. U.S.S. Medusa (AR-1) photograph. Online <http://www.navsource.org/archives/09/09250102.jpg>. 23 March 2003. [Reynolds]

National Archives. U.S.S. General S. D. Sturgis (AP-137) photograph. Online <http://www.navsource.org/archives/09/22137.htm>. 05 January 2004. [Ritchie]

Rogers, Charles. "Attending College At Washington." Undated clipping from unidentified newspaper. Owned 2004 by Ercell Stout, Simi Valley, California. [Rogers, C.]

Rogers, William. "Awarded Nation's Highest Unit." Undated clipping from unidentified newspaper. Owned 2004 by Ercell Stout, Simi Valley, California. [Rogers, W.]

Thompson, Boyd. 32nd Bomb Squadron, 1942-1945. Online <http://www.stauntonweb.com/32nd/index.html>. 10 January 2004. [Rogers, W.]

Ewing, Steve. "U.S. Navy VF-3 Squadron photograph, 05 March 1942." E-mail to author from Dr. Steve Ewing, Historian, Patriots Point Naval and Maritime Museum, Mt. Pleasant, South Carolina, 11 February 2003. [Rowell]

Lundstrom, John. *The First Team, Pacific Naval Air Combat from Pearl Harbor to Midway.* Maryland: Naval Institute Press, 1984. [Rowell]

Army. The U.S. Army Campaigns of World War II: New Guinea. Online <http://www.ibiblio.org/hyperwar/USA/USA-C-NewGuinea/>. 22 January 2004. [Scates]

Danko, John. "Golden Gate Cemetery, Walter E. Scates photograph." E-mail and photographs to author, 31 July 2003. [Scates]

U.S. Coast Guard. Celebrating Women of Courage & Vision. Online <http://www.uscg.mil/hg/g-w/g-wt/g-wtl/women/sld007.htm>. 10 January 2004. [Schwartz, E.]

Air Force. 341st Bomb Group, H.Q. 14th Air Force, 1943-1945. Online <http://www.341stbombgroup.org>. 23 January 2004. [Settle, R.]

Navy. Doolittle Raid on Japan – Ships. Online <http://www.history.navy.mil>. 05 January 2004. [Sherlock]

AFFA. "American Fighter Aces Association Album." E-mail and photograph to author from Jim Sterling at <http://www.web-birds.com>. 12 December 2002. [Stambook]

Gaskill, William. *Fighter Pilot – World War II in the South Pacific.* Kansas: Sunflower University Press, 1997. [Stege]

Stege, John. "John Stege Active in North Africa." Antelope Valley Ledger-Gazette newspaper. 10 December 1941. Lancaster Library, Lancaster, California. 19 July 2002. [Stege]

Army. 26th Infantry Division History World War II. Online <http://www.ww2-museum.org>. 15 February 2002. [Weaver]

National Archives. Air Raid Pearl Harbor. Online <http://www.navsource.org>. 17 Feb 2003. [Westerfield]

U.S. National Park Service. U.S.S. Arizona Memorial: U.S.S. Arizona Casualty List. Online <http://www.nps.gov/usar/AZCas.html>. 28 May 2003. [Westerfield]

Ancestry Database. World War II and Korean Conflict Veterans Interred Overseas. Online <http://www.ancestry.com>. 28 May 2003. [Westerfield]

NOTES